A HOUSE UNITED?

EVANGELICALS AND CATHOLICS TOGETHER
A WINNING ALLIANCE FOR THE 21ST CENTURY

KEITH A. FOURNIER
WITH WILLIAM D. WATKINS

NAVPRESS

BRINGING TRUTH TO LIFE
NavPress Publishing Group
P.O. Box 35001, Colorado Springs, Colorado 80935

144120

The Navigators is an international Christian organization. Jesus Christ gave His followers the Great Commission to go and make disciples (Matthew 28:19). The aim of The Navigators is to help fulfill that commission by multiplying laborers for Christ in every nation.

NavPress is the publishing ministry of The Navigators. NavPress publications are tools to help Christians grow. Although publications alone cannot make disciples or change lives, they can help believers learn biblical discipleship, and apply what they learn to their lives and ministries.

© 1994 by Keith A. Fournier
All rights reserved. No part of this publication may be reproduced in any form without
    written permission from NavPress, P.O. Box 35001, Colorado Springs, CO 80935.
Library of Congress Catalog Card Number:
    94-29886
ISBN 08910-98615

Some of the anecdotal illustrations in this book are true to life and are included with the permission of the persons involved. All other illustrations are composites of real situations, and any resemblance to people living or dead is coincidental.

This publication is designed to provide accurate and authoritative information in regard to the subject matter covered. It is sold with the understanding that the author and the publisher are not engaged in rendering legal, accounting, or other professional service. If legal advice or other expert assistance is required, the services of a competent professional person should be sought. *From a Declaration of Principles jointly adopted by a Committee of the American Bar Association and a Committee of Publishers.*

Unless otherwise identified, all Scripture quotations in this publication are taken from the *New American Bible* (NAB), Copyright © 1970, by P. J. Kenedy & Sons. Other versions used include: the *HOLY BIBLE: NEW INTERNATIONAL VERSION* ® (NIV®), Copyright © 1973, 1978, 1984 by International Bible Society, used by permission of Zondervan Publishing House, all rights reserved; the *New Revised Standard Version* (NRSV), copyright 1989, by the Division of Christian Education of the National Council of the Churches of Christ in the USA, used by permission, all rights reserved; the *New American Standard Bible* (NASB), © The Lockman Foundation 1960, 1962, 1963, 1968, 1971, 1972, 1973, 1975, 1977; *The Living Bible* (TLB), © 1971 owned by assignment by the Illinois Regional Bank N.A. (as trustee), used by permission of Tyndale House Publishers, Inc., Wheaton, IL 60189; the *New King James Version* (NKJV), copyright © 1979, 1980, 1982, 1990, Thomas Nelson Inc., Publishers; and the *King James Version* (KJV).

Fournier, Keith A., 1954-
    A house united? : Evangelicals and Catholics together / Keith A. Fournier with
William D. Watkins.
        p. cm.
    Includes bibliographical references.
    ISBN 0-89109-861-5
    1. Catholic Church—Relations—Evangelicalism. 2. Evangelicalism—Relations—
Catholic Church. I. Watkins, William D. II. Title.
BR1641.C37F68 1994
280'.042—dc20   94-29886
                                                                                 CIP

Printed in the United States of America

CONTENTS

❖

To Jesus Christ, the Evangel

ACKNOWLEDGMENTS

NavPress is a courageous, committed Christian publisher. What I have found in Publisher John Eames, Senior Editor Steve Webb, and the rest of NavPress's staff is nothing short of a prime example of the kind of mutuality of respect Christians need in these desperate times.

I also wish to acknowledge the hard work and assistance of my writing partner and friend, Bill Watkins. He has seen this book through its many editions, helping me make its truths come alive. A devout evangelical Christian who likes to describe himself as a Thomist or a triple-A theist (that is, a Christian in the tradition of Augustine, Anselm, and Aquinas), Bill's sensitivity, intelligence, creativity, dedication, and kindness will always be appreciated. He represents the best to me of a writer and editor deeply committed to Jesus Christ, the Evangel, and to excellence in His service.

Finally, I wish to acknowledge the bold leadership and courage of Chuck Colson, Father Richard John Neuhaus, and the signatories of the bold accord "Evangelicals and Catholics Together: The Christian Mission in the Third Millennium" (see the Appendix). It is my prayer that this accord marks a new beginning for cooperation among Christians that could signal a historic turning point in our mutual efforts to proclaim the many dimensions of the gospel message and demonstrate the mission of the church to an age that so desperately needs both.

FOREWORD

In June of 1991 Keith Fournier arrived in Virginia Beach, at my invitation, to become the executive director of the American Center for Law and Justice (ACLJ). For years I had desired to see a group of lawyers rise up against the growing tide of intolerance toward people of faith, the legal killing of the most helpless human beings—unborn children—and the attack on the family.

Like countless other concerned Americans, I have watched the misuse of our courts by a small group of interest groups. I longed to see an opposing group rise to confront them. That was why I founded the American Center. But, until Keith's arrival, my hope had been only a vision.

Keith and I had crossed paths several times over the years. I knew of his deep Christian commitment, his pro-life convictions, and his dedication to building alliances between evangelical Protestants and Roman Catholics. I knew of his work at Franciscan University of Steubenville, his books, and his legal experience. I also knew the people of faith were under attack as never before by common enemies so virulent that it was essential that we lay aside certain concerns over legitimate theological differences to join together and support those things upon which we all agreed, such as the sanctity of all human life. As an evangelical Protestant I welcomed Keith, a conservative Roman

Catholic, as an ally in an important cause.

I have watched with great joy over these years as the ACLJ has grown from vision to the foremost Christian public interest advocacy group in the United States. I have rejoiced over its victories from the Supreme Court to the local school board. And, in it all I have watched Keith's leadership and commitment to true Christian unity prove once again the importance and effectiveness of building alliances to engage and transform our culture.

When I was invited to sign the historic accord "Evangelicals and Catholics Together: The Christian Mission in the Third Millennium" I didn't hesitate. I am convinced of the importance of such united efforts. Not "humpty-dumpty solutions," which Keith also mentions in this book, but true alliances rooted in our common faith in Jesus Christ and dedicated to serving Him together for the sake of our country and our world. There are many theological issues I, a Baptist, differ on with Roman Catholics. These differences are very important. But even more important is the common ground on which we stand and the vital mission we share at the close of this century and into the next. We have a moral imperative to join together in our efforts to oppose the killing of the unborn, the hostility toward and censorship of the Christian message, and the wholesale assault on the traditional family. The next seven years are crucial if we are going to make any inroads against the pressing darkness of our age. The lives of thirty-one million children alone, killed in the womb by legalized abortion, cry out for judgment. But, if we have any hope of turning the tide, we must come together in our efforts.

Keith Fournier is one of the most dedicated men in the American legal profession. He is also an extraordinarily gifted writer. *A House United?* is an example of both his gifts and his prophetic convictions. His passion for religious liberty, the pro-life cause, and the family flow through the book. So too, his deep dedication to helping to heal the divide that has not only separated the Body of Christ but all too often impeded our ability to be more effective as Christians.

A House United? is a compelling, and historic book. It will be controversial as is the accord, "Evangelicals and Catholics Together," which is published in its appendix. But I welcome such controversy if it helps to rouse all of us who love the Lord to united action. But the book is also practical, built on Keith's experience of building such alliances for many years and, most recently, in building the ACLJ, which proves the effectiveness of such alliances.

When darkness threatens all of our freedoms, it is time to raise the

light of truth and lead the way to solutions. *A House United?* does just
that with a message of hope that motivates the reader to effective action.
May the words of the prophet Habakkuk be fulfilled in our day: "For
the earth will be filled with the knowledge of the glory of the LORD as
the waters cover the sea" (Habakkuk 2:14, NIV).

—Pat Robertson,
Founder of the Christian Broadcasting Network

WHEN TROUBLE KNOCKS

The entire free world recently paused to commemorate the fiftieth anniversary of the central event that turned the tide of the Second World War: D-Day. On June 6, 1944, the Allies launched the largest and perhaps most risky amphibious invasion in world history. The landing occurred at Normandy and other key European sites, beginning the longest day of the war and Hitler's worst nightmare.

Fifty years later, those who fought for freedom linked arms once again with those they liberated. Together they shared their memories of that great day. For those of us who weren't there in body, we were taken there in spirit by our televisions, radios, and newspapers. Through them we saw and heard about the sacrifices, dedication, and vision of those who participated in that heroic struggle against a darkness that threatened to sweep the world. We saw the veterans of that crusade gather at the graves of their slain comrades and embrace each other. For a brief moment, we were privileged to watch them refocus on what had brought them together in the first place: common ground, common ideals, and a common need to defeat a common enemy.

I, along with the millions worldwide who witnessed these events, was deeply moved and inspired. But I was also stirred with concern. The culture of death the Allies fought so hard against in World War II has not disappeared. It has reappeared in the lands they liberated a half century ago, and it has come across the Atlantic and invaded our own shores. We are in a new war, a war for the soul of Western civilization, and our enemy is every bit as insidious as the enemy the Allies faced in World War II.

The great historian Christopher Dawson reminded us that Christianity is the soul of Western civilization. When we look around us, though, we see terrible evidence that the West, particularly America, is losing her soul. And with this loss, America is also forfeiting her moral leadership in the free world.

I'm not a pessimist. As a Christian, I can't be. Hope is central to my faith, for I know that in Christ the victory over evil in human history is assured. I also know that history has proven that the vibrant influence of Christianity on the secular order has liberated countless numbers from injustices, tyrannies, immoralities, and the many other manifestations of the culture of death. That's one of the missions of the church. The City of God is called to challenge, contend for, redeem, and transform the city of man. So I believe there's hope for the restoration of America and the rest of the West.

But something very dangerous is impeding this effort. The very people who, with the mighty resources of God, can loose the grip of the culture of death and restore a culture of life are members of a divided house. Unlike the Allies who were united to make common cause, the Christian community is split, not only into different camps but also in its attempts to deal with the strengthening darkness. As a result, its ability to launch an effective counteroffensive even remotely similar to what secular nations accomplished during World War II is severely limited, if not virtually made impotent.

There is hope, however. Just as we have had the opportunity to reflect on the principled alliances in the temporal order that helped defend and restore freedom fifty years ago, we Christians need to rediscover how to build principled alliances throughout the Christian community that can help defend and, in many instances, recover the soul of the West. These alliances should recognize and respect the distinctives of doctrine and practice among us, and they should not make light of the mistakes and pain that years of mistrust and suspicion have created in our community. Such alliances will be difficult to build, but build them we must. The stakes are too high not to try, and with the help of our common Lord, we can succeed.

This is the end I've struggled to achieve for over twenty years in various capacities and positions of responsibility. Even today I'm still working toward that end as the executive director of the American Center for Law and Justice (ACLJ) (a public-interest law firm and educational organization) and as the founder and president of Liberty, Life and Family. Both organizations are dedicated to pro-liberty, pro-life, and pro-family causes, and both seek to fight for those causes through alliance-building efforts among Protestants, Catholics, and Eastern Orthodox.

It is because I believe so deeply in the critical need for alliance building among Christians that I have written this book. I know this book will meet with opposition. Much of what I've done in the past has too. I'm no longer surprised by it.

I remember years ago in the early days of the charismatic-renewal movement in the churches that an impassioned debate ensued over the validity and exercise of the charismatic gifts and experience. Some well-intentioned folks, strongly influenced by classical Pentecostal piety and doctrine, insisted that the sign of a person truly "baptized in the Spirit" was the manifestation of "glossolalia," or the gift of tongues. Others, who were in the camp I found myself, believed that the gift of tongues was available to all believers but that it was not the only "evidence" of baptism, or immersion, in the Holy Spirit. This divergence of belief fractured people who otherwise had shared a wonderful experience of grace.

At the height of this controversy, Bob Mumford, one of the early leaders of that renewal movement, was asked what the evidence of the baptism of the Holy Spirit was. "Trouble," he insightfully replied.

I have discovered trouble has dogged me in my efforts to follow what I believe is the Holy Spirit's leadership in alliance building among Christians. For me, trouble has even become a sign of the Spirit's affirmation that I'm doing what He wants me to do. Don't get me wrong. I'm not saying that difficult experiences are always indications that we're going the right way. But if we believe that following Christ will always lead to bliss, we're simply wrong. More often than not, it will lead the way it did for Christ Himself—the way of the cross. And that's a good thing. We often need to be shaken awake from our comfortable slumber. But some of the trouble that comes our way comes not from hostiles but from those who should be our friends.

Over the last few years, I have encountered trouble from some of my Catholic brethren. They have questioned my orthodoxy as they've heard about and seen my work with Protestant Christians. Nevertheless, the fact is, I'm a loyal, theologically dedicated Roman Catholic who actively works in the midst of an evangelical Protestant "Jerusalem." The ACLJ's national headquarters are located in Robertson Hall, the building that houses Regent University's School of Law, School of Government, and School of Divinity, on the sprawling grounds of the Christian Broadcasting Network. Roman Catholics constitute six of the twenty-six full-time ACLJ lawyers in America, and an increasing number of Roman Catholics are becoming part of the ACLJ's financial support base along with thousands of evangelical Protestants.

Among some Protestant Christians, I have fared no better, while others have captured the alliance-building vision. In his marvelous work *The Judgment of Nations*, Christopher Dawson writes about the challenge of desecularizing society and the need for the Holy Spirit's assistance in every effort to transform the contemporary age with the values of the eternal Kingdom. It's in this context he insightfully states:

> The only way to desecularize society is by giving a spiritual aim
> to the whole system of organization, so that the machine
> becomes the servant of the spirit and not its enemy or its
> master. . . . If culture is not to be dynamized from below by the
> exploitation of the sub-rational animal forces in human nature,
> it must be activized from above by being once more brought
> into relation with the forces of divine power and wisdom and
> love. The faith in the possibility of this divine action is the foun-
> dation of Christian thought. We believe that to every fresh need
> there is an answer of divine grace, and that every historical crisis
> (which is a crisis of human destiny) is met by a new outpouring
> of the Spirit.[1]

Dawson is right. The only observation I would add is that those working to effect this kind of transformation should expect trouble, even from those who would normally support them.

I have a feeling that this book will, among other things, generate controversy and bring me more trouble. I hope it will also enlarge my circle of friends and fellow transformers. For we face a multifaceted crisis at the end of this twentieth century that also brings with it an incredible opportunity to see a new outpouring of the Spirit. One of the signs of this movement of the Spirit in our age is, I believe, renewed efforts between Protestants and Catholics to cooperate in their fight against the culture of death. My prayer and plea is that this book will help advance those efforts. We Christians, regardless of our different confessions and traditions, desperately need to become allies to push back the darkness with the light of the Evangel and the empowerment of His Spirit. If we do, we may very well help usher in a new millennium of life, a renaissance of Christianity.

This is a book about commonalities and differences, unity and divisiveness, true ecumenism and false ecumenism. This book is a call, even a plea, to all Christians to pound the weapons they have for too long turned on one another into plows and use them to tenderly plant and fertilize the seeds of the gospel throughout the world and nurture their growth in the life-giving power of the Holy Spirit. We can—and must—do this together. This book is an apologetic for this agenda. And for those who catch the vision and are willing to exercise the courage to embrace it, if this book provides sound encouragement for this winning alliance of Christians, then I will have succeeded in my task.

PART I

A Prodigal's Story

CHAPTER ONE

A HOUSE DIVIDED

*A house divided against itself
cannot stand. . . . Our cause must be entrusted to,
and conducted by its own undoubted friends—
whose hands are free,
whose hearts are in the work—
who do care for the result.*
Abraham Lincoln

I am a Christian.

I am a Catholic Christian.

I am an evangelical Catholic Christian.

It is my belief and experience that these three claims not only describe who I am but are necessary to define my relationship with Jesus Christ and His church and my role in the church's ongoing mission to bring all men and women to salvation in Christ. Nevertheless, many professing Christians cannot accept my description of my faith. When I make these claims, some people hear the blaring horns of confusion, outright contradiction, or even to their minds, apostasy.

Some Protestant Christians, particularly if they describe themselves as evangelicals or fundamentalists, have a hard time comprehending how I can claim to be Christian or evangelical and yet be Roman Catholic. To them, I might as well be talking about square circles or one-ended sticks. If I'm really Catholic in my understanding of Christianity, they argue, I could not be Christian, much less evangelical. Catholics, they say, believe a "different gospel," which is no gospel at all. They allegedly believe that works can save and that the virgin Mary redeems and that church tradition has equal or superior authority to the Bible. But these beliefs contradict or at least undermine the three cardinal tenets of the Reformation: (1) salvation by faith alone (2) in Christ alone (3) by the

19

authority of the Bible alone. Therefore, these Protestants conclude, either I'm not a Christian, not really a Catholic, or I'm very confused.

Over the years, I've repeatedly heard such charges. Most of them I've read in anti-Catholic literature or heard in media interviews generally from people who, despite their sincerity, misunderstand or caricature the faith I unashamedly embrace. An example of this recently occurred in a magazine I usually enjoy.

FAMILY DISDAIN

Not too long ago *Moody* magazine approached me and asked if I would grant them an interview on recent developments in evangelical Protestant and Catholic cooperation. They had been intrigued by my first book *Evangelical Catholics*, and they wanted to use that along with the interview as a springboard for exploring the issue in their magazine. I was thrilled with their offer. I had long respected D. L. Moody, the founder of many of the Moody ministries, especially for his courageous and productive evangelistic and educational work. Having served as an evangelist and educator myself, I had been impressed with the fruit of Moody's labors. If I could further those in some way by cooperating in this interview, I would be well pleased.

The interview went well. The writer, Davis Duggins, asked some very good questions and seemed honestly open and curious about my Catholic convictions. At no time did I sense a judgmental spirit. He said he would be interviewing other people for the article, some of whom would likely be critical of some of my positions. I had no problems with that and wished him well.

The article was published in the November 1993 issue of *Moody*. Entitled "Evangelicals and Catholics: Across the Divide," I thought the article had clearly and fairly articulated what I had said in the interview and in my book. I also thought the writer had achieved a good balance between the form of cooperation I supported and its critics. What bothered me was what some of these critics had to say.

Protestant Bible expositor and educator John MacArthur declared that "Roman Catholicism . . . is unbiblical." He warned evangelical Protestants against joining "forces with Catholicism, Mormonism, or even Hinduism . . . in order to promote the pro-life movement and other common moral aims" because by so doing they "accept precisely the kind of yoke with unbelievers that is prohibited in 2 Cor. 6:14." To this he added that because "there is no suggestion that Rome will ever repudiate its stance against justification by faith . . . I believe the trend toward tolerance and cooperation is a destructive one because it blurs the distinction between biblical truth and a system of false teaching."[1] As far as MacArthur is concerned, my faith is unbiblical, full of false doctrines, and I'm an unbeliever on par with Mormons and Hindus.

Another person interviewed was Jim McCarthy, the head of Good News for Catholics, an organization that basically assumes Catholics are not Christians and therefore has dedicated itself to evangelizing them. In the article, McCarthy chastised evangelical Protestant Christians (for him, apparently, there are no other kind of Christians) who "defend Catholicism." He said such people "are simply not informed." They don't see "the doctrinal errors of the [Catholic] church," among which are being "pro-pope, pro-Mary, pro-mass." Such people, he believes, show a "lack of conviction and understanding of biblical doctrine," which "contributes to a lack of concern about doctrinal differences between biblical Christianity and Roman Catholicism."[2] So from McCarthy's perspective, I represent a tradition with doctrinal error and one that at its heart conflicts with biblical theology. Moreover, those people who may see things differently than he does are obviously theologically ignorant and apathetic. I suppose that must include me.

Reformed theologian and apologist R. C. Sproul was also interviewed. Though he indicated his pleasure that evangelical Protestants and Catholics are "behaving in a much more charitable fashion" toward each other, he warned that "the things that divide orthodox Protestantism from official Roman Catholic doctrine are greater today than they were in the 16th century." Time has not brought the two camps closer together in theology but has created a much wider gap. According to Davis Duggins, Sproul believes that the doctrinal positions that have led to this deeper divorce are Catholicism's official stance against justification by faith alone and its decrees on papal infallibility and the unique role of Mary.[3] Sproul was especially adamant about the Reformed doctrine of justification: "If justification by faith alone is an essential doctrine of Christianity, then any church [that denies that truth], no matter how virtuous it is . . . would have to be viewed as apostate."[4] Hence, according to Sproul, my Catholic convictions are unorthodox, indeed, more so now than they would have been if I had been a Catholic in the sixteenth century. And worse yet, I am a member of an apostate church.

In one of the articles that followed Duggins's, several Protestants were interviewed. Given the article's title—"Finding the Way"—readers were led to the impression that whatever the article presented, it would deal with moving from error to finding the One who is the way, the truth, and the life. The article's author, Rob Wilkins, had interviewed several people who identified themselves as former Catholics, and he reported that all of them now witness to Catholics. One of the former Catholics, Bart Brewer, has an outreach he calls Mission to Catholics that "offers literature and teaching to help evangelicals develop an effective witness to Roman Catholics." According to Brewer, "There is a theory with some evangelicals that the Roman Catholic Church is now a Christian church. I don't understand that. It just doesn't line up with the truth of the Bible."[5] The rest of the article was apparently designed to reinforce that notion.

Of course, nowhere in the article is any mention made of the many former evangelical Protestants, some of whom were ordained Protestant ministers, who converted to Roman Catholicism. Three of the most notable converts in recent years are philosopher and apologist Peter Kreeft, whose many books have been published by Catholic and Protestant publishers; former Lutheran minister and now Catholic priest Richard John Neuhaus, who is the head of the renowned Institute on Religion and Public Life and whose writings have influenced thinkers across the confessional spectrum; and English professor and apologist Thomas Howard, whose book *Hallowed Be This House* still stands as one of the finest explanations of the Christian view of family I have ever read.[6]

Nor did the article's author include any comments from the many evangelical Protestants who have called for cooperation with orthodox Catholics and have actively linked arms with Catholics in pro-life demonstrations, evangelistic outreaches, discipleship programs, spiritual-renewal conferences and retreats, antipornography campaigns, and legal and legislative battles. Among those many Protestants are Dr. Billy Graham, the twentieth century's most famous evangelist; Charles Colson, one of the most prolific and respected Christian spokesmen in the country and winner of the Templeton Prize for Progress in Religion; Dr. Bill Bright, founder and head of the worldwide student evangelistic movement Campus Crusade for Christ; Dr. James Dobson, an ardent defender of the family and founder and head of Focus on the Family; and Dr. Pat Robertson, founder and president of Regent University, the Christian Broadcasting Network, the Family Channel, the Christian Coalition, and the American Center for Law and Justice, of which I am the executive director.

In what ways do such glaring omissions serve fellow believers? I don't see how they serve the Body of Christ at all. They only perpetuate and further solidify the damaging divisions that keep Christians from trusting one another and becoming allies against the forces that threaten believers from all traditions and confessions.

Tragically, what many Protestants have said about Catholics has also been found on the lips of Catholics about Protestants. I have heard my Catholic brethren refer to Protestants as Bible-thumping fundamentalists, narrow-minded bigots, Catholic-haters, unbelievers, and apostates. Both sides of Christ's house have treated the other side with disdain. We must stop our unChristian Christian-bashing. We must hear and obey afresh what Christ prayed for us on earth and undoubtedly still prays for us in Heaven. The results of disunity are obvious in the field of human history. In his famous "A House Divided" speech, one of the great American leaders, Abraham Lincoln, began to rally a divided nation to a vision of national unity. As he said, "A house divided against itself cannot stand. . . . Our cause must be entrusted to, and conducted by its own undoubted friends—whose hands are free, whose hearts are in the work—who do care for the result." That unity was reestablished in fields drenched in blood. The lessons of secular history call those of us with a foot in eternity to sit up and take notice.

HEAVENLY UNITY, EARTHLY UNITY

I do not believe that our Lord Jesus Christ ever intended for His church to be a divided house. Listen to His words. They come from some of the last words He spoke to His disciples before going to the cross to die for the world's sins. In fact, they are from His longest recorded prayer in Scripture, the prayer that drew to a close His last earthly celebration of the Passover meal.

> "Holy Father, protect them by the power of your name—the name you gave me—so that they may be one as we are one. . . .
>
> "My prayer is not for them alone. I pray also for those who will believe in me through their message, that all of them may be one, Father, just as you are in me and I am in you. May they also be in us so that the world may believe that you have sent me. I have given them the glory that you gave me, that they may be one as we are one: I in them and you in me. May they be brought to complete unity to let the world know that you sent me and have loved them even as you have loved me."[7]

Several times Jesus asked the heavenly Father to unite His small band of followers and all who would believe their message. The unity for which He prayed reflects the eternal unity resident in the Godhead. Just as the Father and the Son are one, so should that Body of believers who worship and follow them be one. The distinct identities, gifts, and ministries of believers will not be lost in this unity but utilized to help bring it about. As the Apostle Paul so clearly put it: "It was he [Jesus Christ] who gave some to be apostles, some to be prophets, some to be evangelists, and some to be pastors and teachers, to prepare God's people for works of service, so that the body of Christ may be built up until we all reach unity in the faith and in the knowledge of the Son of God and become mature, attaining to the whole measure of the fullness of Christ."[8]

Unity in diversity and diversity in unity—that's every Christian's calling, yours and mine. And for what purpose? So we can grow up in Christ and so the world will come to understand and believe that the Son of God has really come into the world out of love for all people: white or black, Republican or Democrat, saint or sinner, factory worker or CEO, male or female, American or Australian, model citizen or repeat offender, capitalist or communist. "For God so loved the world that he gave his one and only Son, that whoever believes in him shall not perish but have eternal life. For God did not send his Son into the world to condemn the world, but to save the world through him."[9]

What will influence people to believe? Jesus' crucifixion? His resurrection and postresurrection appearances? His ascension? His teaching, moral example, or miracles? Although these evidences have led many to bow their knee before Jesus and submit to Him as Lord, these are not the evidences Jesus upholds as the most powerful in the apologetic arsenal. What He points to mirrors the nature of the Godhead and can be pulled off by no one else. Only Deity could accomplish it among fallen, hostile humankind. What is it? Nothing less than unifying the ununitable and uniting them everlastingly. Kings have not been able to do it. Presidents and prophets have failed. Dictators and tyrants have never been successful. Civil-rights advocates and legislators have never adequately broken down the many walls that divide people from other people. Only the Creator and Sustainer of the universe knows us and loves us enough to be able to make this miracle a reality. And that He did in His Son, Jesus Christ. Paul spoke eloquently and simply of this mystery in his letter to the Christians in Galatia: "For you are all sons of God through faith in Christ Jesus. For as many of you as were baptized into Christ have put on Christ. There is neither Jew nor Greek, there is neither slave nor free, there is neither male nor female; for you are all one in Christ Jesus."[10]

In Christ we become one. And only in Christ can we stay one.

The greatest tragedy of our day is not abortion, pornography, the devaluing of our schools, the undermining of the family, corrupt government, illegal drugs, AIDS, promiscuity, or homosexuality. As devastating as these activities are and as much as we need to actively address them, they are not our most serious threat. Division within the Family of God is. When the members of Christ's Body are at each other's throats, defaming each other in the name of our Family's Head, the world walks away from our message in disbelief. "How can people who preach grace, love, and forgiveness be so spiteful and vengeful toward their own? If their message was really true, they would be living it, not contradicting it at every turn." This is an indictment we deserve, and it is one we and the world pay for in ways that should bring us in tears and repentance to the foot of the cross.

Today, the Body of Christ is not one. It is divided. All too often some factions consider themselves at war with others. Too many of us fight over theology. We politicize our beliefs and berate fellow believers when their political convictions don't line up with ours. We raid each other's churches and fill our pews with the freed "prisoners." We stick our thumbs underneath our armpits and rock back and forth on our heels, proud we are members of such-and-such a church or denomination and not members of all the others that we believe may have bits of the truth but for the most part are full of heresies and ignorance. Sometimes we even delight when "Christians" we disagree with fall from grace in very public ways. We revel in our doctrinal purity, our ecclesiastical perfection, and our moral virtue. Like the Pharisees who went before us, we see those outside of our camp as lowly, lost sinners, and we thank God we are not like them.[11] Then we look around us and wonder why the world has gone on without us, why it has stopped listening to us and begun looking elsewhere for answers. What will lead us out of our stupor?

I contend that part of the solution lies in remembering what we as the Family of families have obviously forgotten: what it means to be a Christian, a follower of Christ, a fellow son or daughter of the Father over all. All of us certainly need to reflect on our own Christian convictions regarding this identity issue as expressed within our particular church communion. For me, this means going back to the heart of my own Christian vocation, to my opening three claims. I am an evangelical Catholic Christian. Each of those terms conveys an essential element of who I am in Christ.

Let me explain what I mean by these descriptive terms and how I believe they apply to me. Then I would like to show why I believe they can shed light on what it means to rediscover a ground of unity, even as separated brethren, in the Family of Christ.

The Mandate of Unity

Acts 11:26 tells us that first-century believers were first called Christians in ancient Antioch. *Christian* simply means "follower of Christ." The word was coined to describe those who claimed to have a personal relationship with Jesus the Messiah and were committed to serving Him.

I am a Christian. As I will explain in more detail in the following chapters, I have personally placed my trust in Jesus Christ as my Savior and Lord; I have committed my life to following Him. I do not follow perfectly. Like all disciples, I am a learner and less than my Master. But I am still a Christian, a Christ-follower. *Christian* is the noun that defines who I am in relationship to the triune, living God. And as a disciple, I seek to follow on a continual path of deepening conversion, the "perfection" of which Jesus speaks in His discourse with the rich young ruler.[12]

As a Christian, I am also deeply rooted in the doctrinal essentials of the Christian faith. Though first revealed in the Person of Jesus Christ and later proclaimed in the sacred Scriptures, these essentials were reformulated and reaffirmed throughout church history in numerous creeds. One of the earliest was the Apostles' Creed, which reads:

> I believe in God, the Father Almighty, Creator of heaven and earth.
>
> I believe in Jesus Christ, his only Son, our Lord. He was conceived by the power of the Holy Spirit and born of the Virgin Mary. He suffered under Pontius Pilate, was crucified, died, and was buried. He descended to the dead. On the third day he rose again. He ascended into heaven, and is seated at the right hand of the Father. He will come again to judge the living and the dead.
>
> I believe in the Holy Spirit, the holy catholic Church, the communion of saints, the forgiveness of sins, the resurrection of the body, and the life everlasting.
>
> Amen.

The Apostles' Creed is very much like other early creedal formulas, but it was not drafted verbatim by the apostles. It is a product of the early church community's reflections on the faith as handed down from

Christ through His apostles. However, it does accurately restate biblical truth, and it probably originated from the earliest expressions of faith professed by the catechumens (those preparing for baptism) in the second century AD. Similar professions were used throughout the church in the West, but this doctrinal affirmation became the standard in the Western church by the ninth century.

Another ancient affirmation of faith is known as the Nicene Creed:

> We believe in one God, the Father, the Almighty, maker of heaven and earth, of all that is seen and unseen.
>
> We believe in one Lord, Jesus Christ, the only Son of God, eternally begotten of the Father, God from God, Light from Light, true God from true God, begotten, not made, one in Being with the Father, through him all things were made. For us men and for our salvation he came down from heaven: by the power of the Holy Spirit he was born of the Virgin Mary, and became man. For our sake he was crucified under Pontius Pilate; he suffered, died, and was buried. On the third day he rose again in fulfillment of the Scriptures; he ascended into heaven and is seated at the right hand of the Father. He will come again in glory to judge the living and the dead, and his kingdom will have no end.
>
> We believe in the Holy Spirit, the Lord, the giver of life, who proceeds from the Father and the Son. With the Father and the Son he is worshipped and glorified. He has spoken through the Prophets.
>
> We believe in one holy catholic and apostolic Church. We acknowledge one baptism for the forgiveness of sins. We look for the resurrection of the dead, and the life of the world to come.
>
> Amen.

Since the fifth century, the Nicene Creed (also known as the Creed of Nicaea-Constantinople) has been the only creed used in the liturgy of the Eastern churches. It consists of early baptismal creeds used in Jerusalem and the enactments of two early church councils (Nicaea in AD 325, and Constantinople in 381). It is particularly strong in its Trinitarian emphasis because it was drafted in an effort to combat Arianism, a heresy that denied the triune nature of God.

I embrace these creeds as accurate statements of the historic Christian faith. I believe them not only in my mind but also in my heart. I make that claim in the biblical sense, which sees the heart as the seat of our emotions *and* will, the decision-making center of the person.[13] These creeds set forth what the Scriptures reveal and what the church proclaims. My belief in them plants me squarely in the rich soil of two thousand years of Christian belief. To me, there is great stability in that foundation.

No orthodox Christian church denies the proclamations of these creeds, nor do any such churches deny that at its very heart, being a Christian means following Christ. We may disagree about what being a Christ-follower includes, but that it means having Him as our Master, our Teacher, our Savior, our Lord—to that we can and must all consent. This is part of our unity in Him. It is an essential foundation for our unity that we *must* reclaim.

Unity in a Universal Mission

I am also a Catholic Christian. This is not a contradiction in terms. Catholic as a description of Christians has firm connections to even the earliest centuries of the church.

In a sense, *Catholic* is my first name and *Christian* my last. Literally, the word *catholic* means "universal" or "all-inclusive." An early bishop, Ignatius of Antioch, wrote a letter to Christians in Smyrna right before his martyrdom in AD 110. In his letter, Ignatius wrote, "Where the bishop is present, there let the congregation gather, just as where Jesus Christ is, there is the Catholic Church."[14] Not only does this letter, and many similar texts, demonstrate an early episcopal form of church government, but it also shows that the term *catholic* was used when referring to all Christian people. The church is intended to be catholic and to include all believers under its umbrella. Too many of us frequently forget that critical fact. The mission of Christ and His followers is a universal one.

By the second century, errant doctrines began to creep into the church, and splits began over vital issues such as the divinity of Christ. The bishops of the early, united Christian church began to use the word *catholic* to distinguish the church of Christians who held to the true gospel from heretical groups like the Montanists (second century) and the Arians (fourth century) who had varied from it. In other words, by this early date *catholic* was being used like a first name, a defining name. We can even see this in the *Confessions*, a Christian classic written between AD 397 and 401 by the early bishop of Hippo, Saint Aurelius Augustine. In this great work, Augustine recalls how his mother, Monica, revealed her heartfelt prayer to him before she died: "I did have one reason for wanting to live a little longer: to see you become a Catholic Christian before I died."[15]

Throughout Christian history, what was once intended to be an all-inclusive (catholic) body of disciples of the Lord Jesus Christ has been fractured over and over. These fractures threaten to sever us from our common historical and doctrinal roots. I do not believe that such divisions were ever part of the Lord's intention, no matter how sincere or important the issues that undergirded the breaking of unity. Who's to blame is not for me to decide. There's enough blame for all of us to share. So rather than point fingers at each other, I think we need to focus on what Jesus wanted most deeply for His church: *unity clothed in love.*[16] If we are to be effective in winning nonbelievers to Christ and in transforming our culture for Him, we must have room for fellow Christians in our hearts and in our mission. In other words, we should value unity and seek genuine ground for cooperation.

I am not advocating we embrace a false nondenominationalism or superficial irenicism that denies distinctives of doctrine or practice. These differences among us are very real and very important. But there is an increasing darkness sweeping the globe, and it is imperative that all who bear the name Christian get on with the task of piercing that darkness by proclaiming and demonstrating the Light, by advancing the one mission of Christ.

In their marvelous document entitled the "Decree on Ecumenism," the bishops of the Catholic Church show the respect that properly must be afforded to all Christians: "all who have been justified by faith in baptism are incorporated into Christ; they therefore have the right to be called Christians, and with good reason are accepted as brothers by the children of the Catholic Church."[17] So should it be among Christians of all traditions—mutuality of respect, commonality of mission, and commitment to dialogue. We desperately need such traits to permeate our ranks if we are to carry out effectively the evangelical mission the darkness of our age so desperately needs. I will discuss this need and how to fulfill it as the book unfolds, but now let me take you back to the personal.

What makes me a *Catholic* Christian? A fair explanation would take another book. But let me give you six distinctives that help define my Catholic convictions.

First, I am a Catholic Christian who can point to various times of deepening faith or conversion in my life, "evangelical moments" as I call them, not just one experience. This is consonant with my understanding of what is involved in being transformed into the image of Christ. Conversion is a process, and individuals and the church itself are being continually renewed into His image. I believe in a church that is "one, holy, Catholic, and apostolic," and that will one day be fully restored. I believe in a church rooted in a two-thousand-year history of progress and mistakes. I believe in a church that continues to display the wonder of the Incarnation by revealing the Lord's love in "flesh and blood," a church that is not the Kingdom but merely a "seed of the Kingdom," as the Second Vatican Council so clearly stated.[18]

Second, I believe the Bible is the Book of the church, not that the church is the church of the Book. In other words, even though the Old Testament books were completed before the Christian church came into existence, the church preceded the writing of the New Testament books and out of the church's ranks came the divinely inspired human authors of these books. Moreover, it was the leaders of the church who officially recognized which writings were truly inspired by God and therefore would forever have a place of authority in the biblical canon. Theologian Alan Schreck said it succinctly: "The Bible is the inspired word of God and the 'book of the church.' It is the product of oral and written traditions that were handed on within the church, and each writing in the Bible was discerned by the church's bishops to be uniquely inspired by the Holy Spirit and to have irrefutable authority within the church."[19] Every text has a context, and the context of the biblical text is the church. The Bible is part of the church's tradition and the primary authority within that tradition.

This understanding, rather than lessening my love for the sacred Scriptures, deepens it and gives it clarity, consistency, and dynamism. Jesus came to establish a church, a new people who would inherit all the promises of Israel and become the messenger of salvation. The Bible is a gift to that church and a measuring stick (canon) for all her actions.

Third, I believe that Jesus literally meant what He said about the consecrated bread and wine of the Eucharist, or Lord's Supper.[20] I see that as a tremendous gift to the church—indeed, a source of life to all who will believe. I believe it would be disingenuous for Christians who do not agree on the nature of the real presence of Christ in the Eucharist to join this sacrament of unity. On the other hand, I long for the day when it will be possible for all Christians to share this sacred meal either here or in the wedding feast of Heaven, a time of incredible celebration that the Eucharist symbolizes.

Fourth, I am a sacramentalist. I believe that God reveals Himself in sign and symbol, spirit and mud. I remember learning as a boy that a sacrament was an outward sign instituted by God to give grace. I still believe that. Sacramentals reveal through the mundane the love and mercy of a wonderful God.

Fifth, I believe that belonging to Christ must affect our whole life and give rise to an incarnational worldview, a genuinely Christian culture, and an integrated piety. After all, that is what the Incarnation is all about: God revealing His love, His power, and His plan through a human instrument, His divine Son. Fully God and fully man. He calls us to carry on that role of revealing His love, His life, His mission, and His mercy through the instrumentality of our own human life and earthly work.

In my work through the American Center for Law and Justice, I have the privilege every summer, along with our founder and president, Pat Robertson, of giving our highest honor to a man, woman, or ministry that has done the most to promote pro-liberty, pro-life, and pro-family causes. Our honoree in 1994 was Dr. James Dobson for his outstanding work defending the family.

During the summer of '93, one of my heroes, Congressman Henry Hyde, was given the "Defender of Life" award for his tireless efforts on behalf of the unborn, the elderly, and the differently abled. In receiving the award, Congressman Hyde gave an extemporaneous yet profoundly inspired message. While he spoke, I was sitting next to Pat Robertson, who was visibly moved by Hyde's comments. Pat later asked me, "What is it about Catholics like Hyde?" The question was meant to be affirming. As he and I discussed the matter, it became clear that Pat was intrigued by Congressman Hyde's almost natural understanding of making his faith public and taking his passionate Christian convictions into the political arena. After all, Pat has spent much of his life inspiring and encouraging Protestant Christians to make their faith public. He wanted to understand why it was that somebody like Henry Hyde, a devout Roman Catholic, understood this dimension of the Christian mission without much difficulty.

I tried to explain to Pat that from the earliest stage Catholics who are raised in devout Catholic homes are taught that there are two responses to the gospel mandate: what has traditionally been referred to as "the extraordinary vocation" (the priesthood and religious life) and the "ordinary vocation" (or the call of the lay faithful). Though often misunderstood and sometimes misapplied, the use of the word *extraordinary* for the priesthood and religious life does not denote anything superior. Rather, it is extraordinary in the sense that it is an unusual vocation, a highly esteemed one, to forsake marriage for the cause of Christ. To "wed" yourself to the bride of Christ. To stand as a prophetic symbol of the Kingdom that is to come in the midst of the city of man.

Supplementing this call is the "ordinary vocation" of the lay faithful, which is to take the message of the faith into the marketplace. It is the role of the lay faithful, according to Catholic theology, to "renew the temporal order." This is why it was second nature for a devout Catholic such as Henry Hyde to bring his Christian convictions into the political arena. It is simply *not Catholic* to privatize your faith. Thus, the modern aberrations being proposed by certain Catholic politicians about their private convictions versus their public life are not only nonsense but un-Catholic.

Henry Hyde is an example of the Catholic understanding of the incarnational call of every baptized believer. In Protestant circles, this call is often described as being "salt and light" or a "marketplace Christian."

This kind of incarnational understanding of the faith sees no dichotomy between the spiritual and the temporal but a wedding of the two through the mystery of the Incarnation. It is to me one of the great mysteries and gifts of Catholic Christianity. But in reality, it is simply a restatement of classical Christianity. Remember, the church was once one. This wonderful heritage is shared by all of us even though we currently face divisions in our midst.

Sixth, I am thoroughly convinced that the church of Christ must be both hierarchical and charismatic, institutional and dynamic, and that she is indeed the universal sign (sacrament) of salvation still revealing Christ's presence in the world.[21] Therefore I have submitted myself to the teaching office of the Catholic Church and its leadership. I do this willingly and by conscious choice.

Now, to some of my brethren in different Protestant Christian communities, the fact that I submit to the church in this way creates perhaps their greatest problem with me. But for me this is a vital link to a vibrant ongoing relationship with the Lord and a continual asset in my ongoing pursuit of truth. I have often heard friends refer to themselves as "Bible-toting believers." Well, I am too. But as a Catholic, I believe that there is a magisterium, a teaching office, that provides ongoing guidance in the application of that Book to my life. Hence I am a magisterium-toting Catholic. I appreciate the moral clarity the magisterium provides.

I could continue my list, but hopefully these six points bring some understanding to what I mean when I describe myself as a Catholic Christian and why I choose to be one. I want to emphasize, however, that none of these descriptions has any significance apart from my Christian life. Jesus Christ, the Evangel, is the source and summit of it all. He is my life and redemption. Membership in my church—for that matter, membership in any Christian community—is not a guarantee of Heaven. Saint Augustine in his time-honored apologetic *City of God* warned his fellow Catholic Christians that baptism and membership in the church would not assure salvation, though they could offer great assistance in the Christian life.[22] The Catholic bishops of the Second Vatican Council echoed Augustine's warning: "Even though incorporated into the Church, one who does not however persevere in charity is not saved. He remains indeed in the bosom of the Church, but 'in body' not in 'heart.' All children of the Church should nevertheless remember that their exalted condition results, not from their own merits, but from the grace of Christ. If they fail to respond in thought, word, and deed to that grace, not only shall they not be saved, but they shall be the more severely judged."[23]

The challenge I have as a Catholic Christian is the same as any Christian's: to bring people to Jesus Christ, to a personal decision to accept Him as Savior and Lord, to bring them to personal repentance and conversion. But for me that is only the beginning. That salvation must be sustained, nourished, and deepened. It must also lead to personal transformation and holiness through implantation into Christ's Body, the church. The church is not an option, an extra we can accept or reject. It is the ark, the ship of God, and her mission is to help rescue and restore the drowning. This has always been her primary mission. The church exists to evangelize and disciple toward personal and corporate transformation, a mission entrusted to her by her Head, Master, and Lord, the Evangel Himself, Jesus Christ.

You may not see the working out of your Christian faith in the many ways I do. But if you are an orthodox Christian, whatever your church community, the roots of Christian history lead you to embrace the one mission of Christ as universal and identification with His Body as essential (*catholic* with a small *c*), in all her glory and weakness. The church is under the continual protection of her Bridegroom. Jesus said that not even the gates of hell would prevail against His church.[24] Hell has indeed tried, but Heaven has kept its promise. In that, at least, we are already united and protected.

A Common Commitment to an Evangelical Witness

Defining myself as a Christian is not a problem for most people, though some cringe or look at me with surprise. When I add to that the term *Catholic*, however, many Protestant Christians raise their eyebrows, flinch, or even get upset. Unfortunately, some have chosen to build whole "spiritual careers" on defining my church as a nonChristian cult or worse. But when I add *evangelical* to these terms, sparks fly—and not just among Protestants. Many of my Catholic brethren also believe I have attached a term that contradicts my understanding of what it means to be a Catholic Christian. For them, *evangelical* is a label, a synonym for a small sect of "fundamentalist" or "Bible-pounding" Protestants who are ardently anti-Catholic. If this were what *evangelical* meant, I would not use it to define myself. But if you would step back with me to gain a clearer vision of this term, you would see that not only can I use *evangelical* to describe myself, but I should. It should be—and indeed is—a most proper description for all Christians, be they Protestant, Orthodox, or Catholic.

The root of *evangelical* (*euaggelion*) literally means "good news" or "gospel."[25] It has been used to refer to the essential message of the gospel—salvation by faith in the life and death of Jesus Christ. In its action-verb form (*euaggelizo*) it means "to proclaim the good news."[26] So the word in its most basic sense covers both the message and the proclamation of the Christian faith. Today many Christians use the term *kerygma* to refer to the oral proclamation of the gospel and the word *euaggelion* to denote the written message. Nevertheless, both of these designations are properly contained in the root word *evangel*.

An evangelical Christian, then, is one who believes the good news about Christ and proclaims it. In other words, an evangelical Christian is a proclaiming Christian. Anyone who knows Christ as Savior and Lord and tells others about Him can legitimately attach the adjective *evangelical* to the noun *Christian*. In fact, it's hard to imagine what a Christian would be without also being evangelical in orientation. Putting the two words together almost results in redundancy. It's close to talking about buildings that lack structure or ordering a hamburger without the meat. If it's a building, it has structure. If it's a hamburger, it has meat. You don't get one without the other. Likewise, if someone is a Christian, he or she should be an *evangelical* Christian. One who truly follows Christ not only believes the gospel but shares it.

So in the truest sense of the term, I am an evangelical Christian. And if you are evangelical in your relationship, convictions, and obedience to Christ, you are a Christian too. Since I am also Catholic, I am an evangelical Catholic Christian. I am this without contradiction in terms, logic, theology, or history.

If you are a Catholic reading this book and you've never considered the term *evangelical* applicable to you, please consider two things.

First, most vibrant movements in the church today are evangelical in this sense. And second, John Paul II opened his pontificate with an impassioned plea to all who would listen to "open the doors to the Redeemer." Following in the great legacy of Paul VI's letter "Evangelization in the Modern World," John Paul II has continually called the whole church—and in a profound way, the lay members of the church—to a renewed evangelization. You as a faithful Catholic are called to respond to that mandate to embrace and participate in what is often called "the New Evangelization" in Catholic circles. In that you are being challenged to be an *evangelical* Catholic Christian. To keep alive your personal relationship with Jesus Christ and His family, begun in baptism, confirmed by you in the sacrament of confirmation, and reaffirmed at every liturgy. But not just to keep it alive—to give it away as well. To tell people about Jesus Christ and bring them into His people, the church.

If you are a Protestant Christian and you have never considered the possibility of a Catholic being evangelical in this sense, you haven't spent time with some of the millions of Catholics, some identified with renewal movements in their church, who love the Lord with great affection and demonstrate that love in an evangelistic and missionary life. These believers are a vibrant force for evangelization. They are bringing a profound dynamism not only to the Catholic Church but far beyond to the unchurched and to many Christian communions that are lukewarm in their love for Christ.

For those Protestants and Catholics who are uncomfortable with my use of *evangelical*, perhaps the real problem isn't the term or my application of it but a deeper struggle. The great divorce in our two-thousand-year-old Family has given rise to very serious language barriers. I've often thought that one of the greatest starting places in our efforts at cooperation and our faithfulness to what I believe is the Lord's plan for convergence would be a glossary. We have all picked up a lot of jargon that sometimes, though not always, makes it hard to recognize one another as brothers and sisters in Christ.

But even a sincere effort at learning one another's language is only a beginning. The pain and consequences of our division should lead us to mourning. Let me share some of my grief.

FAMILY GRIEF

It sometimes seems that no matter what I or my Catholic brothers and sisters say or do, we are still anathema to many Protestant Christians. A case in point. Catholic scholar Pastor Richard John Neuhaus, whom I deeply admire, was recently interviewed in that highly respected literary voice of evangelical Protestantism, *Christianity Today*. The article was entitled "A Voice in the Relativistic Wilderness," and it was a very positive treatment of Neuhaus and the many facets of his apologetic and prophetic work. Some of the follow-up letters to the editor, however, were not so supportive.

One man wrote, "The 'voice' that Neuhaus writes about definitely has a different agenda and should be viewed with much suspicion."[27]

A woman exhorted *Christianity Today* to "let go of R. J. Neuhaus and his pope. The very word *pope* should be revolting to you," she added. "To a Protestant, it is clear that anyone who is Roman Catholic has misused Scripture. To say, at the head of the Neuhaus article, that you want help from such believers is pathetic. It is also useless."[28]

And Protestant ethicist Harold O. J. Brown, whose work on behalf of the unborn has been widely appreciated and used in Catholic circles, queried, "Is it really in a good evangelical tradition to praise the man who calls himself the Vicar of Christ on earth without noting that it was papal claims like his that have contributed to the existence of the evangelical movement to which you and we belong?"[29] If honoring a fellow Christian is not part of "a good evangelical tradition," then we are in sorry shape indeed.

These comments are very disturbing, particularly when one considers that Father Neuhaus has been one of the greatest Christian thinkers of this century. Long before his decision to enter the Catholic Church (what he considered both "coming home" and "being faithful to the Reformation"), he and his great cultural insights were highly regarded in devout, intelligent Protestant circles. Has his decision to stand in another church communion undone his value to our mutual effort to engage and transform the secularized darkness of our age? Even among those who sincerely disagree with his theological journey and convictions about the nature of church, it seems illegitimate, if not absurd, to throw him out of the Christian universe when he is still saying many of the same things he said prior to his decision to pursue full communion with Rome.

This kind of backlash is heartbreaking. It causes scandal to our common efforts to reach our age with the claims of Christ. I am not making light of the very real and serious differences between Protestant and Catholic Christianity, but I am convinced that our efforts to ensure that the twenty-first century is the third millennium of Christianity compels

us to at least recognize one another as Christians and, better yet, to cooperate to transform our culture for the sake of the Kingdom.

I grieve for our divided house, and I long for the day when it will be
reunited once again. That may not happen in terms of a full communion, at least on this side of the Second Coming, but it can certainly
progress through cooperation. Tragically, many Christians don't think
that's even possible; some of us even actively fight against it. Maybe
that's because we and our ancestors have lived in a divided house for
so long. We have inherited deep prejudices and destructive misunderstandings. And each of us has done his or her share to perpetuate those
mistakes.

As the book progresses, we'll take a critical look at the fallout of
divorce within the Family of God. By coming to grips with it through
understanding, repentance, and forgiveness, I believe we can break the
deepening cycle of schism. Just as people with destructive appetites or
from abusive family backgrounds can take definite steps to move out in
healthy directions, so can we.

To help us, we'll also look closely at our common Family history.
There we'll find a Christian Family that always wrestled with family
problems and managed to work them out, at least for the first thousand years of its existence. What did that Family do right? Where did
it break down and why? How did it manage to survive divorce within
its midst? We'll probe these kinds of questions to find answers that
will help us begin to restore shattered relationships within our Family.
Taking the appropriate steps to begin healing the wounds of Christ's
Body will also go far in bringing genuine, visible hope to a despairing
world. The hope of North America and of Western civilization is bound
up in Christ and His church. What we do or don't do now will count
for eternity.

I believe these things, and I've verified their truth on a very personal level. And perhaps that's the best place to begin. With my story. With
my relationship with the Family of families and some of the joys and
struggles I've encountered there, and the lessons I've learned, sometimes the hard way. My story is a prodigal's story. It's a search for truth
that led me thousands of miles from home and right into the arms of
Him who is the Truth. It also led me to the greatest adventure of my life,
an adventure all Christians can share together by God's grace.

CHAPTER TWO

OVER THE RAINBOW

And without faith it is impossible to please God,
because anyone who comes to him
must believe that he exists
and that he rewards those
who earnestly seek him.
Hebrews 11:6, NIV

I opened the letter. It was postmarked Jerusalem, Israel, and dated April 1972. It had been several years since I had heard from my longtime friend, Fred.

Fred had been my closest friend since the fifth grade. When he met me, I was a new kid in a new town, and I was deeply afraid of rejection. He reached out to me at a point of real need in my life.

We searched for truth together, each of us somehow believing that what we needed were roots, but neither of us knowing where to find them. Eventually, Fred learned that he needed to find his meaning, purpose, and Jewish heritage in Israel, the land of his forefathers. So he went his way.

I still missed him and had wondered many times if he had made it to Jerusalem. Periodically, he sent unusual updates to my parents' house. For instance, once he sent pieces of a broken stained-glass window from a cathedral in France.

Fred was a romantic, a poet, a young man who felt deeply. When we parted company, I felt a great loss.

Now I was thousands of miles away, standing alone on a beach in Santa Cruz, California, tired, frightened, and without a place to stay. By this time I had traveled across the United States in my search for meaning, purpose, and truth. But I had come up empty.

I looked down at Fred's letter and began to read:

Dear Keith,

As I sit on the Mount of Olives I read these words: "How can a young man keep his way pure? By living according to your word. I seek you with all my heart. Do not let me stray from your commands. I have hidden your word in my heart that I might not sin against you. Praise be to you, O Lord. Teach me your decrees. With my lips I recount all the laws that come from your mouth. I rejoice in following your statutes as one rejoices in great riches. I meditate on your precepts and consider your ways. I delight in your decrees. I will not neglect your word." (Ps. 119:9-16)

Some of these words were vaguely familiar to me. I remembered reading them at home in the insert of our large family Bible, the one with a picture of Pope Pius inside, that Mom and Dad kept on the shelf in our parlor.

Following these words of Scripture was Fred's moving description of his encounter with Yeshua, the Messiah. I felt challenged by what Fred said. I realized that even though I had been Catholic, and supposedly Christian, all of my life, I did not know this Jesus the way my friend did. Jesus had come alive for Fred, but for me He seemed little more than a theory out of my past.

I thought about all of this as I felt the warm sand beneath my feet and tried to ignore the intense hunger pangs rippling through my stomach and the fears clawing at my soul. I was at the end of a cross-country journey that had begun when I left my home in Massachusetts at the age of seventeen. Of course, the preparations for my journey had begun much earlier. Don't get me wrong. I had not left with enough money, adequate transportation, or any confirmed hotel accommodations. In fact, from day to day I didn't know where I would be, how I would get by, or where I would sleep. But I did know that it was a trip I had to take. That sense of destiny, of determination, began building very early in my life.

UPROOTED

I grew up in Dorchester, Massachusetts, an inner-city section of Boston with an intensely Catholic culture. The church and the Christ she proclaimed were my life. Even as a young child, I enjoyed a peace flowing from a Catholic family life, a life rooted in the church. When I was in first grade, I can still recall being asked by a stranger, "Where are you from, kid?" "Saint Matthew's," I replied. The parish, the church, and the faith that it stood for were my culture and my greatest source of identity.

Over the years, I have heard horror stories about the experiences others had with parochial education, but I was a Catholic kid who experienced it only as a blessing. My first-grade teacher was a nun named Sister William Patricia. She told me that I could talk to Jesus anytime and that, in addition to the prayers I was learning, I could speak to Him "from my heart." So I did. Often I knelt in front of my favorite statue of the sacred heart of Jesus, pouring my heart out to Him. To some people, this might have appeared idolatrous, but I knew I was praying to the One whom the statue represented, Jesus the Christ, not to the statue itself.

The beautiful church adjacent to my school held daily mass in the main upstairs sanctuary as well as in the sanctuary downstairs. I frequently sneaked upstairs and sat alone, looking at the beautiful stained-glass windows and enjoying the fragrance of the votive candles as it filled the air. I admired the stations of the cross on the church walls that recounted the different stages of Jesus' courageous climb up the mountain of Calvary. I knew Him then and I loved Him. For me, even as a child, these times of private devotion were "evangelical moments."

As soon as I was able, which was around the third grade, I served dutifully as an altar boy at the altar of sacrifice. Even though I didn't understand the Latin spoken in the Catholic liturgy of that time, I knew that I was a part of something supernatural. Even then I had a metaphysical appreciation of the presence of the all-holy God. I believed what I had been taught: At the moment of consecration, I stood at the foot of the cross, in some miraculous way becoming a part of the timeless event of Jesus' crucifixion on Calvary. Sadly, I would later wander from the cross, but the memories of those evangelical moments would linger, albeit buried beneath the grave of my fears and confusion.

As I completed the fourth grade, my family experienced a personal tragedy that rocked us with the devastation of a terrible earthquake. Our home's oil burner exploded, causing our house to go up in flames. I'll never forget the experience.

We had come home from school as usual and left our shoes on the landing. The smell of chicken cacciatore filled the house. We sat down to eat and to be entertained by my father's wonderful humor. But within minutes the security of routine, home cooking, and a carefree father would be consumed in flames.

Suddenly, we heard the woman who lived in an apartment below cry, "Fire!" My father looked at us sternly and directed us to leave the house immediately, stopping to take nothing. He then ran downstairs and I followed him. As he opened the basement door, flames singed his eyebrows and hair. Again he directed me to leave.

My father then went into the bottom apartment and helped a mother and her children escape. I ran outside into the night. Heavy rain quickly drenched me as I watched the crowd that had gathered to watch my family's life burn away.

The deep loss and fear of that moment were indescribable. The trauma would influence my life for years to come.

I finally got into a car for shelter in time to watch one last explosion bring the roof in and seriously injure two firemen. I looked across the street and saw my mother sobbing.

Things would never be the same. Our house had been desolated, and with it the practice of our Catholic faith began to wane. Although it took a few years for the devastation to show through our lives, we eventually stopped praying and going to mass regularly.

Our misfortune happened on the heels of the Second Vatican Council in the Catholic Church (1964), which unfortunately became a significant source of confusion for many Catholics worldwide.[1] My family, along with many others, became secularized. For us, to be "Catholic" became more of a cultural statement and less of a religious one. In time, I stopped going to mass altogether. I began to rely on my own devices and the world's values to make it in life. Those values soon left me spiritually bankrupt but not intellectually or culturally inactive.

By the ripe old age of fourteen, I must have appeared to many as a successful junior high school student in a quaint southern New England town. But inside I was a cauldron of anger born of disillusionment, fear, and insecurity. Much of that anger released itself in rebellion.

I edited the first underground newspaper in my high school—a politically radical paper we called *Metamorphosis*, which, ironically, was just what I was looking for in my own life. A transformation. But I didn't know how to find it. Others weren't very helpful either. Because I expressed my discontent in creative ways, I was encouraged by well-meaning teachers. They, however, didn't see the pain and desperation behind my activities.

SEARCHING

Although my anger was fueled by the fire that had destroyed my home, my search for meaning and purpose came about another way—quite innocently, in fact. It began with a highly inquisitive mind. While other boys were playing baseball at the age of thirteen, I was away from the baseball field asking existential questions:

Why am I?

Who made me?

Why are there poverty and injustice in the world?

If there is a God, why do people suffer?

I hungered for answers to these and many other questions, and in my open-mindedness I wanted to give every philosophy a fighting chance to provide those answers. So at thirteen I turned eastward, as so many other young people were doing at the time. I began reading the works of Hermann Hesse as I sought to understand the *Bhagavad Gita*, a book of Hindu scriptures.

Fred had also hungered for answers as a young boy. Though he joined with me in most of my pursuits, he still focused much of his energy on art. He wrote inspiring poetry, painted murals, even composed some music. In all that he did, he showed himself to be a dreamer in search of meaning. He was deeply intrigued by my childhood Catholic faith. Jesus Christ and all things related to the Christian faith fascinated him. Even though he had a religious home life, his Jewish upbringing had not satisfied his spiritual hunger. So he kept looking—searching for more answers to what seemed to be an unending list of questions.

Thus, our search began together. Though we were younger than most of the pilgrims on the countercultural journey of the sixties, we, like them, embraced it all. Our search encompassed the areas of religion, politics, and philosophy. We read the great spiritual classics from both Western and Eastern traditions and dabbled in every New Age religious group available. And there were plenty; they were springing up in Boston like weeds. We attended Scientology lectures and listened to that version of how to find true meaning in life. We danced with Hare Krishnas on the Boston Common and tried to converse with them about the *Upanishads*. We even visited some of the darker elements of the growing new religions, including a group called "The Process," which years later would be clearly identified as satanic.

My parents, like many during the sixties and early seventies, were confused over my behavior. They didn't know what to do with me, so they responded with well-intended tolerance.

But despite all my early searching, I found no answers to my questions. No matter what system of thought I probed, it did not fill the emptiness in my soul. Paradoxically, though, no matter where my searching took me, I stayed fascinated with Jesus—the One who claimed to be *the* way, *the* truth, and *the* life. I frequently felt pulled back to this Jesus who had offered Himself on the cross, this Jesus of whom I had learned as a child, this Jesus who was meek and humble of heart.

Spiritual journeys were not all that preoccupied me, however. I became consumed with the plight of the poor and oppressed, a concern that was molded for a while by the "new Marxists." They attempted to recruit me and my friends, playing not only on our social concern but also on our anger over the war in Vietnam. Inspired by two friends of mine who lived in a "political collective" in Boston and gave me Marxist literature to convert me, I became fascinated with Che Guevara and other so-called revolutionaries—people who sought to overthrow what they viewed as an oppressive political or economic system for the sake of liberation. Soon I wanted to be like them. And for a season, I was.

In 1969, I linked arms with a virtual sea of quasi revolutionaries and, armed with a desire to stop war and expose injustice, marched on Washington, D.C. During these days of political enthusiasm, I also handed out leaflets against the Chicago Eight's trial, convinced they were victims of an oppressive system.

Fortunately, I eventually saw that in spite of their rhetoric, most of these "new revolutionaries" were as self-centered as the "they" they railed against. Like the alleged oppressors, these "liberators" were preoccupied with self-advancement and self-love. I eventually concluded they were paper revolutionaries, so I abandoned my fling with radical politics. My searching, on the other hand, intensified.

At the age of sixteen, I had accumulated enough credits to graduate from high school, but under Massachusetts state law, I was unable to graduate because of my age. So I dropped out. I didn't want to be just another cog in the "Establishment" wheel. I wanted to make a difference. In my egocentric adolescence, I decided to become an individual about whom books are written. So I enrolled in a "free school," one of the many begun by the so-called counterculture of the day. The name of the school was Satya, which is Hindu for "the truth," a fitting name for a school attended by one who considers himself a seeker of truth. The school was certified by the state of Massachussetts. I enrolled in classes on Eastern philosophy, pottery, and other esoteric or trendy subjects, and simply bided my time. Once I fulfilled the state requirements, I received my high school diploma and began my journey to "greathood" by leaving home.

It was the early seventies. Eastern philosophy was making incredible inroads into Western thought. Bookstores were giving more and more shelf space to what we now know as the New Age Movement. Self-professed gurus were finding followers among the hippies, musicians, and artists scattered throughout the country. Their mystical ideologies were attractive, but they only added to the already confusing array of choices.

It was also a time when many young people were experimenting with drugs in their search for significance. Songs by such groups as Jefferson Airplane, Cream, Buffalo Springfield, Ten Years After, and the Beatles had heralded mind-altering drugs as the doorway to personal peace and happiness. Many took the songs at their word, tasted the forbidden fruit, and soon discovered that it delivered a nightmare rather than a blissful dream.

I was seventeen, a fallen Catholic, a pursuer of the elusive dream—the dream that would open the world of answers to me. And I was sure that I could capture this dream if I left Massachusetts and hit the open road. So, like many other young people at this time, I enlisted a traveling companion. His name was Stuart Baker. Like Fred and me, Stuart was a seeker. However, he was much more interested in feeling than thinking. He was daring, heroic, and reckless. Deeply into the music of the time, he lived his life song to song in a fast-paced, frantic stream of consciousness. He had already hitchhiked across the country the previous summer and lived in the Hollywood hills. He so often shared his wild experiences with me that I was ripe when he invited me to join him again in a new adventure.

We set out as pilgrims, hoping to find our personal promised lands. Our search was not unlike Dorothy's in the *Wizard of Oz*, a favorite film of mine. Maybe we too would find our answers "somewhere over the rainbow."

My clothing for the journey was the typical uniform of the day: an army jacket, a T-shirt, bell-bottomed jeans, and earth shoes. We wore these clothes thinking we were making a statement that we were nonconformists. Ironically, though, all us nonconformists dressed alike. So much for individuality. The rest of my meager belongings were a toothbrush, a hairbrush, and a change of underwear and socks.

Everything fit into my backpack.

My transportation was my feet. My emotional and spiritual preparation for the journey, next to none. I was totally unprepared for what I would encounter.

Stuart and I left Boston and traveled through the Midwest, sleeping in rest areas, cars, and church hostels. We camped on the plains of Kansas and stayed in a cheap hotel in Denver with other guests of the crawling variety. We saw the stark beauty of Arizona's deserts, and after several months we finally arrived in what we hoped would be our promised land—Los Angeles.

While on the road, we ran into many young seekers like ourselves—people who also sensed that there was more to life than just school and career. What that more was, none of us knew for sure; we only knew that it was supposed to be better than what we had or had been offered. But because we couldn't define the "more," any road that promised more got our attention. Drugs, sex, alcohol, transcendental meditation, revolution, social activism—no road was left untried. Of course, all of us didn't try every road. But that didn't matter. What did was that it seemed none of us were finding anything more than dead ends. As our journey kept producing little to nothing, our optimism waned while pessimism and hopelessness grew.

Although Stuart and I found lodging in a variety of places, many times we had no *safe* place to sleep. Fear often kept us awake. Sometimes our fear came as the result of experiencing the unfamiliar. For example, since I had spent my early childhood in the inner-city of Dorchester, Massachusetts, I was not used to the sound of coyotes. One evening as I slept outside on the plains of Kansas, I heard coyote cries shatter the silence of the night. I nearly crawled out of my skin in fear.

At other times, our fears were anchored to real dangers. While hitchhiking, we traveled for two days with a man we thought was a fellow pilgrim. Tired of what he called his "banal life," he was headed for the coast. We spent two days traveling, partying, and discussing what we were going to do once we arrived in L.A. He was going to drive us the whole way. We and our tired feet were thrilled. Stuart had a pair of bongo drums, and as we sped down the open highway, we turned up the radio to a decibel level unfit for human ears while he beat a mesmerizing rhythmic pattern to the music. For a while, the music and bongos dulled our fear.

But this dream situation didn't last long. One evening we pulled into a remote rest area to sleep. Because the weather was so pleasant, we decided to sleep under the stars. As the night wore on, however, the stars disappeared and the sky opened with a fierce downpour. I remember waking and finding myself at the curbside, soaked with runoff water. The sky was pitch black because the moonlight was gone. And so was our ride. Our driver had abandoned us. He had even taken our few belongings with him. We were wet, cold, hungry, and broke—a state with which we had grown all too familiar.

When we ate, which sometimes happened only once every several days, our meals often consisted of day-old bread and water. A meal that included meat and almost anything green, except for mold, was a treat we relished.

When we weren't sleeping, fearing for our lives, chasing an elusive meal, or working a little to get some money, we read. Two books that caught my attention were with me wherever I went. In my top left jean-jacket pocket was the "little red book," *Quotations from Chairman Mao Tse-tung,* which I had received from a well-intentioned friend, who in his own search for truth had become a dedicated Maoist and revolutionary. He had joined the Students for a Democratic Society and even belonged to its militant faction, the Weathermen Underground. For him, truth involved the violent overthrow of the American government. I had dinner with him on several occasions at a political collective in Boston. There my friend Stuart and I listened to this group's plans to promote violent activities for the sake of the revolution. The walls of their apartment were covered with large portraits of Che Guevara and Mao Tse-tung. The little red book was my friend's gift to me, a gift he hoped would lead to my conversion to his system of thought.

In my right pocket was a New Testament given to me by other friends, a Pentecostal couple from Sharon, Massachusetts—a little town where I lived from the fifth grade through my sophomore year of high school. They opened their home on Friday evenings to anyone who needed a place to get warm. During those gatherings, they read from the gospels and talked about Jesus to anyone who would listen. Many Friday nights I found myself going to their home for warmth, potato chips, and Coke with a group of many other young people. Thank God for their courage and evangelical fervor. I would look back later and understand that those evenings were evangelical moments for me. Though I didn't know it at the time, the love I saw in their eyes was the love of Jesus Christ. Yet I was like a Teflon pan; their proclamation never seemed to stick to me.

FINDING THE WAY

Then, after months of traveling, I sat on that beach in Santa Cruz, California, with Fred's words swirling around in my mind. I faced the emptiness I had been unable to fill. I looked back on my journey, realizing that it had not turned out as I had expected. Instead of the promised land, I had found hunger, sleeplessness, disappointment, disillusionment, despair, and fear.

Through all of this, and always at the most frightening times, certain questions and answers rolled through my mind:

Who made you? God made you.

Why did God make you? To know, love, and serve Him in this world and be happy with Him in the next.

These were the words of the Baltimore Catechism I had learned as a child. They had stuck in my mind. Why? I wasn't sure. And I never really knew what to do with them. Not until that moment on the beach. In the midst of my confusion and fear, the Baltimore Catechism and Fred's letter of his startling conversion to Jesus Christ penetrated my awful fog. His letter was on fire with the good news, telling me what the catechism had taught me: God is real, He loves me, and He understands me more than I understand myself. Fred's letter also told me what I needed to do: Tell God that I love Him, confess my sin to Him, admit my weakness to Him, and ask for His forgiveness. If I simply invited "Yeshua," Jesus, God's Son, into my heart to be my Savior, He would renew my life. In Him I would find the meaning, purpose, and truth I had been so desperately searching for. Although I had heard these claims many times before and thought I had embraced them, I realized at that moment that my heart had grown cold and my relationship with my Lord had grown distant.

How clear it all was now! The hand of the Lord had been upon my whole life—even during my early teen years of questioning; even during my brief encounter with radical politics; even during my honeymoon with the "counterculture" of the sixties; even during my long, arduous, despairing trek across the United States. He had spared me from so much destruction while allowing me to get lost in the fog of my idealism and egocentricity so I would be ready to see Him more clearly and accept Him more readily.

My recollection of all of this, evoked by the words in Fred's letter, culminated in a deep longing and heartfelt cry to God. I had tried everything but Him. He was my last hope to find the truth. The urgency of this evangelical moment swept through my soul.

"Lord, I want to believe," I cried out. "If You are real, please come to me and save me. I confess my sin, and I ask Your forgiveness. I invite You, Lord Jesus Christ, to be my Savior."

It was the most important evangelical moment of my life. On that day, on that beach in 1972, I encountered the Evangel, the Good News, the God who became flesh, Jesus Christ. I stood at the foot of the cross. I found the Answer—the One from whom all the other answers to my questions would flow. My spiritual and intellectual journey wasn't over, but for the first time it was guided by faith rather than by a false drive for self-discovery. My life was changing from the inside out.

That internal change impacted my external life right away. I knew that my decision for Christ required a change of lifestyle, a change that immediately affected my relationship to Stuart and my current housing situation.

Stuart would be difficult to talk to because he had never understood my spiritual journey. Although he was culturally Jewish, he had no real faith *in* the God of Abraham, Isaac, and Jacob. So I didn't know how he would respond to my newfound faith.

Our living situation was another matter entirely. When Stuart and I first arrived in Santa Cruz, we slept for days in the basement of a local church until a small advertisement on a church bulletin board caught our eyes: "One young man needed in return for room and board." We didn't need to know any more than that. Though the ad requested one applicant, we both applied for the job and got it.

It was wonderful to have a warm bed and good meals, all for a little daily labor. We were so exhausted it took us about a week to recover from our cross-country travel, but when we did, I sensed something strange in that house. The man who hired us was more than a bit unusual. He sent us out daily to pick wild spearmint, bay leaves, and other herbs used in his "potions." It all seemed quite funny to me until calls from all over the country began to come in the middle of the night. Callers were looking for wealth and success and magical solutions to their problems in this man's potions. Stuart also picked up on the oddity of all this, but both of us were so tired of traveling and grateful for a place to settle that we didn't challenge any of it.

But now—sitting there on the beach, fresh in the Lord—I knew that I couldn't keep silent. I had to confront the lies I was living, the owner of the house whom I now knew was deceived, and my own fears and insecurities about my newly rediscovered faith. My initial evangelistic challenge was to share my faith with this man of potions.

To say the least, my outreach attempt was shoved back in my face. And that wasn't all that got attacked. Late one evening I entered the house and found the owner sitting at the kitchen table either drunk or high on drugs. He wanted to know why I was reading the Bible so often. I told him I had given my life to Jesus Christ and wanted to get back to my childhood faith.

"What?" he shouted angrily. Then he lunged across the table and tried to grab my throat to choke me.

As he came at me, the only thing I could think to do was scream a Scripture verse I had read that same day. In the heat of the moment, I even misquoted it. At the top of my lungs I yelled, "Greater is He that is in me than he that is in you!"[2]

My employer cursed me with vile profanity, stopped his assault, and stumbled out of the kitchen. What an evangelistic encounter!

Later I learned that he was heavily involved in the occult. I didn't know it at the time, but even the symbol on his hat was a pentagram, a satanic symbol. I also discovered that earlier his emotional problems had been serious enough to require institutional treatment.

As traumatic and frightening as that experience was, I felt the power of God surging within me. This time it would stick.

The next morning I confronted my friend Stuart. I told him about my disillusionment and discouragement with Marxism, the political left, and the false spiritualities we had encountered. I spoke to him about my childhood Christian faith and my return to faith in Christ. But he wasn't interested. He believed there was more of life for him to experience before he would consider settling into one "system of belief," as he put it. Stuart was not engaged in a spiritual journey. His search was of another kind.[3]

I felt bad about Stuart, but I knew I had to break away and build on what God had begun in me. So I took the little income I had earned from doing odd jobs around that house, called my parents, boarded a bus, and began the long trek back across the country. But this time the only book in my army jacket was the Good Book.

CHAPTER THREE

THERE'S NO PLACE LIKE HOME

I am the bread of life.
He who comes to me will never go hungry,
and he who believes in me will never be thirsty.
Jesus Christ, John 6:35, NIV

Like Dorothy in *The Wizard of Oz*, I discovered the emptiness of what I thought would be my Oz and the futility of my journey on the Yellow Brick Road. I longed to go home. But it would take much more than clicking the heels of ruby slippers and saying out loud, "There's no place like home." It would take a Greyhound bus ticket, a willingness to say goodbye to my friend Stuart, and another step in faith.

Just before I had begun my trek back across the United States, my parents had moved from Boston to a small city in Florida called Lakeland. Upon my return, I had no sooner walked in their door when I began blurting out my experience of encountering Christ and having my faith come alive. With good intentions but not much tact, I tried to "evangelize" them. They responded much differently than I had imagined they would.

"Son," my father replied, "if you're going to get religious, for goodness' sake, please stay Catholic!" My mother agreed. As time passed, my parents grew to better understand my love for the Lord, but at that point it was more important to them that I stay Catholic.

FRIENDLY SUPPORT

I enjoyed spending time with my parents, but before long my need for deeper Christian support and for people who could help me study the

Bible outweighed my desire to stay home. Ever since that day on the Santa Cruz beach, I hungered to know the Word of God. I spent hours poring over chapter after chapter of the Bible, never failing to find words of strength and encouragement. Nonetheless, I wanted more. I wanted to study the Scriptures more deeply and to discuss different perspectives of what they taught. So I began searching for a quality Bible study, one that would help meet my growing need. Strangely enough, I found one in an unexpected corner of my past.

When I left Massachusetts to cross the country, Chuck, a friend of mine from Boston, moved with my family to Florida. He played lead guitar in a rock band. Everyone called him Spider because of the black widow spider tattooed on his arm. Every time his arm moved when he played guitar, so did the spider.

How he got that tattoo is a story in itself. It began as a dare one evening. Chuck and I were at his home in North Attleboro, Massachusetts. We challenged each other to make a physical statement about our independence from the "Establishment." The statement had to come in the form of either a tattoo or an earring. After sealing our pact with a handshake, we climbed into Chuck's green '64 Chevy and traveled to Rhode Island. I watched Chuck get a tattoo. That was enough to convince me to pierce my ear.

Thankfully, my momentary madness healed quickly. You can't tell now that my ear was ever pierced. Chuck hasn't been so fortunate. Today he leads a lay community of Reformed Christians at New Hope Presbyterian Church in Indiana. At one time he edited a marvelous periodical on spirituality for pastors called *The Country Parson*. The spider still moves when he flexes his biceps. An ode to a time past. But the Lord has taken Chuck's raw creative energy and baptized it. It is now being wonderfully used for the Kingdom.

During our rebellious adolescent years, Chuck, like me, wandered from his Christian upbringing, swept up in the craziness and confusion of the age.

When I returned to Florida to "evangelize" my parents, I looked up Chuck, who was living only one town away from my parents' place. I found his trailer and knocked on the door. While waiting for him to answer, I heard the words of a song I had heard before. The song was "Welcome Back," and its lyrics did not fit the Chuck I had left behind.

You thought you could turn away and
no one could see through your eyes.

But I can see that you know better now.
You never were the untruthful kind,
And I'm so happy now to welcome you back.
Welcome back to Jesus.

"Come in. Door's open," came the familiar voice.

But when I walked in, I saw a very different Chuck. His hair was much shorter, and he looked happy. A stark contrast, indeed. When I had last seen Chuck, his deep black, curly hair cascaded past his shoulders. He had been fond of "muscle man" sleeveless T-shirts. And when he didn't wear those, he wore short-sleeved T-shirts with a package of cigarettes rolled into one sleeve. No matter what shirt he wore, however, he defiantly exposed the spider on his arm. But in the Chuck I now saw before me, the old defiance was gone. He was a new man.

"What happened to you, Chuck?" I asked. "You look so different."

"I've become a Christian, Keith."

"You're kidding! Me too."

We embraced each other and laughed as we spent the rest of the day recalling our different yet similar journeys. I now know that when I encountered Chuck that day, I also encountered Jesus Christ, who lived within him. This was another evangelical moment. And it led to the beginning of a wonderful summer—the summer of my conversion honeymoon.

Chuck and I, along with two other men who had a deep faith in Christ, rented a home and began studying the Bible together. One man was a member of the Assemblies of God; one was a Southern Baptist; Chuck was Presbyterian; and I, of course, was a fallen-away Catholic. And all of us were now deeply Christian, in love with Jesus, and committed to knowing His Word.

THE SPIRIT AND STUDY

We soon heard of a prayer meeting being held at night in a small private home. We decided to attend.

At our first meeting we saw excited people worshiping God, and we heard them speaking in a language we couldn't decipher. My curiosity got the best of me. I asked the leader of the group to explain what was happening. He opened his Bible and took me through the Acts of the Apostles, showing me that I was witnessing the very manifestations of spiritual gifts that had occurred in the early church.

I fell to my knees. If there was "more of God" to be had, I wanted it. So I prayed and received an abundance. The power of the Holy Spirit was manifested in me more deeply than I had ever experienced before. The participants at the prayer meeting called this the baptism of the Holy Spirit. For me it was another evangelical moment.

In later theological reflection, I realized I had experienced a deepening of what had already begun on that beach in California—indeed, what had begun in me as a child at baptism and had grown stronger as I became a confirmed Catholic. Without a doubt, something special happened to me that night: The Holy Spirit began to lead me in a new way. In the wider context of my life, this event was yet another sign of God's involvement.

Soon after this prayer meeting, I discovered a Bible college in my area. My passion for studying the Scriptures had been steadily increasing, and I knew I needed to learn more. So I enrolled in the college, thinking it would be the best way to study the Scriptures intensively. As it turned out, I was one of only a handful of Catholics who had ever enrolled there, although there were plenty of former Catholics and anti-Catholics among the student body.

During my first semester, I met some wonderful people who were on fire for Jesus Christ and for spreading the good news. With them, I fully embraced my study of the Scriptures and took advantage of every possible opportunity to worship God. I was gradually becoming aware that to belong to Jesus meant to belong to His church, His community of faith. I discovered a wealth of teaching on *koinonia*, Christian fellowship, in the New Testament letters.

Saint Paul's letters were written mostly to bodies of believers, to communities of believers, not just to individuals. Even those written to individual disciples were filled with instructions for community life. For example, Paul's letters to Timothy were directed not only to his personal life but to his leadership of the church at Ephesus. Community life was normative for early Christians. To belong to the Head, Jesus, meant to belong to His Body, the community called the church.

I searched for that experience of belonging. I tried many different churches: Baptist, Presbyterian, Assemblies of God, Church of God, Church of God of Prophecy . . . and the list went on. At each church, I experienced the Lord's presence and found people in love with Him, but I somehow knew I was not yet home. That did not stop God from working in my life, however.

Another evangelical moment occurred while I was involved at an

Assemblies of God church. In their zeal for evangelism, this community of believers sent busloads of young people to a particular downtown park during secular rock concerts. These young people walked through the crowds, freely sharing their faith in Christ. I was inspired to join them one Saturday, and they teamed me up with a real dynamo. He was on fire for Christ. He shared that fact freely with anyone who would listen. How? By telling his own conversion story with honesty, humility, and power. For the first two hours, I simply accompanied him, marveling at his courage and learning from his example.

Then I went out on my own. Mustering up enough courage and filled with spiritual zeal, I witnessed to the first concert participant I could find. I sensed God's presence as I told this young man how I had placed my faith in Jesus Christ. Much to my delight, he really listened to my message, and the Holy Spirit began to move him visibly. I asked him if he would like to meet the Jesus I knew. His eyes lit up as he nodded yes. During the next moments, I had the privilege of introducing him to Jesus, the Evangel. I simply said, "Jesus, I want You to meet my friend, Rick. He wants You to be his Savior." Rick confessed his sin and invited Jesus Christ into his heart. What an evangelical moment!

From that time on I desired nothing more than to bring people to Jesus Christ and begin them on the road to eternal life. Personal evangelism became as natural as breathing.

I experienced this and many other evangelical moments during my stint at the Bible college, and I know that many of these moments were possible because of my study of God's Word. Nothing else cuts like a two-edged sword. I will always be grateful for the intense exposure to Scripture I received there. But I eventually became perplexed by the very classes that had once inspired me.

My experience in one class is still vivid. We were discussing the sixth chapter of John's Gospel, where Jesus claims to be "the bread of life."[1] This passage served as the springboard for discussion of the Assemblies of God doctrine of the Last Supper. As the professor explained the Assemblies' perspective, I realized how different it was from my own understanding. In my parochial school and catechism classes, I was taught to believe that the bread and the wine of the Last Supper miraculously become the body and blood of Jesus Christ. For me it was the Eucharist, where Jesus in His flesh and blood was actually present, not simply being remembered by a group of His followers. It was the heart of the Christian life, not just a tangential religious act.

My professor, though, argued that the words of Jesus in John 6 were figurative. Jesus really did not mean that He would give His flesh to the disciples to eat. "That, after all," he said, "would be tantamount to cannibalism."

His explanation and reasoning amazed me. Up to this point in the course, we had studied the Gospel of John with a literal approach to all of its verses. In other words, in all other instances what the text said it meant and what it meant it said. This included Jesus' discourses. I had admired the consistency and clarity of this hermeneutical approach. On this day, however, the approach changed dramatically. The switch disrupted my newfound literalist approach to Scripture. I couldn't bring myself to accept this hermeneutical shift of gears. Which interpretative approach was right? Were Jesus' words to be understood within their grammatical-historical framework? Or were they to be treated as allegory with hidden meanings? Somehow, I believed there was more to what we were studying. There was a profound gift and mystery that was not being grasped.

I went up to the professor at the end of class and asked him why the same Jesus who literally meant everything else He said spoke figuratively in sections of John 6. He didn't answer my question. Instead, he gave me a discourse on his understanding of the Lord's Supper.

Undaunted, I asked him another related question: "Why is grape juice substituted for wine at many Protestant communion services when Jesus and His disciples drank wine?" Once again, the professor didn't answer my question. Rather, he told me that "new wine" in the Scripture referred to unfermented grape juice. But this didn't square with the biblical accounts. How, for instance, could people get drunk on "unfermented grape juice"? And why would people who knew the quality and power of good wine berate the host of a wedding for allegedly withholding the best of his brew until the end of the celebration? And why, if wine was such a bad thing, would Jesus miraculously supply not only wine but the best that had been served at this wedding feast?[2] Certainly they weren't complaining about the host's withholding the best of his grape juice!

I was confused. I wanted to know the truth, but I believed the truth was being suppressed. I questioned and questioned, but my hunger for answers went unsatisfied.

TRADITION REDISCOVERED

So I began to look to the past for answers. I started by delving more deeply into Protestant church history. First I read the Reformers—men such as Luther and Calvin. I discovered that their teaching about the Gospel of John and the Lord's Supper was significantly different from what I had heard in class. While poring through their works, I began to discover the church before the 1500s. It was not the church I had been told it was at the Bible college. The church of the Middle Ages wasn't perfect, but neither was it the perpetrator of a spiritual dark age. On the contrary, I found it to be a church of great intellectual and spiritual vitality coupled with a strong missionary and evangelistic zeal. It didn't take long before I found that Christianity had a wealth of tradition and that *tradition* was not a bad word. We had recently sung a verse in the Bible college's chapel assembly: "Tradition had me bound but Jesus set me free!" What I was finding was both Jesus and freedom *in my tradition*.

The Reformers and medieval theologians took me back to the early church Fathers: Ignatius, Polycarp, Tertullian, and numerous others. They were wellsprings from which I drank insatiably.

Another personal discovery was the *Didache*, the earliest compilation of post–New Testament writings currently extant. The *Didache* helped me see that very early on Christians had gathered for liturgy. Ignatius of Antioch in his ancient letters showed me that church government was not a later addition to Christian history. Over and over again, the more I unearthed the church's past, the greater my appreciation grew for its incredible wealth of worship, wisdom, and biblical understanding.

My thinking definitely needed to be reshaped. I knew I had not yet found my religious home, but I was now centuries closer. Still, I kept on with school, even though I found its instruction increasingly unsettling.

One day I received a homiletics assignment that would woo me closer to my religious home. We were told to give an oral report on a great Pentecostal hero. After several hours of research and reflection, I decided to speak on Saint Francis of Assisi, also known as Francis Bernardone, the "little poor man." He was my favorite saint from my childhood years. I still remembered the sisters' stories of his proclamation of the gospel and the miracles worked through his prayers. So I dug into his life and writings and discovered a man filled with the Holy Spirit and an evangelical fervor that rivaled many of his contemporaries, not to mention many of us today. Studying the renewal movement he inspired, I discovered that all of Europe had been set aflame by one little man so in love with Jesus and with the church that even when he saw inconsistencies within her, he refused to abandon her. He had truly lived his life touching the lives of others with supernatural power and compassion. This for me was another evangelical moment, an encounter with the good news of the church.

To the chagrin of my professor but to the interest of my classmates, I gave my first sermon on this great Pentecostal hero.

My college studies also led me to great evangelical Protestants like John Wesley, Charles Finney, and Smith Wigglesworth, and also to such mendicant evangelical Catholics as Saint Dominic.

But I found myself most drawn to that little poor man of Assisi, Francis, who while praying before the cross at San Damiano received a commission from the mouth of the Lord: "Francis, go and rebuild my church which, as you see, is falling down in ruins around you." Francis had seen so much that needed to be rebuilt in the church of his day that, had he responded on a purely human level, he might have rejected God's call. Yet he understood the deep mystery: To belong to Christ is to belong to His church. I knew I had to belong, as well. My call and my place were in the church of my childhood. This, too, was an evangelical moment, an encounter with the Lord who still incarnates Himself through His church. I did not, however, return immediately to active participation in the Catholic Church.

One morning while at prayer, I opened my Bible to the prophet Isaiah and read about his commission. These words from the pages of the sacred Scriptures came alive: "Then I heard the voice of the Lord saying, 'Whom shall I send? And who will go for us?' And I said, 'Here I am. Send me!'"[3] Another evangelical moment. Through this passage I heard the voice of the Lord commissioning me. But what my commission would be was still not totally evident.

I believe that part of it, which was also a fervent personal desire, was to see my family come back to faith in Christ. I knew, however, that a major obstacle for them was my attending a Protestant Bible college. Every time I broached the topic of religion with my parents, they gave me the same response: "Son, will you please get back to the church?" Although their question had frustrated me, I became increasingly aware that my behavior was a stumbling block to them. Moreover, my constant need for "something more" was ever more strongly drawing me back to my Catholic roots.

WELCOME HOME

One Saturday morning after personal prayer, I borrowed my father's truck and drove through the streets of Lakeland, Florida. I noticed an advertisement for Saint Joseph's Catholic Church, and I felt compelled to find the church. This was a strange feeling. I had not been a practicing Catholic since the fifth grade. I had attended an occasional liturgical service, but that was all. So why such a strong pull on my heart to locate this church? Could it be of the Holy Spirit?

After I passed the sign, I came to a railroad track and was forced to stop because of an oncoming train. Waiting, I looked around, exploring a part of town I had never given a second glance. What immediately caught my eye was a Christian bookstore. I pulled in to kill some time.

The minute I walked through the door of the store, the first book that caught my eye in a crowded book rack was entitled *Catholic Pentecostals*, by Kevin and Dorothy Ranaghan. *Is there really such a group?* I thought. With my father in mind, I bought the book. But as I began to read it, still standing in the bookstore, I was fascinated by story after story of Catholics like me who had returned to a deep faith in Christ, had been empowered by the Spirit, and had never been the same as a result. Now more than ever, I felt led to find Saint Joseph's Catholic Church.

I got back in the truck and started to drive. Minutes later, I found the church. As I walked inside, I recognized the familiar aroma peculiar to older Catholic churches—the scent of burning votive candles. The candles, the statues, and the tabernacle all reminded me of the wonder of God. I felt drawn into His presence, filled with a sense of mystery and awe.

I slowly made my way up the aisle. The closer I came to the altar, the more my heart was filled with an unspeakable Presence, an excitement that made my whole being attentive. Reaching the altar, I fell prostrate and cried out, "O God, I need to find my home in Your church."

I could have lain there for hours, lost in the homecoming, but within seconds the church lights went on. I was startled, torn from the intensity of my petition and worship. I hurriedly stood up and moved toward the exit, all the while realizing that something had happened within me, but too frightened to find out what.

As I began to leave the church, an elderly woman was coming in the door. She invited me to stay for the mass that was about to begin, but I declined her invitation and left. Within a matter of minutes, however, I knew I had to return. So I did.

I sat through the mass and felt everything come alive—the words of the Scriptures, the words of the canon, the words of consecration. Each point of the mass pierced my heart. I wept openly.

Afterward, I approached the priest and told him my whole story—

my encounter with Jesus Christ, my new birth, and my empowerment through the Holy Spirit. He smiled and welcomed me home. He then told me about another Catholic church in town that held a charismatic prayer meeting. Coincidentally, the group was to meet that evening.

So I went to mass again that day at the other church. How remarkable to attend mass twice in one day after a hiatus of nine years. The name of that Catholic community was Resurrection Church, appropriate for me as I was entering new life there, encountering the power of Jesus' resurrection in a personal way.

After that church's mass, which was another powerful experience, I shared my story a second time with this other priest. My heart was racing when he introduced me to the couple who led the prayer meeting, Chris and Pauline Earl. The Earls were gracious hosts. They took me home that night and gave me dinner, then later drove me to the church hall for the prayer meeting.

When we walked into the back of the church, I saw about twenty-five elderly Catholic men and women with their hands raised, singing "Alleluia." Something inside me immediately clicked. I knew at that moment I was finally home. This was where I belonged. This was the ark. This was the place where God would show me His plan for my life.

In the months that followed, I fell deeply and passionately in love with the Catholic Church and was obsessed with learning more about her. I went to the Lakeland Public Library and found more books on the early Fathers, which I pored over day after day. I studied about Saint Polycarp, whose heroic martyrdom greatly inspired me. I studied the lives of many other saints as well, but none moved me as much as did the life of Saint Francis of Assisi. My fascination with him led me to write to a Franciscan friar about whom I had read in a popular magazine. His name was Father Michael Scanlan.

At that time, he was the rector president of a seminary in Loretto, Pennsylvania. I sought his advice for my vocational direction. As a Catholic man in love with Christ and His church, I aspired to the priesthood and was attracted to the Franciscan spirit. Father Mike's written response marked the beginning of a friendship that endures to this day.

For a time, I continued discerning my vocational goals and growing deeper in my knowledge and love of God. Once I went to a weekend retreat at which a holy Benedictine abbot, David Gaerets, gave a powerful message on conversion. By the time the weekend retreat ended, he had invited me to visit his Benedictine monastery in Pecos, New Mexico.

Abbot David inspired within me a hunger for genuine Christian community. He had a vision for the renewal of the church that was based on Saint Benedict's model. In the sixth century, Saint Benedict planted powerhouse monastic communities in the centers of villages that were as stones cast into ponds. The heroic lives of the Benedictine brothers and sisters rippled out by example into the surrounding villages like concentric circles. Their ministry outside of the monastic walls strengthened the townspeople in their resolve to live fully for God. Considering this order's historic work, Abbot David asked a simple question: "Couldn't Saint Benedict's approach still do the same thing today?"

He helped me realize more clearly that to belong to Christ I must be a part of His people, not just in theory and theology, but in fact. I embraced this vision. Young, single, in love with Jesus Christ, and seeking His will for my life, I spent the next year and a half aspiring to the monastic life under the tutelage of Saint Benedict and Abbot David. I studied the *Philokalia*—the writings of the Eastern church fathers—and further rooted myself in a sacramental and incarnational catholic Christian worldview. I experienced genuine relationships of brotherly love. Church and family came together for me, and I encountered Christ through His incarnational revelation of Himself in His people. This was yet another evangelical moment.

At monastery youth retreats, I proclaimed Christ and the gospel to young visitors and invited them to make a personal commitment to Him. I loved to preach the gospel of grace. I was an evangelical Catholic Christian, an aspiring young monk, and my time and ministry at the monastery were some of the most wonderful months of my life. But I soon understood that I was not called to remain single for the Lord and the church, although I was convinced of the dignity and holiness of this extraordinary vocation that had been chosen by the Apostle Paul and so many other believers throughout Christian history.

When I finally left the monastery, I wanted to complete my college education. I had my high school diploma, even though I had left school for my cross-country journey before graduation. I had also taken the opportunity to complete the freshman year at the College of Santa Fe as a Benedictine seminarian. But now I wanted to earn a college degree. Most of all, I wanted to keep studying the Scriptures in an environment where my faith would be nurtured, not attacked. I had received my notice of acceptance and a grant of scholarship monies to Boston College. To a Boston-bred Catholic that meant a lot.

So I returned home to Boston to enroll. Within days of being on campus, however, it appeared to me that the school lacked a strong faith-nurturing environment. I am sure many people there were strongly committed to the Christian faith, but the environment of the school was quite secular at the time. And what a culture shock that was for me after spending a year and a half in a monastic community. It was too much for me. I couldn't stay. But where could I go instead?

During my stay in the monastery, Father Michael Scanlan and I had corresponded several times, and at one point he had even come to visit me. Before I left the monastery, he moved from Loretto and accepted a position as president of the College of Steubenville.

Confused about where to attend college, I called Father Michael on the phone. "Father Mike, I want to go to school where my faith will be strengthened. Is there any more room at the College of Steubenville?"

"Keith," he replied, "there's always room for you—take the next plane."

I felt the little poor man of Assisi beckoning me to "rebuild the church." So following the lead of the Holy Spirit, I moved to Steubenville, Ohio, to join in Michael's Franciscan mission.

Dr. Carl Henry, one of the foremost deans of evangelical history, in a talk entitled "The Christian Scholar's Task," defined an evangelical as "one who affirms the good news that God forgives sin and gives new life to sinners on the ground of the substitutionary death of Christ and His bodily resurrection."[4] He was quick to add that the message to be proclaimed must be scripturally controlled and scripturally authenticated. I would soon discover that just such a proclamation would become the secret to the success of an evangelical Roman Catholic college in Ohio. It would become caught up in what Protestant Christians call a revival.

CHAPTER FOUR

CLASSICAL REVIVAL
AT A CATHOLIC COLLEGE

Where there is no vision, the people perish.
Proverbs 29:18, KJV

Vision is the world's most desperate need.
There are no hopeless situations,
only people who think hopelessly.
Winifred Newman, *Quotable Quotations*

In the late sixties and early seventies, the College of Steubenville suffered from the disease that afflicted many church-based schools—secularization, the purging of God and a God-grounded ethic at least from the public arena of life. Alcohol, drugs, sexual immorality, and depression, symptoms that so often accompany this illness, were rampant. Though the situation at Steubenville was not unique, a search committee recognized the need for action and assembled to find a captain to steer what appeared to be a sinking ship. In 1974, they chose Father Michael Scanlan to fill this role.

After a trip to Assisi, Italy, to rekindle the Franciscan fervor in his own spirit, Father Mike stepped onto the campus of the College of Steubenville. What he met was a board of trustees whose hearts had been prepared by the Lord to cautiously relinquish control of their plan for the college and make room for God's plan for the renewal of Christian and Catholic values—the values of the college's founders—that would disrupt and upset the existing campus lifestyle. The rather tenuous but open acceptance of Father Mike's nomination for the college presidency was the first step in a series of slow yet steady efforts, under the direction of the Holy Spirit, to begin the restructuring and revival of the Steubenville campus. And what a revival it would be!

Though the board of trustees accepted his new leadership, many of the faculty and students did not. That was not surprising. Secularization had infected the entire campus, and it would not be easily cured. Father Mike saw its damaging effects throughout the faculty and student body.

Some among the students were using alcohol and drugs to ease their depression. One-night stands and other forms of promiscuity were common attempts to find love in their love-starved environment. Many admitted they had no friends on campus, no one with whom they could talk or share their lives, no one they could love or who would really love them in return. Attempted suicides, though not unusual for college campuses, were a visible sign of the student body's brokenness and woundedness.

The faculty was not much better off. The demoralization of many professors dramatically illustrated their loneliness and despair. Some had even spurned their Catholic roots so thoroughly that their classroom lectures and other public expressions heralded a worldview and ethical perspective antithetical to Christian orthodoxy. A few had even gone as far as advocating alien ideologies devoid of any concept of God, much less a Christian one.

In describing these early years, Father Michael stated in his published talk "Making and Keeping Catholic Colleges Catholic":

> In our own situation, we went through some very difficult situations, which resulted in separating people from the university. One involved a faculty member promoting atheistic Marxism. We went through a separation process with a faculty member who was promoting secular humanism and the *Humanist Manifesto*. There was a former faculty member who promoted feminism courses and lesbianism as a priority over a Christian commitment. There were lecturers in theology promoting exegesis and relativism in ways that obscured the truths of revelation. I am talking about individual situations that are no longer present at the university. There was also a former student personnel administrator who regularly promoted skepticism regarding eternal values and absolute truth. In drama, there was a struggle with a director who believed that art for art's sake was the ultimate value rather than a commitment that came under serving the glory of God.[1]

Secularization showed up in still other ways. Though the college was a Catholic school, faculty and student attendance at even Sunday liturgies was virtually nonexistent. The school's financial condition and physical state were as poor as its student life. Enrollment was dropping sharply. Two dorms were empty, and an extraordinary outburst of vandalism was destroying the appearance of the campus.

The college was a war zone with spiritual ruin visible everywhere. Father Mike's mission was clear, and he went at it armed with divine wisdom and love, a vision of the truth, the strength and conviction to bolster the vision, and the willingness to undergo persecution to carry it out.

Father Michael spent the early months of his first year as president getting to know the students. He talked seriously with them; relaxed with them by playing tennis, football, basketball, and volleyball; ate in the cafeteria with them; learned about their lives. Although he saw blatant sin and ill-fated escapism, he realized these were symptoms of deep emptiness and loneliness inflicted by the cancer of secularization, and it moved him to compassion. He worked to cure the disease, not to shame or destroy its victims.

Father Michael also spent a good deal of time getting to know the faculty. He dialogued with them about their views and prayed for their spiritual revival. Although some strongly opposed his efforts, others welcomed him, wooed by his genuine concern for their personal lives.

I arrived on the scene in the initial stages of Father Michael's work of renewal, and in the process I embarked on a new stage in my personal walk of faith.

I will never forget my arrival in Steubenville, Ohio, in 1975. As I rounded the bends of West Virginia Route 2, I saw the smokestacks of the Weirton Steel Mill protruding into a dingy gray skyline. I felt somewhat unsettled as I recalled some of the beautiful landscapes that I have enjoyed living in over the years. I was raised amidst the beauty and strength of the New England countryside. And I had just spent a year and a half sixty-nine hundred feet up in the mountains of New Mexico, nestled in the Sangre de Cristo (Blood of Christ) mountain range. As I pursued the monastic life there, the countryside offered me peace and strength. To say the least, I was not prepared for the geography, the climate, or for that matter, much else that I found in Steubenville.

I was unsettled, but somehow it didn't really matter. I was here for a purpose: to complete my education in an environment of faith. I had long since decided that the most precious thing to me was Jesus Christ. I wanted to give my whole life to Him in service, and I didn't want to be in an academic setting that would threaten my commitment. Little did I know, however, the challenges ahead or how much my faith would be tried and refined by them.

What I found shocked me. The College of Steubenville was barren.

An air of despair hovered in the minds and hearts of many. But not in Michael Scanlan. In him I saw hope, vision, conviction, and the fire of God's Holy Spirit. Proverbs 29:18 says, "Where there is no revelation, the people cast off restraint; but blessed is he who keeps the law" (NIV). Or, as another version puts it, "Where there is no vision, the people perish" (KJV). There was no lack of vision in Father Mike.

When I arrived on the Steubenville campus, one of the first things I noticed was an etching in the administration building of Saint Francis carrying a stone. I didn't know then that the etching would later become the symbol of a great movement of God to raise up a mighty fortress where His name would be praised and adored.

As a young man, Francis of Assisi had a dramatic conversion. He heard the Lord tell him to "go and rebuild [restore, revive] my church, which as you see is falling down around you." Responsive to God's call, Francis Bernardone immediately set out to restore physically the small churches that had fallen into misuse and disrepair. Stone by stone he started to rebuild them. But his focus wasn't merely buildings; he also sought to rebuild souls. He gathered around himself the misfits of his time, the lepers, the impoverished, and the many others society had rejected or ignored. As he followed the Lord, he prayed fervently for revival, and God added to his group others who were on fire for the divine mission. Eventually Francis came to see that the ruins of which the Lord had spoken were the *living* stones—the living members of His church—not the physical structures they used for worship.

The Apostle Peter describes us as living stones in his first letter: "As you come to him, the living Stone—rejected by men but chosen by God and precious to him—you also, like living stones, are being built into a spiritual house to be a holy priesthood, offering spiritual sacrifices acceptable to God through Jesus Christ."[2] I thought of this verse and Francis of Assisi many times in the initial years of rebuilding the Steubenville campus. Yes, buildings needed repair and other physical and financial matters needed attention, but none of these was as important as addressing the deep personal needs of the college's "living stones." Franciscan Michael Scanlan clearly saw this order of priority.

Following in the heritage of Saint Francis, Father Mike began assembling around him living stones for the work of revival. His formula was simple and consisted of these parts:

◆ Prayer
◆ Repentance

◆ Conversion
◆ The power of the Holy Spirit
◆ Mission

The nature of revival hasn't changed since the first century. When these essential elements are genuinely embraced and lived out, revival occurs. The great Protestant and Catholic revivalists understood and practiced this and saw God bring incredible results. The College of Steubenville would experience no less.

THE PRAYER FACTOR

As a resident student, I had to move into one of the college dormitories. Space was not a problem given the low student population. But at Father Michael's suggestion and my request, I moved into Saint Thomas More Hall, which was nearly empty, except for a group committed to all the elements of revival. They called themselves the "Heart of Mary Household," and they occupied a small section of the dormitory. Joined by many laypeople from the local area, they had begun meeting for protracted prayer sessions, beseeching God to send His Holy Spirit to resurrect and renew the dry bones of the campus.

Inspired by their efforts, I moved onto the dorm's third floor and began what would become the first student faith household. The Heart of Mary was comprised of volunteers and employees of the university, which was fine and good. But part of Father Michael's vision for the college's renewal was the building of a genuine *koinonia*—a Christian community—of students. He believed that one of the greatest impediments to experiencing the faith at many Christian colleges, and for that matter in many Christian churches, was the lack of true fellowship. So he longed to see dormitories where men and women would gather on their respective floors, commit their lives to love the Lord as well as one another, and truly become fellowship groups.

Father Mike suggested I seek other young men who were willing to commit themselves to live in the same wing, pray together daily, study the Scriptures, attend the Eucharist, and engage in missionary work together. I embraced his vision and watched God work.

In that first household, I was soon surrounded by some wonderful men: Craig Brotz, David Reuter, Rick Peters, John Heit, Dave Anderson, Rich Stepanski, and Frank Kelly. We all had our shortcomings. We were young and didn't know the first thing about building a genuine experience of Christian community and fraternity, but we all loved the Lord and knew how to pray. And how we prayed! Every day. Every night. Without fail. Always expecting God to honor the humble requests of His people.

In time, we joined forces with other committed Christians on campus and in the surrounding area, constantly interceding for the College of Steubenville. As a household, we prayed with those of the Heart of Mary Household, who were also growing spiritually stronger by the day. On yet another floor in our massive dormitory were some religious women—Sister Barbara, Sister Anne, and Sister Loretta—who had also experienced a fresh anointing of the Holy Spirit and a call to be a part of His great work on our campus.

God provided other sources of encouragement and inspiration as well. Several priests in Steubenville played an important role in moving me to give myself totally to Jesus Christ. Perhaps the one I remember with the greatest affection is Father Philip Bebie, who has since gone on to be with the Lord. He loved God and had a joy and vibrancy that I had never seen before. He and the other priests taught me much about living a holy, inspired, and radical life for our Lord.[3]

Finally, there were the laypeople who gathered in the college chapel on Thursday evenings to pray: Bob and Betty Burns, George and Mary Gable, Dick and Doris Skibicki, George and Lois Fyke, and of course, one of the early leaders, Tom Kneier, who later, with his wife Madeline and Father Michael, would become a founder of the Servants of Christ the King Catholic Community.

All of us became a team unified in vision and prayer, continually pleading for the Holy Spirit to move on the campus and revive it to new life. We had no idea what our prayers would bring. We just knew God would answer.

COMMITMENT IN THE FACE OF OPPOSITION

As my household began to see the fruits of our prayers, our life together deepened. We took on a new name, Heart of Jesus, which better conveyed our desire to discover the depths of Christ and love Him more faithfully. In the process, we grew to know one another, wrinkles and all. We learned to support each other as we struggled through the processes of growing up, pursuing academic study, and adjusting to college life. The greatest challenge we faced, however, was what the church has always faced when she faithfully follows her Lord—tremendous opposition.

Not everyone at the college accepted the vision of its new president.

I will never forget the day when a contingent of students decided to march up to Father Michael's office carrying a coffin to signify their outrage at the state of affairs on campus. I was extremely concerned about him because my loyalty to him, even then, ran deep. When the students mounted the top of the hill leading to Father Michael's office, he came out of the building with a smile on his face. With Christian charity, he then welcomed them into his office to discuss their concerns. They were surprised, but they accepted his invitation. Later, campus leaders arose out of that group of students. They turned their opposition into support and worked to help bring the president's vision into reality.

Another expression of opposition I remember well concerned the efforts to build the second household of faith in another residence hall. A group of pious and devoted young men wanted to have an alternate faith-household experience. One of their number, Tony Corasaniti, invited me to come and address them one night on how my household got started. But some in this group didn't welcome my presence. They thought that the very existence and behavior of the Heart of Jesus were saying, "Nobody else is truly Christian." Fortunately, their opposition was short-lived, and under the leadership of Tony Corasaniti they would later become known as "Precious Blood," the second faith household on campus. This marked the beginning of a system that gradually became the mainstay of the school's social activity.

THE RENEWING WORK OF REVIVAL

What happened in the dorms also began taking place in the chapel. A small local prayer meeting started to grow as its members experienced God's love in genuine repentance and conversion. The Lord's work among them was magnetic. Soon, the prayer meeting swelled in size until it frequently packed the college chapel.

Revival was breaking out all over the campus with a power that could not be contained. We didn't use the term *revival* to describe what was happening. *Revival* is not a familiar word in Catholic circles. Instead we called these happenings "renewal in the Holy Spirit." But having studied revivalism, I was and still am comfortable using the term *revival* as a rough synonym for what Catholics mean by renewal. Just as the revivals of nineteenth-century America evoked repentance and deeper commitments to Christ among believers, so did the revival at Steubenville. God's Spirit was mightily at work.

By the time I graduated in 1977, two years after my arrival, the college's spiritual dimension was really beginning to flourish. The prayer meeting that developed in the chapel had become a vibrant, evangelical Catholic lay community called the "Community of God's Love." Members of that community, many of whom were alumni, faculty, and staff of the college who had been deeply affected by the revival, began serving voluntarily and assuming leadership positions in the school. Years later, the Community of God's Love became a formal lay Catholic covenant community that became known as the Servants of Christ the King. It proved to be a vital resource in the university's ongoing renewal.

I have watched God build these monuments of faith from the ashes of secularism. The more I saw His transforming work in action, the more inspired and awed I became. Campus ministry began to thrive. Campus prayer meetings grew rapidly in frequency and size. The lack of attendance at daily mass had been replaced by a need for more liturgies to handle the ever-increasing number of worshipers. Students who were meeting the Lord in a new and fresh way were evangelizing and desiring to spread the gospel beyond the local community. And the Lord kept calling faithful laborers—new faculty, staff, and other devoted Franciscan friars—to develop and manage the work He had graciously begun in answer to the prayers of a handful of His people.

"Life in the Spirit" seminars began on campus and in the local area. They were basic, seven-week proclamations of God's love, repentance, and forgiveness and calls to prayer, faith, and mature Christian living. They literally transformed lives and enabled the fire to spread from log to log, ever burning brighter and stronger.

During this time the Community of God's Love became the Servants of God's Love and then the Servants of Christ the King. The name changes reflected a progression—a move from a prayer group to a community of believers committed to a common way of life according to a covenant. And the transformation happened within a clear and committed Catholic context centered on the Eucharist and faithful to the teaching of the Roman Catholic Church.

From its inception this community identified with the revival at the college by sending volunteer workers to help oversee the burgeoning faith-household movement. Household by household the work spread throughout the campus, leaving in its wake a reinvigorated, genuinely evangelical Catholic culture. Indeed, the whole framework of life began to take on a new dynamism; it was even reflected in the names each of the student faith households picked to identify their individual charisms and convictions. To this day, all over the campus at what is now called Franciscan

University, you can find sweatshirts, T-shirts, banners, and intramural team rosters bearing the names of groups of men and women differing in gifts but walking in the same Spirit. It is not unusual to see a flag-football game between "Mustard Seed" and the "Lion of Judah," or a basketball playoff between "Magnificat" and "The Handmaids of the Lord."

A MATURING CHRISTIAN WORLDVIEW

All that has happened on Franciscan University's campus has been carefully guided by the clear apostolic, pastoral, and prudent leadership of Father Michael. Even the school's name change was a result of Father Mike's untiring work. Because of the college's increased enrollment and ability to offer fully accredited graduate programs, the College of Steubenville became the University of Steubenville in 1980. Then, by decision of the board of trustees, the name of the university was officially changed to Franciscan University of Steubenville to reflect more clearly the charism and Christian commitment of the school.

Franciscan University, in addition to a full array of undergraduate majors, now offers graduate degrees in philosophy, theology, business, and counseling. In short, after more than two decades of revival, a mature Catholic worldview has emerged on campus.

Student government positions are seen as opportunities for service to the Lord, His church, and His people. Clubs and organizations arise regularly to prepare students who will go into the marketplace as missionaries of the future—God's servants in the business world, the political arena, and foreign service, as well as in explicit church service. An ideal of Christian family life has been demonstrated through the faculty and the local community and is being taught on campus with the mission of enabling the students, many of whom have suffered the blight of family breakdown, to find healing and restoration so they can move ahead with a vision of the Christian family as the domestic church.

Academic instruction has matured as it has been touched by the wind of renewal. Due to the outstanding leadership of Dr. Michael Healey, Franciscan University's academic program has consistently moved toward excellence. It has virtually reintroduced a classical Western liberal-arts education in an orthodox faith environment. And it is producing some of the brightest and best leaders for the future.

The school also has the largest number of theology majors on any Catholic campus in the United States, which is another sign of God's remarkable grace. In the early seventies, a general recommendation was made that the college stop teaching theology classes because of the lack of student interest. This happened on other Catholic campuses as well. But the college's post-revival experience has made it an exception to the norm. Now the school has men and women touched by the Holy Spirit, eager and hungry to learn about the Scriptures, the history of the church, the elements of Christian living, and the doctrines of the faith.

When people grow in their experiential and intellectual knowledge of God, their love for Him increases. The overflow of this love manifests itself in all types of ministries, and at Steubenville many of these outreaches developed from within the student body. For example, groups of students travel every spring to evangelize in various locations. Student music groups perform at various high schools. Student evangelistic teams engage in local outreach. The thriving Works of Mercy programs care for the shut-ins, developmentally handicapped, and elderly. The university has founded an Austrian campus from which students also serve and at which they rediscover the riches of their Catholic heritage. All of these ministries are the fruit of the Holy Spirit in a Catholic Christian environment. He has brought a classical revival at a Catholic college—renewal within an evangelical and apostolic institution and community.

THE ELEMENTS OF CLASSICAL REVIVAL

These are merely a few of the details of the Steubenville miracle. More of the story is recorded in *Let the Fire Fall*, a wonderful book written by Father Michael Scanlan. What occurred at Franciscan University is a telling example of a classical revival and its perpetuation of spiritual renewal. All the elements of revival were evident on this campus.

Prayer
A prevailing hunger for depth of prayer and an understanding of the power of intercession and spiritual warfare pervaded the university. Visitors could nearly always find students praying in the eight available Eucharistic chapels or at informal gatherings. Prayer was (and is) proclaimed, taught, demonstrated, and expected. Indeed, now there is a "reverse peer pressure," as Father John Bertolucci called it, toward Heaven and away from worldliness.

Repentance
This prevailing spirit of prayer led to a penitential lifestyle, not of heaviness or despair, but of true joy. The word *penitential* has been used

throughout Christian history to denote those men and women who have grasped that repentance is not a one-time affair but a call to continual conversion—a call to acknowledge our sin and God's greatness. There is tremendous joy and freedom in surrendering ourselves to the healing touch of the Lord.

Francis of Assisi and his spiritual brothers considered themselves a penitential movement and their work a penitential renewal. Their heritage was revived at Steubenville. Twice a week, long lines formed for the sacrament of reconciliation. Students, faculty, staff, and local community members gathered, all seeking freedom from their sins and reconciliation to God. In honest relationships, people acknowledged their faults and responsibilities and set one another free, obeying the admonition, "Therefore confess your sins to each other and pray for each other so that you may be healed."[4]

The great seasons of the liturgical year are now celebrated with the fervor and vibrancy that characterize a true spirit of revival. Before I left the school to begin another chapter in my life, I remember celebrating the forty days of Lent and watching throngs of students pack the chapel on Ash Wednesday to receive the ashes on their heads as a sign of their call to repent and believe the good news. That call to a life of repentance is a sign of God's movement among His people in any Christian confession or tradition, be it Protestant, Catholic, or Orthodox.

Conversion

Such prayer and repentance led to dramatic and continual conversions among students, faculty, administrators, and even visitors. For example, I remember one particular man, a Muslim, who had come to do some engineering work in the local Ohio Valley. He stayed on campus for a month and paid room and board in what was called the Renewal Center, but later was renamed the Saint Thomas More dorm. By the time he left, he had met Jesus Christ as a result of the prayers offered up for him. His life was transformed.

Many lives were changed by the touch of the fire that spread from Steubenville and went out to the nations. An ever-deepening conversion was clearly evident in the lives of the young men and women at the university, many of whom began coming to the campus precisely because of the unmistakable signs of God's presence.

In the final analysis, what changes hearts is not what we do but what God does. Yes, we must allow Him to penetrate our lives. We can shut Him out. But when we open our soul's door, He touches us with the tenderness of His love. Franciscan University became a testimony to that fact. Through prayer, liturgy, and communal support, the school received the overwhelming experience of God's infinite, unconditional love.

The preaching from the pulpits, the teaching in the classrooms, the pastoring from the Franciscan friars all became geared toward an understanding of conversion as the continual call of the Christian to become fully complete and mature in Christ, demonstrating through his or her life the fruit of the Spirit: love, joy, peace, patience, kindness, goodness, and self-control.[5]

The Power of the Holy Spirit

And then there's the power. The power of the Holy Spirit became so tangible on campus that at times it seemed as if one could squeeze it from a hypersoaked sponge. Part of that real presence was a result of the operation of the gifts of the Spirit. At the school they became operative and seen as normative, not as exceptions to His work. In the early stages of Steubenville's revival, the campus was often viewed as a center of charismatic renewal, but that label eventually dropped away. The campus is now more accurately described as deeply Christian and fully Catholic.

Father Michael reminded everyone that it is *normal* for a Catholic college to believe in Jesus Christ, to follow Him, to be filled with His Spirit, to receive and use the spiritual gifts given for the upbuilding of His church, and to be faithful to the teaching of Scripture as well as to the teaching authority of the Catholic Church.

Normal is one of those words we need to recapture. The secularization prevalent in our contemporary age is *abnormal*, indeed, the result of disordered appetites. The secular mind-set is just another piece of bad fruit coming from the Fall. It's not the good fruit of God's desire for His human creatures. It does not, nor can it ever, bring what it claims: lasting freedom, joy, and peace. Only the power of the Spirit of God breaking forth into the human experience and transforming individuals and communities can bring those evidences of grace into our lives. And those evidences became commonplace at Franciscan University, because the power of God's Spirit was at work in God's people.

Mission

On the Steubenville campus, the work of evangelism was understood by all to be the responsibility and privilege of every Christian. The evangelical task of proclaiming the gospel is not limited to clergy or professional evangelists. It is a mandate binding on all Christians. Through life and lip, we are called to penetrate this age with the good news of salvation in Christ. By advancing with this message and its transforming power, we can regain lost ground in our culture and advance the cause of Christ. No matter what our career or vocation, our primary task is to be the church and do what the church does. And among the church's many tasks, she "has the obligation and also the sacred right to evangelize all men."[6]

WORLDWIDE REVIVAL?

My evangelical Protestant friends will likely recognize the blueprint for revival evidenced in my description of what happened in Steubenville. For many it may seem strange to hear of a classical revival flourishing in a Roman Catholic context. But what Franciscan University experienced is not precedent setting. Revival has occurred throughout church history; it is clearly a part of our common evangelical heritage. Revival flourishes where Jesus Christ is proclaimed and honored as Lord. It has been this way since the first Pentecost. And it will always occur in any Christian tradition where believers once again invite Him in and open themselves to the tangible manifestation of His Spirit.

Some of my Catholic friends, however, may object to my use of the word *revival*. Perhaps you associate it with tents, hellfire preaching, and emotional but superficial commitments to Christ. But you must realize that some great work has come out of tents. Indeed, that occurred frequently each summer on the campus of Franciscan University. Furthermore, some of our heroes, such as Saints Dominic and Francis, were responsible for revival movements during their own day. And these were revivals that positively affected church history, even into the twentieth century.

Unfortunately, Christians often limit revival to one confessional tradition or another. Many have made it an exclusively Protestant concept, while others have narrowed it further, relegating it to certain segments of Protestantism. This is not only tragic but narrow-minded and untrue. Revival is a work of God, not of man. And He has amply proven that He works transconfessionally. Thank goodness He does. For what we need is a classical revival to sweep *all* of today's Christian churches. We need genuine, divinely energized revival—the kind that will release the work of the Holy Spirit in the hearts of *all* of God's people. Then can the sleeping giant—the Christian church in all of its beauty, communions, and traditions—rise up and respond to the desperate hunger of our spiritually starved age.

But such a sweeping, dynamic revival will not happen in a fragmented Christian community. Of course, it can begin, as it did in Steubenville, with the prayers and spiritually sensitive actions of a handful of dedicated, visionary Christians. It can even start with the prayers of one believer. Yet, as long as we see ourselves as disconnected, even polarized, communities, we will never experience the full benefits of a genuine worldwide revival. What Steubenville experienced will be experienced elsewhere, but only in localized doses. A global sweep of God's Spirit throughout His church will elude us.

We don't have to accept this state of affairs. We can change our perceptions of and attitudes toward each other. We can reembrace the biblical truth that we were meant to be one church united under one Head for the purpose of carrying out a threefold mission: proclaiming the gospel, maturing in Christ, and contending for the culture. Remember, the divisions in our two-thousand-year history have been recent. And though on our own we cannot recapture that lost unity, we can begin to work together.

Even though the differences between us are still too great for us to fellowship together at the Lord's Table—the liturgical sign of Christian unity—I do not believe they are so great as to hinder us from making common cause to transform our culture for the sake of our common Savior and Lord. Even when I was privileged to be a part of the Steubenville miracle, I firmly believed in the necessity of Protestant, Catholic, and Orthodox Christians becoming allies in the battle for the mind and soul of America, Western civilization, and the rest of the world. We have too much to fight for and against for us to battle alone or turn our guns on one another.

It was the driving force of that belief that eventually led me from the university setting and back into the full-time practice of law. Not that a school of higher education can't also be a place to prepare people to confront the culture. Franciscan University certainly did that, as do many other Christian schools across the country, including Regent University. But my training was in law. It was my career and not by accident but, as I began to see, by plan. I knew the Spirit of God was leading me back to it. What He would do through it would amaze and challenge me, and it would begin yet another chapter in my life. A chapter marked by alliance building among Christians that would seek to recapture law and justice in an increasingly oppressive and unjust society.

CHAPTER FIVE

Fighting for Law and Justice

Do not despise this small beginning,
for the eyes of the Lord rejoice to see the work begin.
Zechariah 4:10, TLB

For precept must be upon precept,
precept upon precept,
Line upon line, line upon line,
Here a little, there a little.
Isaiah 28:10, NKJV

I'll never forget the look on my children's faces when we pulled up to the front of the cottage at the Lake of the Woods in Virginia. I knew then it would be an Easter vacation we would never forget. I believed this for a lot of reasons, not least of which was that a tree had fallen through the roof of the cottage. The scene was like something out of Chevy Chase's movie *Summer Vacation.*

"You've got to be kidding," said my son.

"Are we really staying here?" asked one of my daughters.

With reassurance and sage fatherly advice, I said to all of the children and my wife, Laurine, "This will be a great week." My statement proved to be very true. It would be a week that would forever change our lives.

We had decided to take the vacation at a critical time in our family's life. I was in the midst of career discernment. I had already served many years as general counsel at Franciscan University, not to mention my work there in the capacities of dean of students, dean of evangelization, and presidential assistant. I had been a lay leader in a large Christian community and had carried on a private law practice and served on the prosecutor's staff of Jefferson County, Ohio. But Laurine and I knew it was time to move on to a new chapter of our lives. We had come to this decision through prayerful discernment and practical evaluation.

After the decision was made, the only real issue was timing. Our oldest daughter was just about to enter high school, and we had four more in line. If we were going to relocate, we knew this would be an ideal time to do it. Through the discernment process, I had sought the trusted advice of my dear friend Chuck Colson. Chuck had recommended me to a law firm in the District of Columbia that represented major Christian ministries. He had also suggested some other ideas. He knew my passionate desire to continue to integrate my law practice with my Christian ministry and convictions. After all, I had been doing that for years, wearing various "hats." But two threads were clearly woven through all my work—evangelism and cultural apologetics. I wanted those to remain; how, though, I wasn't sure.

So Laurine and I decided that taking the week after Easter for a little rest and recreation was just what the family needed. My dear friend, Bill Beatty, who at the time served as the executive director of the National Service Committee for Catholic Charismatic Renewal, had just relocated his family and that ministry to the Lake of the Woods in Virginia. He invited me and my family to come and see the beautiful countryside.

Having been raised in Boston, my geography, particularly as it related to the South, was not the best. Unfortunately, New Englanders tend to have an inflated opinion of New England. Anything below Connecticut is considered the South. I had never really seen much of the Virginia countryside. I was in for a real treat.

We all packed into our van and with excitement drove to the Lake of the Woods. I had made arrangements to rent for a week what I thought was a small home. Bill had tried to get me the best deal. Two days before we left for the trip, he told me in a passing telephone conversation that because a tree had fallen on the property, he had been able to get the price down. I thought he was joking. But sure enough, when we arrived we discovered a very big tree had fallen right on top of our lodging. That's how our vacation began, but its end would be more surprising still.

THE OFFER

One of the goals I had set for myself professionally during that week was to travel to Virginia Beach, Virginia. I had long known of the efforts of Dr. M. G. "Pat" Robertson's Regent University to integrate Christian principles into professional graduate education. I wanted to see how that was being worked out in their law school. That venture seemed singularly exciting in a field of increasingly secularized church-related law schools. Regent was openly evangelical in conviction and making serious attempts to integrate Christian faith and values into the legal educational process. I wanted to see the campus and get a better feel for the work being done there. I also wanted to visit the headquarters of the Christian Broadcasting Network (CBN).

So early one morning I set out for Virginia Beach. While traveling, I had a tremendous opportunity to pray and reflect on my life and the Lord's blessings on my family. I was alone in the van, no children's voices. It was finally quiet. I knew the Lord had been faithful to us as a family in the past. Now I was wondering what He would call us to do in the future. A sense of excitement gripped me as I focused my prayer and reflection on anticipating the things to come.

When I pulled into the stately campus that houses not only the Regent University buildings but the entire CBN complex, I was deeply impressed with the grandeur and permanency of the Georgian architecture. It all spoke loudly of a long-term institutional plan to make a difference in the nation, to still be standing a century from now.

I spent some time visiting with the dean of the law school and was deeply impressed with the philosophy and educational convictions he expressed. During the course of our conversation, I asked him whether the law school had adjunct faculty members. I thought perhaps that if I relocated to the Virginia area, I would enjoy teaching law. Teaching is one of my favorite pastimes—to communicate to others truths concerning both the Christian faith and, in a particular way, how to integrate that faith into the legal profession. The dean told me they welcomed adjunct faculty members and that if I were to relocate, they would certainly be interested in having me teach.

He then proceeded to tell me of something much bigger than teaching. He told me of Pat Robertson's desire to bring together a group of lawyers to "take on the ACLU and other interest groups that have wreaked havoc on this nation." As he started talking about this vision, my spirit leaped within me. *Why not? It's about time*, I thought.

I was all too familiar with the efforts of many misguided public-interest groups in the last thirty years. They had literally besieged the courts with strategic test cases to change the cultural landscape. They had opened the doors to the legalization of abortion on demand, sanctioning it as a "reproductive right." They were assaulting the family from every front and, in a perverse way, they were using the First

Amendment to increasingly censor the free-speech activities of people of faith. In the world of these public-interest practitioners, anything they perceived as religious, and particularly Christian, was deemed politically incorrect.

My excitement about the concept of launching a legal counteroffensive became obvious to the dean. In fact, I found myself later that day spending time with the chancellor of the university, the president of CBN, the chairman of the board of the Family Channel, the founder of the Christian Coalition, and the leader of a host of other enterprises, all of which were bound up in one amazing man, Pat Robertson.

Our paths had crossed on numerous occasions before this meeting. We had mutual friends such as Harald Bredesen, a giant of the Christian faith, and we had met at a couple of meetings regarding efforts to activate Christians in the cultural and political arenas. In fact, my only other time of real conversation with Pat in person had come several years before when he convened what was called the American Congress of Concerned Christian Citizens. It was an effort to bring together Christians from various confessional communities who shared a deep concern over the state of America. I had attended the congress as the representative for Father Mike and Franciscan University.

On this day at Regent, Pat and I talked almost two hours. Within a very short time, I felt I had known him for years. We discussed our faith, our convictions, and the current state of the culture. Pat is a Yale University–trained law graduate and a man deeply concerned about the current state of America. We exchanged war stories of our work in various ministries. He seemed particularly delighted as I shared with him some of my own experiences in the courtroom. He, in turn, shared with me his vision for a Christian counterpart to the ACLU, a public-interest law firm he called the American Center for Law and Justice. I was deeply inspired. I had often wondered why lawyers who believed in the constitutional right to life, true religious and civil liberty, the right influence of religious faith in American society, and the primacy of the family didn't come together and seek to right some of the damage done in the last thirty years by some of the so-called public-interest groups.

As our time together unfolded, I grew in my appreciation for Pat's intellect and insights into the current state of America. I, like many others, had heard third- and fourth-hand reports of his alleged narrowness on the issues. But what I found contradicted these claims. Pat showed himself to be an astute, intelligent, passionate, concerned citizen and leader. I also saw him as a bold entrepreneur and founder.

As our meeting began to close, Pat asked, "Keith, what would it take to get you here?"

I was somewhat taken back. In my own mind I expected some reticence about my assuming a high-profile role with an organization he was attempting to found. After all, I am a loyal Roman Catholic and he a loyal Protestant. But again, I, like so many others, failed to see the depth and breadth of the man's vision. "What do you mean?" I asked.

"Would you consider becoming the executive director of the American Center for Law and Justice?" Pat responded.

"Pat, this is a surprise. I am honored, but I can't go backward professionally. This will be a new work and it will likely need to begin with a low budget. I have five children looking at college ahead of them, and I have a career that can supply their needs. I have to give this a lot of thought."

"And prayer," he added.

"Of course," I replied.

We then prayed on the spot.

He was aware I was Catholic. In fact, he had a copy of my first book, *Evangelical Catholics*, on his desk. We discussed the concept of bringing Christians together to make common cause for social change. I shared the image of the Allies joining forces to fight a common enemy in World War II, and he smiled broadly.

Then I simply told him, "Pat, I'm not a constitutional lawyer. You don't learn constitutional law in a general law practice. You're going to need people with constitutional experience to make this new work effective."

"Well, I'm not sure you need to be a constitutional lawyer," he replied. "What do you think you are?"

"I'm an alliance builder, a mouthpiece, a communicator, and an entrepreneur."

"Well," he replied, "that might be just what we need."

As I left his office we exchanged brotherly support and agreed to discuss the matter further. Laurine and I spent the rest of our time in Virginia enjoying our family and praying about the possibilities.

When my family and I returned from our vacation, I faced a heavy schedule in my law office. In fact, the next Monday morning I had a criminal trial in juvenile court arising out of the arrest of three teenagers dealing crack cocaine. At the time, I was the juvenile prosecutor for Jefferson County, Ohio. It was a part-time position that really consumed much more time. And back then, that was very significant, for I held three other jobs.

On Monday morning, I ran into my office to pick up my trial folder. The witnesses were waiting for me in court along with the Bureau of Criminal Investigation representatives who would be testifying in court. As I grabbed the file off my desk in the offices of Spon and Fournier, the phone rang. I was asked to be available at six o'clock for a call from Pat Robertson. I agreed and proceeded on to court. Fortunately, less than fifteen minutes into the trial, the offenders confessed guilt.

The rest of the day my mind was on the conversation I was to have at six o'clock. I was intrigued, so much so, in fact, that I had a hard time getting my work done in my law office. *Why would Pat be calling me so soon after we had talked?* My thoughts swirled, and my eyes kept flirting with the clock.

When 6:00 p.m. finally rolled around, the phone rang. As I picked it up I heard, "Hello, Keith, this is Pat Robertson. I'd like to invite you to become the executive director of the American Center for Law and Justice. It's going to be big."

I was ready. Laurine and I had given a lot of thought and committed a lot of prayer to the possibility of this offer. If it was going to be workable, a number of matters had to be settled. Within minutes, Pat and I got down to discussing what my father always called "brass tacks." It didn't take long for us to agree on terms. But there was someone else who needed to agree also. So I told Pat I wanted to discuss the offer with my wife and that we would pray about it and get back to him. He concurred and that drew our conversation to a close.

My mind reeled. A Roman Catholic at CBN heading up an organization founded by a highly influential evangelical Protestant leader. That was a remarkable scenario to ponder.

To be frank, though, when Laurine and I began to work through all the various issues connected to a move and a job change, we got very practical. We had been through the meat grinder of Christian ministry and career changes. We had ridden the waves of excitement and failure. I was not starry-eyed anymore. I knew this venture would be risky—professionally and personally. So the real question that had to be answered was, Is the opportunity worth the risk? *After all,* I thought, *I have five children and a lot of responsibility and opportunity where I am now.* I had just rejoined the law firm I had founded in 1982 with my dear friend, John Spon; I was representing Franciscan University and still deeply involved in evangelism and apologetics work as a lay Catholic; and I and my family were living in a wonderful home in the country. Then there was the tremendous risk always associated with starting a new organization. But as Laurine and I considered the opportunities to change the nation, to fight to restore constitutional protection to unborn children, and to further integrate my faith and my law practice . . . well, the offer seemed hard to resist. How many opportunities does one get like this in a lifetime? Not many. Often, only one.

Nevertheless, Laurine and I took the next couple of months to ruminate on the offer. We weighed the pros and cons, we committed the process to God. Finally, we decided it was worth the risk. So we sold our home, closed my law practice, and completed all the various and sundry practical details involved with a move. All the while, we kept thinking ahead about what the Lord might have in store for us as we ventured into the next chapter of our walk in faith as a family. Little did we realize that what would greet us in Virginia Beach would be more stark and challenging than discovering an old cottage with a tree fallen on its roof. Our faith would certainly be tested.

THE CHALLENGE

One day after rolling into Chesapeake, Virginia, with my wife, five children, and our cat, I found myself in the offices of the new American Center for Law and Justice (ACLJ). In reality, however, what I discovered was a vision in need of substance. Fortunately, one person had preceded me. His name was Norm Berman, a dedicated Jewish believer in Jesus and a superb development expert, who is still a vital member of the ACLJ's continued work. There were also two part-time graduate students, along with two old, wooden desks belonging to Regent University and some used furniture from Colonel Zed's, a local second-hand furniture store. Everything and everybody were crammed into two back offices in a Regent classroom building. So far, that was the extent of the embodiment of Pat's vision for the ACLJ.

I sat down at my desk—it appeared to be of World War II vintage—and began to reflect on the challenge that lay ahead. Aside from staff, office space, and equipment needs, we had to have a base of independent financial support, which was extremely inadequate at the time. I had definitely arrived on the ground floor, or more accurately, at the ACLJ's ground breaking. We needed to lay a foundation and begin to build. The question was, Where do we start?

On my second day at my new job, I sat with my head in my hands and thought of the words of the prophet Jeremiah:

Oh LORD, you deceived me, and I was deceived;
   you overpowered me and prevailed.
I am ridiculed all day long;
   everyone mocks me.[1]

I was deeply discouraged, to say the least. Then Pat Robertson arrived with his typical infectious enthusiasm and encouraged me. "It's going to be big, Keith," he said. By the time he left my office, I was inspired. The discouragement that had overwhelmed me dissipated like dew off grass under the heat of the sun.

Several weeks later, I learned a bit more of what keeps this man motivated. I visited the dressing room where Pat prepares for his daily commentary on the "700 Club." Over the door I noticed a wall hanging that apparently was an old gift from a friend. It read, "Have a vision so big that it will only fail if God is not in it." This interesting perspective on life reveals a lot about Pat's philosophy of life and leadership.

Pat lifted my spirits on that gloomy second day, and I didn't waste time letting them soar. After he left my office, I sat down and, having been trained in strategic planning for business, wrote out some objectives for myself as the executive director of this new organization. In retrospect, I realize now that I was either insane or inspired. History is proving perhaps that a little of both is correct.

The first objective I gave myself was "to build the General Motors of Christian public-interest advocacy."

My second objective was to "engage in litigation where rights and liberties are at stake, particularly in defense of religious freedom and civil liberties under the First Amendment in an opposition to anti-religious hostility."

The third was "to develop and effectively execute a strategy of exposing and opposing the American Civil Liberties Union and its anti-family, anti-life, and anti-liberty pursuits."

The fourth was "to establish a network of attorneys who will provide counsel, assistance, and services to clients on a referral basis."

My list also included developing the ability to provide legal counsel and advice for those who would call in for help; filing what's called friend-of-the-court briefs; assisting clients as lead counsel; publishing in law reviews, popular periodicals, and numerous other types of publications; developing an educational outreach; cooperating with the Regent University Law School in continuing education seminars; developing an ACLJ journal; creating an extern and intern program utilizing law students. And on the list went. *If you're going to think big, you might as well plan big*, I thought. And so I did.

But after drafting all these objectives, reality really hit me. I had very little money and a less-than-bare-bones staff. I was the only lawyer. But that didn't discourage me this time. Instead, I leaned back in my chair and virtually said out loud, "What an incredible opportunity!"

THE IMPLEMENTATION

One of my biggest draws to accepting the challenge of building the ACLJ was what could be done through it to help save the lives of North America's most vulnerable. The passion of my professional life has always been the pro-life cause. I am deeply and unqualifiedly pro-life. I am convinced that respect for life (the unborn, born, infirm, elderly—all life) is the litmus test of civilization. It is certainly the fundamental issue currently facing our culture. So I decided that the best thing I could do was to begin to defend some people who were being persecuted for their heroism on behalf of unborn children. Over the next few weeks, I did just that. I began appearing as legal counsel on behalf of pro-lifers while trying to build a public-interest law firm.

At the same time, I and my small staff started developing a program for utilizing direct-mail fund-raising, and I began to survey the terrain for lawyers to join our effort. Who was already doing this kind of legal work? How could I build effective alliances with them? And who was going to be a part of this future national public-interest law firm and educational group? I was committed to building an institutional presence that would be around fifty years from now.

I also developed a mission statement. I had learned long before, particularly during the time I was privileged to work with Father Scanlan, that a mission statement was essential to the birth and growth of any enterprise. In particular, it becomes a continual well of strength to an organization dedicated to Jesus Christ and to securing the place and role of people of faith in the culture. So I worked on the ACLJ's mission statement, which reads:

> The American Center for Law and Justice is a not-for-profit public-interest law firm and educational organization dedicated to the promotion of pro-liberty, pro-life and pro-family causes.
> The American Center engages in litigation, provides legal

services, renders advice and counsel to clients, and supports attorneys who are involved in defending the religious and civil liberties of Americans.

The American Center is also developing a national network of attorneys who are committed to the defense of these liberties, and cooperates with other organizations that are committed to a similar mission and serves the public through educational efforts concerning First Amendment and religious liberty issues.

As a not-for-profit organization that does not charge for its legal services, the American Center is dependent upon God and the resources He provides through the time, talent, and gifts of people who share our concerns over the erosion of our religious and civil liberties.

The mission statement underscores the tripod upon which I decided to build the ACLJ: the defense of pro-liberty, pro-life, and pro-family causes. It seemed to me that under each one of these three headings most of our litigation would occur.

Lessons From the Opposition

I also embarked on a detailed study of the history of public-interest groups like the ACLU, the NAACP Legal Defense Fund, and the National Organization for Women. How did they become such influential forces for social change? How did they utilize the vehicle of public-interest law to effectively alter the culture? Though I disagreed with many of their results, I thought I could learn a lot from their strategy.

I spent most of my time studying the history of the NAACP Legal Defense Fund. I had long been convinced that the result of the landmark civil-rights case *Brown v. Board of Education* was important for this nation. "Separate but equal" among races was not equal, as the Supreme Court rightly noted in their decision on this case. Government-mandated segregation and racism are intrinsically wrong. I thought that the work of Thurgood Marshall and his early colleagues in that effort was brilliant. Though to this day I believe that the internal reasoning of the judicial opinion would have been better had its decision been premised on a legal analysis based on inalienable rights and natural-law premises, I believe that the ultimate result was correct.[2] It ended legally sanctioned segregation and racism. I also found the idealism and the energy asserted by those early pioneers in a public-interest legal movement not only inspiring but a great model for the work I was striving to start.

In fact, here is where I departed from some of my colleagues. Many Christian lawyers are legal purists. They want to work within the letter of the law, including the precedents that have led to our current statutes, in order to defend their clients. In a word, they are legal conservatives. I am not. The word *conservative* literally means "to maintain the status quo." I didn't want to do that in a legal climate that sanctions abortion and calls license liberty. I didn't want to build on a group of legal precedents that undermine the primacy of the family as the first government, the first school, the first church, and the first charity. Perhaps in a sane legal environment, I could be a legal purist, but in the current climate I've chosen to be an activist. I believe we must undo the mess caused by the legal engineers of the latest cultural revolution.

I learned a great deal studying the strategies of the legal activists of the last thirty years, among which was how to begin to undo the damage they've caused and restore some sanity to our jurisprudence. We needed a form of what I called "incremental pragmatism" in our legal strategy. I knew we could not change things quickly; getting from A to Z would not occur overnight. It had taken years to institutionalize murky relativism and judicial insanity. It would take years to undo it and restore sanity. We needed to be prepared to struggle from A to B, then from to B to C . . . all the way to Z. This action principle has become the ACLJ's hallmark.

During my second week on the job, I sat in my office and sketched two diagrams. Those diagrams became increasingly important in building and growing the work of the ACLJ. The first was an arrow. The arrow reflected the use of public-interest legal practice to effect social change. The point of the arrow consisted of test cases. The NAACP and other legal groups had intentionally postured test cases in a strategy aimed at changing the law. They didn't take on every case that came across their desks. (Indeed, no law firm, public-interest or otherwise, has the ability to handle every case, nor would it be prudent for it to do so.) Instead they focused their efforts on those cases that had the potential of changing the law. That point of the arrow, the test case, pierced the legal and social armor, and they used it effectively to work changes into the culture through lower court decisions, agency involvement, and the development of a public educational effort that centered on apologetics and debate. I knew this was the way to weave change into the fabric of a culture. I knew it was the course the ACLJ needed to follow in our efforts as well.

The second diagram was a body. In particular, an upper torso. The body had a head, arms, and shoulders that reflected the current state of

American society at the end of the twentieth century. The body also had a heart, which represented the center of emotions and dynamism—the affective center of change. It was clear to me that strategic legal cases were the heart of any work geared at changing the fabric of the nation. The heart provides the blood and the excitement to the rest of the body. These cases had to do that for the ACLJ. They also needed to be able to rouse concerned people to action throughout the nation.

A Winning Record

I also understood how important it was to win. People of faith every-where were tired of seeing true liberty undermined and life overtaken by the culture of death and selfism. But many of them didn't quite know what to do about it, and many more were too discouraged to do any-thing at all. For they had heard the disenchanted proclaiming "Chicken Little" messages at every available opportunity and with evangelistic zeal. Do you remember the "Chicken Little" story? He kept telling other animals that the sky was falling. Soon he had quite a following of believ-ers until he and his supporters ended up in a wily fox's den, never to be heard from again.[3] The "Chicken Little" proclaimers had gained an incredible following. Christians were retreating from the culture in droves, giving up and giving in. I wanted to reverse this trend before the fox of secularism devoured more escaping victims.

The unmistakable fact of Christian history is that the church exists for times such as these. We have been through worse times, and at no time is our calling to retreat. Our vocation is to hold the sky up, to proclaim the message of Heaven, to engage and transform whatever culture we find ourselves in. We're to move forward, not backward. I knew that with God's help and careful planning, victories in strategic legal cases could help reinvigorate discouraged Christians throughout the nation. Then, with their help, we could bring lasting change.

Tertullians for Today

I also knew, however, that the heart alone does not change the long-term direction or orientation of a person or a nation. What changes people and cultures for the long haul takes place predominantly in the mind and the will. The mind of the nation had to be changed on the impor-tant issues of the day: issues such as the nature of liberty and freedom, the sanctity of life, and the primary role of the family. We had fallen a long way from the inalienable rights recorded in our Declaration of Independence. We had turned away from the American heritage of liberty and the philosophical heritage of Western civilization. What we needed was another generation of apologists. Men and women like Tertullian, one of my heroes, whose valiant efforts had helped transform the corrupt Roman Empire. We needed a new generation of leaders who could debate in the public square and contend for the grand ideas that shape any culture. We needed true, courageous defenders of the faith.

Back to Our Roots

The losses in the courtroom of such fundamental values as the sanctity of life, the free-speech rights of people of faith (because of the content of their message), and the undermining of the primacy of the natural family have to be stopped. But first, we had to stop the hemorrhaging. We had to wrap antiseptic bandages tightly around the bleeding wounds of Western civilization before it collapsed and died. And we had to stop the assaults of judicial activism prompted by the legal cultural revolutionaries. We had to turn back the clock on some of the horrible legal decisions that had wreaked such havoc in the nation. Decisions such as *Roe v. Wade* that unleashed the horror of the killing of millions of unborn children with the sanction of a judicial imprimatur; the growing body of court cases attempting to redefine the family and insert in its place profane counterfeits. These court decisions and many like them are geared toward redefining the very understanding of the nature of liberty in the American proposition. If we were to challenge them effectively, we had to return to the founding fathers' understanding of liberty.

I knew from my study of American history that our founding fathers understood liberty to be ordered liberty. It was not freedom from responsible living but freedom for responsible living. The revolution that took place on the shores of what is now the United States was significantly different from the revolution that took place in France, the home of my ancestors. The French revolutionaries used the word *liberty* as well. But to them it meant something very different. In the name of their kind of liberty, they unleashed an antitheistic reign of terror on rulers and ruled alike. The awful result was the persecution of the church, the slaughter of clerics, political anarchy, and the near end of civility. The persecution of the church was at the heart of the French Revolution. In fact, the ideology and philosophy of the French Revolution gave rise to the antitheist movements of the twentieth century. Among these movements are Marxism, which has tyrannized and shackled entire nations, promising to create a "new man" without God, and secularism, which has attempted to cleanse religious principles from the public arena.

On the American continent, the word *liberty* was understood in a very different context with a much different heritage. The concept of "ordered liberty" flowed out of the great heritage of Western civilization, particularly that influenced by the Judeo-Christian worldview. In the United States, it gave rise to institutions that defended and protected true liberty and to judicial precedent that supported the inalienable rights of the people. The founding fathers saw these rights as divine endowments on all human beings. These rights were not culturally relative or politically determined. They came from the Creator, therefore human government had to protect them, not pass laws or enforce policies that would undermine or violate them in any way. This was the unique genius of the founders and their gift to all of us.

Yet, many modern court decisions have assaulted the word *liberty* and the institutions built upon it. I refer to this phenomenon as the institution of a destructive cultural revolution. Its legal component is very strong. Strategic cases, filed by groups advancing the cultural revolution, have attempted to redefine the very meaning of terms such as *liberty*, *life*, and *family*. And they have often succeeded, which is why the threat to true freedom is increasing at such a dramatic pace. Part of this revolution involves just what it did during the days of the French Revolution: promoting and sanctioning a growing hostility toward people of faith.

Armed with these convictions, I knew the ACLJ had plenty of opportunities to occupy its time and resources. After all, given current legal trends, the door was closing on the right of free speech for those considered "religious" by the increasingly hostile secular order. If that door closed, the voices of people of faith would not be heard. Because of the imminency of this threat, I knew that the first thing that demanded my attention was the litigation work. The ACLJ needed to be a legal counteroffensive. Developing the cultural apologetic work that burned so deeply within me would have to come later.

People with the Right Stuff

As I looked over the legal field, I knew there were several men, women, and organizations doing great work in the arena of religious liberties and pro-life activity. I also discovered many groups that had started with a flash but were unable to sustain their efforts. Our adversaries had done a much better job at funding and institutionalizing their work. They had learned how to build effective organizations, such as the Alliance for Justice, an alliance of pro-abortion, left-leaning, so-called public-interest groups. I wanted the ACLJ to last in the public-interest arena.

One of the tasks it would need to perform was to reclaim the term *public-interest law*. I found that when the term *public interest* was used in most periodicals, it was presumed that all groups that organized themselves under the public-interest law umbrella were pro-abortion, anti-family, and in my opinion, did not understand true civil and religious liberty. In other words, many of the efforts of public-interest groups were truly not in the public interest. So I set about the task of building a public-interest law firm that was unqualifiedly pro-liberty, pro-life, and pro-family.

I started to look for lawyers who were ready to fight a battle. I remembered the gargantuan task Abraham Lincoln had when he took the president's office and began his search for generals to lead the North in the Civil War. When he finally found the right general, Ulysses S. Grant, he refused to let go of him even in the face of opposition. He said to those who opposed Grant, "I can't spare this man . . . he fights."[4] That's what the ACLJ needed: lawyers who would fight. So I decided to pursue the lawyer who clearly had done the most for our movement, Jay Sekulow.

Freedom Fighter

I had heard of Jay's victories in courts throughout the United States and was particularly aware of his U.S. Supreme Court victory in *Westside Community Schools v. Mergens* (1990). The *Mergens* case involved an effort to challenge the constitutionality of the Equal Access Act, an act of Congress that simply declared that when a high school opened itself up as a "public forum" by allowing noncurricular clubs to meet on its campus, it could not discriminate against those clubs based on their viewpoint or content. The act covered much more, but that was the particular bone of contention when Bridget Mergens found herself having to go all the way to the U.S. Supreme Court because she started and led a Bible club on her high school campus. The forces of militant secularism would not allow what they perceived as a religious intrusion into their secularized environment. A rather frightening turn of events in a republic founded by people of faith.

It seems bizarre to me that in an age when students have to go through a metal detector before they can enter a high school classroom, there are those who wish to strip those students of the only valid weapon against the malady that afflicts our whole culture—the Bible and the truths it reveals. To have the Bible become a banned book and those who wish to study it banned as well is ludicrous, not just illegal.

In his argument before the U.S. Supreme Court, Jay Sekulow brilliantly defended Bridget Mergens, and in so doing defended all Christian and religious clubs, the First Amendment, and the Equal Access Act. That would not be the last time he ventured before that august body. In the case *Board of Airport Commissioners v. Jews for Jesus* (1987), Jay successfully defended the right of Jewish believers in Jesus to distribute religious literature in airports. A deeply devoted Jewish believer himself, he would also later defend the right of a Hindu sect, the International Society for Krishna Consciousness, to do the same.[5] Not because he believes in their message but because he believes in their right to speak.

As I surveyed the turf of lawyers who were dedicated Christians litigating in the pro-liberty, pro-life, and pro-family arena, Jay Sekulow stood head and shoulders above them all. He was obviously and uniquely anointed and gifted for the task. I wanted him to serve as chief counsel for the American Center for Law and Justice.

Having had some previous encounters with Jay, I had some idea of what to expect. For instance, I knew he was a whirlwind of energy. Meeting him is like confronting your first wave in a long-awaited summer vacation at the ocean. It is at once exhilarating, overwhelming, refreshing, and startling. Additionally, no matter how firm you stand, you can't help but be moved by its energy. He is definitely a uniquely gifted man.

I knew too that Jay and I were like-minded in some important ways. This became clear at a gathering we both attended in the nation's capital. I had been invited to attend a round-table discussion on legal strategies geared toward changing the nation in cooperation with other "conservative" religious-liberties groups. The then dean of the Regent University Law School had asked me to come. Interestingly enough, the meeting occurred the same week I had seen a Hallmark Hall of Fame television special on the early days of the NAACP Legal Defense Fund's efforts. The television special confirmed what I had read about this organization and only reexcited me with the possibilities of using a public-interest practice as a vehicle for social change.

Around the table were leaders from various Christian legal groups. Among them were Jay Sekulow and Ben Bull, who at the time served as general counsel to the American Family Association. The participants spent the first hour getting to know one another. I immediately discerned a high level of suspicion and mistrust in the group. Turf wars and broken promises, intentional or unintentional, had caused quite a bit of pain. But I knew throughout the meeting that this was the seed of what could change North America. We desperately needed to build alliances among

Christians who were dedicated to influencing the culture and making common cause.

As it turned out, Jay had watched the same television special I had that week. Charged by the special, I tried to share with the group about drawing on the NAACP Legal Defense Fund's history as a model for our efforts. But many participants winced while I spoke. Some likely misunderstood me, perhaps thinking I agreed with many of the current political positions of the NAACP or many of the legal positions of the NAACP Legal Defense Fund's current leadership. I didn't, of course. I was simply using the group's history as an example of how motivated lawyers, dedicated to changing their country, can make common cause for good and move the social equation.

Jay rose to my aid in that meeting and told the participants that he had seen the same television special and had also been deeply inspired by it. At that point Jay and I both knew there was common ground between us. We also realized that we broke a mold.

Jay is a Jewish believer and his ethnic identification is refreshing and unique. I spent much of my childhood in a Jewish town in Massachusetts. I have always had a great admiration for the Jewish culture, and I've long esteemed the Jewish people. In fact, as I said, my decision to reembrace my faith in Jesus Christ at the age of eighteen was precipitated by the witness of my best friend, who had become a believing Jew in Jesus while rediscovering his Jewish heritage. Over the years I have been deeply influenced by many other Jewish believers in Jesus. Some of the messianic Jewish groups in the early seventies published or distributed literature that helped me in my then-neophyte faith. The ministry and work of Monsignor Arthur Klyber and other Hebrew Catholics have been a great inspiration for me as a Catholic Christian. So Jay's very Jewishness was a great source of comfort for me. After all, in many respects I, like Jay, felt somewhat like a fish out of water. I was the only Roman Catholic in a group of predominantly evangelical Protestant Christians. (Indeed, that's been a common occurrence over much of my last almost twenty-five years of alliance-building efforts.) As a messianic Jew, Jay wasn't exactly fitting in either.

Aside from these factors, though, the most important thing about that Washington meeting was the philosophical and strategic connection that occurred between Jay's convictions about how to change the nation and my own. That meeting also provided a great framework for a later one-on-one meeting Jay and I would have. But that one would become foundational for our developing a friendship and brotherhood that would deepen in the months and years that lay ahead.

Jay and I decided to meet again later in Washington, D.C. Because both of our schedules were too demanding to permit an early meeting, we decided on a late-night one.

We began our discussion around ten o'clock that evening and concluded around four the next morning. We prayed, laughed, shed some tears, shared our mistakes, failures, and limited victories in our mutual efforts to serve the Lord Jesus Christ and to integrate our faith with the practice of law. We also shared a common vision and excitement about changing North America, about effectively and strategically using test cases to turn back some of the mistakes and errors of the last three decades. Jay and I saw things in a very similar light.

We also realized we had been through many common experiences, among which were the joys, struggles, and pains of Christian ministry. But neither of us had lost our hope, our resolve, or our faith. Our meeting was clearly a serendipitous event, a moment I knew was divinely ordained. I realize that's a very strong statement to make, but I believe the last few years have borne out its truth.

Initially, Jay and I decided to work together on a case-by-case basis. Jay and his wonderful wife and partner in life, Pam, had founded and led a dynamic religious-liberties organization called CASE, an acronym for Christian Advocates Serving Evangelism. Through the vehicle of CASE, Jay and several other religious-liberties lawyers had done outstanding work over several years. It was important to me for that work to continue. But it was also important to me that the alliance effort of the ACLJ begin. Using the ACLJ as the institutional wheel, I began to develop a long-term working relationship with CASE as the first spoke in that wheel. After many cases, months, discussions, and much prayer, CASE became the ACLJ's Atlanta office. It is now more fully and completely integrated under the institution of the ACLJ.

Jay serves as chief counsel to the entire ACLJ effort. The title chief counsel is very appropriate for Jay. I believe he is the Thurgood Marshall of our work. In fact, though not even forty years old, he has been to the United States Supreme Court eleven times. A great number of state supreme courts, intermediate appellate courts, and trial courts have also experienced his advocacy on behalf of people of faith. Over the years we have worked together, I have had the privilege of serving with Jay as co-counsel in two very significant U.S. Supreme Court cases that he argued: *Bray v. Alexandria Women's Health Clinic* (1992) and *Lamb's Chapel v. Center Moriches School District* (1993).

The first case, *Bray*, involved an incredible effort by pro-abortion groups to cripple pro-life demonstrators by using the Ku Klux Klan Act—a civil-rights statute aimed at opposing racist groups such as the Klan that engage in terrorist activities. The National Organization for Women (NOW) argued that opposition to abortion was discrimination against women. This is an absurd argument when you consider the overwhelming number of women involved in the pro-life cause.[6] It was one more example of what Jay calls "the abortion distortion."

Although the Ku Klux Klan Act is good legislation, NOW was using it to try to achieve an insidious end—the censoring out of the pro-life message from public debate. The threat to freedom that case presented required an extraordinary effort. I will never forget Jay's argument before the Supreme Court and his passion for the cause. Fortunately, we won the *Bray* case by basically arguing that NOW's case was not only bogus but a clear violation of the U.S. Constitution's First Amendment. The First Amendment stands as the trump card against the politically correct in their efforts to squelch the speech of pro-lifers. Jay knew this and used it to win a legal and moral victory for the pro-life cause.

In the *Lamb's Chapel* case, another critical victory, secularists lost in their efforts to cleanse the public arena of religion. That case involved a small nondenominational church in New York that attempted to show the James Dobson film series *Turn Your Heart Toward Home* in a public high school auditorium after school hours. The high school routinely opened its auditorium to local community groups after the end of the school day as long as the groups' events promoted the welfare of the community. But when this small Christian church wanted to show a film on family life, the state of New York responded with a vengeance.

The state argued that since the film was "religious," it was somehow a threat to the public order. Insane? You bet. But it highlights the fury behind some secularists' efforts to purge religion from the public arena. Imagine, that case had to go all the way to the U.S. Supreme Court in a country that prides itself on preserving human rights, among which is the right to practice one's religious convictions according to one's conscience. Once again, Jay argued with passion on behalf of the rights of that church and the rights of all people of faith and people of good will in this country.

Jay's case was built on a principle very similar to that argued in the *Mergens* case, which involved the principle of equal access. In this country, a person or agency cannot censor out of the public arena a message simply because of its content. The *Lamb's Chapel* case involved the state doing just that because the content of a film series was deemed religious. This principle is at the very heart of the purpose of the First Amendment and constitutional democracy in this country. Can you imagine the state of New York spending its citizens' tax dollars to take a case like this all the way to the U.S. Supreme Court?

By God's grace, with a lot of hard work, and with the great advocacy skills of someone who has given over his career to a cause more important, freedom won. In a unanimous ruling, the U.S. Supreme Court stood up for freedom of speech and the first freedom, freedom of religion.

Advocate for Life

The next person I went after in my efforts to build a legal alliance was Thomas Patrick Monaghan.

"Pat" Monaghan and Professor Charles Rice of the University of Notre Dame School of Law were cofounders of Free Speech Advocates, a project of Catholics United for Life. I had long been aware of the valiant efforts of this group in opposing the abortion power of the state and defending unborn children and their mothers, the second victims of the lies of the culture of death. Pat Monaghan had also worked very closely with Jay Sekulow over the years.

Like the popular country song that goes, "I was country when country wasn't cool," Pat Monaghan was pro-life when pro-life wasn't cool. He was pro-life when a pro-life law practice meant maxing out your credit card to defend this new civil-rights movement without knowing whether you'd be able to return home from a court date due to lack of funds. Pat's commitment to the pro-life cause, like his commitment to Jesus Christ, was bedrock.

I knew he was also an articulate speaker and a brilliant writer and a committed family man. Every silver white hair in his head has been earned both through raising ten children along with his wonderful wife, Mary Louise, and through defending pro-lifers and people of faith for years.

Also a devout conservative Roman Catholic Christian, Pat was the kind of gifted and dedicated man we needed in our corner of the ring.

As I recount our history, you can see already the intriguing alliance that was forming. Evangelical Protestants, devout Roman Catholics, and Jewish believers in Jesus coming together to make common cause to engage and transform the culture and stand up for liberty, life, and family.

Pat Monaghan had led Free Speech Advocates for a long time. But in just a matter of months, he brought all of the litigation efforts of Free

Speech Advocates under the ACLJ umbrella. This organization became one more spoke in the wheel, with the ACLJ providing the institutional foundation, strength, and resources necessary to keep the wheel moving. With the blessing of the ACLJ, Free Speech Advocates, however, continued on in its apologetic efforts to persuade the mind of the nation that the killing of unborn children was not reproductive and it was not right.

With the change made, Pat began serving as our senior counsel. The title senior counsel is very appropriate for Pat. His wisdom, garnered of age and battlefield experience, provides a tremendous source of strength to the ACLJ's work.

Today, Free Speech Advocates is evolving into Free Speech International, an organization that defends the rights of the Catholic Church to proclaim the truths of the faith throughout the world.

Constitutional Prowess

Along with Pat Monaghan came another great resource to the ACLJ: Professor Charles Rice. Dr. Rice is one of the foremost constitutional scholars in the country. He is a man with impeccable academic credentials, and he possesses a longstanding commitment to the cause of religious freedom, life, and family. A prolific author, committed Catholic, and tireless advocate, he has served on the faculty of Notre Dame University in the School of Law for more than twenty years. I am honored to have him serve as a senior fellow to the ACLJ. He provides a tremendous intellectual wellspring of scholarship, understanding, and experience out of which we frequently draw in our litigation work.

THE SPREADING VISION

As I write this chapter, the ACLJ has twenty-six full-time lawyers and fifty staff in five offices nationwide. Among the lawyers are Protestants, Catholics, messianic Jews, and Eastern Orthodox believers. The ACLJ staff are just as diverse in their faith affiliations.

Our national headquarters is located in Virginia Beach, Virginia, and our Washington, D.C., office houses our Appellate Court Center and our Office of Government Affairs, which monitors the government's treatment of people of faith. We also have offices in Kentucky, Georgia, Alabama, and Arizona.

The ACLJ also has more than 450 affiliate attorneys throughout the United States, and we have begun reclaiming students training to be lawyers through a program called the Law Student Advocate Program.

Student chapters are on such university campuses as Regent, Notre Dame, Harvard, Puget Sound, Emory, Detroit Mercy, and Duquesne. Our goal is to have a chapter on every law school campus in North America.

But our efforts can't be restricted to just the United States. All of Western civilization has fallen prey to the seduction of secularism. So in 1993, we supported efforts to launch the Canadian Centre for Law and Justice, which is located in the federal center of that nation, Ottawa. There, Gerard and Renauld Guay, two deeply dedicated Christian advocates, oversee an entire staff engaged in defending faith, family, and freedom throughout the dominion.

We have come a long way from two old, wooden desks and a vision. But we still have a long way to go. One of my favorite passages in Habakkuk is, "For the vision is yet for an appointed time, but at the end it shall speak, and not lie: though it tarry, wait for it; because it will surely come, it will not tarry."[7] The vision does press on to fulfillment. We need more gifted people to join us, more people to pray for and support us, more groups to align with us in the vast array of litigation work left to be done.

But I'm not naive. I know a society cannot change through litigation alone. We need to develop a clear, creative, and aggressive apologetic that will move people's minds and wills to embrace the truth and the One who is the Truth. That vision is what led me to begin yet another chapter in my life, one that now runs concurrently with my litigation work.

CHAPTER SIX

RESTORING LIBERTY, LIFE, AND FAMILY

Don't be afraid of them.
Remember the Lord, who is great and awesome,
and fight for your brothers,
your sons and your daughters,
your wives and your homes.
Nehemiah 4:14, NIV

When a Hebrew cupbearer to a pagan king heard that the protective wall and high gates of Jerusalem, the city he dearly loved, lay in ruin, he wept, fasted, and prayed for days. He petitioned the God of Heaven to forgive the sins of His people and to grant him favor before the king. Nehemiah wanted leave from his position in the royal court so he could return to Jerusalem and rebuild its fortifications. God answered Nehemiah's pleas, and through a foreign ruler gave Nehemiah the building materials and travel papers he needed to gain safe passage.

Once Nehemiah arrived in Jerusalem and assessed the damage for himself, he rallied and organized the people there to take on the rebuilding project.

Not everyone supported his plan. In fact, Nehemiah and the builders were mocked and verbally terrorized. Some people even threatened to wage war against the city's inhabitants if the construction continued. But in spite of the mounting opposition, Nehemiah and the city's citizens kept at the rebuilding project. To ensure its continuance and the safety of the builders, Nehemiah posted a round-the-clock guard patrol, and he "stationed some of the people behind the lowest points of the wall at the exposed places, posting them by families, with their swords, spears and bows."[1] He also divided up the work force. To put it in his own words:

Half of my men did the work, while the other half were equipped with spears, shields, bows and armor. The officers posted themselves behind all the people of Judah who were building the wall. Those who carried materials did their work with one hand and held a weapon in the other, and each of the builders wore his sword at his side as he worked. But the man who sounded the trumpet stayed with me.

Then I said to the nobles, the officials and the rest of the people, "The work is extensive and spread out, and we are widely separated from each other along the wall. Wherever you hear the sound of the trumpet, join us there. Our God will fight for us!"[2]

All of Nehemiah's opposition, however, did not come from outsiders. Some among God's people threatened the success of the work by engaging in immoral activities.

Regardless of the source of the perils, Nehemiah stood firm, and he called on the Jerusalem populace to do the same. As he saw it, God was greater than any enemy and He was on the side of His people, not of their enemies. Therefore Nehemiah exhorted the people not to fear the enemy: "Don't be afraid of them. Remember the Lord, who is great and awesome, and fight for your brothers, your sons and your daughters, your wives and your homes."[3] The people listened and worked and courageously stayed ready to defend the work. Consequently, the people held together as one and completed the wall's reconstruction in a record fifty-two days.

This historical account provides a powerful image and framework for understanding our role as God's people in rebuilding the walls of civility in a decaying, secularized culture. Jerusalem was the center of God's people then and generations later is still a type of the church, the "New Jerusalem." Just as Nehemiah and the Jews had to engage in a rebuilding project in the midst of opposition, so must we. In society, part of our task is to establish and preserve a moral foundation to achieve an ordered culture. In every generation, God's people must face the challenge of bringing eternal values to bear in the temporal order. And like Nehemiah and the rebuilders, we too must put one hand to the reconstruction work while we arm ourselves against opposition in the other hand. Rebuilding and contending, that's our dual task.

It's not an easy job to take on. We live in extremely difficult times, and they don't appear very conducive for the inculcation of Christian values, much less the many other aspects of the Christian worldview. Indeed, many cultural commentators have described America as *post-Christian*, roughly meaning that it still bears some of the marks of its Judeo-Christian heritage but it has gone a long way toward cutting itself off from its religious roots. While that may be true, I don't think it's the best way to think of the United States.

For one, it engages us in debates about how Christian America ever was. Historical records show that America was certainly strongly influenced in many ways by the Judeo-Christian worldview, but other influences were at work as well,[4] as they have been in every other country on the face of the earth. No society, culture, or nation has ever been thoroughly Christian, nor will any until the Second Coming.

Furthermore, by calling America post-Christian we spin our wheels trying to determine what aspects of its past we should return to. After all, if it shows only the remnants of a Christian past now, then we need to determine what's missing and restore it to what it once was. But this misses the point too. America was never perfect in its adherence to Christian principles or anything else for that matter, so why try to return to a pristine past that never existed?

I think it's far better to think of America—indeed, all of Western civilization—as *pre*-Christian. Whatever it used to be isn't nearly as important as what it now is, and its current state clearly demonstrates that as a culture it does not embrace distinctively Christian values, principles, or truths. America has a pagan mind-set, not a Christian one. Once we come to grips with this fact, it will revolutionize our approach to engaging and transforming American culture.

I've already talked some about Saint Francis of Assisi, but elements of his story are relevant here too. Like us, Francis lived at a time of great cultural and spiritual decay. In the church and in the European culture of his day, the signs of barbarism and paganism seemed to overshadow the influence of Christianity. For part of his life, these influences dominated Francis. Born to a wealthy family, he lived a life almost completely untouched by the claims of the Christian faith. While he was off at war, however, he began to reexamine the existential questions that can only be answered in Christ: Why are we here? Who put us here? What is the purpose of our life? During his wrestling with these questions, Francis experienced a profound conversion, an evangelical moment. He laid aside everything for the sake of serving Christ. He founded a fantastic renewal movement that literally transformed the Europe of his day. Its influence is still felt even into our century.

Francis touched the lives of the untouchables—those people no one else wanted anything to do with. He, like Jesus his Master, embraced them as brothers and sisters. He also sought to rebuild, not only physical churches, but the church of Jesus Christ itself. Francis and his followers established a way of life that challenged the corruption of the culture and the church. He never gave up on the church or culture. Believing the church represents the City of God in the midst of the city of man, he worked to support her in her task. He knew that Christ and His church were the keys to changing the hearts and minds of individuals and to transforming culture. He knew that no matter how devastated she becomes, she and the message she bears are still the only hope for a fallen race.

The Apostle Peter reminded the dispersed Christians of the first century, "As you come to him, the living Stone—rejected by men but chosen by God and precious to him—you also, like living stones, are being built into a spiritual house to be a holy priesthood."[5] The recipients of Peter's letter were scattered throughout Asia Minor, and they had been facing persecution and were expecting more to come. They were strangers where they resided, and they were confronted with various forms of pagan practices, everything from idolatry to promiscuity, from infanticide to slavery. And yet, they brought the claims of Jesus Christ and the promise of His Kingdom into the midst of that social sewer.

The church's task hasn't changed for two thousand years. Those who walk under the banner of Jesus Christ and who bear the name Christian are called to engage and transform their cultures. This is the task of the church in every age and in every culture. And just as it did in Nehemiah's day and in Francis's, our cultural work will involve both the sword and the trowel.

EFFORTS OF THE SWORD

I see the litigation efforts of groups like the ACLJ as the sword. They help us fend off the social marauders, those who are stripping away the remnants of civilization, suppressing people of faith, and substituting a new culture in the United States which, in spite of its lofty rhetoric, is in fact a resurgence of ancient paganism. This new culture elevates being wanted and useful over the dignity and sanctity of the individual human person. It ruthlessly seeks to censor out of the public square any message that speaks of eternal values and accountability to God.

It glorifies pleasure over principle, vice over virtue. It goes under many names: pro-choice, assisted suicide, population control, planned parenthood, relativism, gay rights, the New Age Movement, cleansing the gene pool, secularism, and on the list goes. But regardless of the labels and the claims that go with them, they are as ancient as death and just as deadly. We must set our swords against the verbal, social, and even religious masks of all "arguments and every pretension that sets itself up against the knowledge of God."[6] No exceptions.

I have always been convinced that our litigation efforts, as important as they are, are a means of keeping critical doors open while buying time for more important means of advancement. Christian lawyers will not be able to turn this culture around. What we can do is use our legal resources to reopen and keep open doorways of free speech so the gospel message can be heard again in our country's streets, markets, and meeting places. It is that message, and the hope that it brings to bear upon the human condition, that will lead to the conversion and transformation of this culture.

Put another way, a litigation strategy, including that of the ACLJ, will always be incomplete. It needs to be supplemented with a new generation of Christian apologists—defenders of the faith who will engage in a strategy of cultural apologetics and thereby provide reasons to believe the answers Christianity can provide to the vast array of contemporary social issues.

APOLOGETICS—THE WORK OF THE TROWEL

Apologetics is an ancient discipline that was born out of the church's experience of persecution. The word *apologetic* comes from the Greek term *apologia*, which means "defense" or "reply." The word appears eight times in the New Testament,[7] and in each instance it comes within the context of "contend[ing] for the faith that was once for all entrusted to the saints."[8]

Throughout Christian history, and particularly at critical times, God has raised up men and women apologists. One of them was Justin Martyr. He is a part of the heritage of all Christian traditions and a brave example of heroism in the face of state-sponsored hostility toward people of faith.

Justin was born in Samaria at the beginning of the second century and converted to Christianity as a young man. He opened a school in Rome where he trained fellow defenders of the faith. These men and women were skilled in debate and would engage the leaders of the Roman Empire on critical issues of the day. Their goal was to move the Roman culture away from barbarism to a higher level of civility by influencing that culture with the values of the Christian faith. To bring eternal truth into temporal turf.

In the year 165, Justin and several of his companions were seized and brought before the prefect of Rome. He was asked by the emperor, "What system of teaching do you profess?"

Justin replied, "I have tried to learn about every system, but I have accepted the true doctrines of the Christians."[9] He then proceeded to share his Christian faith with the prefect.

I wish I could say the prefect saw the truth of Justin's arguments and was persuaded to faith, or at least that he changed his position on some vital issue. But history records a different result. The prefect tried to coerce Justin and his companions to renounce their faith and their positions, which, for a Christian, amounts to false worship or idolatry. Justin and his compatriots refused. Justin even told his persecutors, "You can kill us, but not hurt us."[10] So they were sentenced to death and beheaded.

Time, however, proved Justin right. Though the government tried to silence him, his followers, and their message, their martyrdom spoke volumes to their generation and the generations that followed. Inspired by their sacrifice, other apologists rose up and took their place. And when some of those shed their blood for the truth of the Cross, still others took their place. No matter what Rome tried, they couldn't censor or marginalize the truth because Christians stood their ground regardless of the personal cost. As the apologist Tertullian said, "The blood of the martyrs is the seed of the church." Persecution grew the church; it didn't stifle it, much less kill it.

Today, Christians are still giving their lives in defense of the truth, but not all forms of martyrdom result in physical death. Georgetown University Professor James V. Schall writes about this:

> The modern form of death or martyrdom—I do not forget that
> there are probably more real martyrs for the faith in this century
> than in the rest of history put together—consists in a kind of
> public execution that comes from the rejection of the presuppo-
> sitions found in the laws or public opinion of the polity. We have
> no natural law, only civil laws, which we make ourselves with
> no other guidance but our unrestricted liberty.

The cruelest form of death, I have no doubt, is not physical death. Rather it is that public death which comes from the killing of ideas about God, about natural law, about the real dimensions of what loving means. It comes from not talking about good and evil, from being too modest even to bring them forth.[11]

This accurately describes the current climate in America. We have become a culture of death. Recognizing this fact and its many ramifications, Cardinal James Hickey of Washington, D.C., recently wrote to President Bill Clinton and rebuked our government's efforts to export its pro-death policies to the rest of the world. On behalf of the entire conference of Catholic bishops, Cardinal Hickey wrote: "When our government advocates population control through abortion, contraception and sterilization, it is not a force for freedom, but an agent of coercion."[12]

To some people, these comments may be viewed as disrespectful, unpatriotic, or maybe even treasonous. Language like that has carried a price tag in every age. But Cardinal Hickey and his brother bishops are right, and their willingness to make their position public shows refreshing courage. More of this type of heroic leadership is needed today, leadership a new generation of apologists must prepare to provide.

In Rome, there were the Justins. In the Third Reich's Germany, the Dietrich Bonhoeffers and Maximillian Kolbes. And in the former Soviet Union, the Aleksandr Solzhenitsyns. The truth must be proclaimed and defended, even before presidents, emperors, führers, and bureaucrats. And it must be done no matter the cost. We desperately need Christian women and men of courage who are willing to put their comfort and reputation on the line as they intelligently and articulately defend the faith.

In my work over the years, I have met men and women who qualify for this mission. But they must be identified, encouraged, and given a platform. This is the reason I founded Liberty, Life and Family in 1992.

The Apologetic Work of Liberty, Life and Family

Liberty, Life and Family (LLF) is both an institute and an alliance of Christian lawyers, thinkers, philosophers, apologists, and activists. These people recognize the signs of the times and seek to develop a response that will bring intellectual conversion to a secularized America and even beyond to a decimated Western civilization. Recognizing that the malady that ails the West has reached all levels of academia, the media, the body politic, the consumerist culture, and increasingly secularized churches, LLF is hopeful the illness can be cured. The institute is convinced that the cure for the disease of modernism is Jesus Christ and the truths of the faith founded by Him. We are convinced that the love that alone can resecure lost ground is the love of God, which was manifested perfectly through the incarnation, crucifixion, and resurrection of the Father's divine Son, Jesus Christ. We are dedicated to this Love and the truths that flow from it. These are the truths we seek to lovingly proclaim and defend. These are the riches of a classical Christian worldview LLF is striving to represent and demonstrate to a modernist, pre-Christian age.

In order to accomplish such a monumental task, new thinking and new thinkers must be raised up and networked so they can give a contemporary voice to classical Christian thought. This alliance must cross confessional, racial, socioeconomic, gender, and political lines so it can authentically bear witness to the universality of the Christian message. All those within this alliance should share a common dedication to the evangelical message of the gospel and classical orthodox Christian thinking, and they should come from various Christian churches, communities, and confessions. Building this alliance and giving it the needed platform are the primary goals of LLF.

We who are part of this new institute are committed to recapturing the mind and the culture of America. Our country's very heart and future are at stake, and with it the very survival of ordered liberty, the sanctity of all life, and the value of the family. How can we win this struggle? Numerous factors are involved, and the rest of the book will articulate the key ones. Here, however, I'd like to concentrate on the theological foundation upon which we should build an apologetic response. Then I want to show the building LLF is erecting on this foundation.

The Theological Foundation

In order to articulate the primary vocation of both the individual Christian and the Christian people in relationship to the contemporary age, we must appeal to a solid theological foundation, one that is understood by classical Christians in all major Christian communities. Many Christian thinkers of the last twenty years, seeking to rouse a response from an otherwise lethargic church, have sought to ground this foundation in one of two biblical injunctions. One is called the Great Commission (Matthew 28:18-20). Its focus is on evangelism and discipleship. The other injunction is referred to as the Dominion Mandate (Genesis 1:26-30), and it primarily deals with subduing the created order. While I believe both of these biblical frameworks provide a portion of the foundation needed for explaining the Christian vocation to transform the culture, I think both are limiting.

The Great Commission, when acted upon in isolation from other Christian truths, can lead to a spiritual-secular dichotomy that misses the implications of the Incarnation on the whole of human experience. Helpful in this regard is a corrective principle recently conveyed by the leaders of the Catholic Church: "The faithful should 'distinguish carefully between the rights and the duties which they have as belonging to the Church and those which fall to them as members of the human society. They will strive to unite the two harmoniously, remembering that in every temporal affair they are to be guided by a Christian conscience, since no human activity, even of the temporal order, can be withdrawn from God's dominion.'"[13] God is not just Lord of our souls or local churches or the church universal, but of the entire created order. And when the Father sent His Son to take on a human nature and live among us as a man, He provided for the full redemption and transformation of the total human experience. The Great Commission in and of itself does not cover all this ground, hence it is an insufficient foundation for us to build on in our attempts to engage and transform the culture for Christ.

The Dominion Mandate fares no better. It, too, when seen in isolation, can lead to a misguided marriage of Christianity to secular rule. In this period of human history, our role is not to establish the church as the governing authority over all peoples, be they believers or not. Christ Himself will handle that upon His return.[14] In the meantime, we would be better served by returning to a foundation for true social action that represents a more thoroughly and classically Christian approach while including the Great Commission and the Dominion Mandate without their limitations.

Liberty, Life and Family proposes we rebuild a contemporary apologetic for Christian action that can renew the temporal order, or as some say it, Christianize society. This new yet ancient approach would be rooted in a profound understanding of the mystery and grandeur of the Incarnation. When Deity entered the human experience through the incarnation of the Son of God, He forever changed that experience. Jesus brought with Him salvation for those who would believe. He also elevated and transformed the entire human experience. He gave it a profound dignity and elevated it above the mire it's so naturally drawn to when unaided by grace. The Son did not become man simply to be religious on Sundays or do religious things. He took on our nature and entered into our history so He could dramatically, profoundly, and eternally transform the human experience and reorient the human community's cultural expression toward Heaven. Human societies will never become fully Christian before the Second Coming, but they can become more Christlike. That's the church's mission, and it belongs to all of us corporately and individually.

The author of the letter to the Hebrews reminded the early believers and those who still carry on their mission that "Jesus also suffered outside the city gate to make the people holy through his own blood. Let us, then, go to him outside the camp, bearing the disgrace he bore. For here we do not have an enduring city, but we are looking for the city that is to come."[15] This verse bears witness to one of the challenges Christians have faced throughout the centuries: dealing with the tension between the now-and-not-yet nature of the Kingdom. We live here and now, but as Christians we're citizens of a Kingdom that's partially here and now yet more fully later. This sets up an eschatological tension. We're between two worlds, two kingdoms, two cities. And it's in this state that we're called to renew the earthly city incarnationally while seeking the heavenly City still to come. This tension, however, isn't bad. In fact, it serves to protect us from numerous errors (many of which I'll talk about in chapter 13).

Achieving a balance between the two sides of this tension is not easy. Throughout Christian history, the church has experienced various successes and failures in this attempt. The accord "Evangelicals and Catholics Together" has sought to articulate a sound approach to achieving this balance when it comes to contending for American culture.

> Together we contend for the truth that politics, law, and culture must be secured by moral truth. With the Founders of the American experiment, we declare, "We hold these truths." With them, we hold that this constitutional order is composed not just of rules and procedures but is most essentially a moral experiment. With them, we hold that only a virtuous people can be free and just, and that virtue is secured by religion. *To propose that securing civil virtue is the purpose of religion is blasphemous. To deny that securing civil virtue is a benefit of religion is blindness.*[16]

With all of our past mistakes, we are still called to Christianize society, to renew the temporal order, while we sojourn in its midst. We are called to influence, evangelize, and elevate the culture. Ironically, when the church has perceived that it is fully within the camp and to some extent even beginning to run the camp, she has gotten far off track and lost her prophetic call. Perhaps this is part of the mystery of God's plan in allowing what historians have called the "American experiment" to reach its current frightening low. We thought we had more influence on the minds and hearts of men and women than we truly did. Rather than give up because of our mistaken judgment, though, we must reassess our failures and successes and try again. This is what LLF has set out to do in its own sphere of influence.

The Apologetic Building

We at LLF believe Christians must be salt and light; we must be agents for change in this increasingly secularized nation. But we must not underestimate the magnitude of the work that lies before us. As I'll show throughout the rest of this book, we have much to do to refashion society so it values liberty, life, and family; so it executes justice and exercises mercy; so it stops discriminating against people of faith as well as people of color and poverty; so it reintroduces absolute truths and ethics into every level of education; so it genuinely protects all our human rights from the womb to the tomb without granting special rights to those who engage in immorality or to those who seek to undermine marriage and the family through legal and legislative fiat. LLF is seeking to address these issues and the many others we face through a number of avenues. Here are six.

Reclaiming intellectual conversion—The classical understanding of the role of intellectual conversion has all but disappeared in many Christian traditions. Consequently, though people may be genuinely committed to the faith in their heart, many of them have not been transformed by the faith in their mind. In a recent insightful article entitled "Can Evangelicalism Survive Its Success?" the authors cite Charles Malik, a prominent evangelical Christian, who reminded us, "the problem is not only to win souls, but to save minds. If you win the whole world and lose the mind of the world, you will soon discover you have not won the world. Indeed it may turn out that you have actually lost the world."[17]

Jesus Christ came to save the whole person, an aspect of which is the mind. This is why the Apostle Paul exhorts us to present ourselves as "a living and holy sacrifice, acceptable to God, which is your spiritual [literally, "rational"] service of worship. And do not be conformed to this world, but be transformed by the renewing of your mind, that you may prove what the will of God is, that which is good and acceptable and perfect."[18] If we took Paul's admonition seriously, we would be thinking more like Christ, more incarnationally. Instead the fruit of our thinking frequently looks more like the decaying fruit grown by the spirit of this age.

In other words, if we were truly thinking Christianly, our own house would be in better order than it now is, and we would have more energy to turn outward to contend for the mind of the culture. We, of course, must do both simultaneously, which is why LLF is committed to renewing the minds of believers as well as the minds of unbelievers.

Some of you may question my claim that the nonChristian mind can be renewed, at least to some degree, before the unbeliever accepts Christ as his or her Savior and Lord. To verify my claim, all you have to do is consider the lives of people such as Justin Martyr, Saint Augustine, and C. S. Lewis, to name just a few. These and countless others came to accept many truths before finally accepting Jesus as the embodiment of truth, the One to whom all truths point and from whom they come. Consider also the many nonChristians who have adopted and defended positions on social, historical, philosophical, economic, and even moral issues that are compatible, if not identical, to those found in a distinctively Christian worldview. God is always rewarding those who seek Him, even if they don't know they are pursuing Him. All truth leads to Him, so those who find and accept truth learn more about He who is the truth, and in that way their minds begin to undergo at least a partial renewal.

Removing linguistic limitations—In many of our evangelistic and apologetic efforts, we have developed a language that limits our ability to speak to the contemporary age. We use what I call "Christianese" or "religionese." Rather than being sensitive to our culture and what it can comprehend, we use words we are familiar with and then simply expect our culture to catch on. For instance, in a society that disavows moral absolutes and distances itself from personal responsibility, talk about sin seems not only outdated but nonsensical. However, if we define *sin* by explaining it with words such as *wrongdoing, going wrong, messing up, missing the target, hurting ourselves and others, a sense something is amiss,* or *violating a law that carries severe consequences,* we'll have a better chance of gaining a hearing as well as some understanding.

Another way to handle the sin issue is through the experience of guilt. Everyone experiences guilt. And even though there is such a thing as false guilt, most guilt is genuine and associated with real sin. The only way to rid oneself of the guilt of sin is by forgiveness and reconciliation, and those are only available through faith in the death and resurrection of Christ.

Men and women of all ages wrestle with guilt, even if they don't connect it with the word *sin*. And they also know they can't deal with this problem on their own. When I talk to moderns about guilt and their struggle with it, I often take them to Romans 7, where the Apostle Paul describes his struggle with guilt and sin. When they hear Paul say, "I do not understand what I do. For what I want to do I do not do, but what I hate I do," they usually readily identify with him. People's struggle with the human condition is universal, so when we appeal to their attempts to deal with it and tell them we have the answer to that problem, they are much more willing to listen to the gospel message. After all, isn't that what the good news is basically about—namely, that freedom from guilt and sin are found in Jesus Christ and what He did for us on Calvary?

Another problematic word for moderns in the Christian's vocabulary is *God*. American society is secularistic and pluralistic. In part that means various religious persuasions abound but their expression and practice are largely relegated to the private sphere. So when we start talking about God, we run into at least two problems: (1) public conversation about God is unexpected and often disregarded or regarded with contempt; and (2) when it is allowed, our God-talk can be interpreted in enough ways to fill an encyclopedia on world religions. The first problem often leads to acts of religious cleansing and other forms of religious bigotry. The second problem, due to a resurgence of paganism and Eastern forms of mysticism (such as the New Age Movement), can frequently lead us into conversations with people who think of themselves as gods and goddesses. Therefore, we must clearly define what we mean and don't mean by *God*, and we must speak up about Him with courage and conviction.

LLF is dedicated to using language that those caught up in our pre-Christian culture can understand. After all, what value is there in speaking, dialoguing, evangelizing, and writing if no one understands what you say?

Knocking down caricatures—Once we win a hearing and can speak intelligibly to a modern audience, we must be prepared to clear up distortions about Christians and our common faith. We have all too often been caricatured by those who oppose our positions and seek to undermine them by distracting people from listening. Sometimes we have played right into their hands. We have looked, talked, and frequently presented ourselves in a manner quite easily mocked by a hostile, secularized world. In some ways, we have earned the caricatures we have received. This wouldn't be so bad if the distortions were really related to our attempts to live according to the example set by Jesus Christ. Too often, however, this isn't the case.

Many nonChristians see Christians as boring, stupid, mirthless, irrational, superstitious, easily led, and more defined by what they don't do than what they do. Compare this with the reputation Jesus gained during His short sojourn on earth. Wherever He went, to whomever He talked, He broke the mold. His activities and self-presentation were so extraordinary that not even His reputation could be clearly pegged. Some thought He was a great prophet or an authoritative teacher. Others saw Him as a mighty healer, while some scorned and feared Him as a sorcerer. Many people thought He was a political messiah come to break the yoke of Roman rule. He was even viewed as "a glutton and a drunkard, a friend of tax collectors and 'sinners.'"[19] He was known for going to parties and providing the best wine at a wedding feast. People knew about the time He spent with lepers, prostitutes, the poor, and the other social outcasts. And they had seen Him soundly refute any and every argument that conflicted with divine truth.

Jesus was anything but stereotypical. That's why He was seen as such a threat. That's why He couldn't be ignored. More of us need to follow in His footsteps. This won't stop the caricatures, but it will certainly raise them to a new high and make them much harder to develop and stick.

And when caricatures do arise, we need to challenge them. Jesus certainly did. He constantly corrected people's misunderstandings about Him and His mission. We must do the same.

There are a number of different ways to attempt such a task, and they must be studied and tried. Included among them, and a major commitment of LLF, is to build interracial and interconfessional networks of relationships among Christians.

Like Francis of Assisi who passionately gave his all to transforming both the culture of the church and the culture of the European continent, so must we. Right before his death, Francis gathered his brothers around him and said, "My brethren, we must begin to serve our Lord and God. Until now we have done very little."[20] That kind of dedication to influencing and redeeming the mind and the culture is absolutely essential if we are to be effective.

Recovering the academy—You likely won't find any Christian who believes that most of today's educational institutions in the United States are pro-Christian. If anything, most are religiously intolerant, and many display outright hostility to the specific claims of the Christian faith. Recently George Marsden, an evangelical Protestant who teaches at the University of Notre Dame, commented on this problem before a group of scholars: "Unless the major universities change, they should add a footnote to the phrase in their catalogues announcing that they 'welcome diverse perspectives.' It should read: 'Except, of course, religious perspectives.'"[21]

Christians can counteract this form of discrimination in a number of ways. One is by penetrating America's schools as teachers and administrators and using such positions of authority to keep classrooms free of religious bigotry. Another is to strengthen the efforts being made in many Christian schools to reclaim education.

Just recently, LLF embarked on its "Recovering the Academy" project. In our first effort, we have brought together Regent University and Thomas More College, linking like-minded evangelical Protestant and evangelical Catholic schools of higher learning in an effort to restore education to its rightful place in the Christian community and the culture at large. After all, any serious effort geared toward cultural change must resecure the ground lost. And that involves rebuilding Christian educational institutions and building new ventures. If we do not recover the academy, we simply *will not* recover the culture.

Under the dynamic leadership of Dr. Terry Lindvall, Regent University is an example of a new institution committed to integrating the highest ideals of university education with evangelical Christian faith. The same is true of Franciscan University and Thomas More College. I count it a privilege to serve on the Board of Thomas More College. Under the thoughtful, reflective, and brilliant leadership of Dr. Peter Sampo, Thomas More is a small but powerful example of an academic community dedicated to the great-books tradition of a truly liberal education and to orthodoxy in Christian teaching and doctrine.

There are many other schools I could mention. I hope they will join us too. Through our "Recovering the Academy" project, we hope to see Catholic and Protestant institutions of higher learning find common ground for dialogue and cooperation in our mutual efforts to reclaim civilization by raising and training future leaders and scholars.

Utilizing the available tools—Christians also need to draw on every available outlet to present and defend a Christian worldview. This means we need to access radio, television, newspapers, magazines, journals, books, the movie industry, theater, music, art—every possible avenue of communication.

Through LLF, we are building a network of the emerging generation of effective apologetic writers. One of these, for example, is E. Michael Jones, a prolific author and profound contemporary Christian thinker. His most recent works include *Degenerate Moderns* and *Dionysus Rising*. He is also the editor of an insightful and intelligent journal called *Fidelity* that predominantly reaches out to Catholic Christians. Michael has caught a big vision and has joined LLF in working out a five-year apologetic publishing strategy. In part this will involve the publication of a magazine that will squarely face the cultural war raging around us. This magazine will provide a monthly commentary on the struggles I discuss throughout this book.

Bill Watkins, who has been my writing assistant and close personal friend all these years, has also joined the publishing effort of LLF. Drawing from the well of his many years in the publishing industry and many activities as an apologist, he has worked with me on researching and writing the booklets *Religious Cleansing in the American Republic* and *In Defense of Life*, and the full-length book *In Defense of Life: Confronting the Culture of Death with the Message of Life*. Bill and I also put together a publishing plan of which this book is a part. Indeed, *A House United?* is the first title in an entire product line. This brings me to my sixth point.

Building apologetic alliances—As I've said, LLF's primary mission is to educate and engage in apologetic discourse. Our goal is not only to influence Christians, but more importantly, to bring contemporary moderns to the faith. In other words, to engage in precisely what Justin Martyr and Francis of Assisi and so many other Christians have for centuries. Thus, many months ago, Bill Watkins and I embarked on an effort to involve a major publisher in our mission. I must confess I did not expect what occurred.

We sent out proposals to most of the major Protestant and Catholic publishing houses. The proposals set forth the vision of Liberty, Life and Family and laid out the groundwork for developing a publishing partnership to produce a line of apologetic-oriented products. This line had a dual purpose: (1) it would raise the intellectual water level among Christian people and engage those who do not share our faith on vital issues; and (2) it would seek to raise up the next generation of Christian apologists and provide a platform for their efforts.

We received interest from a number of houses, but the greatest enthusiasm came from John Eames, Steve Webb, and the other leaders of NavPress. When I first heard of their excitement over the product line, I must admit to a little Catholic bigotry. I assumed NavPress, having been birthed by The Navigators, had limited its mission and purpose to the evangelical Protestant world. I also thought they probably had a certain inherent anti-Catholic sentiment. I was wrong. What I found was a publishing house on the cutting edge of bringing the gospel and the claims of Christ to bear in the contemporary age. What I found was an openness to all Christians who shared their passion for evangelization and mission.

I will never forget the day Bill and I visited their headquarters in Colorado Springs, Colorado, at NavPress's invitation. When we first walked into the meeting room, I was struck by the friendliness of their publisher, John Eames. In his laid-back, warm, and gracious manner, he made me feel very welcome. As other people began filing into the room, I experienced the same kind of genuine Christian acceptance and a strong spirit of cooperation.

With that level of support, Bill and I openly shared our conviction about building alliances among Christians and engaging and transforming the culture. The more we talked, the more I saw excitement grow in the eyes, demeanor, and remarks of every person in the room. In fact, I would say it truly was an encounter in the Holy Spirit.

Our conversation and discussion flowed on literally for hours. When the meeting drew to a close, we prayed together and parted company realizing we were caught up in something bigger than all of us. We had shared a serendipitous move of the Lord. I sensed a common bond with these women and men, a bond that can only be found in Christ.

My sense of the meeting was confirmed when NavPress came back to us with their publishing decision. They were willing to take the risk and join in a publishing venture with LLF. In fact, they weren't only willing but delighted. They too came to see the desperate need for carrying out the apologetic task in the publishing arena and doing it through an alliance-building effort.

In the months and years ahead, we look forward to working alongside NavPress to bring to the forefront women and men of various ethnic, racial, socioeconomic, and confessional backgrounds who will demonstrate with passion, clarity, and power the veracity of classical

Christianity and its relevance to rescuing culture from the quicksand of destruction and reestablishing it on the bedrock of pro-liberty, pro-life, and pro-family.

THE VIEW FROM HERE

We will soon approach the end of two millenniums of Christianity. From our humble start in Jerusalem in the first century, the church has come a long way. She has made many mistakes but accomplished much good as well. And there is still plenty for her to do. The question isn't, What shall we do? Christ has given us our mission. Nor is the question, Can we do it? Christ has given us the Holy Spirit to help us fulfill our mission. The burning question is, Will we seek to accomplish our mission separately or together, as a people divided or a people united? If the answer is separately, we will never accomplish what Christ has called us to. Only together will we fulfill the fullness of our destiny in Christ.

The culture is slowly dying. The barbarians are at the door. Will the church respond as she should? Will we build the alliances necessary to win our culture to Christ? To beat back the barbarians? Indeed, to Christianize them?

If we are to get serious about this task, we must come to grips with the barbarism crashing down upon us. We must be able to identify it, expose it for what it is, and refute it in the marketplace of ideas. Put another way, if we are going to defeat our enemy we must understand him. And that's just what we're going to strive to do in the next two chapters.

PART II

Making Common Cause

CHAPTER SEVEN

BARBARIANS
AT THE DOOR

Woe to those who call evil good and good evil.
Isaiah 5:20, NIV

*Cleaving [which is what occurs
in a traditional marriage]
is an activity which should be left to snails
for cleaning ponds and aquariums.*
Jane Rule

I had heard Michael preach hundreds of times. He was always inspiring. But today's message was different. It grabbed me in a life-changing, foundational way. He spoke of his memories of the "war effort" during World War II and his own family's participation in it. Threatened with a dark cloud of totalitarianism, nations joined together to combat common foes. On the front lines were different people with deep and important differences. Yet they made an alliance to confront a shared enemy; they made common cause and fought together.

On the home front, people also joined the war effort through sacrifice and solidarity. Michael remembered even saving tinfoil and gum wrappers to be melted down for munitions productions.

While sitting there listening to Michael talk about this not-too-distant history, I was particularly struck by the passion in his voice. The years had not eclipsed the strong feelings and impressions these events had first evoked in him. And for good reason: From the greatest sacrifice of shedding blood abroad to the daily sacrifices at home, Michael had lived through one of the greatest united efforts in world history, an alliance that succeeded where individual efforts had miserably failed. He could recall how the darkness was pushed back and freedom, at least a form of it, arose victorious. In fact, to this day, veterans of that world war and their families still speak of being allies in a common cause.

The analogy to our current age grabbed me and has never let me go. It has become the passion of my life in both my professional and my evangelical work. For I believe we live in a time in which a new darkness is sweeping the globe. It is a new kind of barbarism, which in some respects is even more threatening than the barbarism demonstrated by the totalitarian political movements that gave rise to World War II and the Allied response. And ironically enough, it has found a home in the very nations that physically resisted the darkness of national socialism and the threats of the Axis powers only half a century ago. Yet, it is surprisingly similar in its philosophical underpinnings and practical outworkings. And it is spreading at an alarming rate.

In the United States alone, it has infiltrated virtually every sector of our society, from our courtrooms and classrooms to our churches and homes. Even the highest levels of our governing bodies show the horrific influence of this invader. But you won't find its proponents wearing brown shirts and swastikas or shouting feverishly into microphones. Instead you'll see them dressed in neatly tailored suits and usually speaking calmly and civilly before judges, legislative assemblies, or the press. But the change in dress and demeanor should not fool us. The fruit of their tyranny is producing a holocaust of body and spirit all too reminiscent of that perpetrated on the human race just decades ago.

In this new age of darkness, once again good has become evil and evil good. Thousands of years ago, in stirring words spoken through the prophet Isaiah, God warned the nation of Israel about those who . . .

> call evil good
>   and good evil,
> who put darkness for light
>   and light for darkness,
> who put bitter for sweet
>   and sweet for bitter.
> Woe to those who are wise in their own eyes
>   and clever in their own sight.[1]

Their descendants appear to be thriving in America today, and they are attempting to refashion the culture in their own image.

These social engineers are substituting a culture of death for a culture of life. We can see it most clearly in the disdain for unborn life, the growing intolerance toward the infirm and the elderly, and the increasing cheapening of life itself. The lies of the age are squeezing out the truth, including the One who is Truth. Just take a quick look at some of the many disturbing facts.

THE STATE OF THE UNION

In his book *The Index of Leading Cultural Indicators*,[2] former secretary of education under President Ronald Reagan, William Bennett, points out that since 1960, America's population has increased by 41 percent, her domestic product has nearly tripled, and the total social spending at all levels of government has risen from an annual $142.73 billion to $787 billion. During that same time period, however, violent crime has increased 560 percent, illegitimate births have gone up 400 percent, divorces have quadrupled, the number of children living in single-parent homes has tripled, the teenage suicide rate has increased by more than 200 percent, and the SAT scores of high school students have dropped an average of seventy-five points.

In 1940, when teachers were asked to identify the top problems in America's schools, they listed talking out of turn, chewing gum, making noise, running in the hall, cutting in line, dress-code infractions, and littering. In 1990, teachers answered the same question with a very different list: drug use, alcohol abuse, pregnancy, suicide, rape, robbery, and assault.

When the United States is compared to the other industrialized countries of the world, the severity of our condition looks even worse. As Bennett observes, "We are at or near the top in rates of abortions, divorces, and unwed births. We lead the industrialized world in murder, rape, and violent crime. And in elementary and secondary education, we are at or near the bottom in achievement scores."[3]

Since the U.S. Supreme Court's decision in *Roe v. Wade* and its companion cases, we have methodically and legally slaughtered nearly thirty million children. That's about four times the number of people in or outside the womb who had their lives extinguished under the policies of the Third Reich. "Today, one out of every three children conceived in the United States is aborted. In more than fourteen metropolitan areas, abortions outnumber live births."[4] Every twenty seconds, abortion takes the life of another baby.

Once a baby is born, life isn't assured either. For children born with unwanted disabilities or diseases, medical personnel may snuff out their lives or even advise parents on how to do it. More and more physicians are recommending infanticide as a "management option." As one medical writer reported, the practice is becoming a routine procedure in America's hospitals: "The decision to withhold or withdraw treatment from extremely sick, premature, and/or deformed newborns is probably being made at least once every day by anguished parents and doctors in one of the nation's more than 500 intensive care nurseries."[5] It's not safe to be a baby in America anymore.

Then there's the matter of assisted suicide. Whether the assistant is a spouse, a friend, a physician, or Jack "Dr. Death" Kevorkian himself, an increasing number of people are choosing to die rather than live. According to the founders of the Hemlock Society, "Mercy killings rose ten times in the 1980s compared to any five-year period since 1920, while murder-suicides, double suicides, and assisted suicides involving the terminally ill increased forty times."[6]

Americans are accepting this grisly practice in ever-increasing numbers. "A 1990 Gallup Poll revealed 69 percent of those surveyed approved of voluntary active euthanasia if the patient and the family requested it. Only 37 percent supported this view in 1947, with the percentage dramatically increasing to 60 percent by 1977."[7] Other recent polls support Gallup's numbers. *USA Today* conducted a survey in which "68 percent of those polled felt that terminally ill people should be allowed to end their lives. Another poll, by the Maturity News Service, showed that just over half the Americans surveyed felt that life-and-death decisions should be made by family members; 25 percent felt that life support should be removed only if the patient had expressed this preference; and only 7.2 percent said that life support should be continued until a patient died or recovered."[8] Some states, such as Washington and California, have entertained voter initiatives to legalize physician-assisted death for the terminally ill. Many other states—such as New Hampshire, Maine, Iowa, Michigan, and Oregon—have considered legislation that would legalize certain kinds of euthanasia.

Space doesn't permit a detailing of all the telltale signs of a culture gone corrupt. Suffice it to say that we have fallen far from the Christian understanding that life is sacred, that our children are one of our greatest blessings, that morality is grounded in the eternal God and not in the changing mores of individuals or societies. We have also undermined our constitutional rights, the inalienable rights to life, liberty, and the pursuit of happiness. Today our right to life can be stripped from us at any time from just moments after our conception to just moments before we would die naturally. Our rights to speak freely, especially if our speech is religious or politically incorrect, are being minimalized and even stripped away with threats of arrest, prison time, large fines, and law-suits. Our freedoms to pursue economic opportunities in support of our-selves and our families are being squelched by heavy taxes and unnec-essary governmental intrusions. Liberty is being construed as moral license to satisfy one's disordered appetites. Its original meaning as involving individual and corporate responsibility linked with an authen-tically moral code of conduct has been all but abandoned.

We are definitely in desperate straits. The state of the union is tragic indeed.

THE DIFFERENCE INDIFFERENCE MAKES

What has happened to us? Why have we fallen so far?

In his incredibly insightful speech before the Heritage Foundation in late 1993, Bennett related a story that provides a key to answering these questions. He told about a Polish high school student named Paulina who is studying in the United States. When she first came to the U.S., she was stunned by the way teens spent their time. "In Warsaw," she said, "we would talk to friends after school, go home and eat with our parents and then do four or five hours of homework. When I first came here, it was like going into a crazy world, but now I am getting used to it. I'm going to Pizza Hut and watching TV and doing less work in school. I can tell it is not a good thing to get used to." As different and unacceptable as she found American teenage behavior and values, Paulina has done her best to fit in, even though she realizes "it is not a good thing to get used to."[9]

In our culture, we have adapted as Paulina has. Just thirty years ago we would have been appalled, even outraged, by the decadence and debauchery that daily fill our streets, television shows, movie screens, music and art, video games, businesses, and political bodies. But today we rarely give it a second thought. Indeed, we often give it our approval, or at least fail to speak out against it. We have gotten used to it all, even though it is not a good thing to get used to.

As a society, we have gotten used to illicit sexual relationships, adolescent promiscuity, abortion, cheating, lying, stealing, prostitu-tion, rape, divorce, selfism, and even murder. We have gotten used to financial mismanagement on both civil and personal levels. We have accepted political corruption. We have rejected personal and social responsibility and learned to blame anyone or anything else for our problems and failures. In short, we have surrendered. We have given up our dignity, abandoned our values, sacrificed our futures. We have traded in our infinitely valued divine image for a nickel-plated pagan shrine erected in honor of self-interest, immorality, and social apathy. It's me first to do what I want, when I want, to whom I want, regardless of who or what it may hurt.

These are the signs of a society gone wrong. America is no longer the leading civilization of the world. It is becoming decivilized. Like fruit left on the ground in an orchard, America is rotting—not from the outside in but from the inside out. America is undergoing the degeneration of its heart and soul. The moral, spiritual, and aesthetic character and habits of American society—what the ancient Greeks referred to as society's *ethos*—are wasting away.

At the heart of America's increasing demise is the sin of sloth. The ancients called it *acedia*. It does not refer to laziness but, as Bennett says, to "an aversion to and a negation of *spiritual* things. *Acedia* reveals itself as an undue concern for external affairs and worldly things . . . [and] an absence of zeal for divine things." Aleksandr Solzhenitsyn put his finger on it when he said, "In the United States the difficulties are not a Minotaur or a dragon—not imprisonment, hard labor, death, government harassment and censorship—but cupidity, boredom, sloppiness, indifference. Not the acts of a mighty all-pervading repressive government but the failure of a listless public to make use of the freedom that is its birthright."[10] Tough words to accept, but they are much too true to ignore.

Dorothy Sayers, in her collection of insightful essays called *The Whimsical Christian*, reminds us of the slippery nature of this malady: "The sixth deadly sin is named by the Church *acedia* or *sloth*. In the world it calls itself tolerance; but in hell it is called despair. It is the accomplice of the other sins and their worst punishment. It is the sin that believes in nothing, cares for nothing, enjoys nothing, loves nothing, and remains alive only because there is nothing it would die for. We have known it far too well for many years. The only thing perhaps that we have not known about it is that it is a mortal sin."[11]

America is inflicted by a corrupted heart and a decadent mind. Claiming to be a tolerant people, we have embraced a new barbarism. We have turned to the wrong things for help and hope.

INSTITUTIONALIZING BARBARISM

How did all this happen to us? The same way it occurs in many other cultures: methodically and incrementally.

A great Christian of our time, Malcolm Muggeridge, while discussing the deterioration of Western civilization, used the example of a frog and a kettle. When a frog is placed in a kettle of boiling water, it recognizes the danger immediately and quickly leaps to safety. On the other hand, if that same frog is put in a pot of tepid water that's very gradually heated to a boil, the frog won't try to escape. Its body heat will adapt to the slowly rising temperature until it's too late for the frog to save itself from death.

The same has happened to the U.S. Social changes came slowly, sometimes almost imperceptibly. And while a few prophetic voices warned us of impending dangers, as a culture we ignored them and simply adapted to our surroundings. Now we're close to boiling to death, and many of us don't even mind because we don't feel the heat. Indeed, it's even pleasurable to us. The changes cater to our selfish desires, and we like that. Who among us is willing to give up what makes us comfortable and brings us pleasure? As educator Neil Postman says, "We are a people on the verge of amusing ourselves to death."[12] We have not been oppressed as people were in George Orwell's novel *1984*. What we have experienced is much closer to the fictional scenario portrayed in Aldous Huxley's *Brave New World*. Postman explains:

> Contrary to common belief even among the educated, Huxley and Orwell did not prophesy the same thing. Orwell warns that we will be overcome by an externally imposed oppression. But in Huxley's vision, no Big Brother is required to deprive people of their autonomy, maturity and history. As he saw it, people will come to love their oppression, to adore the technologies that undo their capacities to think.
>
> What Orwell feared were those who would ban books. What Huxley feared was that there would be no reason to ban a book, for there would be no one who wanted to read one. Orwell feared those who would deprive us of information. Huxley feared those who would give us so much that we would be reduced to passivity and egoism. Orwell feared that the truth would be concealed from us. Huxley feared the truth would be drowned in a sea of irrelevance. Orwell feared we would become a captive culture. Huxley feared we would become a trivial culture, preoccupied with some equivalent of the feelies, the orgy porgy, and the centrifugal bumblepuppy. As Huxley remarked in *Brave New World*, the civil libertarians and rationalists who are ever on the alert to oppose tyranny "failed

to take into account man's almost infinite appetite for distrac-
tions." In *1984*, Huxley added, people are controlled by inflicting pain. In *Brave New World*, they are controlled by inflicting
pleasure. In short, Orwell feared that what we hate will ruin us.
Huxley feared that what we love will ruin us.[13]

We have become a culture so caught up in having our carnal wants
fulfilled that we have exchanged life for death, liberty for license, family for fornication, virtue for vice, character for condoms. This change
didn't happen overnight. But it has occurred.

Many books could be written on how it happened and through whom,
but in broad brush strokes I would paint the scenario by focusing on
four distinct methods that have slowly ripped apart our social fabric and
rewoven a new utopia that's no dream world at all.

Verbal Engineering

Perhaps the most important strategy used to bring about the new social
(dis)order has been redefining words. Words are powerful tools. The
Apostle James told us, "If anyone considers himself religious and yet
does not keep a tight rein on his tongue, he deceives himself and his
religion is worthless. . . . Consider what a great forest is set on fire by a
small spark. The tongue also is a fire, a world of evil."[14] Some things
haven't changed. Words have been used as potent weapons throughout
human history. Sometimes for good. Sometimes for bad.

In the first year of law school, students learn that whoever frames the
issue first often wins the argument. And the issue is framed with carefully selected words combined with finely crafted definitions. This is
one of the ways America has been reshaped. In the process, many people
have been confused, co-opted, and crucified.

What has happened is what C. S. Lewis called "verbicide; the murder of a word."[15] People must be led to believe that the old ways are out
of touch, passé; that they are keeping society from realizing its full potential. The established good must appear evil, and the new thought must
appear good. So the new social engineers have gone to work to change
the language and thereby recast the issues.

For example, just a quarter of a century ago, the word *abortion*
clearly meant "prenatal murder." Since then, those who have favored
abortion on demand have reframed the issue by redefining the word.
Pick up just about any newspaper or magazine or listen to almost any
television report and you'll find that *abortion* now means "reproductive

right" or "reproductive liberty" or "pro-choice" or "pro-family plan-ning" or "responsible child-rearing" or "a constitutionally protected right" or "a necessary medical procedure in a woman's total health pack-age." In reality, of course, abortion is none of these things. It's not repro-ductive or right since it eliminates life. It's not pro-choice or libertarian since it destroys the free choice of its most innocent victim. It's not a form of family planning or child-rearing since it executes the child that leads to family. It's not a constitutional right since the U.S. Constitution contains no such provision for killing one's offspring with impunity. And it's anything but a health option for the mother since it often leads to physical complications, some of which cause permanent physical damage including death, and it creates a myriad of emotional, psycho-logical, and relational problems, which therapists have summed up under the label "postabortion syndrome." Nevertheless, the new social engineers manage to ignore or cover up these facts. They won't let anything or anyone stand in the way of their achieving their social agenda. This includes the unborn.

Consider also homosexuality. Even through much of the "free love" movement of the sixties, homosexuality was not a hot topic of conver-sation. As William Dannemeyer has pointed out,

> You didn't hear it discussed on talk shows or depicted in movies. You didn't see so-called gay pride parades in our major cities. You weren't bombarded with political pronouncements on the subject. You didn't have homosexuals militantly proclaiming to the general public the propriety of what they did in the bed-room. Certainly prominent political figures did not announce to the world that they habitually committed homosexual acts and were proud of it. If someone engaged in such acts, he kept the matter to himself, not only because there were laws against homosexual conduct but also because the community at large disapproved of it as much as it disapproved of any kind of abnormal sexual behavior.[16]

Today, you routinely hear about a "gay pride march" or another homo-sexual "coming out of the closet." Now homosexual advocates have as much access, sometimes more so, to the airwaves and print media than advocates of other movements do.

What happened? The language was altered. Homosexuality went from being an abnormal condition frequently due to a mental or emotional

disorder to a predetermined condition every bit as natural as heterosex-
uality. Paradoxically, this so-called biological trait was also touted as a
"sexual preference" and an "alternative lifestyle," which indicated it
was a matter of personal choice in a smorgasbord of sexual and lifestyle
options. Even the words *family partners* are now being used by homosexual couples to describe themselves so they can "be allowed all the
perquisites of married heterosexual partners, including tax exemptions
and other legal advantages, as well as the right to adopt and rear children
on an equal basis."[17] Homosexuals even compare their social struggle with
that of blacks and other minorities, and on that basis seek civil rights
for themselves that will really give them a special-rights status in
American law.

Please understand, I do not believe that this social restructuring is
being funded or conducted by a secret or elite society. Certainly there
are groups who are working to reshape the cultural landscape, but there
are many individuals not connected with any activist group who are
involved as well. They are not a part of a conspiracy but a philosophical movement with worldview beliefs frequently contrary to the Judeo-
Christian perspective. These beliefs often even conflict with each other,
so one cannot say that these social revolutionaries are propelled by a
single belief system. Nevertheless, what they are seeking to achieve in
the social arena, however genuinely motivated, is socially destructive.

Consider now the family. Since the family is the basic cell of society, the church, and education, whoever controls it controls the key elements of any culture. To make room, therefore, for a "new morality"
(really no genuine morality at all) founded on a new social order, the
new social engineers must supplant the normative definition of family
as a married man and woman in a loving, lifetime union that involves the
procreation and raising of children. Instead, family must be changed in
order to make room for sexual promiscuity, militant homosexual and
feminist ideology and practice, and other new-regime goals.

Then there are those involved in the weird alliance now calling
itself "liberalism." The word *liberal* itself is the victim of verbicide.
Liberals of the last century abhorred big government; championed individual responsibility; and spoke valiantly of morality, family, church,
and culture. If they were alive today, they likely would not even recognize the eclectic group of statists, collectivists, and politically correct forces currently using their once-proud label. This contemporary
illiberal alliance has embraced as its own what was once almost a swear
word to many new-left utopians, and it is using "family" rhetoric to

promote national "family" policies. But it doesn't have the natural family unit in mind anymore than many homosexuals and feminists do. Rather, under this new regime the current welfare state is the new mother. Rights formerly viewed as "inalienable" and derived from outside the government are being redefined by the government (or, as in the case of the right to life, removed) and new "rights" are being doled out by mama-state to her favored children.

C. S. Lewis tells us that "Men often commit verbicide because they want to snatch a word as a party banner, to appropriate its 'selling quality.'"[18] The new cultural revolutionaries are doing just that as they work to construct and sell us a new order that turns life into death and family into elastic social groupings. Their new-order products, however, are poisonous. Their attack on the family alone is potentially devastating.

To whom will we listen? To the new cultural revolutionaries? Or to the One who made us and instituted marital and family life?

The word *church* has also been made a target of verbicide. On February 25, 1994, Surgeon General Joycelyn Elders addressed the National Family Planning and Reproductive Health Association, which represents four thousand "family" planning centers. She told the crowd, "We always talked about the separation of church and state. . . . I want to forget about the separation. Let's try to integrate church and state so we can come together and begin to do things that make a difference to people in our community. The churches have a lot to offer us. They have prestige, power, and money. You can't do better than that. They can provide education, day care, and other services people need."[19] Apparently, among the "services" this "church" should provide are access to abortion, distributing condoms, blessing homosexual unions, and preaching a pop feel-good spirituality that assuages the conscience of moderns.

If we are to reverse these destructive trends, we must stop the co-option of the language. We must refute the attempts to redefine and reframe the issues in absurd rhetoric, and we must redeem the art of rhetoric for the cause of Christ.

Social Engineering

After reframing the issues and redefining the terms, the architects of our new social order have attempted to redefine society in their own image. The social agenda of these new cultural revolutionaries includes death on demand, the eradication of a Judeo-Christian understanding of marriage and family, the abandonment of sexual mores, the creation of government as the new parent, and the restructuring of the American experiment into a nightmare of intolerant secularism.

While I believe homosexual practice is morally wrong and unnatural, I must also say that many Christians have steered the public debate away from this truth by strident rhetoric. Some Christians have engaged in homosexual bashing frequently out of a lack of compassion and understanding of the homosexual struggle. They have caricatured and maligned people and promoted stereotypes. This is just as wrong as the caricatures some homosexuals have made about Christians and their beliefs.

Homosexuality is a disordered appetite much like many other disordered appetites (such as adultery and premarital heterosexual sex). Regardless of its causes (which are varied), those who have been trapped by it need our help, not our condemnation. They need the resources of Christ and His church, among which are genuine love, undying hope, and compassionate mercy. While we need to stand up for what's right, we must do so with the spirit Jesus did when confronted by a woman caught in adultery. Without condoning her sin, He challenged the self-righteousness of her accusers: "He who is without sin among you, let him throw a stone at her first."[20] With those words, her accusers slowly dispersed, realizing they were all sinners. Jesus then turned to meet the fearful woman's needs with grace rather than judgment.

Verbal engineers must not be allowed to make homosexual practice appear to be normal or morally acceptable. On the other hand, Christians must not engage in their own form of verbicide where they depict homosexuals as monsters ready to pounce on unsuspecting victims. Homosexuality is a sin, but like any other sin its causes are multiple, it is forgivable, and those caught up in it need the compassion and courage of Christians to come alongside them if they are ever to control it, much less beat it.

These social architects have succeeded in getting numerous aspects of their agenda accepted. Especially hard hit has been the American family. Once the strongest single protection against the erosion of true liberty and strong moral values, the family in America today is collapsing under the moral and legal onslaught of the new utopians. While studying the demise of the American family, Bryce Christensen came upon a chilling parallel we would do well to ponder.

> Family historians Becky Glass and Margaret Stolee have examined the reforms in family law now being promoted by many Western lawyers, legislators, and academics, finding them strikingly similar to the measures enacted by the Bolsheviks when

they first came to power in Soviet Russia. These Bolshevik initiatives included easy divorce, abolition of the distinction between legitimate and illegitimate birth, collectivized child rearing, and broad definitions of family. Such moves were central, not incidental, to Bolshevik governance because Marxist theory called for the dismantling of the family as a necessary preliminary to the creation of a utopian classless society.[21]

What has this search for utopia by subverting the family brought us? Social chaos. Again, citing Christensen's research:

Psychiatrist Boris Segal views "the breakdown of the traditional family" as part of "the crisis of our culture," a crisis evident in several trends: "disillusionment in religious and secular ideologies; decline of the intellectual authority of the Church and loss of unity with God; the disappearance of old taboos and restrictions; the loss of a sense of continuity and belonging; . . . and the growth of sensualism and the exploitation of sex." Sociologist Viktor Gecas likewise suggests that family disintegration must be acknowledged as a cause of "increasing alienation, antagonism, delinquency, personal destructiveness, . . . drug use, teenage pregnancy, teenage runaways, school dropouts, teenage suicide, and violent crime." Gecas believes that family disorder creates an appetite for themes of "violence, nihilism, and exploitative sex" in popular culture.[22]

At every level of society, including the media, public education, government, and sadly enough, within much of the church community itself, the new social engineers have been hard at work to recreate a new society in their own image. As we look at it and suffer under it, is it a society we really want?

Christians must strive to reshape society toward the image of Christ, not the image of unredeemed man.

Political Engineering

With the language captured, the issues reframed, and a new social agenda being pursued, the new engineers have gone after positions of power with a vengeance. They are filling political offices, they are working for and running activist law firms, they are lobbying for laws and policies that will further their agenda. Over and over again they have sought to put the power of law and the penalty of punishment behind abortion on demand and homosexuality. They have utilized the power of the public school education lobby to usurp parental rights. They will not stop until their social agenda is enforced from the top down.

The entire Christian community is already reeling under their victories. We and our children are paying for these "successes," and our children's children will likely reap some of the consequences as well. But we dare not surrender simply because we've lost some battles. We're in a culture war. Some battles will be won, others lost. There will certainly be tragedies along the way. But losing some skirmishes, even some significant battles, will cost us little compared to what the entire culture will lose if we are defeated in the war.

It must be said, however, that as a believing community, we do not fight alone. In His sovereign power, only God will bring ultimate victory. We will never see a culture fully won to the Judeo-Christian view this side of the Parousia (Christ's Second Coming). But until then, we must be involved, we must contend, we must struggle.

We must fight on at the ballot box and challenge the new cultural revolutionaries in political races throughout the country and at every level of the social order. School boards, state legislatures, Congress, and even the White House are not off limits. People of faith should take their role in politics seriously and go after it carefully. We avoid the challenge of civic leadership at our own peril and that of the culture's.

Legal Engineering

Through the strategic use and abuse of the court system, these new engineers have used litigation to turn wrongs into rights. They have achieved this not only through such infamous court decisions as *Roe v. Wade* and its progeny, but also through other court cases they intentionally filed to create new legal precedents. In so doing, they have substantially changed American jurisprudence.

Their public-interest legal groups have been at work changing the social landscape much longer than ours have. In the name of "civil liberties," these groups often oppose free speech when the content of that speech does not agree with their own positions. As a result, a new barbarism is being legalized, and it's being enforced by legislators and federal judges. The law is being used to intimidate those who oppose the new protectors of the status quo. I call these protectors "statists," because once they secure legal and public-policy support for their social agenda, they strive to squelch any and all voices that rise up against it.

The American Center for Law and Justice is one of these voices. We are actively challenging the legal engineers from the local to the federal level. Among the groups most upset with our activities is the American Civil Liberties Union (ACLU). In recent fund-raising letters, the ACLU's president, Ira Glasser, characterized the ACLJ's work as society's greatest threat in order to garner financial support for the ACLU. Frankly, I was flattered by some of what he said. Glasser complained that the ACLU's "resources are in danger of being overwhelmed." "Never before," he wrote, "has the ACLU faced a single antagonist able to combine political and legal strategies with financial resources so effectively and widely in so many local communities at once." Without immediate help, "the ACLU will be unable to meet the growing challenge." According to Mr. Glasser, this formidable force is the "religious extremists across America—especially those led by Rev. Pat Robertson, founder of the . . . American Center for Law and Justice (ACLJ)."[23]

At times, at least, Christians have set the new statists on the defensive and even forced them to back down. We must keep doing this if we are going to win the heart and mind of our culture for Christ.

RECIVILIZING AMERICA

Now that we have identified our social disease, why it has come upon us, and how, what is our cure as a culture? Turning from the wrong things and back toward the right things.

And what are the right things? What they have always been. An understanding that God is and that we have been made His image-bearers. The realization that He created us to be in a right relationship with Him, and until we make that choice we will never achieve our true happiness, the blissful end we were made to enjoy forever. The willingness to obey His counsel as it is revealed in nature, in His Son, in Scripture, and in the church. The courage and conviction to speak light into the darkness and to live as citizens of the City of God and as simply sojourners in the city of man. The endurance to keep doing what is right regardless of what others do or say to the contrary. The willingness to fight for the sanctity of all life and protect the vulnerable. The desire to love the unlovable because God loved us even when we didn't love Him. The self-discipline and enlightened common sense to live in monogamous, committed marriages and families that serve as islands of sanctity and hope in the midst of the modern madness of false liberation.

This is the truth, these are the right things, but the enveloping darkness is pushing them aside. It is squeezing out the truth, including the One who is Truth, with lies.

Two thousand years ago, our Lord Jesus stood before Pilate, falsely accused of treason. Treason against the Roman Empire, and treason against the Zeitgeist, the spirit of the age. The King of kings and Crown Prince of all creation, the Truth made flesh, was on trial before a prince of this age, a delegated military power, an agent of Caesar, merely human government. The charge against Jesus was that He claimed to be a king. His answer to the charge? Yes, I am, and all who follow Me are on the side of truth.[24] Pilate's response is telling: "What is truth?"[25]

Pilate's question has echoed down twenty centuries of history marked by great struggles between belief and disbelief, obedience and rebellion, truth and error. What is truth? That is the heart cry of all men and women, and Christians have the answer. Truth can be known and Truth has a name—Jesus. He still calls out to each one of us, "I am the way, and the truth, and the life."[26] And His call can still be heard in the voices of His followers. Recently they reverberated in the words of John Paul II through the opening to *Veritatis Splendor:* "The Splendor of Truth shines forth in the works of the Creator, and, in a special way, in man, created in the image and likeness of God. Truth enlightens man's intelligence and shapes his freedom, leading him to know and love the Lord."[27]

Contemporary society needs the truth, and in many darkened corridors and on bloodied streets, it is crying out to hear the truth. We Christians must present it, and that includes above all presenting the gospel in its fullness. The first and fundamental human right, a right that comes before all others, is the right to hear the truth, the right to hear about He who is Truth incarnate and the way of life He has provided for all who trust Him by faith.

I know many Christians are working to present this truth, but despite all our efforts to get our message out, it is not getting through. The darkness is growing and our light is dimming. Why? I believe it's because all too often we are not delivering the truth to our culture *together.*

I believe that Christians of all confessions—Protestant, Catholic, and Orthodox—must build an alliance to confront the hungry darkness we all face. We must engage in a war effort together, not as individual camps. Some of us will engage our common enemy on the front line, many of us will save the equivalent of tinfoil on the home front, but all of us must participate in the war effort. It is a steep challenge, and it will require a willingness to risk, to make mistakes, to be misunderstood and even wrongly caricatured (even by those we respect). But we must try to make common cause anyway. Civilization itself is at risk. And it is we, Christian people, who are the leaven in the loaf of civilization.

Undoubtedly, this is a desperate hour, but our God is great and His resources infinite. As long as we rely on Him, we will persevere and enjoy the ultimate victory. In the process, we must dedicate ourselves to recivilizing the culture, and we must do this together. Just as the political Allies of World War II joined forces to combat the darkness of socialism and fascism in their day, so must we build alliances among ourselves so we can effectively challenge the spiritual, moral, and intellectual darkness covering our world with the stench of death.

We can learn much from the Allies' experience. Their foe had parallels to the foe we face, and their struggle to build an alliance can provide us with some helpful insights as we make strides to cooperate to defeat an even more insidious threat. Like any other alliance-building effort, the Allies made mistakes, even after they had achieved an earlier victory. Let's take a look back to the beginning of the twentieth century, to a time of celebration that eventually led to a new tyranny and the greatest alliance-building effort the world had yet seen. Let's learn some relevant lessons from history. Let's delve into the story that inspired Michael's sermon that day.

CHAPTER EIGHT

SHARING FOXHOLES—AGAIN

The people of this world
are more shrewd in dealing with their own kind
than are the people of the light.
Jesus Christ

The Allies were ecstatic. Germany had acknowledged her willingness to surrender and had agreed to a cease-fire. The end of the Great War was finally in sight. Soldiers, who had been living in muddy trenches that reeked of the decaying bodies of their comrades in arms, stepped out into no-man's land, singing and dancing. They shot off fireworks, exchanged prisoners, swapped food for American cigarettes or French cognac. The stench of the war's effects was everywhere, but the smell of peace was sweeter still.

For Germany's aggression, the French and Italians wanted revenge, and they wanted to ensure that Germany would never be a formidable foe again. So they drafted their desires into the Treaty of Versailles. Although the German people opposed the treaty's terms, they were in no condition to negotiate. So on June 28, 1919, a German delegation arrived at the glittering Palace of Versailles, about fifty miles outside of Paris, and there signed their country's future over to the Allies. A war-weary world rejoiced.

In the ensuing years, worldwide euphoria flowered into a rich bed of new peace-loving organizations and pacts. Peoples and governments believed what Woodrow Wilson had proclaimed: the Great World War was "the war to end all wars." To ensure that, the League of Nations was formed, the American Committee for the Outlawry of War was organized, and, amid much pomp and circumstance, the Kellogg-Briand Pact was signed in Paris, France, in 1928 by fifteen countries: Germany, France, Great Britain, the United States, Japan, Canada, New Zealand, Australia, India, Belgium, South Africa, Italy, Ireland, Czechoslovakia, and Poland. Later, the Soviet Union along with thirty-one other nations signed the agreement, which "renounced war as an instrument of policy and promised to solve all disputes . . . 'by pacific means.'"[1] The world press heralded the signing of the pact as a tremendous achievement.

With peace finally secured for all generations to come, the U.S., along with the rest of the Allies and many other countries, turned inward and took stock of its own needs and wants virtually exclusively. Isolationism became much of the world's foreign policy by choice. The stock market crash of 1929, which ushered in the Great Depression in the United States and quickly to the rest of the industrialized world, made it even easier for isolationism to become a way of life and diplomacy. That's probably why few noticed with any seriousness the darkness slowly enveloping parts of Europe and her red neighbor, Russia.

In southern Europe, Benito Mussolini, already an accomplished revolutionary with a long history of using violence to get his way, had turned Italy into a totalitarian state. Mussolini had also won tremendous popular and international support because of the perception that he had done so much good in Italy.

Just east of Europe, the son of peasants and progenitor of a long line of serfs had already discovered that the revolutionary spirit mixed with the flow of human blood was an intoxicating elixir. Calling himself Joseph Stalin (*Stalin* meaning "man of steel"), he was determined to leave his mark on Russian and world history. And that he did. After Vladimir Lenin's death in 1924 and by the time of the Great Depression, this blood-thirsty, ambitious revolutionary had finally seized total control over his homeland. Stalin was now the dictator of Russia.

In northern central Europe, yet another insatiable, angry young man had moved to the top of the political ladder. Many years earlier while he was still in his young teenage years, one of his teachers described him as "definitely gifted, but only in a one-sided way, for he was lacking in self-control, and to say the least he was regarded as argumentative, willful, arrogant and bad-tempered, and he was notoriously incapable of submitting to school discipline. Nor was he industrious. . . . He reacted with ill-concealed hostility whenever a teacher reproved him or gave him some advice. At the same time he demanded the unqualified subservience of his fellow-pupils, fancying himself in the role of a leader."[2]

Now it was August 1934. Adolf Hitler was not a disruptive teenager anymore but a forty-five-year-old terror. Craving absolute freedom and total control, Hitler had bullied, charmed, deceived, and murdered his way through the German democratic process of government. He had recruited many of the most vicious, despotic men the world had ever encountered, and he had already conceived the "legal" apparatus needed to carry out the infamous and grisly "final solution"—the extermination of the Jews. With the death of Germany's president, Paul von Hindenburg, Hitler immediately assumed the president's office legally, then abolished it and declared himself Führer and Reich chancellor. Rudolf Hess, one of Hitler's henchmen, told the German nation: "Do not seek Adolf Hitler with your brains; all of you will find him with the strength of your hearts. Adolf Hitler is Germany and Germany is Adolf Hitler. Germany is our God on earth." All over Germany the masses roared back: "Heil Hitler!"[3]

Three thugs were now dictators of three of the most powerful countries on earth. Throughout the 1930s, all three men sought to solidify their ability to achieve their dreams of worldwide prowess and power.

But the democracies slept on. Still focused on their internal struggles, they ignored the many signs of impending disaster.

In the meantime, on the other side of the globe and under the leadership of Emperor Hirohito, a militaristic and highly imperialistic Japan was invading Manchuria, China, and Mongolia, and it had its eyes on Southeast Asia, the Philippines, the Dutch East Indies, and numerous other neighboring islands.

Like a great volcano awaking from its slumber, the world was erupting into war.

But still the democracies slept.

It wasn't until Hitler and Stalin signed the German-Russian Nonaggression Pact and invaded and conquered Poland in 1939 that the democracies' slumber was finally shaken. France and Britain declared war on Germany. Both began mobilizing their armies. But the American public and political opinion still strongly favored noninvolvement.

Hitler, Stalin, and Mussolini began dividing and conquering Europe. Soon the war jumped the English Channel and put Britain on the defensive. It didn't take long before the Middle East and northern Africa also became embroiled in the war. Still, America stood by, divided more within regarding whether to maintain her commitment to isolationism or to joining her struggling comrades against a superior, united foe.

Then, in the morning hours on Sunday, December 7, 1941, more than two years after the outbreak of WWII in Europe, America received a wake-up call. It came from Japan, and it was delivered with devastating blows from the Japanese air force upon the unprepared American Navy anchored in Hawaii's Pearl Harbor. When the air raid had ended, America's navy was crippled beyond even Japan's expectations.

The next day, President Theodore Roosevelt addressed a joint session of Congress and asked it to declare war on Japan. Congress did. Germany and Italy responded by declaring war on the United States, upon which America responded in kind.

By now all the countries that had signed the Treaty of Versailles, the treaty that was to put an end to all war, were reengaged in another world war of a much greater magnitude than the one they had fought less than three decades earlier. The Allies, which now included Russia due to Germany's betrayal of the Nonaggression Pact, had risen in number to thirty-five countries. For the most part, these were the countries that had signed the 1928 Kellogg-Briand Pact, which was supposed to put an end to using "war as an instrument of policy." In order to effectively combat the German-Italian-Japanese Axis, the Allies began working together, planning joint strategies, sharing commands, drawing upon one another's many resources to fight the common enemy side by side.

At first, Allied victories were few and far between. And the loss in human life was always costly on both sides. But the Allies were committed to standing together to make common cause against a darkness with an insatiable appetite for grandeur and power. In time, the Axis began to suffer defeats with heavy losses. Battles for such places as Guadalcanal, Midway, Saipan, Guam, Normandy, Rome, Paris, the Rhine, Leningrad, Stalingrad, Iwo Jima, and Okinawa were etched on the minds of military strategists, the bodies of those who fought there, and the hearts of those who lost loved ones there. However, waterway by waterway, street by street, city by city, farm by farm, the Allies advanced and the Axis fell back upon itself.

As the summer of 1945 drew to a close, the most devastating and extensive war in human history came to an end. A staggering fifty million human beings had lost their lives. The great bulk of Europe, western Russia, northern Africa, the Middle East, Japan, the Philippines and neighboring islands, and southeast Asia lay in ruin. Except for Stalin, the dictators East and West had been vanquished. The Allies had won once again.

Though the world celebrated, this time realism instead of optimism settled in. There was no talk of this being the war to end all wars, nor did the victors withdraw into dealing with internal concerns alone. The world was now everyone's concern. No doubt dictators would still rise and attempt to extend their rule by force, but this time the world would not sit back and simply watch. This time the Allies would strengthen their ties, maintain and increase their armaments, and whenever possible contain and eliminate threats to world peace before they could be actualized.

The world had finally learned that darkness could loom at any time, anywhere.

FOR SUCH A TIME AS THIS

United we stand, divided we fall. This is not simple folk wisdom, but a profound truth that applies to every level of human society. Whether we're in a marriage, part of a family, a member of a local community or church, an employee of a company, or a citizen of a country, when we enter into a relationship with other people, that relationship will not last unless we commit ourselves to developing, strengthening, and protecting it. If we fail to make or keep that commitment, we run the very real risk of losing that relationship.

The Allies would never have succeeded against the Axis countries if they had not made previous commitments to each other and then kept their promises when tyrants crashed through their borders. Divide and conquer—that was the strategy of Hitler, Mussolini, Stalin, and Hirohito. And it was a successful strategy, at least at first. In the beginning, the Allied countries were too self-absorbed and complacent to honor their alliances with one another, even when some of their friends were being bullied into submission. But as the invaders pressed on, the ties that bound the Allies cried louder for attention. Eventually, the Allies broke away from their isolationism, linked armaments and armies, and aimed them at the Axis.

People of vastly different cultures, speaking different languages, living according to different customs and convictions, fought side by side against a common foe in order to save their native lands and preserve all they held dear. They didn't always get along with each other or even understand each other. Sometimes they got on each other's nerves. They argued among themselves and teased one another and even competed against each other. They often failed to grasp each other's jokes or tolerate one another's food. But they also marched and strategized together. French soldiers helped American soldiers learn unfamiliar terrain. American and British pilots trained together and flew joint bombing missions. The Allies gave each other courage, patched each other's wounded, even buried each other's dead. American, French, British, Polish . . . no matter the political affiliations or nationalistic commitments, they gave everything they had so they could make common cause against a shared threat until the danger had been eliminated. Then they sought to strengthen their alliances with one another so they would not be overwhelmed ever again.

If political and national entities can embrace their many differences while joining forces to make common cause, why are Christians, who are joined in a common relationship with Jesus Christ and a spiritual bond far more powerful than a political alliance, so reluctant to cooperate in an age so gripped by a spiritual blindness and darkness?

WALLS OF ISOLATION

Christian communities are not unlike nations. Both are made up of human beings who have mortgages, marry and raise families, develop and maintain forms of government, work, eat, play, and worship. Both draw boundaries around themselves and want those boundaries respected. Both draw up and seek to obey certain rules of conduct, and both devise disciplinary proceedings to handle those individuals who disrupt the approved order.

In at least one critical way, however, Christian communities differ from nations. The members of Christian communities have a dual citizenship within which lies a higher allegiance. Christians are citizens of Heaven and of whatever earthly nation is their native home. But these citizenships are not on equal footing. Our heavenly citizenship commits us first and foremost to the Kingdom of Heaven; it takes priority over any and all of our commitments to any other kingdom. This dual citizenship and hierarchial allegiance makes us a people within a people, a holy nation within secular nations.[4] I am a Christian first, not an American, Frenchman, Egyptian, or what have you. I may live in a democracy, or under socialism or fascism, or be ruled by a king or a dictator. Indeed, Christians have lived under all types of political systems throughout the world. But none of those affiliations is nearly as important as a Christian's allegiance to the Ruler over all and to His everlasting, incorruptible Kingdom.

I'm not saying Christians cannot be patriots. I love being an American. What I am saying, however, is that our first obligation is to the King of kings. We are His. And as His people, we are challenged to bring the values of the City of God into the city of man. It is an incredible task. Without God's power we would surely fail. But He empowers us so we can accomplish what He asks us to do, and He has called us to do it, not only as individuals but also as His community. He has made us a people, a nation. He has made us dependent on each other. We need one another by divine design.[5]

Nevertheless, instead of looking to each other for help, we often turn inward. We keep to our own groups. We isolate ourselves. Most nations understand they cannot survive, much less thrive, in a dangerous world if they fail to build adequate alliances with other nations. Yet, many Christians, it seems, have not learned this lesson. Rather than build alliances, Christian groups spanning the confessional spectrum tend to retreat into themselves.

Modern-Day Gnosticism

Isolated, these groups can begin to believe they are the truly faithful, perhaps the only ones left. They may even come to see themselves as having the corner on truth and how it should be lived out. This self-perception often leads to a modern version of Gnosticism. Gnosticism was one of the earliest heresies in the church and appears to be one of the most enduring. Early Gnostics believed they alone possessed the "hidden knowledge" and were the only ones saved. When I use *gnosticism* to describe some modern-day believers, I mean it more figuratively to refer to the propensity among many Christians to exclude others who don't live up to their convictions. Such people usually end up viewing other Christian communions as either apostate or at least teetering on the precipice of dangerous ignorance. Hence, they believe these straying communities must be enlightened, saved from themselves. These gnostic-like Christians may start out with sincere intentions, but they often become uncharitable and injurious toward other Christians. Rather than maintain the "purity" of the faith, they pollute it with destructive attitudes and practices.

Evangelism Gone Awry

One of the ways this comes out is through what I call evangelistic raids. Many times those who believe they have the corner on truth raid the groups they believe don't. They corner the "apostate" members, try to "evangelize" them to their way, then urge them to come away to their group. Once there, these "new" believers are taught by the "true" believers that their old ways and beliefs were filled with half-truths at best.

The "new" believers are encouraged to leave their old tradition behind, even to despise it; after all, it was "merely a tradition of man," not of God, and we all know what the Apostle Paul said about that: "Beware lest anyone cheat you through philosophy and empty deceit, according to the tradition of men, according to the basic principles of the world, and not according to Christ."[6] In time, the "new" believers are convinced. They become full-fledged members of the "true" group and begin to join the raids on other groups.

Often, I find that some of the strongest anti-Catholic Protestant Christians are former Catholics who were unevangelized and poorly catechized (assuming they were ever catechized at all). In other words, they never "owned" what they professed week after week in the liturgy. Consequently, when they experience an encounter with the Lord in a Protestant environment that views the Catholic Church as a false church, they frequently become the most ardent anti-Catholics and look back on their past participation in the Catholic Church as "years wasted." Many of them eventually grow beyond this adolescent period of spiritual discernment. Some, however, never do.

The converse occurs as well. Sometimes, when nominally Christian Protestants encounter the Lord in a Catholic context, depending on how they are catechized, they can become anti-Protestant in an uncharitable way.

When either shift occurs, the judgmental and disrespectful attitudes that often accompany it may finally pass on and give way to a more charitable, gracious spirit. On the other hand, if these attitudes are not properly dealt with, they will fuel the cycle of mistrust, prejudice, and hostility that continues to divide the Christian community from within.

I don't want to be misunderstood here. There are times when those who profess to be Protestant, Catholic, or Orthodox are not truly followers of Christ. They need to know Him personally as their Savior and Lord. When we come across such people, we need to present them with the gospel message so they have the opportunity to move from disbelief to belief, from a faith that's no faith at all to a faith that saves. On the other hand, I believe that once people make a true confession of faith, if they are in a recognized Christian tradition, we should not try to convince them that our particular confession is true and the other one false. If they make such a change in the course of their spiritual growth, that's one thing. But when we work to undermine one Christian tradition in order to bring believers into our own, we're furthering the divisions already present in the Body of Christ. That's simply wrong. I agree with what the precedent-setting accord "Evangelicals and Catholics Together" says about this matter:

> It is understandable that Christians who bear witness to the Gospel try to persuade others that their communities and traditions are more fully in accord with the Gospel. [But] There is a necessary distinction between evangelizing and what is today commonly called proselytizing or "sheep stealing." We condemn the practice of recruiting people from another community for purposes of denominational or institutional aggrandizement. At the same time, our commitment to full religious freedom compels us to defend the legal freedom to proselytize even as we call upon Christians to refrain from such activity.
>
> Three observations are in order in connection with proselytizing. First, as much as we might believe one community is more fully in accord with the Gospel than another, we as Evangelicals and Catholics affirm that opportunity and means for growth in Christian discipleship are available in our several communities. Second, the decision of the committed Christian with respect to his communal allegiance and participation must be assiduously respected. Third, in view of the large number of non-Christians in the world and the enormous challenge of our common evangelistic task, it is neither theologically legitimate nor a prudent use of resources for one Christian community to proselytize among active adherents of another Christian community.
>
> Christian witness must always be made in a spirit of love and humility. It must not deny but must readily accord to everyone the full freedom to discern and decide what is God's will for his life. Witness that is in service to the truth is in service to such freedom. Any form of coercion—physical, psychological, legal, economic—corrupts Christian witness and is to be unqualifiedly rejected. Similarly, bearing false witness against other persons and communities, or casting unjust and uncharitable suspicions upon them, is incompatible with the Gospel. Also to be rejected is the practice of comparing the strengths and ideals of one community with the weaknesses and failures of another. In describing the teaching and practices of other Christians, we must strive to do so in a way that they would recognize as fair and accurate.[7]

Toxic Religion

Another problem with isolationism, especially when it becomes coupled with this contemporary version of Gnosticism, is that it tends to breed suspicion and lead to suppression within the very groups that have cut themselves off from others. Let's look at an example. Though fictitious and somewhat facetious, it reveals a dynamic that occurs fairly often in some Christian groups.

Susan overhears Brenda question even a minor point of the True Believers' seventy-three-point doctrinal position. She has never been told that some in "True Believers" believe that the seven in seventy stands for completion (like the seven days of God's creative activity and rest that led to a finished creation), and the three in seventy-three stands for perfection (like the perfection of the three Persons of the Trinity existing as one God). Susan then learns that Brenda has raised her doctrinal questions with a few other church members. She is threatened.

Sensing a growing movement of subversion, Susan makes an appointment to see Don, the group's doctrinal policeman. Don listens intently to Susan's claims, then calls for a meeting of some of the other church leaders. This august body convenes, solemnly discusses the matter, and decides they should call Brenda before them to answer some critical questions.

Acting on behalf of the group's leadership, Don contacts Brenda and asks her to come to his office to discuss some concerns that have been raised about her understanding of the truth as embodied in the group's seventy-three points. Somewhat confused and surprised, Brenda tries to tell him that she has not embraced any teaching that contradicts True Believers' convictions but has only raised some questions about a minor matter or two. Don reminds her that no teaching of True Believers is minor and that divergences in even one "small" area would undoubtedly lead to apostate beliefs if allowed to fester. Brenda tells Don she'll come, but after she hangs up the telephone she halfheartedly considers taking a lawyer with her. Don hadn't seemed willing to talk but ready to accuse. Nevertheless, she convinces herself that the leaders of True Believers really have her best interests in mind and that they would probably be the best people to answer some of her minor yet nagging questions.

Within moments of entering Don's office, Brenda wishes she had brought a lawyer. Don and four other church leaders are there sitting in chairs facing hers. Brenda feels she's on the witness stand about to be cross-examined by a hostile judicial bench.

Two hours later she leaves Don's office. Hurt and outraged, Brenda now realizes that her enlightened group is afraid of questions. Its leaders had accused her of sowing discord, of questioning "God's teaching," which they had identified fully with their own. They wouldn't allow the possibility that any point of their teaching was less critical than any other point, and they certainly wouldn't entertain the notion that a theological jot or tittle in their doctrine might be even slightly askew. Of course, Brenda had never said that she disbelieved any of True Believers' doctrinal stance, only that she wondered what support could be offered in defense and clarification of a couple of the lesser points. But she now knew that any questioning would be interpreted as potentially subversive, so her only options were to stay and keep her questions to herself or to leave True Believers and perhaps try the Real Believers group down the street.

Brenda decides she doesn't want to leave her friends, and she is afraid to make any more waves lest she be perceived as a "problem." So she quietly submits to the True Believers' leadership and attempts to shut down her critical faculties. However, no matter how much she tries, Brenda can't squelch her questions. So she quietly and privately pursues answers to them on her own. She reasons that True Believers would never find out as long as she remains discreet.

For True Believers, Brenda's case is viewed as a victory. Brenda has once again become a supportive member of their seemingly united, intentionally isolated community. Besides, the leadership reasoned, even if she had chosen to leave, their community could have rejoiced, for their "doctrinal purity" would have been preserved. So regardless of what happened, True Believers thought God would be pleased by their actions.

Unfortunately, this fictional scenario commonly occurs in some form in sick religious groups. Even religion and the dynamic of a religious community can become, to use an overused modern term, "dysfunctional." Such communities can begin to behave more like extended dysfunctional families with unspoken dynamics and manipulative techniques designed to repress questions, doubts, doctrinal explorations, and certainly any hint of cooperation with groups who don't think and behave exactly as "we" do.

Brenda's pursuit of truth is typical of many people who either discover the Lord as adults or have their faith reawakened. I for one never accepted the idea of checking my brain at the front door of the pursuit of religious faith. Pursuing the truth and the implications of being a Christian is a lifelong process.

In the New Testament letter of Hebrews, we read about great

examples of faith in Abel, Enoch, Noah, Abraham, Jacob, Joseph, Moses, and numerous other saintly heroes. The author refers to them as "so great a cloud of witnesses."[8] These women and men were persevering seekers and doers. They followed God and believed His promises, some even to the point of death. They knew what the author of Hebrews tells us: "without faith it is impossible to please [God], for he who comes to God must believe that He is, and that He is a rewarder of those who diligently seek Him."[9] This kind of mature faith is active. It involves a continual seeking after God, which is at the heart of the biblical understanding of conversion and transformation.

In groups like True Believers, this kind of faith is discouraged. Growth and risk cannot occur without questioning and inquiry, but these traits are feared in Gnostic-like communities. Instead the traits that reign are intimidation, legalism, manipulation, false guilt, and abusive forms of leadership. Thinking is sequestered, blind faith exalted. No group, whether Catholic, Protestant, Orthodox, or even "ecumenical," is immune from toxic religion. I know. I have experienced it and, unfortunately, helped to foster it in various stages of my own journey. Wherever it occurs, it usually poisons lives and whatever influence for good its victims might have had on those within and without the Body of Christ.[10]

The Perils of Isolationism

Of course, I'm not denying that there is a core of true doctrine and right practice at the heart of Christianity. There certainly is and must be. The church's creeds are a great place to begin to discover these truths and values. They have withstood generations of inquiry.

What I am referring to, however, is an attitude of judgmentalism and exclusivity that marks many Christian groups and individual believers. Few groups or individuals start out with a full-blown version of this attitudinal perspective; it occurs incrementally. It seems to go part and parcel with withdrawing from the world in a wrong sort of way and emphasizing a misguided notion of doctrinal or moral purity. The mandate of the church is to preach the gospel and make disciples throughout the world. And yet that mandate, long called the Great Commission by Protestant Christians, has often become instead a Great Omission that looks more like retreating from the world in order to protect the gospel and those who believe it. We must understand that love cannot be contained. True love gives itself away, and as it does, it multiplies and embraces those in its path. Love knows not isolationism, except that it resides in hell, shut up with its companion, selfishness.

Again, the paths of secular nations can teach those of us who ultimately belong to the eternal Kingdom a great deal.

Imagine what would have happened if after the bombing of Pearl Harbor, America had remained steadfast in her conviction that isolationism was still the best policy. Or what if America had fought against Japan but never lifted a finger to help her European allies? Or if Britain had remained neutral even after Hitler overran France? Likely, Europe would have a much different political configuration than it does now. Certainly democracy and civil freedoms would be restricted even more than they now are.

Since we're allowing ourselves to imagine different historical scenarios, we can construct one better: In the 1920s (rather than in 1939 and later), suppose the Allies had heeded the red warning lights flashing at them from Italy, Germany, the Soviet Union, and Japan, and managed to work together to take the necessary steps to curtail the rising tyranny and avert a second world war. Impossible? Not at all. When we take a backward glance and realize that America, Britain, France, and the other Allies had the opportunities to divert disaster but failed to take advantage of them, we cannot ignore the fact that the Allies bear some of the responsibility for the outbreak of World War II.[11] If they had only looked beyond their borders through the eyes of realism instead of fantasy and strengthened their unity instead of allowing it to fall into disunity, they may very well have been able to isolate the darkness, perhaps even cause it to self-destruct. But isolationism and self-centered protectionism won out. And that gave the darkness the time it needed to grow and devour close to half the world.

The Allies, though they discovered their mistakes too late to divert a world catastrophe, did finally pool their resources and fight side by side to defeat the enemy. And in doing so, they won. The church must do the same, despite the mistakes she has made in the past. Jesus once said that "the people of this world are more shrewd in dealing with their own kind than are the people of the light."[12] We who belong to His community must heed the lessons of history if we are going to have any long-lasting impact on the current age, for the darkness we face makes the threat of the Axis powers dwarfed in comparison.

THE HOVERING DARKNESS

The Axis dictators are dead, their schemes crushed. But like a radiation cloud blowing with the wind and dropping deadly ash and rain

over everything it passes, the darkness that was at the root of their movement is always hovering, blowing here then there, infecting all it can,
even through channels that are meant to bring renewal and refreshment.
The darkness comes in many shapes. Some are philosophical and theological. Others are scientific and technological. Still others are political and sociological. Nonetheless, all its forms begin as ideas in someone's mind, and most are incarnated by human beings who experiment
with them on a small scale before they advance to higher degrees of
destructive power.

Take Mussolini, for example. Born in poverty, he came into the
world with two influences who would vie for his destiny: a devout
Roman Catholic mother who had hung a portrait of the Virgin Mary in
their home and did everything she could to ensure that Mussolini
received a Christian education; an ardent socialist father who had hung
in the house a portrait of the revolutionary liberator of Sicily, and who
was so engaged in violent antigovernment activities that he was under
constant police surveillance. In Mussolini's life, his father's influence
eventually prevailed.

By the age of eight, young Benito had already become an unwill-
ing and unwelcome church participant. He regularly pinched worshipers
and spoke out loudly during mass. When he was finally banned from
church for his disruptive behavior, he sought revenge by pelting the
church and its celebrants with stones and acorns.

His escapades in school were no better. He fought with students and
teachers with equal vigor and delight. On one occasion he threw an ink
pot at a teacher, and on another he stabbed a fellow student in the but-
tocks with a pocketknife.

He was proud of his reputation as a rebel, and he worked at it with
the zeal of an artisan determined to become world renowned for his contributions to his craft. One art he practiced regularly was public speaking. He would hole up in his room and give speeches to imaginary
crowds. During one of these practice sessions, his mother heard what
sounded like a stream of nonsense flooding through the walls of her
son's room. Frightened by what she heard, she rushed into Benito's room
and found him standing in the middle shouting at the four walls. Benito
smiled with pleasure at the signs of fear on his mother's face. "I am
preparing," he finally announced, "for the day when all Italy trembles at
my words."[13]

Mussolini mixed his dreams of attaining dictatorial power with the
writings of revolutionaries such as Victor Hugo and Karl Marx, men

who spoke of the valiant struggles of the oppressed against the injustices allegedly perpetrated on them by priests and capitalists. He came to view intimidation and violence as the means for achieving justice and revenge and the satiation of his many carnal appetites. One of these appetites was a lust for women. In his autobiography, he described his ruffian style for winning female companionship: "I caught her on the stairs, throwing her into a corner behind a door, and made her mine. When she got up weeping and humiliated she insulted me by saying I had robbed her of her honor and it is not impossible she spoke the truth. But I ask you, what kind of honor can she have meant?"[14]

Over time, he identified his enemies as the Christian church, the Italian king, the military, the government, the current established order, even Jesus Christ Himself. At trade-union meetings and strike demonstrations, Mussolini would attack these alleged enemies of the common work force, using them to whip crowds into a frenzy, bringing them to their feet crying out to him *"Duce! Duce! Duce!"* which meant "Leader! Leader! Leader!" Openly atheistic, anticlerical, and antisocial, Benito Mussolini made a name for himself, seized Italy's highest seat of political power, and with revolutionary hatred painted everything he touched with human blood.

Ideas have consequences—for good or ill. And like most everything else in life, ideas begin small, find small ways in which to enter the world of flesh and blood, and bear small consequences. If they are good ideas enacted by good people in good ways, they will spawn good consequences. But if any part of this chain breaks down and evil, even unintentional evil, creeps in, the consequences that flow will expose the invader.

Most of Mussolini's life, even as a young boy, testified to greater destruction to come. The signs were there for anyone to see. His mother saw them all too clearly, and she did all she could to tame the anger and rebellion within her son. The Italian people saw them too, but not enough people rose up to contain Benito's increasing rage. Even the Allies saw the signs of trouble, but they were too preoccupied with their domestic problems and dreams to bother with a distant maniacal schemer. So the terror grew and grew until it gripped all Italy and brought her neighbors and many beyond to their knees. Not until the signs of danger became ravaging, roaring monsters did the Allies break from their isolationist fantasies and begin raising up and uniting their forces to engage an enemy already deeply entrenched and thoroughly despotic.

CONTEMPORARY CHAMELEONS

The enemies of civilization and the church did not disappear with the toppling of the Axis dictators. Like chameleons, they change their colors to blend into the surrounding social and political terrain. Then slowly and methodically, wishing not to attract suspicion or undue hostility, they move about testing their ideas, winning converts wherever and however they can, training an army of ideologues who will parrot and help establish the "new wave" of thinking and behaving.

Such a scenario surrounds us as we come to the end of the twentieth century and the beginning of the twenty-first century. Will it be a century of new forms of barbarism? Or the beginning of the third millennium of Christianity and a rebirth of civilization? In many respects, how Christians respond in the current hour will determine the outcome.

The forces of darkness in the contemporary age are marshaling new troops. They have public-interest groups backing them, many legislators carrying out their bidding, and the forces of political correctness enforcing their attitudes and new definitions.

But they know they will not win the culture war if people of faith, especially Christians, are allowed access to the public debate. So they have turned their war machine on us. They are engaging in what I call "religious cleansing."

Religious Cleansing

With adequate controls achieved over a culture's language, one can more easily gain control over its educational organizations and public policies. Through these, then, one can reeducate the populace in the "new truths" and the "new morality" and enact and enforce laws that will ensure the implementation of the new order's ideology. Part of this strategy must be neutralizing the church's effectiveness. This is made easier when the church is so disunited that its many organizational manifestations—such as movements within the Catholic Church, Protestant denominations, nondenominational churches, parachurch organizations, and increasingly secularized church-related schools—ignore or even distrust one another. In that condition, the Christian community cannot speak with a united voice or act with a united front. It only has as much clout as each individual part has, which is very little when compared to the potential of the whole. But even the individual units can be made weaker if they can be silenced in the public arena. This I have witnessed firsthand.

We dare not underestimate or ignore the fact that we are in the midst of a cultural revolution in America and the rest of the West. In our century we have seen cultural revolutions (such as Lenin's and Mao Tsetung's) come and go, and we have seen that they are generally achieved through bloodletting and severely restricting human liberty. The same is occurring in the United States.

In aborbuaries, almost thirty million children have been sacrificed on the cultural revolution's altar, and to that number one can add the increasing number of victims of infanticide, euthanasia, and some practices related to genetic engineering.[15]

On the liberty side, our constitutionally protected freedoms are being slowly choked, especially those that are being used to challenge the new regime's ideology and practices. This is occurring through what was once thought to be the least dangerous branch of government, the courts.

Through the ACLJ, we have joined forces with others to defend people against religious cleansing in the American republic. *Religious cleansing* is a term I use to describe the current hostility and bigotry toward religion and people of faith that are leading to covert and overt attempts to remove any religious influence from the public arena. Just as ethnic cleansing attempts to rid certain ethnic groups and their influence from public life, so religious cleansing attempts to do the same with religious groups, their beliefs, and their values. How? Not by physical extermination—at least not in the United States—but by political and legal containment. You see, if as Christians all of our views on contemporary major issues are seen as "religious"; if "religious" views are to be kept in church buildings or behind the front door of our homes lest we somehow violate certain contemporary notions of the separation of church and state; and if taking positions on the critical ideas—such as liberty, life, and family—that shape culture is somehow deemed "improper" for a religious person, then what are we left with? No voice in the marketplace of ideas. Sure, we can sit around in our homes and churches and discuss political, moral, and social issues. Yes, we can vote our conscience. But if we move beyond these borders and step into city hall or the courts or the public schools or federal offices or virtually any other public arena, then we become trespassers—violators who need to be pushed back to the private sphere where our ideas cannot impact, or even threaten to impact, anyone but ourselves.[16]

Yale University professor and political liberal Stephen Carter confirms these observations in his highly acclaimed book *The Culture of Disbelief*. He challenges what he calls the contemporary "intuition" that "encourages a tendency to say of religious belief, 'Yes, we cherish you—now go away and leave us alone.'" Continuing, he writes:

> It is an intuition that makes religion something that should be believed in privacy, not something that should be paraded; and if religion *is* paraded, it is this same intuition that assures that it likely will be dismissed. This intuition says that anyone who believes that God can heal diseases is stupid or fanatical, and the same intuition makes sure that everyone understands that this belief is a kind of mystic flight from hard truths—it has nothing to do with the real world. The same intuition tells the religious that those things that they know to be true are wrong or irrelevant. . . . At its most extreme, it is an intuition that holds not only that religious beliefs cannot serve as the basis of policy; they cannot even be debated in the forum of public dialogue on which a liberal politics crucially depends.
>
> The intuition says, in short, that religion is like building model airplanes, just another hobby: something quiet, something private, something trivial—and not really a fit activity for intelligent, public-spirited adults. This intuition, then, is one that in the end must destroy either religion or the ideal of liberal democracy. That is a prospect that can please only those who hate one or the other or both.[17]

What Carter says here is true, but I believe he has underestimated the destructive impact of this secular "intuition." From what we are witnessing, especially on the legal and political sides of the social landscape, this politically correct practice of religious cleansing will destroy both religion and democracy, not just one or the other. It will lead to the public dismissal and ridicule of religious faith and practice, and in the process it will undermine and likely topple American democracy. All this is already occurring in small yet increasingly larger increments.

This is what we face as we near the end of the twentieth century. The only hope for lasting change is the truths of Christianity. Yet those of us who adhere to these truths are all too often unaware of the darkness around us and the vulnerable condition in which our disunity places us. If we do not come out of our isolationist slumber soon, we will find ourselves captives in a much more hostile land—a land where religious teaching and practice will have no place or value *whatsoever*, except perhaps in the privacy of our homes or churches. That world is much closer than most of us think. And it will never be effectively challenged until we join our voices to make common cause and reassert the influence of the Judeo-Christian worldview in American culture and Western civilization.

NEEDED: A NEW ALLIANCE

Recognizing the signs of the times and the desperate need of the hour, at least some Christians are beginning to come together to engage the culture. They are a part of an evangelical wave that is sweeping Christian churches of every tradition, including my own. In its wake it is leaving renewed and committed believers who are striving to reevangelize their churches and evangelize the nations with the truth of the Christian worldview. Although they recognize that longstanding historical rifts, deep-seated doctrinal differences, misunderstanding, mistrust, and even spiritual pride have played devastating roles in keeping fellow Christians from working together, these believers are determined to overcome these barriers in order to better penetrate the contemporary darkness with the light of the gospel.

But I also believe that we should not come together on a false foundation. What divides us is important, so important that full communion between Christians is not possible at this time. Many Christian groups believe that receiving Communion, or the "Lord's Supper," with other Christian groups is a means to unity. But to Catholics, Anglicans, and Orthodox Christians, it is the sacrament or sign of *full* unity. Moreover, all Christians don't agree on the nature of the event itself. Therefore it would be disingenuous for us to partake together. But rather than create hostility among us, our inability to come to the table together should cause us to grieve over the brokenness of the one Body of Christ and to seek to rediscover our common ground and mission. We can stand together on the essentials of the Christian faith while not denying our important and genuine distinctives in doctrine and practice. This is our high calling, our mission, and it is civilization's greatest hope. We can make common cause to influence our culture even though there are differences among us.

Two Christian leaders I greatly admire and am privileged to know have taken a courageous and historic step to speak to their traditions—evangelical Protestant and Roman Catholic—about this mission and hope. Charles Colson and Pastor Richard John Neuhaus recently announced the finalization of a twenty-five-page accord that took two years to draft. Entitled "Evangelicals and Catholics Together: The Christian Mission in the Third Millennium," this accord exhorts Christians from all traditions and confessions to advance united against the many foes that threaten the church and culture.

The original list of signatories (more are being added almost weekly) attached to this accord is a virtual who's who of Christian leaders spanning Catholic and Protestant persuasions. Besides myself, Charles Colson, and Pastor Neuhaus, the forty signatories include such notable leaders as William Bentley Ball, Bill Bright, Os Guinness, Nathan Hatch, James Hitchcock, Peter Kreeft, Ralph Martin, Richard Mouw, Mark Noll, Michael Novak, John Cardinal O'Connor, Thomas Oden, Elizabeth Achtemeir, J. I. Packer, Pat Robertson, Avery Dulles, Richard Land, Jesse Miranda, Herbert Schlossberg, George Weigel, and John White.

Along with these believers, I am committed to Christ and His commission. And I believe that we stand on the threshold of an unprecedented opportunity to reach the world for our Lord.

The more I travel, read, and listen, the more I discover pockets of believers who have not allowed their differences to divide their efforts. Many of these are members of movements that have sprung up among the laity, but some others have been birthed by professional church leaders. All saw the light of day when they lifted their heads above the fog of divisiveness and caught the glittering rays of unity founded on a common agenda—penetrating and transforming the culture with the gospel of Christ. And this was made possible, oddly enough, by retaining rather than rejecting their doctrinal and ecclesiastical distinctives as they sought to cooperate with other Christians. We Christians have differences—important, critical differences. But we have far more in common in belief and in a dedication to the one mission of Christ. These believers have built on their commonalities without denying their differences. As a result, they are making a difference.

If nations could band together to oppose the threats of the Axis powers and their ideology, cannot Christians band together to fight the culture of death and threats of militant secularism? The answer to this question may well depend on at least two factors: our committing to a cease-fire so we stop shooting at each other, and our ability to once again rediscover our common Christian heritage.

I think it's time we look back to a time when unity thrived in the church. It was a time when schisms threatened but failed to succeed. It was a time of persecutions and martyrs, the rise and fall of heresies and a deepening understanding of orthodoxy. It was a time of fighting against religious cleansing and moral perversity. It was a time not too unlike our own. It was the church's first millennium.

PART III

Children
of the
Great Divorce

CHAPTER NINE

WHEN UNITY THRIVED

There is one body and one Spirit,
just as you were called in one hope of your calling;
one Lord, one faith, one baptism;
one God and Father of all,
who is above all, and through all, and in you all.
Paul, the apostle

The blood of the martyrs
is the seed of the Church.
Tertullian, the apologist

One within their midst betrayed their Leader with a kiss in exchange for thirty pieces of silver. The other eleven of the group fled from His side when He needed them the most, at the time of His betrayal and arrest. Not one of them arose to defend their Master and Friend during His trials. After He was tortured, crucified, and buried, they cowered together out of fear for their lives. They even disbelieved the initial reports of His resurrection from the dead, and some still wrestled with doubt even after they saw and heard their transformed risen Lord.[1]

If you had been a gambler and bet that these eleven men would ever become a unified force for change in the Roman world, you would have been considered an easy take. And yet, after they had spent forty days with the resurrected Messiah and watched Him ascend toward Heaven, they courageously returned to Jerusalem, the city of His execution and site of their cowardice. There they met together "with *one accord* in prayer and supplication, with the women and Mary the mother of Jesus, and with His brothers."[2] Then with Peter leading them, the eleven apostles chose a new apostle to replace Judas the betrayer.[3] These men were changing. Challenged and inspired by the risen Lord Himself, they were preparing together to receive the promised Spirit, and through Him the empowerment to carry out the Great Commission "in Jerusalem, and in all Judea and Samaria, and to the end of the earth."[4] The jump-start they got must have startled even them.

On the day of Pentecost, while "they were all with *one accord* in one place," the Holy Spirit descended on them as a mighty wind and baptized them with the fire of foreign tongues.[5] Devout Jews from the world's nations heard their own languages come out of the mouths of the enraptured apostles. Amazement and perplexity gripped them. Some mocked the apostles, claiming they were overcome by the influence of "new wine." But Peter rose up and defended the strange happenings as the fulfillment of prophetic utterances that had long been embedded in the Hebrew Scriptures. Then he went on and explained and defended the life, death, resurrection, and teaching of the Messiah of the New Covenant, the covenant He had enacted and secured by His sacrificial death and miraculous resurrection.

That day three thousand people repented of their sins, accepted Jesus as their Savior and Lord, and entered the ranks of the church, where "they continued steadfastly in the apostles' doctrine and fellowship, in the breaking of bread, and in prayers." We're also told that "all who believed were together, and had all things in common, and sold their possessions and goods, and divided them among all, as anyone had need. So continuing daily with *one accord* in the temple, and breaking bread from house to house, they ate their food with gladness and simplicity of heart, praising God and having favor with all the people. And the Lord added to the church daily those who were being saved."[6]

The repetition of the words *one accord*, first used with the apostles, then with those the Lord added to their number, stresses the unity of the early church from the top down. The church began in unity and grew in unity despite the many pressures that threatened to divide and destroy her. The church's oneness, however, was not a unity of sameness; rather, it reflected the unity of God. The church confessed that there is one God and one God alone, but she also maintained that God exists as three co-eternal, uncreated Persons. These Persons—Father, Son, and Holy Spirit—are all equally God, yet They are distinct, not separate. They are not three gods but one. Nevertheless, Their unity exhibits plurality and Their plurality, unity. The Father is not the Son or the Spirit; the Spirit is not the Father or the Son; the Son is not the Father or the Spirit. But They exist together, in eternal harmony, in the same divine nature. Three Whos in one Who. A true Tri-Unity.

The church, like her triune Head, was to be a plurality expressed in unity. Individuals were not to melt into an indistinguishable whole, but to come together and form a community that embraced and celebrated diversity for the health and growth of the whole. Each person was redeemed, gifted, and being transformed to play a vital role for the sake of others. Individuality expressed in community; community confirmed in individuality. Diversity in unity; unity in diversity. This was the church. And she revealed her oneness in a number of diverse ways, all of which exhibited a sharing of a common culture.

THE CULTURE OF THE CHURCH

According to *The Social Science Encyclopedia*, "Culture is the way of life of a people. It consists of conventional patterns of thought and behaviour, including values, beliefs, rules of conduct, political organization, economic activity, and the like, which are passed on from one generation to the next by learning—and not by biological inheritance."[7] History bears out the truth of this definition in the life of the church from even its New Testament conception.

The church is a people. In the Apostle Peter's words, "a chosen race, a royal priesthood, a holy nation, a people he claims for his own to proclaim the glorious works of the One who called you from darkness into his marvelous light. Once you were no people, but now you are God's people; once there was no mercy for you, but now you have found mercy."[8] Commenting on this text, New Testament scholar D. Edmond Hiebert rightly observes:

> The word "people" (*genos*, "kindred, race") denotes the descendants of a common ancestor and thus designates a people with a common heritage, sharing the unity of a common life. The term pictures Christians as a people united by their common heritage through the new birth (1:23). Because of its spiritual birth, the new race transcends all natural distinctions of ancestry, languages, or cultures. But the word "chosen" ... reminds us that it is the divine initiative that has made Christians a distinct people who no longer belong to the world. It "removes all boasting and yet establishes a dignity of heredity that enables a chosen one to point to God as the father of his race." The oneness of believers in Christ is a reality to be treasured, especially in times of persecution.[9]

This people is united in Christ, within whom "there is no longer Jew or Greek, there is no longer slave or free, there is no longer male and female; for all of you are one in Christ Jesus."[10] A people united in "one body and one Spirit, ... called in one hope of [our] calling; one Lord, one faith, one baptism; one God and Father of all, who is above all, and through all, and in [us] all."[11]

If we are followers of Christ, we are His people, united in Him. Our race, our station in life, our gender, even our national or worldly associations cannot abolish the fact that He has brought us together and called us His own. We are now more than just citizens of some earthly country or members of the black, white, Hispanic, Asian, or Indian communities or even members of the larger category, humanity. We are adopted sons and daughters of the Family of God; we are citizens of His Kingdom; we are kings under His rule and priests in His temple; we are visible lights of His grace and mercy because He has been gracious and merciful to us; we are heirs of His infinite estate and unfailing promises. We are one, sharers in a common identity, common origin, common purpose, common inheritance. You and I, along with everyone throughout human history who has given himself or herself to God in Christ, stand together under one roof with our common Savior as the Chief Cornerstone of the entire structure and us as living stones, His building blocks for constructing a spiritual house.[12]

As this people, we have a shared way of life, a common culture. We always have. Even when the church first began, she demonstrated common values and beliefs; common rules of conduct; a common organizational structure; a common mission; common Scriptures, values, and practices; common threats and defenses; and a common commitment to pass on her treasures to each generation of believers. In all these ways, Christians set themselves apart as citizens of an unearthly kingdom, as travelers and aliens in this world and seekers after the next. The church has always had this otherworldly quality, and for that reason she has won converts while enraging her enemies, obeyed a higher law in the face of suffering under the penalties of a lower law, and transformed even hostile cultures as she's strived to understand and preserve her own. And for the first thousand years of her experience on earth, she did all this as one visible body under her Head, Jesus.

Here I want to help you catch a glimpse of the church united during the time of her life when unity thrived—the first millennium of her existence. I want you to understand her as a people dedicated to a way of life, a common culture, a culture she believed had come to her under the authority of her common Lord and by the guidance of her common

Spirit through the teaching of her common apostles. Perhaps that's the best place to start, with the twelve apostles.

Shared Leadership

From the very beginning of the church, the twelve apostles were recognized as the church's key human authority figures. Among the list of offices given in the New Testament, the apostolic office was always listed first, for it was viewed as the highest, most authoritative office in the church. Those who held it had been eyewitnesses of the life of Jesus from His baptism by John the Baptist to His ascension into Heaven.[13] They of all people could bear witness to who Jesus was, what He taught, why He died, and that He conquered death and ascended to the right hand of God the Father until the time of His Second Coming, at which time He would return as the world's Judge rather than as its Savior.

Moreover, to the apostles, Jesus gave "power and authority to overcome all demons and to cure diseases. He sent them forth to proclaim the reign of God and heal the afflicted."[14] After His resurrection, Jesus appeared to the apostles and commissioned them to carry on His ministry by giving them the ability to understand Scripture and the authority to baptize, teach, preach repentance and forgive sins, and make disciples of all nations. The Lord had commissioned them, and He had promised to be with them always.[15] The early church knew this and esteemed the apostles because of it.

Furthermore, unbelievers first heard the gospel message through the apostles, and when unbelievers became believers, they looked to the apostles to guide them in their spiritual pilgrimage. As Luke records in Acts, the newly baptized "devoted themselves to the apostles' instruction."[16] When the Twelve spoke, Christians listened, and in the voice of the Twelve, believers could hear the revelation of God in Christ through the power and witness of the Holy Spirit.

The Twelve also directed the church's communal life, centering it on the worship and service of the crucified and risen Lord through the Eucharistic liturgy, prayer, evangelism, and meeting even the physical and economic needs of fellow believers.[17] The church likewise looked to the apostles to adjudicate disputes, carry out and authorize church discipline, defend Christian doctrine, teach and exemplify Christian morality, and identify and confront heresy.[18]

The apostles also established different levels of leadership, at first to keep themselves free to focus on the ministry of the Word of God, but also in response to the gifts the Holy Spirit was pouring out on the church for its ongoing edification and evangelistic work. Just as Moses could not handle the Israelites' needs alone during the wilderness wanderings, so the apostles could not meet all of the church's needs or fulfill its mission on their own.

One office established by the apostles was that of bishop or elder, which carried on the special apostolic ministry of "teaching the authentic gospel message, and defending it against attack and false interpretations."[19] Bishops were selected in every city to watch over the local assemblies and to serve them as administrators, pastors, teachers, and apologists. They were called to rule over the churches as shepherds would take care of their flocks. They were spiritual overseers of the souls of the people who had been placed under their care, and one day they would have to account to the Lord for the way they carried out their responsibilities.[20]

The office of deacon was also instituted by the apostles. Those who filled this office were primarily responsible for the church's material needs, and they assisted the bishops in various administrative and liturgical functions, especially in the celebration of the Eucharist. The office was established in order to relieve the apostles and bishops of burdens that would interfere with their ministry of spiritual oversight.[21]

According to theologian Alan Schreck:

> As the early church developed, three roles or "offices" of leadership and service came to be recognized in the local Christian communities: The bishop or overseer (*episcopos*), the elders or presbyters (*presbyteroi*), and the deacons or servants (*diakonoi*). The writings of the early church demonstrate beyond question that the one who led the others and exercised "apostolic" authority in the church was the bishop. The role of the bishop assumed increasingly greater importance as time went on. . . .
>
> The development of basic offices of leadership in the local churches reached its final phase by the middle or late second century. By that time, every local Christian church was led by a single bishop who was assisted by presbyters (elders) and deacons (servants). This basic pattern was the only generally accepted model of local church leadership for hundreds of years.[22]

The church from the beginning had a distinctive leadership, and it was a leadership style and system that grew out of the church's experience and was shared by all the local churches.

Shared Beliefs

All Christians also shared the same core of beliefs, which came to them from the apostles and was first memorialized in creeds. The earliest creedal statements show up in the New Testament. These creeds pre-date the writing of the New Testament books in which they are cited. They show what beliefs Christians shared verbally even before those doctrines were written down years later in the pages of what became the New Testament Scriptures.

Bible scholars have identified several New Testament texts that record these oral confessions: Luke 24:34; Romans 1:3-4; 4:25; 10:9-10; 1 Corinthians 11:23-26; 15:3-5; Philippians 2:6-11; 1 Timothy 2:6; 3:16; 6:13; 2 Timothy 2:8,11-13; 1 Peter 3:18; and 1 John 4:2. Some of these oral traditions clearly came down from the apostles themselves: "I received from the Lord what I handed on to you"; "I handed on to you first of all what I myself received."[23] While other creedal affirmations more than likely grew out of the Christian community's capsulization of the apostles' teachings.

All of these early creeds, probably formulated between AD 30 and 50, focus on the Person and work of Jesus of Nazareth. They show what even the pre–New Testament apostolic church was taught and believed about the central Figure of the faith. These core beliefs included twelve historical facts:

(1) Jesus died by crucifixion and (2) was buried. (3) Jesus' death caused the disciples to despair and lose hope, believing that his life was ended. (4) . . . the tomb in which Jesus was buried was discovered to be empty just a few days later.

. . . (5) the disciples had experiences which they believed were literal appearances of the risen Jesus. Because of these experiences, (6) the disciples were transformed from doubters who were afraid to identify themselves with Jesus to bold proclaimers of his death and resurrection. (7) This message was the center of preaching in the early church and (8) was especially proclaimed in Jerusalem, where Jesus died and was buried shortly before.

As a result of this preaching, (9) the church was born and grew, (10) with Sunday as the primary day of worship. (11) James, who had been a skeptic, was converted to the faith when he also believed he saw the resurrected Jesus. (12) A few years later, Paul was also converted by an experience which he, likewise, believed to be an appearance of the risen Jesus.[24]

These creeds also affirm the humanity and deity of Jesus Christ, His death for our sins and resurrection for our justification, His exaltation to power and authority at the Father's side, the eventual universal acknowledgment among humankind of Christ's lordship, the promise of our future resurrection and reign with Christ, the way of salvation He provided, and His establishment of the Eucharist.

In short, even prior to the writing of the New Testament, the basics of the Christian message were being accepted, taught, and evangelistically proclaimed by the entire Christian community. Oral transmission and tradition played a primary role in accomplishing this.

Of course, this does not mean that problems of interpretation or application never arose. They did. And when they surfaced, the apostles, or those to whom the apostolic hand of authority was extended, addressed them. Many of the New Testament letters deal with such matters. For example, in 1 Corinthians, the Apostle Paul confronts several issues that the Christians living in pagan Corinth had asked him about—namely, issues surrounding marriage (7:1-40), Christian liberty (8:1–11:1), the role of women in worship (11:2-16), the observance of the Eucharist (11:17-34), spiritual gifts (12:1–14:40), the bodily resurrection of Christ and believers (15:1-58), and the offering for the needy saints in Jerusalem (16:1-4).

Paul also tackles several disturbing matters that had been brought to his attention about the Corinthian assembly. The believers in Corinth were making several unwise moral decisions. They had failed to discipline a fellow believer involved in open immorality (5:1-13). They were taking each other to pagan law courts rather than resolving conflicts within their own midst (6:1-11). They were engaging in sexual immorality with prostitutes (6:12-20).

But even worse than these errors, the Corinthian Christians were threatening their unity by dividing over their alliances with different teachers—alliances these teachers neither desired nor promoted. Some of the Corinthians said they were followers of Paul, others of Apollos or Peter, and others of Christ Himself (1:12). In response to this, Paul chastises them for dividing the Body of Christ, refers to sectarianism as carnal and spiritually immature, and calls on the Corinthian believers to accept the remedy for divisiveness: understanding and embracing the apostolic message of Christ crucified and of His followers as servants of God (1:18–4:5). God is one and His Son came to die to make a people one. With Jesus as the foundation and the Holy Spirit as the Equipper, Empowerer, and Sanctifier, God is cobuilding with His followers a beautiful, everlasting temple made of holy, living stones (3:9-17). For those who build with the right material, their work will be rewarded; for those who don't, their work will be consumed in the fire of divine judgment, even though they "will be saved, but only as one fleeing through fire."[25]

It's in this light that Paul pleads with the Corinthian believers, "in the name of our Lord Jesus Christ, to agree in what you say. Let there be no factions; rather, be united in mind and judgment."[26] And the best way to do this, Paul later explains, is by following the most excellent way of love. Sectarianism flows from pride, jealousy, foolish human wisdom rather than divine wisdom. Sectarianism pits people against each other, bringing out the worst in human behavior instead of the best. The way of love reverses this ugly trend. By its very nature, love seeks and preserves unity. How so? Paul tells us in one of the most powerful passages in all of Holy Scripture: "Love is patient; love is kind. Love is not jealous, it does not put on airs, it is not snobbish. Love is never rude, it is not self-seeking, it is not prone to anger; neither does it brood over injuries. Love does not rejoice in what is wrong but rejoices with the truth. There is no limit to love's forbearance, to its trust, its hope, its power to endure. Love never fails."[27]

A Body marked by love cannot divide. The Corinthian assembly needed to pursue love and put the One who is Love at the center of their church life.

Second Corinthians tells us that Paul's counsel and admonishments in 1 Corinthians did help effect significant change in the church at Corinth.[28] Nevertheless, some misunderstandings and disputes within the Christian community were too explosive to handle through letters or even apostolic visits. At such times, the leaders of the early Christian community found it necessary to come together as a council to prayerfully and thoughtfully decide on potentially divisive issues. The first recorded instance of this kind of authoritative gathering is found in Acts 15.

The First Ecumenical Council

The council meeting was occasioned by a group of men from Judea who went to Antioch and told the Christians there that they had to be circumcised according to the Mosaic Law in order to be saved (Acts 15:1). These Judaizers, who were "zealous for the law," believed that only through Israel and Judaism could Gentiles (all non-Jews) have a part in God's redemption and the blessings that accompanied it.[29] As far as they were concerned, Christianity was merely an extension of Judaism. Yes, one needed to believe in Christ by faith to be saved, but one also needed to comply with all the stipulations of the Mosaic Law as interpreted by the rabbis, including circumcision, dietary prescriptions, the moral code, and the strict conditions of table fellowship.

The controversy and dissension that arose because of the Judaizers' claims eventually led to the church's first ecumenical council. It was held in Jerusalem around AD 49 with the apostles and presbyters presiding. All sides of the issue were represented and discussion was open and vigorous. After much debate had ensued, the Apostle Peter took the floor and addressed the assembly. He briefly recounted what he had seen God do for the Gentiles and how He had "purified their hearts by means of faith" just as He had done for Jews who believed.[30] "Why, then," asked Peter, "do you [Judaizers] put God to the test by trying to place on the shoulders of these converts a yoke which neither we nor our fathers were able to bear? Our belief is rather that we are saved by the favor of the Lord Jesus and so are they."[31] Peter's close brought the entire assembly to silence.

After awhile, Paul and Barnabas broke the hush and "described all the signs and wonders God had worked among the Gentiles through them."[32] Then James spoke up and supported Peter's case with an appeal to the inspired writings of Isaiah, Jeremiah, and Amos. With apostolic testimony, accompanying reports of miracles, and prophetic support behind him, James conveyed a decision that the entire council embraced. Salvation by faith, not by law, was upheld and the only concessions made to the Judaizers were that Gentile believers should "abstain from meat sacrificed to idols, from [eating] blood, from the meat of strangled animals, and from illicit sexual union."[33]

In other words, to the question "Must Gentile Christians be circumcised and keep the other stipulations of the Mosaic Law?" the answer was no. To the question, What practices should Gentile Christians avoid for the sake of maintaining unity between Gentile and Jewish believers during social and table fellowship?, the answer was they should freely submit to three dietary restrictions and one moral one.

This was a precedent-setting decision. As historian Paul Maier put it, "The resolution at Jerusalem, while not 'compromising' (in the negative sense) a syllable of the gospel, still found a 'compromise' solution (in the positive sense) between opposing viewpoints, for the sake of harmony in the Church."[34] This approach to resolving conflicts within the church would be utilized time and time again throughout the centuries to come. The church would call other council gatherings to resolve doctrinal disputes and combat heresies, resting and relying on the biblical promise that the Holy Spirit was working in her midst to bring her to maturity in unity and to guide her into the fullness of the truth.[35] And in those cases, the prayerful desire would be to compromise in the positive sense so that unity could be preserved, but not at the expense of the faith's essentials.

Shared Scriptures

Christianity spread rapidly throughout the Roman Empire. A great road system, free and vigorous trade, a common political and legal structure, and a policy of religious tolerance (for the most part, at least) were just some of the factors that eased Christianity's advance. But with growth comes growing pains, and one of the ways those were alleviated within the church was through correspondence.

Almost all of the New Testament books are letters. The only exceptions are the gospels of Matthew, Mark, and John. But even these, along with the other New Testament books, were circulated widely among the local assemblies in the Roman Empire and perhaps beyond. And this sharing frequently occurred at the insistence of the apostles. They wanted their instructional letters read to the original recipients as well as passed around to other congregations.[36]

This same truth is borne out by the writings of the church Fathers, those bishops, lay leaders, theologians, and apologists who guided the church through her first few centuries following the Apostolic Age. One of these men, Clement, the bishop of Rome, wrote the believers in Corinth around AD 95 and told them, "Take up the letter of the blessed Apostle Paul,"[37] which assumes they had the letter in their possession. Polycarp, the bishop of Smyrna, wrote the Philippian Christians (between AD 110–117) and exhorted them to pore over Paul's letters because through them they would "be built up into the faith."[38] The evidence is similar for the other authors' writings that found their way into the New Testament canon.[39]

Of course, the early church also understood that the Hebrew Bible, what we call the Old Testament, was divinely inspired and authoritative. While oral tradition and the firsthand testimony of the apostles taught believers about Jesus the Messiah, the New Covenant He initiated, and the new people He was forming called the church, the Hebrew Scriptures provided God-breathed material "useful for teaching, for reproof, for correction, and for training in righteousness, so that everyone who belongs to God may be proficient, equipped for every good work."[40] But this use of the Old Testament had a distinctly Christian twist to it. As New Testament scholar Ralph Martin explains, with the advent of Christ, the Old Testament had to be viewed in the revelatory light of His coming and commission:

> On its own and without the interpreting and complementary witness of the New Testament, the Old Testament is a book of unfulfilled prophecies, unexplained ceremonies, and unsatisfied longings. Yet as a witness to Christ and a preparation for His advent and Kingdom, it holds an unrivalled place; and its place and importance in the worship of Christ's people are assured. The Lord's own words recorded in Luke xxiv, 27 have been the guide and incentive to the Christians' study of the Old Testament in both private devotion and public assembly.[41]

One of the most prized possessions of the early church was the Scriptures, which were Jewish (the Old Testament) and Christian (what was becoming the New Testament). Our ancient forefathers strove to live out the counsel these writings preserved and provided, and they frequently died the death of martyrs for their efforts. They certainly would not have sacrificed so much if they had not embraced the truths embedded in those timely yet timeless writings.

Shared Practices and Values
When one looks at the early church, one cannot divorce practice from values. For the most part, Christians conducted their lives according to their moral convictions and religious beliefs, even if it meant losing their possessions and their lives. One of the most revealing observations of this fact is conveyed by an early Roman governor, Pliny the Younger.

Pliny was appointed imperial legate of the Roman province of Bithynia in northwest Asia Minor around AD 111. While carrying out the duties of his office, the greatest of which was to keep peace in the empire, he ran into a situation where he had to deal with the "Christian problem." According to a letter he wrote on the matter to the emperor Trajan, it seems that Pliny had received numerous complaints about the Christians. They had penetrated every social class, age level, gender, city, village, and countryside with their message and won so many converts that the surrounding vicinity had suffered some important financial and employment losses largely due to the huge drop in devotion to the pagan gods.

When people became Christians, they abandoned their old ways and took up new ones. What were these new ways? Pliny provides an objective, telltale description extracted from his interrogations of

Christians: "They maintained that their fault or error amounted to nothing more than this: they were in the habit of meeting on a certain fixed
day before sunrise and reciting an antiphonal hymn to Christ as God, and
binding themselves with an oath—not to commit any crime, but to
abstain from all acts of theft, robbery and adultery, from breaches of
faith, from repudiating a trust when called upon to honour it. After this,
they went on, it was their custom to separate, and then meet again to
partake of food, but food of an ordinary and innocent kind."[42]

Fascinating, isn't it? Pliny's description of some of the practices and
values of the early Christians corresponds to those taught by Jesus, the
apostles, and the other New Testament writers. Pliny's list also finds
parallels in the writings of the church Fathers. What all of these show is
that Christians met on the same day for worship (Sunday), sang hymns
together and shared public readings from sacred Scripture or other prized
writings, centered their worship on Christ as God incarnate, shared the
Eucharist, and corporately committed themselves to living virtuous lives.

The church also honored virginity, chastity, and marriage between
one man and one woman for life. Divorce, homosexual practice, premarital sex, and adultery were taboo. The natural family was seen as the
social foundation of the church—the domestic church—and it wrapped
its arms around aunts, uncles, nieces, cousins, grandparents, great-grand-
parents, widows, and orphans, not just around mother, father, and their
children. Christians held human life in high regard, believing it to be a
creation and gift of God; therefore they believed abortion, infanticide,
euthanasia, suicide, human sacrifices, and murder were wrong. They
honored and obeyed human governmental authorities as long as those
authorities allowed them to live according to their Christian dictates.
They strove to be at peace with all and to help as many as they could.
They prayed for their persecutors, fed the hungry, clothed the naked,
adopted the orphaned, shared their possessions with the needy, settled disputes among themselves rather than in the pagan courts.

They assumed the manners and customs of the cultures that surrounded them, but did so critically; they embraced what they found
was true and good and sought to avoid or redeem the rest. They worked,
played, rested, attended various social gatherings and events, accepted
political appointments, saved and spent money, educated themselves
and their children, purchased property, engaged in commerce—in short,
they performed the normal functions of any human being in a given
cultural milieu. But Christians did so according to the cardinal virtues
of justice, wisdom, courage, and moderation, and the theological virtues

of faith, hope, and love.[43]

What Christians did was noticed, and even among their enemies their deeds were often praised, sometimes reluctantly. The Roman emperor Julian, for example, witnessed the Christians, whom he called atheists and "godless Galileans," outshining the followers of his own religious persuasion. As he must have painfully wrote, "Atheism has been specially advanced through the living service rendered to strangers, and through their care for the burial of the dead. It is a scandal that there is not a single Jew who is a beggar, and the godless Galileans care not only for their own poor but for ours as well; while those who belong to us look in vain for the help that we should render them."[44] Church historian Henry Chadwick rightly observes, "The practical application of charity was probably the most potent single cause of Christian success. The pagan comment 'See how these Christians love one another' (reported by Tertullian) was not irony. Christian charity expressed itself in care for the poor, for widows and orphans, in visits to brethren in prison or condemned to the living death of labour in the mines, and in social action in time of calamity like famine, earthquake, pestilence, or war."[45]

In short, the church as one followed her Master's message and model. And by doing so she thrived, eventually winning the respect and admiration of Jews and pagans alike, including that of many of her enemies.

Shared Mission
At the heart of the church's life was the commission she had received from her Head through her apostolic leaders: "Full authority has been given to me both in heaven and on earth; go, therefore, and make disciples of all the nations. Baptize them in the name of the Father, and of the Son, and of the Holy Spirit. Teach them to carry out everything I have commanded you. And know that I am with you always, until the end of the world!"[46]

The church faithfully carried out this commission, beginning in its hub of origin, Jerusalem, and like the spokes of a wheel reaching out to the uttermost parts of the world. We have good reason to believe, for example, that the Apostle Paul made it all the way to Spain planting churches throughout the Mediterranean area. Ancient writings, oral traditions, and other archaeological findings indicate that the Apostle Matthew took the gospel as far as Ethiopia; the Apostle Andrew to Scythia (which was north of the Black Sea); the Apostle Bartholomew to Arabia and India; the Apostle "Doubting" Thomas to India as well; Mark the evangelist (writer of the gospel that bears his name) to Egypt, where

Eusebius says he became the first bishop of Alexandria; the Apostle James the Great may have gone as far as Spain; the Apostle Simon to Persia. And this is just a sampling of what Christians, laypeople and church leaders alike, did to spread the good news and establish the church to the "ends of the earth."[47]

Another expression of the church's commission came from Jesus' Sermon on the Mount. There He spoke of believers being "the salt of the earth" and "the light of the world."[48] Light, of course, illuminates the darkness, and in the ancient world, salt's primary uses were as a preservative and a flavoring. Light is ineffective if it is covered up, and salt becomes almost worthless once it loses its abilities to flavor or preserve food. Believers therefore are to live out their faith in a dark, decaying world in such a way that unbelievers see their "good works and glorify your Father in heaven."[49] This high calling led Christians to play three different yet interrelated roles in the many cultures they found themselves.

Lift Up

One of these roles was *redemptive* and *transformative*. The early Christians knew that because human beings are made in the image of God, even unredeemed people will mirror, however dimly, the nature and work of their Creator.[50] So when Christians found truth, beauty, justice, or goodness outside of the church, however marred it was by sin and error, they extolled it, stripped it of the dross that polluted it, and attempted to build upon it as God had intended. In other words, they reclaimed it and transformed it, restoring it to its rightful place in the created order. As a result, they lifted philosophy out of the mire of the likes of skepticism, gnosticism, polytheism, and despair. They gradually turned a rationalistic and anthropocentric science based on fate or caprice into an empirical science that assumed and gloried in the Grand Designer and cosmic Creator-Sustainer. They shifted artistic and architectural genius and inspiration away from immoral and idolatrous images to grand exaltations of the infinite majesty of the Triune God; the radiant beauty of a creation in harmony with its Creator; the miracle of the Incarnation; and the incredible story of redemption in the pages of Holy Writ and church history. Music, sculpture, theater, literature, law, politics—everything Christians touched, they sought to redeem and transform.

Speak Out

They also played a second role, that of *prophet*. A maxim many Americans live by is, "If it ain't broke, don't fix it." As Christians grew in their understanding and application of the faith, they came to see more and more in the world that was broken and needed to be fixed. They were often able to penetrate those problematic areas of the culture and solve them from the inside out. Christians changed politics by becoming politicians, law by becoming judges and lawyers, music by becoming composers and musicians. They also shared their faith with unbelievers from all walks of life and social strata, saw them converted, taught them in the truth, and guided them in transforming their own jobs and areas of discipline.

Many times, however, Christians had to stand on the outside looking in, or found themselves standing inside alone after penetrating a particular level of society or attaining a certain occupational status. In these instances, they not only modeled the truth in their lives but called the surrounding society to account as well. Like the prophets of Israel and Prophet of prophets, Jesus Christ, these Christians pointed out injustices and immoralities of all sorts and in all social spheres. They believed that nothing was off limits to the scrutiny of the Christian faith. God was Lord of all even though some members of the human race thought otherwise. And through His Son and chosen apostles, He had commissioned the church to stop society's decay.

There was much to stop. In the Roman world, life was cheap, sexual immorality rampant, and social injustice commonplace. Vice was Roman society's mainstay. Adultery; homosexuality; prostitution; slavery; repressive economic practices; the brutal elimination of the elderly, infirm, and unwanted; bigotry and socially acceptable injustices toward women and all who were not Roman citizens ... you name it, somewhere in the ancient world it could be engaged in with impunity.

This was the world the church had to face. It was here she had to be salt and light. Here she had to carry out the Great Commission. Here she had to be a model and prophet of virtue. It was in this horribly cruel world she had to learn how to turn the other cheek when struck, love and pray for her enemies, and persevere in the faith no matter what. But she did all this and more. Sin abounded much, but Christians faithfully confronted it, protested it, and worked to stop it. Sometimes paying the highest price of all—their own blood.

Pray Much

A third role Christians played in confronting the culture around them was that of *priest*. They believed with the Apostle Paul that the real battle was not "against flesh and blood, but against principalities, against powers, against the rulers of the darkness of this age, against spiritual hosts of wickedness in the heavenly places."[51] A spiritual war had to be fought with spiritual weapons, and one of the mightiest weapons in the Christian's arsenal was prayer.[52] Believers prayed for fellow believers; that was to be expected. But they also lifted their eyes toward Heaven on behalf of civil authorities, even when those officials were hostile to the faithful. This was not expected, at least not by Christianity's enemies.

Jesus Christ had prayed for forgiveness for His persecutors from the cross.[53] The deacon Stephen had done the same just before he died from being stoned.[54] These examples would be multiplied countless times throughout church history: believers exercising mercy even on those who were merciless toward them.

This loving outpouring of prayer flowed from a deep, abiding conviction that this life was not the end. There was another life and another death beyond the grave. For those who had believed in God and given themselves to Him by faith, there was the expectation of living forever with Him in immortal, uninterrupted bliss. Therefore any hardship Christians would face in this life simply paled in significance when compared to the new life death would bring.[55] But believers also knew that for unbelievers who died in unbelief, a second death awaited them, one of incredible, unending torment.[56] Christians knew Jesus had come and died and risen from the dead so no one who believed in Him would have to face the second death. That was part of the good news they proclaimed, and it motivated them to have mercy on unbelievers, which was exercised in part through prayer.

Jesus' teaching on this matter must have echoed resoundingly clear, however difficult at times it must have been to carry out: "I say to you, love your enemies, bless those who curse you, do good to those who hate you, and pray for those who spitefully use you and persecute you, that you may be sons of your Father in heaven; for He makes His sun rise on the evil and on the good, and sends rain on the just and on the unjust. For if you love those who love you, what reward have you?"[57]

So Christians linked their proclamation and performance with prayer. The combination turned the world upside down within just three centuries of the church's birth. The church could not have accomplished so much so quickly if she had been divided rather than united. She understood her mission, and she carried it out vigorously and well.

CHAPTER TEN

UNITY IN THE FACE
OF PERSECUTION

When I was delighting in the doctrines of Plato,
and heard the Christians slandered,
and saw them fearless of death . . . [I] perceived
that it was impossible that they could be living
in wickedness and pleasure.
Justin Martyr

Ironically, the church's effectiveness in carrying out her mission is what brought her grief. She enjoyed incredible early growth in the midst of the same city that had tried to abort her by killing her Lord and by squelching her claims about His resurrection. She was even the vehicle God used to work signs and wonders among the populace so they would join her ranks in salvific belief.[1] But she was not to enjoy all this without paying a price. For almost from the day of her birth, the church would experience the forging fires of the furnace of persecution.

OPPOSITION WITHIN THE HOUSEHOLD

Jesus had come to the Jewish people. He was a rabbi. He wanted to see the deliverance of Israel, and He died to bring that about. Yet, the first flames of persecution against His followers flared up from among some of the religious leaders of Judaism. They were found among the Pharisees, Sadducees, chief priests, and scribes. Even the high priest got involved. As far as they were concerned, this so-called new movement of God within Judaism was scandalous and absurd. Not all of the Jewish leaders agreed with their assessment, nor did many among the general Jewish populace. In fact, the first believers in Jesus as the Messiah came from the ranks of Judaism. Nevertheless, some Jewish leaders opposed the

176

Christ-followers and their claims. They believed that Jesus of Nazareth had been rightly executed for several reasons.

One reason was *political*. Many people had heralded Jesus as the expected political deliverer of Israel, the One who would crush Roman rule and free Israel from her Gentile oppressors. Caiaphas, the worldly-wise high priest, predicted that if this occurred, the precarious balance of authority that had finally been achieved between Palestine and Rome would be shattered and lead to direct occupation by Roman legions rather than the present representative rule by Rome's own Pontius Pilate. Hence, Caiaphas reasoned, "It's to our advantage that one man dies for the people rather than the whole nation be destroyed."[2]

Another reason for Jesus' execution was *economic*. He had threatened the commercialization of Temple worship. He had chased out the merchants who had set up shop in the Temple's outer courts to convert foreign currency and provide for monetary exchange so worshipers could purchase memorial trinkets and the appropriate sacrifices needed during the Passover celebration.[3] The religious establishment "controlled all concessions on the Temple premises, and, while one day's loss was not that significant, Jesus was setting a precedent that might well rouse the rabble to future assaults on the Temple and disrupt worship and sacrifice."[4] This could not be tolerated.

Yet another motive for destroying Jesus was *personal*. He had thoroughly refuted the Pharisees and Sadducees who opposed Him in their public encounters, claiming they were hypocrites and false teachers who were leading the people astray from the true meaning and spirit of the Mosaic Law—the very Law they prided themselves in correctly interpreting, applying, and protecting. In one encounter He had referred to them as "son[s] of hell," "fools," "blind guides," "whitewashed tombs," "vipers," devourers of "widows' houses," and murderers.[5] They felt humiliated by Him; they would not stand for that.

There was also a *religious* reason for seeing Jesus terminated. The same Jews accused Him of blasphemy for claiming He could forgive sins as only God could do and for proclaiming Himself to be the Son of God who would soon rule with God and one day return to judge humankind. He had also performed numerous healings, which some of the religious leaders had explained away as demonically empowered acts. The populace had showed signs of believing Him. So before He could lead Israel into "apostasy," He had to be stopped.

And silenced He was by the occupiers of Israel, the Roman government . . . or so they thought. Just when they believed the sedition of the Jesus movement had been squelched, Jewish apostates calling themselves apostles were publicly heralding Jesus as the long-awaited and prophesied Messiah. That was too much to accept, not only for some of the Pharisees and Sadducees and other religious leaders, but also for many among the general populace. You see, to most first-century Jews, a crucified Messiah was a contradiction in terms. They expected a political Messiah who had God's ultimate favor and would come to break the cruel yoke of their Gentile rulers through military force. After judging Israel's wicked oppressors, He would forever establish Israel as the world's most blessed nation. The Messiah would rule the world from David's reestablished throne in Jerusalem, and the Jews would no longer have to fear persecution from anyone, including any foreign power.[6] Jesus of Nazareth, however, this carpenter's son, appeared to be anything but a divinely favored military deliverer. He had not challenged Rome's political rule over Israel during His entire ministry, and He had died a tormenting death at the hands of Israel's enemies. Moreover, He had been crucified, which seemed to show clearly God's disfavor toward Him. The Torah was explicit about this, stating, "God's curse rests on him who hangs on a tree."[7]

The apostles were very aware of these stumbling blocks to the Jewish acceptance of the messianic claims of Jesus. Their defense centered on three primary facts: Jesus' resurrection, messianic prophecies, and miracles. The apostles argued that God vindicated Jesus as His Son and Israel's Messiah by raising Him alive from the grave. They appealed to the prophetic writings in the Hebrew Scriptures that foretold the Messiah would suffer. The apostles also performed miracles, especially miracles of healing, as further confirmation that Jesus was alive and well and active in Israel's midst.[8]

For this testimony, followers of the Way were scorned, threatened, beaten, imprisoned, and even killed. But through it all they, like the apostles, "rejoic[ed] that they were counted worthy to suffer shame for His name."[9] The fearful had become fearless; the powerless, powerful; the forgiven, forgivers; the repentant, revolutionaries.

Their numbers grew dramatically. And so did the persecution against them.

THE PAGAN CAMPAIGN

Although the forge of persecution was first fueled by some Jewish unbelievers, it didn't take long before the Romans were confronted with what they first perceived to be a new sect of Judaism. And what they found did more than arouse their curiosity.

To many Romans, Christians were strange, superstitious, and even subversive. Seutonius, a Roman historian who around AD 120 wrote about the lives of the first twelve caesars, said that Christians were "addicted to a novel and mischievous superstition."[10] An apt description from the Roman perspective. Look at it from their point of view.

First of all, Christians worshiped a man from Galilee named Jesus as if He were a god. And this Jesus wasn't just any man, mind you, but a man who had been scourged and crucified—a form of humiliating and excruciating punishment the Romans reserved primarily for "hardened criminals, rebellious slaves and rebels against the Roman state."[11] The point of crucifixion was not so much to punish the criminal but to deter others from attempting to subvert Roman rule.

> In the provinces Roman rule was held together by the popular perception that any challenge to her authority was doomed. It was thus imperative that any serious challenge to Rome's rule be met not only victoriously but also turned into a public demonstration that in the end the rebel had submitted. Having condemned a man to die for his rebellion, Rome required him, as his last act, to display submission publicly to the authority against which he previously had rebelled. This was done by having him carry the instrument of his judgment through the city to a public place while wearing a sign which said that he had been a rebel. But as all could see, he was now submissive.[12]

As far as many Romans were concerned, Jesus was a subversive criminal, rightly condemned and executed for His rebellion against the *Pax Romana*. After all, hadn't He called Himself the King of the Jews, and didn't His followers refer to Him as the King of kings and Lord and lords?[13] But there could be only one ruler in the Roman Empire, and that was Caesar. Granted, Pontius Pilate, the Roman procurator of Judea, had said Jesus was innocent of the crimes with which some of the Jews had charged Him.[14] That was beside the point. He had been executed to appease His Jewish accusers and thereby preserve the peace and unity of the empire. That was sufficient cause.

Christians had also claimed that after their Savior had been crucified and buried, He rose bodily from the grave, appeared to His followers several times over a forty-day period, then ascended into Heaven.[15]

The Romans thought this idea was repulsive. They had inherited the Greek attitude toward the body, which was that the corruptible body is a drag on the immortal soul. At death, the soul finally sheds the body so it can pass into the realm of the divine—that is, if while embodied the soul had performed good rather than evil. This postdeath condition was believed to be free of pain, deformity, and any other burden of mortal, embodied existence. So when Christians talked about the resurrection of the body, its reunion with the soul, and that "concoction" living forever in the realm Romans had reserved for disembodied, incorruptible souls, they had made a claim repugnant to Roman ears. No Roman or Greek poet, philosopher, seer, or priest had ever propounded such a distasteful view of the afterlife. This was quite an obstacle, especially for pious Romans, to overcome.[16] This is why the Greek philosophers mocked the Apostle Paul when they heard him at the Areopagus on Mars Hill tell them about the "unknown God," and the One He has appointed to "judge the world in righteousness," whom He also raised "from the dead."[17]

Third, the followers of this crucified and resurrected divine Man swore off all the gods and pledged their allegiance to Him alone. Even for the tolerant Romans, this was a difficult practice to accept. They had no problem permitting the peoples in their empire to worship their own deities in the ways they chose as long as their religious commitments "did not encourage sedition or weaken morality."[18] This is where the Christians ran into the steel fist of Roman rule. You see, the Romans heard stories that Christians were citizens of another kingdom, one that had authority over the Roman Empire, which the conquering Romans found unacceptable.

The Romans also came to believe that these Christ-followers were engaged in unlawful and vulgar practices in their often-secret nocturnal assemblies. The Romans thought they engaged in incest because of their references to loving their brothers and sisters. Another charge leveled against the Christians was cannibalism, because they spoke about eating the flesh and drinking the blood of Jesus, their God.

The charge of atheism also arose. Wherever Christianity flourished, the pagan temples emptied and the sale of pagan idols and the meat of sacrificial animals became a bust. This greatly upset those merchants and prostitutes who made their living from pagan worship, as the Apostle Paul so quickly learned.[19] It also raised the suspicions of the Romans who believed the gods had granted them favor, which was why they thought they had been able to conquer and rule much of the then known world. The Christians' allegiance to only one God, their abhorrence of all other gods, and their refusal to pay homage to the emperor as a god were viewed by the Romans as acts of subversion against the state and blasphemy against Roman religion.

As the Romans saw it, Christianity was, at its heart, antagonistic to the established order. The God of this new "superstitious sect" supposedly hated all other so-called gods and had vowed to crush them. This God demanded that all peoples give their ultimate and total allegiance to Him, and He promised to severely judge those who refused to bow to Him and unreservedly serve Him. The Romans could tolerate belief in one God. They could even assimilate new religious practices. But they could not understand, nor would they tolerate, such inherently hostile beliefs toward their state-approved religious order. As far as they were concerned, partaking in even "the minutiae of religious ceremonies [to the gods] . . . was a mark of piety that contributed to the well-being and success of the Roman Republic."[20] When Christians refused to participate in any of these practices, they were viewed as endangering the warp and woof of Roman society. To be antigods was to be anti-Rome, a precarious position to be in while living within the boundaries of the Roman Empire.

Pagan "Justice"
So the Romans struck out at the church.

The first great persecution came under the hammering blows of the emperor Nero in the empire's capital. After a devastating fire broke out in Rome and lasted nine days and consumed ten of the city's fourteen districts and brought incredible suffering to the one million inhabitants, Nero was charged by his political enemies with starting the blaze. Nero, however, was not to be disenfranchised so easily. In an attempt to exonerate himself of the accusation, he pointed his imperial finger at the Christians in Rome and blamed them for the fiery tragedy. Cornelius Tacitus (c. AD 55–120), who has been called the greatest historian of ancient Rome, recounts the persecution that followed:

> An arrest was first made of all who pleaded guilty; then, upon their information, an immense multitude was convicted, not so much of the crime of firing the city, as of hatred against mankind. Mockery of every sort was added to their deaths. Covered with the skins of beasts, they were torn by dogs and perished, or were nailed to crosses, or were doomed to the flames and burnt, to serve as a nightly illumination, when daylight had expired.

Nero offered his gardens for the spectacle, and was exhibiting a show in the circus, while he mingled with the people in the dress of a charioteer or stood aloft on a car [that is, a chariot or a cart]. Hence, even for criminals who deserved extreme and exemplary punishment, there arose a feeling of compassion; for it was not, as it seemed, for the public good, but to glut one man's cruelty, that they were being destroyed.[21]

It was under Nero's reign of terror that the Apostles Paul and Peter lost their lives, Paul by beheading and Peter by crucifixion.

Though not all of Rome's emperors were hostile toward Christians, many were, and they found a role model in Nero. When social problems flared and accusations flew, political careers were saved at the expense of the church. Torturing and killing Christians even became a sporting event. Many Christians died of starvation or disease as they sat in their own filth, shackled by heavy irons in hot prisons. Others were sentenced to work in fields and mines. "Half naked, underfed, beaten for low production, the damp ground their bed, these believers faced a living death."[22] Just as many Old Testament saints had suffered greatly for their faith in the promises of God, so did the followers of God's Promised One, Jesus.[23]

But not all of the persecution came from the top down. Locals, who were misinformed about, fearful of, or upset at the "atheists" living among them, either took "justice" into their own hands and ran Christians out of town, beat them, or murdered them, or complained to their governing officials until they took stringent measures to handle the problem-makers. An excellent case in point comes from the extensive correspondence of Pliny the Younger to the Roman emperor Trajan.

As I mentioned earlier, Pliny had received an increasing number of complaints about Christians who were upsetting the pagan way of life. Charged with the duty of keeping the *Pax Romana* in his jurisdiction, Governor Pliny acted accordingly to put down the Christian threat. In a letter to Trajan, he described the procedure he followed:

I have asked the accused themselves if they were Christians; if they said "Yes," I asked them a second and third time, warning them of the penalty; if they persisted I ordered them to be led off to execution. For I had no doubt that, whatever kind of thing it was that they pleaded guilty to, their stubbornness and unyielding obstinacy at any rate deserved to be punished. There were others afflicted with the like madness whom I marked down to be referred to Rome, because they were Roman citizens.[24]

Apparently, at least for a season, Pliny's persecution paid off. As he reported to Trajan, paganism was revived: "The temples, which had been well-nigh abandoned, are beginning to be frequented again; and the customary services, which had been neglected for a long time, are beginning to be resumed; fodder for the sacrificial animals, too, is beginning to find a sale again, for hitherto it was difficult to find anyone to buy it. From all this it is easy to judge what a multitude of people can be reclaimed, if an opportunity is granted them to renounce Christianity."[25]

The Gains of Loss
Contrary to Pliny's observation, paganism may have had some revivals due to the persecutions carried out against Christians, but it was those same persecutions that helped loosen paganism's grip on the Roman world. When a Roman centurion watched how Jesus died, he exclaimed, "Certainly this was a righteous Man!"[26] The same frequently occurred when His followers were tormented. A case in point comes from the life of the second-century figure, Justin Martyr.

A Gentile seeker heavily influenced by the Greek philosophies of his day, Justin was profoundly impacted by the courage demonstrated by Christian martyrs. As he recalled, "For I myself, too, when I was delighting in the doctrines of Plato, and heard the Christians slandered, and saw them fearless of death . . . perceived that it was impossible that they could be living in wickedness and pleasure."[27] Partly as a result of the witness of these martyrs, Justin was converted to the Christian faith. He went on to start a private school in Rome where he became a professor of philosophical Christianity. A layman, he traveled a good deal throughout the Roman Empire teaching others about the Christian faith, defending the faith's veracity, and sharing the good news about the salvation available through Christ.

One of the most compelling illustrations of the power of martyrdom comes from the turn of the fifth century. It concerns a monk named Telemachus.

Imagine an Asiatic monk in his cell in quiet meditation. As he listens, it seems to him that God is guiding him to journey westward to Rome. When at last he reaches the Eternal City, Rome is full of excited people. A great victory over the Goths has just been won. It is a public holiday and crowds jostle the monk in the streets. He overhears their excited tale of the programme prepared for them in the Colosseum. Animals are to fight together. Men are to fight animals. Men are to fight men. Telemachus makes his way to the great amphitheatre which seats eighty thousand people. He is on the lowest tier, nearest the sandy floor. A group of men march into the arena, and before they commence to fight one another, they halt before the royal box and cry out to Caesar, "We, who are about to die, salute thee." The soul of Telemachus is revolted, horrified at what is about to happen, that in Rome, where the faith of Christ is spreading, this horrible slaughter should still continue. The brain of Telemachus works like lightning. He sees in a flash why God wanted him to come to Rome. He rises, leaps on the low wall which alone separates him from the arena, and, in the silence which followed the greeting to Caesar, he shouts at the top of his voice, "In the name of Christ, forbear."

Laughter runs round the galleries. What can one man do to stop the amusement of eighty thousand, however revolting it be? But see, the saint has leapt down on the sand. As the gladiators close with one another he rushes to the nearest group and thrusts himself between them. Indulgently they thrust him aside and continue to fight. The crowd roars with laughter. How ridiculous he looks! What a figure he is making! A gladiator strikes him with the flat of his sword. The saint stumbles, is up again, is between the combatants, is imploring them in the name of Christ to cease. The crowd thinks it funny no longer. "Run him through!" is the cry. There is the quick flash of a blade and Telemachus is lying in the sand. Slowly the sand reddens around his body. A man rises and leaves the Colosseum. Another follows. Another. . . . The great amphitheatre begins to empty. The mind of the multitude is changed. They cry for the games to cease. *It was the last time in the Roman Colosseum that gladiatorial fights took place.* One man loved and suffered enough to change the mind of Rome. The power of the Cross![28]

The courage and conviction displayed by the early Christians had a profound effect on their pagan neighbors. Because of the church, pagan practices changed, and so did pagans. As missiologist Stephen Neill notes, there are many "well-authenticated cases of conversion of pagans in the very moment of witnessing the condemnation and death of Christians."[29] Tertullian was right: "The blood of the martyrs is the seed of the Church."[30]

SHARED DEFENSE

Christians rose up to challenge the misperceptions and caricatures of their faith and practice. Two of the greatest defenders recorded in the New Testament were the physician Luke and the Apostle Paul.

Doctor of Defense

Luke, who accompanied Paul on some of his missionary endeavors, was intent to answer several charges against the Christian movement that the Romans had either heard from others or leveled themselves. He did this by writing the gospel that bears his name and the Acts of the Apostles. In the Gospel of Luke, he strives to show that Jesus' life was exemplary. Far from being a seditious rebel against Roman rule, Jesus believed and taught that Rome's subjects, the Jews included, should give to Caesar what belongs to him and give to God what belongs to Him. Religious and state interests could coexist, with the pious being good citizens.

Furthermore, contrary to popular Roman belief, Jesus was not crucified because Rome's representative in Palestine, Pontius Pilate, thought He was guilty of insurrection. Luke points out that no less than four times did Pilate declare his belief in Jesus' innocence regarding the charges brought against Him. So why did Pilate authorize Jesus' execution? Because an influential segment of Jewish religious leaders joined by a hostile crowd demanded it. Because the Scriptures predicted the Messiah would die this way at the hands of Gentiles. Because even though sin would nail Him to the cross, in that very act sin would be defeated because through His death and resurrection the way of redemption from sin for peoples everywhere would be secured. Hence Pilate, freely following an ancient script, reluctantly and against his better judgment, acquiesced to the call for Jesus' execution in order to maintain the peace.[31]

In Acts, Luke continues the story, but this time his focus is the activities of the apostles following the vindication of Jesus in His resurrection and ascension. As New Testament scholar F. F. Bruce observes, Luke "introduces an impressive variety of people in official positions, both Gentile and Jewish, showing good will to Paul and other Christian missionaries or at least admitting that the charges brought against them by their enemies lack any basis in fact."[32] The finale of Luke's case comes when he shows Paul carrying on missionary activities in Rome unhindered, even though he's under constant police surveillance.[33] "If Christianity was really such a lawless movement as was widely believed, Paul would certainly not have been allowed to propagate it by the imperial guard who had charge of him during his detention in Rome!"[34]

With that, Luke rests his case.

The Activist Apologist

Another great apologist of the early church was the Apostle Paul. Prior to becoming a believer in Jesus, Saul (his pre-Christian name) was zealous in his persecution of the Way. He oversaw the execution of believers and worked tirelessly to have them rounded up and imprisoned. This impassioned defender of Judaism became perhaps the church's greatest apologist and missionary after encountering the risen Messiah Himself.[35]

Soon after his conversion, Paul found himself presenting and defending the gospel before Gentiles of all walks of life and strata of society. To them he witnessed tirelessly of the divine Sonship of Jesus Christ, His death and resurrection, and the salvation He promises to all who will believe by faith.

With each group he had a different strategy. To Jews who accepted the divine inspiration and authority of the sacred Scriptures, he reasoned with them from the Law, the Prophets, and the Psalms about what had been prophesied about Israel's Redeemer and how those prophetic utterances had been fulfilled in Jesus. To Gentiles such as the Romans, Paul chose not to begin with writings about which they cared or knew nothing. Instead, he found common ground in their religious symbols, poets, and philosophers, and in the revelation of God in nature and the human conscience. He appealed to their reason, knowledge, and experience, and he relied on the Roman system of jurisprudence to gain a hearing for his case, especially when he found himself before hostile crowds.[36]

Whenever it didn't conflict with his religious and moral scruples, Paul also changed his behavior in an attempt to establish a common base for sharing Christ with others or to remove stumbling blocks that got in the way of preserving unity among believers.[37]

In time his methods, the church's prolific growth, and the increasing volcanic reaction Christianity received in the communities in which it was introduced led Paul to the capital of the mighty Roman Empire, Rome itself. There he spent two entire unhindered years "preaching the kingdom of God and teaching the things which concern the Lord Jesus Christ with all confidence."[38] Since all roads led to Rome, this meant that Paul's message would certainly radiate beyond the capital's boundaries and spread throughout the world.

The Defense Never Rests

For the next three hundred years, many Christians would follow in the steps of the likes of Luke and Paul and defend the faith and its adherents against the challenges of all comers. Among these many apologists were Justin Martyr (c. 100–167), Athenagoras (second century), Irenaeus (120–203), Tertullian (155–235), Origen (c. 185–253), Athanasius (298–373), and Augustine (354–430). These apologists were especially intent on exonerating Christianity of the charges leveled by pagans.

For instance, the philosopher-teacher Justin Martyr granted the pagan charge that Christians were atheists, if that meant Christians refused to confess belief in or show honor to the "soulless and dead" gods that had been created by men and therefore were not gods at all.[39]

Justin also made it clear that the Christian belief in another kingdom did not make Christians potential enemies of the Roman state. If anything, it helped to ensure they would be model citizens:

> And when you hear that we look for a kingdom, you suppose, without making any inquiry, that we speak of a human kingdom; whereas we speak of that which is with God.... For if we looked for a human kingdom, we should also deny our Christ, that we might not be slain; and we should strive to escape detection, that we might obtain what we expect. But since our thoughts are not fixed on the present, we are not concerned when men cut us off; since also death is a debt which must at all events be paid.
>
> And more than all other men are we your helpers and allies in promoting peace, seeing that we hold this view, that it is alike impossible for the wicked, the covetous, the conspirator, and for the virtuous, to escape the notice of God, and that each man goes to everlasting punishment or salvation according to the value of his actions. For if all men knew this, no one would choose wickedness even for a little, knowing that he goes to the everlasting punishment of fire; but would by all means restrain himself, and adorn himself with virtue, that he might obtain the good gifts of God, and escape the punishments.[40]

Against the charge that Christian meetings were seditious and filled with illegal and immoral activities, the prolific apologist Tertullian responded by setting the record straight: "We are an association (*corpus*) bound together by our religious profession, by the unity of our way of life and the bond of our common hope. . . . We meet together as an assembly and as a society. . . . We pray for the emperors. . . . We gather together to read our sacred writing. . . . With the holy words we nourish our faith. . . . After the gathering is over the Christians go out as though they had come from a 'school of virtue.'"[41]

In response to the accusation that Christian beliefs lead to an inferior morality to that of the pagans, the Christian philosopher Athenagoras asked who among the great pagan moral rhetoricians or their followers "have so purged their souls as, instead of hating their enemies, to love them; and, instead of speaking ill of those who have reviled them (to abstain from which is of itself an evidence of no mean forbearance), to bless them; and to pray for those who plot against their lives?" "Among us," he added, "you will find uneducated persons, and artisans, and old women, who, if they are unable in words to prove the benefit of our doctrine, yet by their deeds exhibit the benefit arising from their persuasion of its truth; they do not rehearse speeches, but exhibit good works; when struck, they do not strike again; when robbed, they do not go to law; they give to those that ask of them, and love their neighbours as themselves."[42]

UNITY MARCHES ON

Beat up but not beaten, bloodied but not dead, the church pressed on, never giving up or giving in.

Finally, in the year 313, almost three hundred years after her birth, the emperor Constantine and his coregent Licinius issued an edict giving full toleration to Christianity and its adherents. Then in 324, after Constantine became the sole ruler of the Roman Empire, Christianity finally acquired legal status. In 392, with the rise of Theodosius, Christianity was decreed to be the official religion of the empire and paganism was outlawed.

The tables had turned 180 degrees. No matter how hard Caesar had tried to conquer Christ, in the end Christ was the victor. Eminent historian Will Durant put it well:

> There is not greater drama in human record than the sight of a
> few Christians, scorned or oppressed by a succession of emper-

ors, bearing all trials with a fiery tenacity multiplying quietly, building order while their enemies generated chaos, fighting the sword with the word, brutality with hope, and at last defeating the strongest state that history has ever known. Caesar and Christ had met in the arena, and Christ had won.[43]

The war, however, was not over. The church still faced numerous challenges, not the least of which was handling the political collapse of the Roman Empire. When the seemingly impossible happened, the sacking of Rome by barbarian invaders, the fiery arrows of false charges were once again aimed at Christians. Pagans arose blaming Rome's fall on the Christ-followers and their blasphemous disregard of the gods. The bishop of Hippo, Aurelius Augustine, certainly one of the greatest theologians and apologists in the history of the church, intercepted the pagans' arrows and broke them in two on the rock of the truth. His answer, contained in the magnum opus called *The City of God*, confronts the charge on a number of fronts.

In the first half of *The City of God*, Augustine points out that the gods the pagans had trusted in to save them couldn't save themselves, much less anyone else. Other peoples who had trusted in the gods, including the Greeks, had been defeated and even slaughtered as they stood next to the images of their gods. Then the gods themselves were captured by men who also saved them from destruction. "And these be the gods," exclaimed Augustine, "to whose protecting care the Romans were delighted to entrust their city! . . . Ought prudent men to have entrusted the defences of Rome to these conquered gods?"[44]

Augustine also brought up the fact that it was Christ who had saved many of the pagans. When Rome was invaded by the West Gothic king Alaric in 410, pagans stole into Christian churches, within which they received sanctuary and protection. There many pagans even professed to be Christians in order to save their lives from the barbarian invaders. Amazingly enough, those who took refuge in churches, whether they were pagans or Christians, were spared. That was unheard of in the ancient world, a fact Augustine pointed out with vigor.[45]

So what had made this invasion of Rome any different? Christ and His church. Because of the presence of the City of God within the city of man, Christ had exercised compassion and mercy even on the unjust. By doing so He had given the pagans another opportunity to ponder the grace extended to them and "repent of their wickedness and reform."[46]

Had the pagans taken advantage of Christ's mercy? Not in the least.

The very ones who had found protection in His church "now, in ungrateful pride and most impious madness, and at the risk of being punished in everlasting darkness, they perversely oppose that name under which they fraudulently protected themselves for the sake of enjoying the light of this brief life."[47]

The Christians and their God were not to blame for Rome's fall. The pagans and their gods were the real culprits, and they would have been totally wiped out if it hadn't been for the safe haven provided by the one true God through His people, the church.

In the centuries that followed, the church continued to flourish despite the Roman Empire's continued decline, barbarian invasions, and bitter political fights over territory and the grandeur of power. She continued to grow in her understanding and application of the deposit of the faith that had been entrusted to her. Ironically enough, heretical teachings within her midst helped her plumb the depths of her doctrinal heritage, especially those concerning the Trinity and the Incarnation. In councils and creeds, the church grasped more fully and stated more clearly the treasures of the faith she held dear.

Tragically, though, the seeds of schism were growing too. That unity the church had so prized and protected against outsiders and insiders alike would be ripped apart, and the consequences of the divide would follow the church through the second millennium of her existence.

CHAPTER ELEVEN

THE BREAKDOWN OF THE FAMILY

A Punch in the Mouth
for the Lutheran Lying Wide-Gaping Throats
Title of booklet by Paul Bachmann, Catholic abbot

One Hundred Select, Great, Shameless,
Fat, Well-Swilled, Stinking,
Papistical Lies
Title of treatise by Jerome Rauscher,
Protestant chaplain

All families, regardless of their apparent or real health, have problems. Granted, the type, number, and degree of the problems vary from family to family, but they are always present. Some of the most serious arise out of the depth of injury inflicted on children in a family affected by divorce, drug or alcohol abuse, trauma, or domestic violence. Those children grow up affected in some way by the mistakes and sins of their parents. Then they have children and pass the problems, perhaps in an altered form, on to them. The problems may change form and intensity over time, but unless someone in the family takes the appropriate steps to short-circuit the corruption and its effects, they will continue unabated from generation to generation.

Because this pattern of generational disorder has gotten so much media attention in recent years, we have become much more aware of it. This new awareness has also given birth to a number of new terms to describe the disorder, such as *dysfunctional*. But this generational disorder is not new. It has been with us since the fall of our first parents, Adam and Eve. The Bible records its terrible legacy, but even extra-biblical history witnesses to its destructiveness as well. The Scriptures are right: The iniquity of the parents *is* passed on from generation to generation.[1]

Of course, what we receive from our parents isn't all bad. Much good is transferred as well. Jesus even acknowledged that people marred by sin still manage to pass on good things to their children.[2]

What's true in natural families holds true in the Family of God, the church. We too enjoy the benefits as well as suffer from the sins passed on by our forefathers. In the previous chapter, we saw many of the benefits and how they held the church together. The Family had much in common, and she clung to it, thrived under it, and protected it with courage and tenacity. For a thousand years, the church enjoyed and worked to retain her visible and historical unity in Christ. But even during this time, schisms were a constant threat. Sometimes they challenged the church's common theology, other times her leadership. On occasion her close ties to the state created internal conflicts, or sometimes it was her strained relationships with certain political rulers that led to factious arguments in her midst. Whatever the tension, the church usually did her best to address it comprehensively, fairly, and always with an eye toward maintaining her unity, much like the church did during her first ecumenical council.

Nonetheless, in time the strains became too great and, in some cases, egos and the lure for power too big. The first major church split took place in the eleventh century over political, ecclesiastical, theological, and even liturgical issues. "In 1054, the patriarch of Constantinople, Michael Caerularius, criticized certain Western Church practices, addressed the pope as brother instead of father, and refused for three months to see the pope's legates who had come to Constantinople. These legates finally left a Bull of Excommunication on the altar of the patriarch's church and left Constantinople. . . . A few days later, Michael Caerularius responded by excommunicating the papal legates and the pope."[3] These mutual excommunications marked the split—called the Great Schism—between western and eastern Christians. From that moment, the Roman Catholic Church and the Greek Orthodox Church went different ways.

Although a good deal of reconciliation and healing still needs to take place between Catholics and Orthodox, official steps were begun on December 7, 1965, when Pope Paul VI and Athenagoras revoked the mutual excommunication decrees that had been blocking reunification efforts between the two churches for almost a thousand years. Since then, the work of reunifying the Eastern Orthodox Church and the Roman Catholic Church has been moving along at a welcome pace.

As difficult as the Great Schism was on the church, it didn't leave the depth of hurt, anger, and divisiveness that we now see throughout the church worldwide. That legacy falls on the shoulders of the Reformation.

It began with an Augustinian Catholic monk named Martin Luther and his nailing of "Ninety-five Theses on Indulgences" to the chapel door at Wittenberg. His intent was to open a scholarly debate on the issue toward the end of correcting some genuine abuses in the church. At this time Luther had no plans to leave the Catholic Church. But after a few years, Luther would write "three treatises denouncing the authority of the Catholic Church and the popes, rejecting the sacraments of the Church (except baptism, the Lord's Supper or Eucharist, and penance), and calling for the Christian princes of Germany to rise up and start their own national church."[4] Many of the German princes sided with Luther—and not primarily for doctrinal reasons—and helped him start the Lutheran church. Then at the Diet of Worms in 1521, Luther was formally excommunicated from the Catholic Church. The Reformation had begun.

Some Christians followed Luther, and other like-minded reformers rose up, propounded doctrines different from both Catholicism and Lutheranism, and began more new movements outside the Catholic Church's umbrella. The protest leaders and their followers came to be known as Protestants. Once outside the Catholic Church, however, they had little impetus to stay together and no overarching authority to hold them together. They soon splintered into more groups until today well more than two hundred Protestant denominations exist in the United States alone. And more are still coming into existence.[5]

The church's unity had been shattered beyond anyone's expectations. Now not only East and West were divided but so was the West itself. Christians who had at one time shared the Eucharist together, studied and prayed together, defended each other, protected one another from outside persecutors, and discussed and worked through a variety of issues together with a sense of mutual respect, were now fighting among themselves, accusing one another of not adhering to the "true faith," and even persecuting each other to the point of death. Catholics were killing Protestants, Protestants were killing Catholics, and some Protestants were killing other Protestants. The back-and-forth mudslinging was appalling. Timothy George recounts one instance: "Paul Bachmann [an abbot] published a virulent anti-Protestant booklet entitled 'A Punch in the Mouth for the Lutheran Lying Wide-Gaping Throats.' Not to be outdone, the Protestant court chaplain, Jerome Rauscher, responded with a treatise of his own, entitled 'One Hundred Select, Great, Shameless,

Fat, Well-Swilled, Stinking, Papistical Lies.'"[6] It was a tragic time in the history of the church.

I have no intention to assess blame against Protestants or Catholics for this terrible split. Enough mistakes were made on both sides. Neither do I ignore the positive impact and necessary correctives the Reformation caused in and outside the Roman Catholic Church (which all church leaders, including my own, have acknowledged). But the fact of the matter is that the Protestant Reformation movement and the church's response to it led to a traumatic family split—a radical divorce—and hundreds of years later we are still suffering from its impact. You and I are children of this great divorce, descendants of a single family tree divided by mistrust, failure, and abuse. We can see its devastation everywhere, even in what is left unsaid or ignored.

WEST VERSUS EAST?

When the Berlin Wall began coming down in 1989, I saw several reports on Christian television programs, most of which showed Eastern European Christians packing small Protestant churches. While I was delighted to see believers finally free to assemble and worship in the open, I was disturbed by the underlying message that was being communicated. The message wasn't voiced, but the omission in the images spoke louder than words. These reports did not mention or show any of the countless thousands of Family members in the Orthodox and Catholic churches who lived, worshiped, and ministered in Eastern Europe even while the Berlin Wall had kept East and West divided. What role did these believers play in the wall's collapse? No role at all was the impression viewers received. Instead, the cause of the wall coming down was attributed to the prayers of Protestant believers in the West.

This really bothered me. I find it presumptuous to believe that our prayers in the West alone brought down the Berlin Wall. I'm even more troubled by the underlying assertion that it was the prayers of Western Protestant Christians that cast the deciding blow. What about all those Catholic and Orthodox Christians in Eastern Europe who prayed, fasted, sacrificed for their fellow brothers and sisters in the faith, and even gave up their lives for Christ? Were their efforts not enough to pierce the heavens and rouse our common Father to action? The only way one could answer in the affirmative is if one believed that Orthodox and Catholic Christians are not full Christians or perhaps not Christians at all, or if one thought that their involvement in Eastern European political affairs was negligible or ineffective. That is sad thinking indeed.

We would be much closer to the truth if we saw that in many respects these Eastern believers have earned the name Christian more than we have in the West. Compared to what they faced, our lives have been a picnic. They have suffered through violent revolutions, bloodthirsty dictators, terribly oppressive religious and economic policies, and governmental intrusions into their lives that we can hardly imagine. And out of their struggle have come some of the most dynamic and powerful Christian voices in the church today. Remember, from Poland's bloodied, fertile ground, enriched by martyrs of the faith, has come Pope John Paul II, who now proclaims the gospel in power to all peoples worldwide. And it was from the Gulags of Russia that Aleksandr Solzhenitsyn was tempered in mind, will, and body to become one of the world's most respected modern-day prophets. And, of course, there are the thousands of not-so-famous "white martyrs," those who sacrificially offered their lives for Christ but were not privileged to shed their blood. Some of them suffered the most, and there have been millions of them in Russia, Poland, Hungary, Lithuania, Estonia, and throughout the rest of the Eastern bloc. Pastors, priests, monks, nuns, bishops, evangelists, teachers, preachers, and millions of lay faithful who gave their all so some might be saved.

Who are we Western Christians to believe that our prayers . . . our faith . . . our anything tilted the scales of power? And what should we make of those Christians who dared to suggest that believers from one tradition or confession only, of which many of these Eastern Christians were not a part, were the true remnant, the only fully faithful who had lived for Christ under socialism and communism and fascism?

While I would grant that not everyone who calls himself a Christian is one, I think it's naive at best and arrogant at worst for us in the West to rush into the East to evangelize it under the assumption that there are few if any true Christians there. Too many of us seem to think that unless Eastern professing Christians behave and believe *exactly* as we do that they therefore lack a saving relationship with Jesus Christ. I am not saying we should refuse to evangelize foreign lands, but if the church is already there, let's support her efforts there rather than subvert them with our own brand of religious bigotry, no matter how well intentioned it may be.

If you doubt the church is present in the Orthodox and Catholic churches of the East, ponder the observations of Paul Weyrich, president of the Free Congress Foundation. In 1989 he went to Hungary, Estonia, and what was then still the Soviet Union. What he reported should make all of us in the West sit up and listen.

> One thing that I found fascinating was the situation regarding the Orthodox Church. Some 3,000 churches have been returned to use in the past two years. I attended St. Michael the Archangel Russian Orthodox Church in the outskirts of Moscow on a Sunday where hundreds of believers packed into a building which, up until February of 1989, was used to store tractors.
>
> The main part of the church was under restoration, so the iconographers and plasterers were there trying to restore the church, which meant the services had to be held in a foyer with a temporary altar. People were literally stuffed into this church, and hundreds more were outside.
>
> John Exnicios and I witnessed twenty baptisms, and many of these were young men who, at 18 to 20 years old, were obviously not coerced by their parents, but were stepping forward as believing Christians. The priests officiating couldn't have been more than 22 or 23 years old.
>
> In Zagorsk, the home of the largest operating monasteries in the Soviet Union, I was able to talk to the director of the academic system for the Moscow Patriarchate. He said that they just opened new seminaries this year in Minsk and Kiev and that they are also training priests in parochial schools. But they can't train enough of them so anyone who expresses interest in becoming a priest is being ordained without theological or liturgical training. Because they didn't have 3,000 clergy to operate the churches that have been turned over to them, they have many untrained people running parishes.[7]

Similar reports regarding other Orthodox Christians abound and are paralleled by reports of the heroic faith of Catholic Christians in the Eastern bloc countries. Take a look at Lithuania, for example.

Catholics such as Father Sigitas Tamkevicius and Sister Nijoie Sadunaite have persevered in the faith throughout the Soviet occupation of Lithuania.

On May 6, 1963, Father Tamkevicius was arrested and banished to a labor camp. Among the charges brought against him were delivering anti-Soviet sermons, catechizing children, providing assistance to political prisoners and their families, organizing a Christmas party for parish youth, and organizing an All Souls' Day procession to a cemetery. During his labor-camp term, Tamkevicius was twice offered release if he would sign a confession of guilt. He refused both times. Eventually, however, his sentence was reduced, and he was transferred to exile in Siberias Tomskaya Oblast in May of 1988, where he remained until his release in 1990. He now serves as the spiritual director of the larger of two Lithuanian seminaries training leaders for the church of the twenty-first century.

Sister Nijoie Sadunaite (or Sister Terese, as she is known in her community, the Sister Servants of Mary) secretly professed religious life in Poland because all Catholic religious orders were banned by Soviet law. In her memoirs *How I Became a Target of the KGB*, she recounts her arrest by the KGB in 1974. She served three years at hard labor in Mordovia and three years of internal exile, but none of this took the angelic smile off her face or the gleam of God's love from her radiant eyes. She now frequently speaks internationally of the power of prayer and God's faithfulness.

Not too long ago, I had the privilege of spending the afternoon with Father Tamkevicius and Sister Sadunaite. They sat in front of me and, through an interpreter, shared their love for Christ and their need for prayer. It was a deeply moving evangelical moment for me.

There are so many more heroes of faith like them. And they can be found across the globe. Yet too often Christians gear their most prominent evangelistic efforts toward other Christians. To presume that these other children of the great divorce aren't Christians and to impose an Americanized evangelical Protestant Christianity, with its attendant culture, on them is terribly judgmental and narrow-minded. We should be going to serve them with a basin, towel, and washcloth, recognizing what the Spirit of God is already doing in all Christian churches in Eastern Europe and throughout the rest of the world.

CHRISTIAN VERSUS CHRISTIAN?

Christians from every tradition and confession are members of the same Family. Consequently, as fellow Family members, we should "rejoice with those who rejoice; mourn with those who mourn."[8] Right? That's the biblical ideal, but it's not the usual way contemporary Christians respond to one another. More often than not, our shared rejoicing and suffering don't even involve fellow believers, unless they are our immediate relatives. Most of us don't even recognize our fellow Christians as Christians. Instead we see only those in or close to our theological or ecclesiastical persuasions as true believers; all others are on the outside looking in.

This damaging perspective is found throughout the Christian community. As is often true for the children of a domestic divorce, choosing sides in the division of the church too frequently entails an imputation of righteousness for "us" and unrighteousness for "them." We are all too good at self-justification. "Look at what you did. I didn't deserve that. Besides, think about all I've done for you, and you still mistreat me and refuse to thank me." Perspectives and attitudes like these plague a family suffering divorce, including our church Family. Many Protestants see the Catholic Church as enamored with itself, seeing itself as the "only church" and having little room for adjustment. Many Catholics have felt the same way about Protestant churches. Consequently, Catholics and Protestants often see themselves as the sole possessors of truth. They look upon each other condescendingly, refuse to move toward each other in dialogue but try to evangelize one another, assuming that the "other side" has embraced a false gospel and needs to be set straight. This form of religious bigotry knows no denominational or ecclesiastical boundaries. And when it expresses itself in evangelistic and missionary endeavors, it is particularly harmful and ugly.

So it is with a divorce. Even generations later the effects of the trauma still manifest themselves—not so much in issues, though they cloaked themselves in that language early on, but in prejudice and ignorance. We may not remember or even know what brought about the divorce, but we sure know whose side we're on and *who was "right."*

THE PATTERN IN THE SPLIT

Since 1973, I have been involved in what is often called the Catholic charismatic renewal or the Catholic Pentecostal Movement. (I guess that makes me a Pentecostal, evangelical, Catholic Christian!) For many years I was also directly involved in the communitarian wing of that renewal. The communities, or fellowships, born of this movement literally span the globe. These groups have struggled with many differences of opinion. Indeed, deep and painful rifts have led to separations on occasion. Through all this I have observed a phenomenon that is typically present in our Christian Family history—one we all too often refuse to admit.

What seems to happen before divisions occur is a serious, unresolved relationship struggle, which often takes place between key leaders. The pain of the struggle is so great that it is never properly resolved, hence reconciliation and healing remain elusive. Soon the issues, which often weren't insurmountable at first, become the ammunition everyone fires at each other. People then begin developing theological and philosophical platforms, which they mount first for protection and then for a frontal assault. All too soon, the relationship struggle that had led to the conflict falls to the wayside, and the issues that were generally smoke screens come to the front. Loyal followers of each of the warring leaders embrace the cause, and this escalates the war. All the while, though, a deep, untreated relational wound is lying under the new crusade. It goes untreated because it is now covered over with "righteousness" or "right doctrine," much of which is really laced with misunderstandings and caricatures similar to what Christians experienced at the hands of pagans during the first several hundred years of the church's existence. The longer the wound festers, the more infected it becomes, and the more it poisons many well-intentioned warriors.

I propose that the major splits the Christian church has suffered follow just such a pattern. I am not downplaying the genuine and important issues related to any or all of the splits. But in relationship to maintaining our unity and love as members of the Family of families, these issues pale in significance. We must maintain a focus on our Family relationship. After all, it is the heartthrob of Jesus for us all. As our common Lord prayed, "My prayer is not for them alone. I pray also for those who will believe in me through their message, that all of them may be one, Father, just as you are in me and I am in you. May they also be in us so that the world may believe that you have sent me. I have given them the glory that you gave me, that they may be one as we are one: I in them and you in me. May they be brought to complete unity to let the world know that you sent me and have loved them even as you have loved me."[9]

In my own experience of building community, I have seen some of the wounds of divorce fester, but I have also seen many more heal. Tragically, however, the experience of the broader Christian church is quite different. Catholics and Protestants oppose one another in Mexico, Northern Ireland, Latin America, and many other places throughout the world. And the Devil laughs. He too knows what Jesus told us, that "a house divided against itself will fall."[10] Satan wants the church to collapse in relational rubble, and history shows he has accomplished much toward his objective. Tragically, we have cooperated with him well. We have faithfully passed on from generation to generation the deep injuries of our divorce. Our challenge is to stop the chain of pain by healing the relational wounds festering below the surface of the issues.

HEALING THE WOUNDS OF DIVORCE

As we stand at the end of one millennium and the threshold of another, I believe that the opportunity for such a healing has perhaps never been greater. The drafting and signing of the accord "Evangelicals and Catholics Together: The Christian Mission in the Third Millennium" is a great step forward. Readily acknowledging the presence of important differences between Protestants and Catholics, the accord recognizes the tremendous number of commonalities between those groups and calls upon them to converge and cooperate together for social change and world evangelization on the basis of all they hold in common. The accord also confesses as sin what both groups have done to divide asunder the unity of the Body of Christ. Citing the accord:

> As Christ is one, so the Christian mission is one. That one mission can be and should be advanced in diverse ways. Legitimate diversity, however, should not be confused with existing divisions between Christians that obscure the one Christ and hinder the one mission. There is a necessary connection between the visible unity of Christians and the mission of the one Christ. We together pray for the fulfillment of the prayer of Our Lord: "May they all be one; as you, Father, are in me and I in you, so also may they be in us, that the world may believe that you sent me." (John 17) We together, Evangelicals and Catholics, confess our sins against the unity that Christ intends for all his disciples.
>
> The one Christ and one mission includes many other Christians, notably the Eastern Orthodox and those Protestants not commonly identified as Evangelical. All Christians are encompassed in the prayer, "May they all be one," . . .[11]

That is the message the church so desperately needs. That is the attitude and perspective and understanding we must have toward each other. That is the way toward healing the devastating wounds of divorce. We—Protestants, Catholics, and Orthodox—are members of the same household of faith as long as Jesus is our Head individually and corporately. There really is only "one body and one Spirit . . . one hope . . . one Lord, one faith, one baptism; one God and Father of all, who is over all and through all and in all."[12] The divisions that have come about in the Body are not attributable to God. He did not create them, nor has He condoned them. God hates divorce, whether it occurs in the bonds of marriage or in the Family called the church.[13] No matter how valid our conflicts with one another may have been and perhaps still are, they should never have led to schism and they should not continue to divide us now.

Centuries ago, one of Jesus' disciples told Him that he and the other disciples had come across a man who was casting out demons in Jesus' name. Because this man was not counted among Jesus' regular disciples, the disciples told him to cease and desist. Jesus told them they should not have done that. "'Do not stop him,' Jesus said, 'for whoever is not against you is for you.'"[14] We tend to act too much like the disciples in this way. Rather than applaud and support one another's efforts done in Christ's name, we look at one another with suspicion, we treat each other with disdain, and we do what we can to stop each other. How sad this must make our common Lord. How much energy we waste futilely fighting one another. How much sadistic delight we must bring to the Evil One.

We must be for one another and stop taking sides against one another. We must recognize that the whole Christian church—Protestant, Catholic, and Orthodox—is in need of reevangelization, repentance, renewal, and reformation. Christ instituted a united church. The Spirit gifted the church so it could mature in unity. We have violated that unity. Therefore we need to ask for one another's forgiveness, and we need to seek the mercy of God and ask for His forgiveness as well.

The Lord is waiting. A dying world is waiting. Will we, the church, rise to the occasion? Will we stop pointing our guns at one another and begin cooperating with one another, standing together as a unified beacon of light to penetrate the darkness with the good news about Christ, our common Savior and Lord? Will we start reexamining and dropping our long-held prejudices so we can rediscover our common Family heritage? Will we take the necessary steps to break the insidious cycle of move, countermove, pain, and mistrust?

The primary symbol of division in Europe has finally been torn down. The Berlin Wall lies in ruin, a relic of a political divorce now undergoing healing. From that wall a shout and cry for freedom are leading to a radical restructuring of all of Eastern Europe. The yoke of atheistic communism is falling from the necks of oppressed people elsewhere as well.

Can the church of Jesus Christ, the Family of God, do the same? Can we tear down the walls that divide us and reunite, at least to cooperate in the transformation of culture? If we don't come together to make common cause and recapture the world for Christ, who will? History proves that when goodness leaves a vacuum, evil rushes in to fill it. The church is here to be good and do good, but she cannot do that effectively as long as the evil of divisiveness continues to haunt her.

We must face the current crisis together, confronting it on the basis of a common evangelical agenda—an agenda that acknowledges the existence of evangelical Christians in all Christian communions and recognizes our common apostolic heritage. Advocates of such an agenda must be characterized by mutual respect and a compelling desire to see Jesus Christ loved and honored.

This kind of cooperation, however, means we must strive to overcome the devastation of divorce. That won't be easy. It never is. We will make mistakes. I and those I have worked with have made many errors in our ecumenical efforts. Nevertheless, we can't bring about change if we don't make any moves. Learning comes by doing. We can learn how to work together if we try doing it, but if we don't try we'll never learn, and if we don't learn, the world may never know as it could who Jesus is and why He came to die and what He can do to return sanity and hope to an insane, despairing world.

I believe we can overcome the prejudice and bitterness and misunderstandings that divide us. With God all things are possible, and we know that unity is God's will for His Family. So, as far as I can see, the real questions for us are not, Can we cooperate? or, Should we cooperate? I don't believe our obedience to God and His will for us makes those questions viable. The real questions, I think, are, Will we cooperate? and, How will we do it?

In the rest of this book, I want to focus on these last questions. I want to look at the roadblocks to cooperation and expose some of the pitfalls we should avoid. I also want to propose a doctrinal basis and social agenda upon which we can make common cause. I then want to examine alliance building more closely. What does it involve? Who's building ecumenical alliances and what can we learn from them? There's much we can gain from each other. While I don't presume to have all the answers, I and many others have learned some lessons along the alliance-building way I'd like to pass on to you. I hope you will do the same for me. Together, we can make a difference. We must.

PART IV

Barriers to Family Reunion

CHAPTER TWELVE

Sticks and Stones

With the tongue we praise our Lord and Father,
and with it we curse men,
who have been made in God's likeness.
Out of the same mouth come praise and cursing.
My brothers, this should not be.
James, the apostle

"Sticks and stones may break my bones, but words will never hurt me."

When did you first hear that saying? More than likely, it was when you were a child. Someone said something awful to you. Perhaps the way you dressed or fixed your hair was the object of ridicule. Or maybe your sister, brother, or even parents had been verbally assaulted in some way. Maybe the kind of music you listened to or a comment you innocently made set off the criticism. Whatever it was, the words leveled against you stung like a hundred bees. The poison burned in your soul, wounding you deeply and profoundly.

You ran home looking for solace. You desperately wanted someone you trusted to tell you that what was said was a lie, that you and your family were really okay. You found your mom or dad, perhaps a close relative or even an older sibling. You poured out your heart.

They listened, calmed your spirit, and refuted the criticism. Then they told you that words don't have to hurt so much. That if people had thrown sticks and stones at you, they would have caused you much more pain than words could ever cause. They told you that saying, gave you another hug and kiss, and sent you on your way.

The next time words wounded you, you recalled the proverb "Sticks and stones may break my bones, but words will never hurt me." You repeated this over and over to yourself and even said it out loud to your verbal assailant. Then inside you pushed down the hurt while you clung to the saying. You desperately wanted to believe it while your heart cried out, "It's not true! It's not true!"

Your heart was right. Words can often wound us so deeply that the scars can last our lifetime and even get passed on to our children and to their children and even beyond. Words can irreparably damage reputations. They can lead to financial ruin. They can topple professional and political leaders. They can break up friendships and destroy marriages. They can set brothers against sisters and turn in-laws into outlaws. They can cause far more havoc than sticks or stones could ever cause.

In the Body of Christ, words are to be used to edify and instruct, to offer repentance and to seek forgiveness, to share with others the salvation Christ makes available to all, to spur one another on to live virtuously, to defend one another against false accusations, to give reasons to unbelievers for the hope we have in Christ, to raise our petitions and praises to Heaven.

Tragically, however, words have frequently been used a different way. Flung like spears in the night, Christians have wounded fellow Christians with words. False accusations, vicious caricatures, innuendoes, rumors. No matter how well intentioned or misguided, when Christians have used words in such ways, they have hurt not only individual Family members and groups within the Family but the entire Family of God. The Body is one, not many, even if our visible unity is in disarray. So when we rail at each other as if we were Family antagonists rather than Family members, we bring disrepute to the whole Family. Every member suffers.

I want to address this Family problem. But I want it to be clear that my intention is not to assign blame to any individual or group. Every Christian community has been injured by words. Indeed, if psychology has demonstrated anything, it's that those individuals or groups who seem to operate with the instructions "Seek and destroy" are usually those who have been wounded most deeply by the very tactics they use against others. When you look around the Body of Christ with this perspective, you can see many among us who need counsel and prayer for the healing of their wounded souls.

With this said, I would like to look at several ways words have been used to wreak damage in God's family. Because I'm Roman Catholic, most of my examples will come from anti-Catholic critics. But I readily acknowledge that Protestants could choose many examples from anti-Protestant literature as could Orthodox from anti-Orthodox material. We've all been attacked unfairly.

I would also like to say that not every criticism made against any Christian or Christian group is false just because it's critical or hurts. These proverbs are true: "Faithful are the wounds of a friend"; "As iron sharpens iron, so a man sharpens the countenance of his friend"; "Open rebuke is better than love carefully concealed."[1] But notice the tenor of these sayings. They are talking about needed corrections and challenges that come from true friends and loving family. They are not endorsing vitriolic assaults that create new wounds and pour acid onto old ones.

The Christian church is not perfect; she never has been. We have all made mistakes, we have sinned against one another, and we have turned the church into camps of warring factions. The solution is not to keep justifying ourselves and developing more destructive weapons to turn on each other. The solution is to repent, seek forgiveness, turn our diatribes into dialogues, and treat our mutual seeking after truth with respect.

I love my church, but I am also very aware of her mistakes. So is Pope John Paul II. On June 13, 1994, John Paul opened an extraordinary meeting of cardinals. The meeting's purpose was to plan how the church will mark the beginning of the third millennium of Christianity in the year 2000. He made it clear that one of the church's efforts must be to deal with "the historic failings and negligence of its sons." He referred to a twenty-five-page memo he had written on this matter. "How can one remain silent," the memo said, "about the many forms of violence perpetrated in the name of the faith?—wars of religion, tribunals of the Inquisition and other forms of violations of the rights of persons."[2]

This is not the first time John Paul or others within the Catholic community have owned responsibility for past mistakes and tragedies in order to bring healing to the Body of Christ and better prepare her for the challenge of the future. I'm aware of individuals from other Christian traditions and confessions who have tried to do the same. These are the voices we must heed. We need to join in their chorus and let the truth and humility in their words and actions do their healing work in the church through the ministry of the Holy Spirit. This is my prayer, my dream, my hope.

Aside from owning up to our past, we must also challenge those arguments and perspectives that seek to keep the pain alive and even intensify it. Whatever elements of truth they might contain, we should acknowledge those and act on them. But whatever errors they convey should be challenged and corrected. This is the spirit in which I seek to answer some of the more persistent and often pernicious charges raised against my tradition. I will deal with two: Catholicism teaches a false gospel, and Catholicism is the false religion of the Antichrist.

By even mentioning and answering these charges, I run the risk of lending credence to them. That is not my intention. I believe both of these charges are groundless. But alas, the effects of divorce can be quite ugly, so in an attempt to set the record straight, much as the early Christian apologists did, I have chosen to address head-on what I believe are pseudo-objections based on terrible misunderstandings and miscon- structions of true Catholic doctrine.

Because the first charge strikes at the heart of what it means to be Christian, I will tackle it first and most fully. Indeed, the other charge has little to stand on if the first is shown to be false, which it certainly is!

NOT A FALSE GOSPEL

Many Christians misunderstand the Catholic theology of salvation as one of salvation by "good works." Catholics, they say, try to earn Jesus' acceptance into Heaven's gate by performing deeds that would please Him. That's how such critics explain the fact that Catholics are so often engaged in feeding the hungry, housing the homeless, caring for the sick, and the like. They believe Catholics have rejected the true gospel of sal- vation by faith alone through Christ alone by grace alone. Instead, they charge, Catholics have accepted the false gospel of salvation by faith plus good works apart from grace, which undermines Christ's redemp- tive work on the cross.

Although some Catholics, as well as some Protestants, have adopted the "gospel" of faith plus good works equals salvation, this view does *not* represent Catholic theology. As we will see, there is an integral place for the deeds of faith (not deeds done apart from or in addition to faith) in the salvation process, but this must be understood in light of the *full* expression of the biblical concept of salvation. And this understanding flows from the biblical view of the human dilemma.

Our Dilemma
We sin. In numerous ways and for a variety of reasons, we violate God's directives. Human beings have done this for centuries, ever since our first parents, Adam and Eve, defied God in the Garden of Eden. As a result of our first parents' original sin, we have received a mixed inher- itance: a corrupted condition that separates us from our Creator and

makes it easier for us to rebel against Him.

The consequences of this fallen condition are staggering. Not only has it created a chasm between us and the Lord, but it has separated us from ourselves, from our friends, from our spouses, from our neighbors, and from our world. Our every relationship has been affected. Now instead of exuding the natural outflow of transparency and intimacy, we hide our true selves from others and even struggle with coming to know who we really are in ourselves.[3] *Death*, which means "separation" in Scripture, has permeated our lives. As the Apostle Paul observed centuries ago, "sin entered the world through one man, and death through sin, and in this way death came to all men, because all sinned."[4]

The theological terms often used in an attempt to describe the wounds caused by sin are not always helpful. The most common phrase is "fallen nature," and in many Protestant circles, the word *depravity*. The meaning of "fallen nature" and its extent have been debated among Christians for centuries. Some have understood it to mean that people are in complete bondage to sin; they cannot perform any good deeds, nor can they reach out to God in faith unless He first gives them the faith to exercise. Fallen humans, they say, are intrinsically evil: Sin is now an integral part of their nature; it has virtually destroyed their ability to will freely, to think rationally, to feel compassionately, to behave unselfishly. In other words, humanity is totally and literally dead in sin; like a physical corpse in a coffin, so is humanity—unable to find God, hear Him, or respond to Him.

Roman Catholics, however, take issue with this picture of humankind. They believe that it overemphasizes some portions of Scripture while neglecting the clear thrust of other passages. In contrast, they appeal to the full teaching of Scripture, seeking to allow it to set fuller parameters for a Christian understanding of humankind's fallen nature. Within these broader scriptural boundaries, a different picture develops.

First, the Bible presents several models of human fallenness. One model is certainly that of death: Humans are dead in sin and need new life (Ephesians 2:1-6, Colossians 2:13). But this does not mean we are unable to respond to God; rather, it means that sin has separated us from Him and that we need to be reunited to Him. The other biblical models confirm this. We are sick with sin and in need of healing (Mark 2:17). We are impoverished by sin and need God's riches (Luke 4:18, 2 Corinthians 8:9, Ephesians 2:7). We are polluted or defiled by sin and need to be cleansed (Mark 7:14-23, Ephesians 5:25-27, Titus 1:15, 1 John 1:7-9). We are lost in the darkness of sin and desperately need the light of Christ (John 8:12, 12:35). We are blinded by sin and need our sight restored (Luke 4:18, 2 Corinthians 4:3-6). We are enslaved to sin and need to be liberated from it (Luke 4:18, John 8:31-36, Romans 6:16-18). All of these models depict our sad, desperate condition, but none of them even implies that we cannot respond to God.

Second, the Scriptures resoundingly declare that all human beings are marred by sin (Ecclesiastes 7:29; Romans 3:9-18,23). Catholics, however, believe that one virgin from Nazareth was preserved from this corrupting influence for the incredible task of bearing the Son of God. And in the words of Elizabeth's proclamation, the virgin Mary was and still is "blessed . . . among women."[5] Catholics believe she was kept from any tarnish of sin precisely so she could bear the untarnished One, whose spotless life, substitutionary death, resurrection, and ascension would pave the way of salvation for us. Mary's preservation from sin is a mystery because she, like us, was saved by the One she bore.[6]

Third, because every aspect of humanity has been affected by sin, humanity needs to be sanctified (or purified) entirely. Our minds, emotions, will, body, soul—all that we are has been affected by sin, but sin has not destroyed us or our abilities.

Fourth, "depravity" could not mean that people are evil *in themselves.* Scripture is clear: *Everything* God created is still intrinsically good, and this includes all humankind (Mark 7:14-23; Romans 8:18-23, 14:14; 1 Timothy 4:4; Titus 1:15). In addition, human beings were created as God's image-bearers, and sin's entrance into the world did not destroy the divine image in them (Genesis 1:26-27, 9:6; James 3:9). We still reflect, however dimly, the character and presence of deity (Psalm 8:6).

On the other hand, we have definitely been effaced by sin, much as rust effaces metal or as wind and water efface rock. But humankind is not essentially evil. Evil is a parasite. It exists in good things, but it cannot exist on its own. Protestant apologist Norman Geisler explains this well. He builds his explanation on an understanding of evil more fully developed in the writings of Augustine and Thomas Aquinas:

> A man born without sight is subject to an evil. The evil is the lack or privation of sight—something that belongs to the natural order. . . .
>
> To say that evil is a privation is not the same as saying that it is a mere absence or negation of good. The power of sight is found neither in a blind man nor in a rock. But it is a privation for the blind man, whereas it is a mere absence in the rock. A

privation is the absence (or lack) of something that ought to be there.

As well, metaphysical evil is not a mere negation or unreality. Privations are real and physical. Blindness is a real and physical lack of sight. Being maimed is a positive and real lack of a limb. Sickness is a real physical lack of good health. A rusty car, a moth-eaten garment, and a wounded body are physical examples of real corruptions in otherwise good things. In each case, there is a real lack or corruption that leaves what remains in a state of incapacitation.[7]

Therefore, if we were devoid of good, evil could not exist in us. And if our natures were intrinsically evil, we could not exist at all—not any more than a totally moth-eaten garment or a totally rusted car could exist. In other words, we could not be *totally* depraved, if that means we are devoid of good or Godlikeness.

Fifth, fallen people can and do accomplish good works. Jesus affirmed this when He said, "Which of you, if his son asks for bread, will give him a stone? Or if he asks for a fish, will give him a snake? If you, then, though you are evil, know how to give good gifts to your children, how much more will your Father in heaven give good gifts to those who ask him!"[8] But the Scriptures also state that fallen people cannot perform any good work that could justify them before God (Isaiah 64:6, Galatians 2:16, Ephesians 2:8-9, Titus 3:3-7).

In short, the biblical view of human fallenness is that *all human beings are morally, intellectually, emotionally, volitionally, spiritually, and physically corrupted because of sin.* As a consequence of the original sin of our first parents, we have inherited and surrendered ourselves to a distorted, corrupted nature. We have dug ourselves into a pit so deep that we can't climb out of it. But because we are God's creatures and image-bearers, we are not *totally* depraved or evil.

God's Solution to Our Dilemma
So what's the solution to our dilemma? How can we get out of the pit of sin? We need someone to have mercy on us and reach down to pull us out. We need a rescuer, a savior. But this person can't be someone who shares the pit with us. This deliverer must be above the pit, on the solid ground above—he must be, in other words, without sin. He also must be able to bridge the chasm between God and man, between holiness and corruption. We need a God-man, a sinless Savior, and the only Person

in human history who has ever fit that description and proved it through His words and deeds is Jesus Christ—the Son of God incarnate. When we freely place our trust in Him, God's undeserved gift of salvation from sin becomes ours. As Saint Paul said in his letter to the Christians in ancient Ephesus, "It is owing to his favor that salvation is yours through faith. This is not your own doing, it is God's gift; neither is it a reward for anything you have accomplished, so let no one pride himself on it."[9]

This truth is the mainstay of evangelical Christianity, but to understand it fully, we need to see it in the context of three central ideas of the Christian religion: (1) *grace*, which is God's unmerited and merciful favor; (2) *salvation*, which deals with our complete deliverance from sin; and (3) *faith*, which is the means whereby we receive God's gracious salvation. These are clearly exhibited in Paul's theology of grace, which can be discussed in terms of justification, sanctification, and glorification. Moreover, these three correspond to the Christian virtues of faith, love, and hope. All of these terms and concepts are an integral part of any discussion of salvation.

Grace and Justification

According to Paul, the first and primary grace is God's free gift of Himself to humans, which is indeed "amazing grace." Through Christ, God has communicated Himself personally to each one of us. And because of His gift of free will to us, we have the potential to either accept or reject His gift. By His grace, which is free and undeserved, He makes it possible for us to respond to Him and ushers us into His life when we come by faith. In Catholic theology, faith is the assent of the mind and will to God and to the truth of what He has revealed to us.

When I exercise faith in accepting God's free gift of grace in Christ, the Holy Spirit converts me and thereby brings about my justification. Moved by grace, I'm turned toward God and away from sin. In the biblical imagery, I'm set free from sin, my sight is restored, I'm made alive in Christ, I become the recipient of His matchless riches, my deepest wounds are healed. I am no longer separated from God but reconciled to Him. The corruption sin has wrought is reversed in my life. In fact, in the very center of my being, I am changed. I am not merely forgiven, though that occurs. I am also purified; I am made a new creation. Put another way, justification not only declares me righteous but makes me righteous. "Justification is not only the remission of sins, but also the sanctification and renewal of the interior man."[10] God makes me just, He doesn't just declare me so. He cleans my sin record and purges me of my sins.

With corruption purged, God pours into my being "faith, hope, and charity" and the ability to obey His will.[11] Now I can commit myself more fully to Him (faith). Now I can confidently look forward to and live in the light of beholding God eternally in the Kingdom of Heaven (hope). And now I can love God above all things for His own sake and love my neighbor as myself for the love of God (charity). This is the beginning of a new life in Christ that's empowered by His Spirit.

If you'll notice, no works are mentioned here except for what God does in us in response to our faith. And even our initial act of faith has grace as its precursor. The *Catechism of the Catholic Church* says it this way: "The *preparation of man* for the reception of grace is already a work of grace. This latter is needed to arouse and sustain our collaboration in justification through faith, and in sanctification through charity. God brings to completion in us what he has begun, 'since he who completes his work by cooperating with our will began by working so that we might will it.'"[12]

Some might object to this cooperation language. "Are you Catholics slipping in works through the back door? Are you saying with one voice that God does it all and with another that He doesn't?" What we're saying is when God made us in His image, He gave us the freedom to respond to Him positively or negatively. Sin has hurt our freedom, but it hasn't crushed it. Contrary to the view Martin Luther advocated in his work *The Bondage of the Will*, the Catholic Church denies we are mere puppets doing either God's will or Satan's. In fact, for Luther, every creature is like a hammer in the hands of the divine Carpenter—He uses us where He wants, when He wants, how He wants, and for whatever reason He wants. We have no say in the matter because we have no capacity to will our own actions. Hammers have no wills, only utilities. They can only do that which the Carpenter causes them to do.[13]

Contrary to this understanding, Catholicism teaches that God gives us the gift of causality. We have the ability to decide to accept God's love or spurn it. But God doesn't sit on His hands and wait on us. Being the Lover that He is, He pursues us, woos us, spreads His arms wide to receive us, even when we are raising our fists in defiance and shouting obscenities.[14] In this way, grace precedes our act of faith. God paves the way for us to come to Him. He gives us the freedom to respond to Him, the power to know Him, and the ability to love Him. He creates us with "a longing for truth and goodness that only he can satisfy."[15] Then He seeks us out and uses a variety of means, some of which are painful, to get us to wake up to His presence and respond positively to His marriage proposal. But God won't force us to come. He doesn't conduct shotgun weddings.

When we do accept His love offer, when we find in Him the satisfaction of our longings, He cooperates with our desire, which is His as well, and brings us to Himself. This is why the Catholic Church can proclaim, "The grace of Christ is the gratuitous gift that God makes to us of his own life, infused by the Holy Spirit into our soul to heal it of sin and to sanctify it."[16]

For those who still aren't sure that the doctrine of salvation is truly grace-filled in Catholic doctrine, let's look at the matter of infant baptism.

Infant Baptism: Evidence of Grace—To the Christian, the sign of the invisible reality of conversion is water baptism. Baptism is meant to be the doorway to a new way of living. It symbolically presupposes what is to come and what was left behind as it acts as a sign of the believer's initiation into the new life in Christ. In baptism, the old man—our corrupt sin nature—is submerged, and the new man—our new nature in Christ—emerges clothed in Christ and His transforming power. "This means that if anyone is in Christ, he is a new creation. The old order has passed away; now all is new!"[17]

Although we often think of baptism and salvation as an adult affair, the church recognized centuries ago that they apply to children, even to infants. In fact, we have good evidence that infant baptism was practiced in the church at least as far back as the second century, and perhaps even as early as the period of the apostles.[18] Certainly by the fifth century, infant baptism was universally accepted in the church. This practice arose because Christian couples who began to have children expressed a desire to fulfill the call of Jesus so their children would be saved: "Let the children come to me and do not hinder them. It is to just such as these that the kingdom of God belongs."[19]

This raises an obvious but important question: How can a baby be saved without acknowledging Jesus? It appears to many evangelical Christians that infant baptism renders faith obsolete as the foundation of one's relationship with the Lord. But is this true? As I see it and as the Roman Catholic Church has taught, infant baptism is just one more example of grace. Even our own exercise of faith cannot earn salvation. Faith simply gives us the opportunity to receive God's gracious gift of new life and walk in it. I am not downplaying faith's critical role in God's salvation plan; rather, I am saying that it is the means by which we receive what God freely offers to all. He reaches down to us so that in childlike faith we can unclench our defiant fists, open our hands, accept His salvific present, unwrap it, and spend the rest of our lives here and in the hereafter enjoying the plenitude of its blessings. Salvation is a gift. It cannot be earned. But it can be received—by faith.

Now since an infant cannot exercise faith, what role could baptism possibly play in his or her salvation? The answer involves first understanding the church as the Family of families. Since its inception, a critical presupposition has underscored infant baptism, and indeed the symbolic meaning of even adult baptism: namely, *the children of Christian parents are part of a faith-filled family called the domestic church, and these children are to be raised in the midst of a faith-filled local Christian community.* The church has believed that these two experiences would ensure that children would be raised as believers. It was assumed that the church and the family would instruct, nurture, and lead the newly baptized into a *full* assent to the faith. Full assent has necessarily included a personal decision and commitment to a lifelong relationship with Jesus Christ. Unfortunately, that commitment has sometimes been lacking in contemporary Christian experience. In other words, there are sacramentalized but unevangelized Catholics. The same is true in the Protestant and Eastern Orthodox traditions. In my own Catholic tradition, there is a tremendous effort to rediscover that full catechesis and community experience necessary for infant baptism, but much is left to be done.

Given the fact that baptism must be approached in faith and the church is the Family of families, I return to the original question: How can a baby be saved without acknowledging Jesus? Obviously, the infant cannot respond by faith. On the other hand, his parents, godparents, other believing relatives, and especially the church in its local expression can respond in his behalf. The faith exercised need not be his.

Does this sound radical or new? Actually, it's neither. Remember the paralytic Jesus forgave and healed? One day when Jesus was teaching, some men came along carrying a paralytic on a mat. They were trying to bring him in and lay him before Jesus. The crowd that had surrounded Jesus, however, was too large for them to get through. So they took a different tack. They took their debilitated friend up on the roof, removed some tiling, lowered their comrade into the middle of the crowd, and set him before Jesus. Seeing their faith, Jesus said to the paralytic, "My friend, your sins are forgiven you," and healed him.[20] It was not the faith of the paralytic that prompted the Master's intervention—it was the faith of his friends.

If this could happen to an adult who could have placed his own faith in Christ, how much more so for a tiny baby who cannot? Children, even infants, can be baptized into the faith by the community of the faithful so they can be nurtured in Christ until they are old enough to trust in Him personally. What a beautiful picture of unmerited divine grace in the salvation process. Salvation is truly preceded, undergirded, motivated, moved along, and greeted by divine grace. Infant baptism is evidence of this fact.

Sanctification and Love

"All right," someone might say. "So the Catholic Church teaches that the initial stage of salvation is by grace through faith apart from works. What about the process called sanctification? Are works involved there?" The simple answer to that is yes, but it must be understood in the larger context of the full Catholic doctrine of salvation.

Many Protestants believe that justification is tantamount to salvation: Once someone trusts in Christ by faith, she is a child of God's Family. Christ's righteousness is imputed to her but not infused in her. In other words, God views her through Christ as if she had no sin, but she is still a sinful being. Sanctification, they say, is the process God uses to move her out of a life of sin and into a life characterized by holiness. But sanctification should not be "confused" with justification. Justification by faith alone saves; sanctification purifies but has nothing of any real substance to do with one's salvation, only with the process of making one holy.

Catholics don't see sanctification quite this way. In Catholic theology, justification and baptism help to equip us, by means of God's objective presence within our souls, to live lives continually transformed in love. This is the life to which the Christian is called. It's the process known as *sanctification.* Though we may be justified by faith in a moment, our justification is deepened through the sanctification process. This day-to-day process makes us holy, not at once, but over the period of our lifetimes. God works in our lives through the virtues of faith, hope, and love to bring this result about. And in that process, He gives us the privilege and ability to cooperate with Him. Among these virtues, love is the greatest, as the Apostle Paul told us it was: "And now these three remain: faith, hope and love. But the greatest of these is love."[21] That's the virtue I'd like to focus on here.

In my own church, a document entitled "Dogmatic Constitution on the Church" comments upon the beautiful passage in the letter of 1 John wherein the beloved disciple reminds us that God is love.[22] The document says, "Love, as the bond of perfection and fullness of the law, governs, gives meaning to, and perfects all the means of sanctification. Hence the true disciple of Christ is marked by love both of God and of his neighbor."[23] Love for God and love for neighbor are two sides of the same coin. They must go together. In fact, as the Apostle John reminds us in that same letter, "Anyone who claims to be in the light but hates his brother is still in the darkness. Whoever loves his brother lives in the light, and there is nothing in him to make him stumble."[24] Mother Teresa is a living example of a faith-walk that manifests the two sides of this coin. Her intense love for God is displayed in her intense love for His creation.

So it must be with all of us. Our journey of faith is to manifest its genuineness through the fruit of our lives. If we do not bear fruit, our justification has not been worked out yet in our lives. True justification brings a change of heart, a change in the innermost part of our being. Therefore, if we are truly transformed and being evermore fully transformed into the image of Christ, our lives will show it. This is what James referred to when he wrote, "Show me your faith without works, and I will show you the faith that underlies my works!"[25]

The integral relationship between faith and works has long troubled many believers of all traditions. But the Catholic theological understanding of the biblical teaching is clear: *We are converted to Christ by faith, not because of our good works; and we do good works only because we have the divine grace to do so.* Our good works flow out of our love for God and that which God loves, His creation. Faith must express itself dynamically in a life of love. As Paul describes it, what counts is "faith working through love."[26] Faith and works go together in God's Family-life plan. Without faith, works have no everlasting value. Without works, faith has no everlasting value either. Works apart from faith are dead; faith apart from works is dead also. If faith is genuine, good works will follow, and if good works are genuinely of God, saving faith will be present. Faith and good works are inseparable.

The matter of merit—"So what's all this talk about merit in Catholic theology? Doesn't that signify that the Catholic Church teaches we can earn our salvation, that God owes us salvation for what we do for Him?" Absolutely not! God owes us nothing. We owe everything to Him. We can't even take our next breath without God sustaining us moment by moment in existence.[27] Jesus was absolutely and literally right when He said, "Without Me you can do nothing."[28] The *Catechism of the Catholic Church* confirms this: "With regard to God, there is no strict right to any merit on the part of man. Between God and us there is an immeasurable inequality, for we have received everything from him, our Creator."[29]

With this point clearly in mind, let me explain what the word *merit* means in Catholic theology. Everything good comes ultimately from God, including merit.[30] Merits are the good works we perform by God's grace through the virtues of faith, hope, and love. These virtues are supernatural gifts. Therefore, whatever flows from them occurs because God has made it possible. Again, quoting the *Catechism:*

> The merit of man before God in the Christian life arises from the fact that *God has freely chosen to associate man with the work of his grace.* The fatherly action of God is first on his own initiative, and then follows man's free action through his collaboration, so that the merit of good works is to be attributed in the first place to the grace of God, then to the faithful. Man's merit, moreover, itself is due to God, for his good actions proceed in Christ, from the predispositions and assistance given by the Holy Spirit. . . .
>
> Since the initiative belongs to God in the order of grace, *no one can merit the initial grace* of forgiveness and justification, at the beginning of conversion. . . .
>
> *The charity of Christ is the source in us of all our merits* before God. Grace, by uniting us to Christ in active love, ensures the supernatural quality of our acts and consequently their merit before God and before men.[31]

Heaven and Hope

In summary, then, Catholic Christians do not see good works as a means to justification. The great medieval theologian Thomas Aquinas taught that we are born on the natural level, and nothing we do can merit eternal life. Only the sacrifice of Christ can merit salvation. But when we become justified at that point of inner conversion, we are raised from the natural to the supernatural level. Raised to a new height, our actions on the natural level are redeemed and transformed. They become eternally significant because they are a gauge, a litmus test of the *fact* that we have entered into the process of total sanctification and transformation and of how we are progressing in our spiritual journey toward the fullness of our salvation.

That's right, I said "the fullness of our salvation." As Catholics see it and I've tried to make clear, the Bible teaches that justification is not the end-all of salvation; rather, it marks the beginning of the salvation process. We were created to live in intimacy with God, but sin alienated us from Him. History is the record of God pursuing us, lovingly dogging our steps, reaching out His arms of forgiveness to embrace us and pull us back to Him. For those of us who say yes to the divine proposal, He promises the full restoration of an intimate relationship with Him. But this cannot happen without the complete abolition of all that hinders such an incredible goal. And this He has promised. One day, all of creation, including we who have faithfully trusted in Him, will be set free not only from all of sin's consequences but even from its very presence.[32] Evil and all its bad fruit will be cast away forever. All the good that remains will spend eternity in blissful worship, rest, joy, and celebration with God. This is Heaven, and our experience of it will mark the completion of our salvation, the fulfillment of our deepest longing. Here we will behold God forever in an incorruptible spotless condition. This is our glorification.

The Scriptures exhort us to work toward this day in hope: "Work with anxious concern to achieve your salvation," or as the text reads in another translation, "Continue to work out your salvation in fear and trembling."[33] We hope in God for our complete salvation, and we're confident in what He has done for us; however, we can never be sure that we will always be faithful to Him. Some of us may even turn our backs on Him in apostasy, thereby "holding him up to contempt."[34] So the race belongs to those who persevere to the end, not to those who never start, nor to those who begin but never finish.

Certainly God is faithful whether we are or not. But He is also love, and love is not coercive. He will not force us to love or serve Him. What C. S. Lewis said is true: "There are only two kinds of people in the end: Those who say to God, 'Thy will be done,' and those to whom God says in the end, 'Thy will be done.'"[35] Or, as the Apostle Paul wrote to the young pastor Timothy:

> For if we died with Him,
>   We shall also live with Him.
> If we endure,
>   We shall also reign with Him.
> If we deny Him,
>   He also will deny us.[36]

For such reasons, Catholics believe that we have been saved, we are being saved, and we hope to be saved. I like the way Catholic theologian and friend Alan Schreck puts it:

First, a Catholic can say "I have been saved." It is an objective
fact that Jesus Christ already has died and been raised to save
me from my sin. The salvation of the world has been accomplished by Jesus Christ. This salvation has already begun to take
effect in the life of everyone who has accepted Jesus Christ and
been baptized. As St. Paul said, "If anyone is in Christ, he is a
new creation" (2 Cor. 5:17). In this sense, I can say, "Yes, I have
been saved."

Secondly, Catholics need to say that "I am being saved."
We must realize that we are still "running the race" to our ultimate destiny of heaven. We must turn to the Lord each day for
the grace to enter more deeply into his plan for our lives and
to accept his gift of salvation more fully. "And we all, with
unveiled face, beholding the glory of the Lord, are being
changed into his likeness from one degree of glory to another"
(2 Cor. 3:18). In this sense, I can say, "I am being saved."

Thirdly, Catholics say that "I hope to be saved." We must
persevere in our faith in God, love for God, and obedience to his
will, until the end of our lives. We have hope and confidence
that God will give us that grace, and that we will respond to it
and accept his gift of salvation until the day we die. In this
sense, "I hope to be saved."[37]

That great bastion of evangelical faith, Paul of Tarsus, well understood the challenge to remain faithful to the end. As he stated it, "Run
so as to win! Athletes deny themselves all sorts of things. They do this
to win a crown of leaves that withers, but we a crown that is imperish-
able. I do not run like a man who loses sight of the finish line. . . . What
I do is discipline my own body and master it, for fear that after having
preached to others I myself should be rejected."[38]

Certainly Christians from other traditions and confessions have different views regarding some aspects of the understanding of salvation I've
outlined here. Indeed, if those Christians sat down and discussed the
matter among themselves, they would discover that they have differences between them as well. But differences don't necessarily amount
to heresy or apostasy. John Calvin and Martin Luther strongly disagreed
with each other on a variety of important theological matters, including
some that concerned salvation. And other Reformed groups, such as the
Anabaptists, differed with both Calvin and Luther on several significant
doctrinal issues as well.

On the issue of salvation, however, we all agree that it begins with God, continues with God, and ends with God. Grace surrounds every aspect of salvation. So any role we play in the salvation plan, including the exercise of faith, is ultimately due to God's unmerited, undeserved, gratuitous grace, which comes to us through Christ's redemptive work and the ministry of the Holy Spirit. Christ alone merits our salvation. If this understanding is heretical, if it is truly a false gospel, then all of us—Catholic, Protestant, and Orthodox—stand condemned. But this gospel is not a false gospel. It is the truth. The church has affirmed it as such since her inception. The apostles taught it because they heard it from the Lord incarnate Himself. On this Rock Catholics stand.

This brings me to the second charge.

NOT AN ANTI-CHRIST RELIGION

Some Christians who adhere to a certain interpretation of biblical passages on the "last days" seem to major on how many similarities or parallels they can find between the anti-Christ religion described in such passages as Revelation 17 and 18 and the Catholic Church. They argue that along with a revived Roman Empire, there will come a counterfeit church. It will parade itself as Christian, and it will seduce world political and religious leaders into obeying its dictates. Indeed, it will attempt to bring all humankind under one world religion and align its incredible influence with the political rule of the Antichrist. Together the Antichrist and the head of this false religious system will seek to control the minds, hearts, and actions of all human beings.

When you ask those who hold to this interpretation of biblical prophecy to tell you what qualifies for this false religion and who will be its leader, they will often tell you the Roman Catholic Church and the pope. One of the more popular and vehement promoters of this perspective is Dave Hunt. Here's a sampling of what he says in just one of his books:

> The Roman Catholic Church, as the sole interpreter of Scripture, seduces its members into embracing a different God, a different Jesus Christ, and a different plan of salvation from that taught in the Bible.[39]

> Roman Catholicism has completely corrupted and firmly opposes the gospel which evangelicals preach.[40]

Many of today's leading evangelicals suggest that Protestants can cooperate with Rome in "evangelizing" the world. In actual fact, the Roman Catholic Church is the most powerful and effective enemy of Christianity in history. Its teachings are masterpieces of deception. . . . [T]he Roman Catholic Church itself . . . is the largest and most dangerous religious cult that ever existed.[41]

Partnership with Rome sets the stage for the rise of Antichrist. Although the "whore" is the Catholic Church, all religions will be gathered together under the Vatican.[42]

Today the influence exerted by the head of Rome's "Christianity" extends far beyond the confines of the ancient Roman Empire, making the Pope once again the ideal partner for the Antichrist in ruling what will be a worldwide kingdom of darkness.[43]

This kind of diatribe against any Christian tradition or confession is simply malicious. These comments and the "arguments" Hunt uses to try to support them demonstrate, not only a severely confused and false understanding of Roman Catholicism, but a hateful, vengeful spirit that is much more in tune with the spirit of antichrist than anything he allegedly critiques. This is mudslinging, pure and simple, and it's completely inappropriate for someone who professes Christ as his Savior and Lord.

Because of the poor reasoning and faulty research embedded in Hunt's analysis and that of those who argue similarly, it would take a lengthy book just to unravel and answer all the errors. So here I'd like to make just a few overall responses to the charge that Roman Catholicism is an anti-Christ religion.

Fully Orthodox

Throughout this book, I have presented a Catholic perspective on God, Jesus Christ, the Holy Spirit, the gospel, the Second Coming, and a number of other doctrines central to the Christian faith. At times, I may have communicated a viewpoint new to you or perhaps somewhat controversial to you. But I have anchored my words in the Scriptures and the church's creeds as well as her other expressions of theological reflection and understanding. I have also opened my life to share my own journey in the faith. At no time have I deviated from historic Christian orthodoxy. And yet what I have said is commensurate with my tradition—the Roman Catholic Church.

So why do some Christians, even well-intentioned believers, accuse my tradition of heresy or apostasy? Sometimes such accusations come from ex-Catholics who were poorly catechized or not catechized at all. They don't understand the tradition they left, and they may even be upset or hurt because of some aspect of their experience in it. Frankly, some of these former Catholics came out of theologically liberal parishes, while others came from legalistic, works-dominated churches where divine grace found little foothold. Especially in cases such as these, many Protestants have helped Catholics better understand and truly embrace many of Christianity's essentials. While that's a tremendous service to the Body of Christ, it has also led many of these Catholics to reject and criticize a belief system and church that are not truly Catholic.

Some of Catholicism's critics, such as Hunt, have adopted a particular eschatological perspective that they think leads to the conclusion that the Roman Catholic Church must be the predicted "whore of Babylon." So they look for reasons to believe in this interpretation, no matter how outlandish they are. For instance, Hunt argues that the word "*Vicar* comes from the Latin word *vicarius*. The Greek equivalent would be *anti*, as in Antichrist. Using the Greek, then," and applying it to biblical prophecy, Hunt concludes that the "Antichrist will be the new Constantine, the head of the revived Roman Empire worldwide, while the Pope will be his assistant, the second beast of Revelation 13."[44]

Hunt fails to mention, or perhaps he doesn't know, that the Latin word *vicarius* means "substitute." Jesus was our substitute on the cross. God provided Abraham with a substitute sacrifice for his son Isaac. The Old Testament economy of animal sacrifices is an economy of substitutes. Substitutes stand in the place of others; they are representatives. It's in this sense that Catholics view the pope as the vicar of Christ. He is the representative of Christ on earth and the visible head of the Body of Christ. In one sense, all Christians are vicars of Christ, for all of us visibly represent Him to those we come in contact with. Does that mean the pope and all other Christians in the world are Antichrists?

Hunt also seems oblivious to the fact that some leaders in other Christian confessions have the title vicar. For instance, a cleric in the Anglican Church acting as priest of a parish in place of the rector is a vicar. The same is true of a cleric in the Episcopal Church whose charge is a chapel in a parish. Does that mean that the Anglican and Episcopal churches are in cahoots with the Antichrist?

And what about that Greek equivalent *anti?* Does it mean "substitute"? Sometimes, yes. But in Greek it can also mean "against," "opposite," "instead of," "for," "as," and "in behalf of."[45] When it's joined with the word *Christ*, as in *Antichrist*, it means "against," not "substitute." It helps designate Christ's adversary. The Antichrist, or the spirit of antichrist, is someone or something that opposes Christ, not someone or something that represents Him or stands in His place as His ambassador.[46]

Moreover, just because *anti* is used negatively in some sections of Revelation, it does not mean that *anti* always carries negative connotations, which is what Hunt seems to imply. Whether *anti* is used independently or joined to a word as a prefix, it can have any number of very positive meanings. When the Apostle Paul introduces the Genesis 2 instruction on marriage, he uses the word *anti*, which in this context means "for this cause."[47] When the word *anti* is joined to the Greek word *lambano* in Acts 20:35, it means "help the weak." Even when *anti* is used in the book of Revelation, it doesn't always carry a negative connotation. In fact, in Revelation 2:13, *anti* is part of a person's name, "Antipas," who is called by Christ Himself "My witness, My faithful one, who was killed among you, where Satan dwells" (NASB). Is a martyr of the faith now an Antichrist?

Words must be taken in their context to be properly understood. By tearing *vicar* and *anti* from their contexts and failing to comprehensively consider their history, meanings, and applications, Hunt has managed to come to a ridiculous conclusion concerning the pope and the Catholic Church. And this is just a small sampling of the numerous errors of reasoning and fact found throughout Hunt's work and the works of many other critics who follow in his footsteps.[48]

Such critics of Catholicism would do well to actually read and ponder the official documents of the Catholic Church and the theologians she honors. To read them with the goal to understand first. All too often, Christians propagate false views of Christian traditions not their own because they fail to take the time to really understand those traditions. And much of the time, when these Christians do criticize other perspectives, they do so on the opinion of secondary or even tertiary sources. Let me illustrate.

The case of Thomas Aquinas—Thomas Aquinas is recognized by scholars in all Christian traditions and confessions as arguably the most brilliant systematic theologian of the Christian church. Even those who take issue with some of Aquinas's arguments or conclusions honor him as a theologian's theologian. The Catholic Church considers Aquinas a saint, and she upholds his many theological and biblical treatises as prime examples of theological reflection and reasoning at its best. Because of this honor afforded Aquinas, many Protestants have criticized what they believed he taught. Some of them read Aquinas firsthand, but in many cases not very carefully or comprehensively. Many more of his critics never read him at all. They simply parroted or paraphrased criticisms they had read about him without ever checking out the validity of the critiques. This happens all the time with many nonChristians and the Bible. They voice criticism after criticism of what they think the Bible teaches, but they don't take the time to ever read it themselves. So their criticisms are terribly uninformed.

In recent years, many Protestants have begun to read Aquinas for themselves. And for the most part, what they've found was not the caricature that had been presented to them. The Protestant philosopher and apologist Norman Geisler has been especially adamant about this. After spending many years studying Saint Thomas's writings and reading what various evangelical Protestants said about him, Geisler wrote:

> Often evangelicals hold the same position as Aquinas, only unwittingly, because his view has been stereotyped and/or distorted through the teaching majesterium [sic] of our evangelical college of apologetic "Cardinals." I must shamefully confess for our evangelical cause that after both a doctorate in Catholic philosophy and nearly twenty years of the direct study of Aquinas it is my conclusion that scarcely an evangelical philosopher or apologist really understands the view of Aquinas, and many of them so grossly distort Thomas that they often criticize him for a view he never held. And with striking irony they often teach, in contrast to what they believe Aquinas held, fundamentally the very view that Thomas held himself. Perhaps first-hand and more sympathetic scholarship would have avoided this embarrassment to us.

Geisler makes several suggestions as part of "a proposal for overcoming some of the obstacles to a greater evangelical appreciation of Thomism." The last one he makes is especially pertinent and appreciated: "Finally, a frank ecumenical confession of our prejudice would be commendable. . . . As a mature evangelical, Aquinas is a more articulate defender of the Faith than anyone we have ever produced."[49]

Another evangelical Protestant scholar has voiced his appreciation for Saint Thomas's use of Scripture. In opposition (*anti*) to the charge that Thomas Aquinas ignored Scripture or often misinterpreted it or didn't grant it its proper authority, John Franklin Johnson wrote:

> Thomas [Aquinas] unequivocally bases the doctrines of theology upon the Word of God. Theological science receives its principles immediately from God through the divine revelation given to the prophets and the apostles. "We must keep to that which has been written in Scripture," writes St. Thomas, "as to an excellent rule of faith so that we must add nothing to it, detract nothing, and change nothing by interpreting it badly." Quite a clarion call to scriptural authority for one whom many evangelical[s] are quick to dismiss in tracing their theological roots![50]

When it comes to handing out superlatives about Saint Thomas, I was surprised and delighted to find the Reformed apologist R. C. Sproul toward the front of the line. "I, for one," states Sproul, "am persuaded that the Protestant Church owes a profound debt to Saint Thomas and the benefit of a second glance at his contributions. I remind my Evangelical friends that when Saint Thomas defended the place of natural theology, he appealed primarily to the Apostle Paul and to Romans 1 for its classical formulation. There is a sense in which every Christian owes a profound debt to Saint Thomas." Among the many positive points Sproul makes about Aquinas, he notes that it was Aquinas who effectively engaged the rise of Islam in his day by writing a multivolume critique of Islam and defense of Christianity called *Summa Contra Gentiles*.

As he finishes his praise of this great theologian, Sproul writes, "We need an Aquinas. We need a titanic thinker who will not abandon truth for safety. We need men and women who are willing to compete with secularists in defense of Christ and of his truth. In this regard, the dumb ox of Aquino was heroic."[51] I couldn't agree with Sproul more.

BEYOND STICKS AND STONES

"With the tongue we praise our Lord and Father, and with it we curse men, who have been made in God's likeness. Out of the same mouth come praise and cursing. My brothers, this should not be."[52] Though written nearly two thousand years ago, these words of the Apostle James still have a striking relevance to our day. We should not speak evil of others, but when they are members of the Family of God, it is especially wicked for us to deface them with our words. We all bear the image of God, even if we're not saved. That's enough reason to treat one another with respect and kindness and charity. But when you add that we are Christ-followers and as such are brothers and sisters in the Family of God who are being transformed into Christ's radiant image until we are spotless and flawless, then it's even more imperative that we stop throwing sticks and stones and uphold one another in love.

Let us never forget: "Anyone who claims to be in the light but hates his brother is still in the darkness. Whoever loves his brother lives in the light, and there is nothing in him to make him stumble. But whoever hates his brother is in the darkness and walks around in the darkness; he does not know where he is going, because the darkness has blinded him."[53] Whoever is of the darkness needs the light only Christ can provide. Let's reach out to such a one with the good news of the gospel. For those of us who are of the light, let's not live as though we're still in darkness. Let's embrace one another and do the work Christ has called us to together.

CHAPTER THIRTEEN

HUMPTY DUMPTY SOLUTIONS

We cannot have one savior—
just like the Big Mac in McDonalds,
prepackaged, shipped all over the world.
It won't do. It's imperialistic.
Kwok Pui-Lan, feminist

The Church has always been blessed
by gays and lesbians, . . . witches, . . . shamans.
Judy Westerdorf, clergywoman

I would like to invite you to join with me in a little speculation and reflection. We're going to begin by recalling Mother Goose. That's right. We're going to look at a children's poem, one you likely heard when you were a kid. It goes like this:

> Humpty Dumpty sat on a wall,
> Humpty Dumpty had a great fall.
> All the king's horses,
> And all the king's men,
> Couldn't put Humpty together again.

In case you didn't know or don't remember, Humpty Dumpty was an egg. Apparently, not a very smart one either. As an egg, with arms and legs no less, he should have known how dangerous it was for him to climb up a high wall and sit precariously on top of it with his little legs dangling over the edge. No doubt, Humpty's mother had warned him about the perils of the combination of eggs and gravity in high places, but Humpty apparently thought he was exempt from such dangers—a malady that affects most children and many adults. So Humpty, looking for some new fun perhaps, scaled the wall and perched himself on top of it.

We're not told how long he sat there or what he saw. But at some point, Humpty got a bit too careless, lost his balance, and went plunging to the ground below. When he struck bottom, he did what any other egg would do—he shattered. Perhaps dazed and confused and in a good deal of pain, Humpty cried out for help. Somehow, the king's men got wind of what happened, and they rode out to see if they could bring aid to the ailing Humpty. When they got there, they must have beheld a tragic site. Eggshell everywhere, with Humpty's insides . . . well, you know, somewhat scrambled (it was a hot day!).

The king's patrol went to work, including their horses. Animals and soldiers worked together to collect all the shell fragments, then they put their heads together and did everything they could to put Humpty back together. But alas, all their attempts failed. Humpty was a goner.

Have you ever wondered why all the king's horses and all the king's men couldn't reassemble poor Humpty Dumpty? I'm sure among all the issues in life with which you've had to contend, this question hasn't loomed large. In fact, you may have never even raised this question. What I'd like to suggest is that it's a good question to ponder, especially if we look at this children's poem from a theological angle.

Assume, for imagination's sake, that Humpty Dumpty represents the shattered church. Further imagine that the king is God, and His horses and men are different confessions and traditions within His church. Now God knows His church is divided. He knows it has undergone a great divorce and that the relationships among Family members have been seriously fractured. Many members within His Family are distressed that the church is in such a divided state, so they rush to the church's aid and try to put it back together. But no matter what they try, they can't reunite her.

Why is this so? If Christ wants, even prays, for unity within the church, why can't we bring it about? Because *we* are trying to do it. Unity isn't a work of man but of God. Only God can reunite His church. He broke down the walls between Jews and Gentiles, men and women, slaves and masters through faith in Jesus and His work of salvation. He sent His Spirit to bring peoples of different races, social classes, abilities, educational backgrounds, and the like to form the one Body of Christ. He gave them the charismatic gifts, Scriptures, and leadership needed to guide and equip Christ's Body. So if the Body is to be reunited again, it will be due to God's work, not ours.

On the other hand, as fellow members of the King's royal household, I believe we can and should strive to work together to impact and change our culture. How we do this, however, needs to be carefully thought through. We don't want to deceive ourselves into thinking that through social action we can put Humpty back together again.

Nevertheless, while our task is not to reunite the church, we do know that part of our mission is to work to help put a shattered society back together. I do not claim we can make society perfect. The church cannot repair all the damage sin has caused. But that shouldn't stop us from trying to make this side of Heaven a more humane and moral place to live. After all, our call is to be in the world as salt and light while striving to avoid becoming tainted by the sin of the world. Throughout history, the church has tried to accomplish this mission, and at times she has succeeded better than others. But since she has become divided, her task has become even more difficult. Now she must not only piece together a broken civilization but do it as a broken Family. How can this be done?

I'd like to consider several ways Christians have tried to fulfill their mission and explain why I don't believe these are the most effective ways. I like to refer to them as Humpty Dumpty solutions. It's important that we look at these. If we just examine success stories, we will not be as well prepared to handle all that lies ahead. There are obstacles everywhere. If we know what they look like and understand what they can cost us, we have a better chance of avoiding them. Moreover, all failures are not dismal failures; they can have redeeming qualities. By looking at these Humpty Dumpty solutions more carefully, we can learn not only what to avoid but what we may want to incorporate more prudently in what promises to be a truly effective alliance-building effort.

Before we get into all this, however, we have a preliminary matter to handle.

ECUMENISM—NOT A DIRTY WORD

Aside from exploring Humpty Dumpty solutions, we need to deal with a Humpty Dumpty criticism of alliance-building efforts among Christians. Basically, this criticism boils down to *ecumenism* being a four-letter word.

Some Christians believe that *ecumenism*, along with its adjectival form *ecumenical*, are evil words because they denote evil alliances. They've seen ecumenical movements, such as the National Council of Churches, build themselves on what I call a lowest-common-denominator form of alliance building. They've watched these groups deny their doctrinal and ecclesial distinctives so they could work together on "common ground." Then they heard these groups eventually dilute even their "common ground" until their beliefs and practices looked like a patchwork quilt of Eastern New Age mysticism mixed with Western paganism and a secularized form of a not-so-moral morality. If this is what ecumenism means, then these Christians are right to be suspicious of it and denounce it.

So let me make myself very clear. When properly understood and applied, the words *ecumenism* and *ecumenical* do not denote lowest-common-denominator approaches to building alliances among Christians. I used to utilize these words in the past, but I rarely do anymore because of the bad associations many Christians connect with them. Instead, I normally use the term *alliance building*, by which I mean anything but lowest-common-denominator approaches to bringing Christians together to engage the culture. I believe in always taking the high road, which means that any alliances built between Christians must affirm both what they have in common and what they don't. And this must be done with mutual respect, and even better, mutual admiration for the unique depth and diversity each Christian and Christian community can bring to the common "war effort." This is the form of ecumenism I am striving for and have argued for throughout this book. I've already dealt with this matter some, and I'll cover it even more later, but I wanted to reiterate once again what I meant before I went any farther. The potential for mis-understanding in a united house is great enough, but in a divided house it's staggering. Hence the repeated clarification here.

Now to the Humpty Dumpty solutions. We will look at four: retreatism, elitism, capitulationism, and politicizing.

RETREATISM

Retreatism is the fortress approach to alliance building. Retreatists are not interested in penetrating culture but in pulling out of it. We might put their view this way: "Society is the Titanic. No matter how you deck it out or how much you polish the railing, it's going to sink. And if we stay on board, we'll go down with it. So let's abandon ship, and build and stay in our own communities. There we'll be safe. There we can grow in the faith and teach our children the faith while remaining apart from the corrupting influence of the world."

In some ways, I think most Christians could identify with many of the sentiments of this viewpoint. When we look around us, we do see a culture sinking fast. It pains us to think about our children growing up in a society caught up in the throes of promiscuity, secularism, paganism, drugs, selfism, and a host of other destructive views and vices. At times it does seem as if there's little we can do to combat all of this. Indeed, it seems that when we have fought back, we have lost as much if not more ground than we gained. This appears especially true in the abortion debate. So why engage in a losing battle? Why not let the Titanic sink?

The answer to these questions is simple yet deeply profound: love. What did the Apostle Paul say about love? Love "bears all things, believes all things, hopes all things, endures all things. Love never fails."[1] In other words, love never, ever gives up. How do we know this? God's involvement in human history. The Scriptures tell us that "God is love,"[2] a truth He has verified over and over to us. Regardless of our faithlessness, He stayed faithful. No matter how great our sin, His grace abounded all the more. God even went so far as to send us His Son to be our vicar, our substitute. He took the lashings, beatings, ridicule, humiliation, and judgment meant for us. And He did it because He loves us. "God demonstrates His own love toward us, in that while we were still sinners, Christ died for us."[3] Before His death, Jesus Himself said, "Greater love has no one than this, than to lay down one's life for his friends."[4]

If Love incarnate refused to give up on us even when He knew we would execute Him, how can we who call Him our Master walk away from the rest of those for whom He died? We cannot. We dare not.

Love should compel us to engage our culture, not to retreat from it. It's true that Jesus often withdrew to quiet, out-of-the-way spots so He could pray and renew His strength for what lay ahead. But He didn't stay there. His call was to go into the world to heal the sick, restore sight to the blind, uplift the poor, return joy to the mournful, silence the scoffers, expose and expel the darkness. Then He gave His followers the Holy Spirit so they could continue His mission until He returns. For when He comes back, it will not be to forgive but to judge, it will not be as a lamb but as a lion.

Now someone might retort, "But isn't there a place in your tradition, Keith, for people to withdraw from society and dedicate themselves to a life of prayer?" That's true, and it's a beautiful picture of a dynamic way to live one's life in total commitment to God. But even though this involves a physical withdrawal from society, it does not at all entail a giving up on society. We desperately need people who will storm the ramparts of Heaven in behalf of Christ's church and her work in the world. Our warfare is spiritual, not just political, legal, ethical, theological, or philosophical. Our ultimate enemy is Satan and his horde, and one of the most potent weapons with which to fight them is prayer.[5] Now you don't have to be a nun or a monk to pray, but we could use more people spending more time on their knees for the sake of the church and her work of engaging and transforming culture.

Retreatism isn't the answer to our alliance-building needs.

ELITISM

Another Humpty Dumpty solution is elitism. This describes Christians who band together and decide they and they alone have the answers to society's problems. Unlike the retreatists, elitists will engage the culture; however, they will not link arms with other Christian groups who are fighting the same battles because these other groups don't see eye to eye with them on everything. Elitists tend to be smug and exclusive. It's their way or no way; there are no other viable options.

Once again, I can sympathize with why some believers take this approach. I have played roles in alliance-building efforts where elitist tendencies were fostered. These groups were having a tremendously positive impact in the lives of Christians and the surrounding culture. Success bred success. We knew we had a good thing going. We wanted other people to become a part of it too, and though we took on new ideas from time to time, at least some of us came to the conclusion that if things are going well, why risk making changes that could hurt that progress? Soon, we began to think we were doing so well that we had *the* formula. If other Christians wanted to join us and do things our way, fine and good. If not, well, they couldn't become a part of our group. We weren't trying to be smug or elitist, but in effect that's just what we had become.

When elitist attitudes go unchecked, they often lead to Christians undermining the work of other Christians and even publicly impugning their character and motives. I know this occurs. I have had it happen to me, and I know many other alliance builders, such as Charles Colson, James Dobson, Billy Graham, and Pat Robertson, who have also weathered the storms generated by elitists.

Most often, the elitists who engage in attacking fellow Christians support their cause by claiming they are attempting to preserve doctrinal purity. They have decided what's orthodox, and that's usually whatever their particular tradition teaches about Christianity's essentials *and* nonessentials. Or they may even be operating outside of an established Christian tradition. They may have come to their own conclusions concerning doctrine, and based on that, they determine who believes correctly and who doesn't. In other words, these elitists have either identified one particular belief system along with its distinctives in doctrine and probably practice as the only true expression of orthodoxy, or worse yet, they have created their own version of Christianity and touted it as "true truth." All professing Christians who disagree with them even in the most minute jots and tittles, they treat as deceived or deceivers. They simply can't accept honest disagreement. If people don't believe exactly as they do, well, those people are wrong, perhaps eternally dead wrong.

Now I'm all for preserving the historic Christian faith and protecting it from errors and heresies. Since the church's inception, she has sought to faithfully articulate, defend, and protect the deposit of faith entrusted to her. But it's also true that throughout church history, intelligent, honest, thoughtful Christians have held different beliefs, even on some important matters. When the church deemed these matters critical enough to demand resolution, she brought the different parties together to work out their differences in a spirit of mutual respect and open dialogue. Exchanges could get heated, but rarely did they degenerate into vitriolic verbal assaults on one another. Nor did they usually end up with anathemas being pronounced on one another's views. Most often, differences were resolved, unity was preserved, and the church's theology was enriched.

Elitists, however, have a very difficult time distinguishing between honest theological differences and distinctives among genuine Christians and true departures from the faith. They can't seem to see any viable alternatives beyond their own convictions. Hence if other traditions don't measure up exactly to their beliefs, then those traditions are in error and perhaps even heretical or apostate. In many cases, elitists become so self-absorbed in the "rightness" of their views that they won't even discuss these matters civilly with those they think are in error. Instead they lash out at those they believe are on the "other side." They treat them as opponents to be knocked out for the sake of truth. To elitists who have fallen this far, anyone who isn't for them is against them and "orthodoxy" and therefore against God. These elitists believe such opponents need to be thoroughly exposed for what they are and refuted for what they believe. Then they might listen to the real "truth," the genuine "gospel" rather than the false one they allegedly embrace.

When elitism degenerates this far, it has become nothing less than religious bigotry. It may even verge on blasphemy. When Jesus' Spirit-empowered work of healing was deemed a work of Satan by some of His opponents, Jesus warned them that they were in danger of committing an unforgivable sin: blasphemy against the Holy Spirit.[6] The Spirit of God is uniquely at work in all Christians, and He equips us differently to carry out His work in the created order. When believers defame the Spirit's work in the life of a Christian by attributing it to the Devil, they are perilously close to profaning God.

Contrary to what elitists believe, their approach to alliance building is self-destructive. Eventually they end up with very few Christians who will align with them because they have alienated and damned other believers. Elitism simply does not help the Body of Christ; it hinders and brings pain to the Body. Plainly put, elitism is sin.

The Apostle Paul fought against elitism when he rebuked the Christians in ancient Corinth for snubbing their noses at other believers because they weren't of the right group. The Paul-followers thought they were better than the Apollos-followers, and the Apollos-followers thought they had it all over the Cephas-followers, and the Christ-followers, well, they thought they were head and shoulders above all the other groups. Paul saw that their elitist attitudes and actions were tearing apart the Body of Christ. Christ, Paul said, is not divided. We are fellow believers in the same Body. We have one Father, one Savior, and one Spirit who has united us under one Head and graced us all with different gifts so we can serve one another and reach out to a needy world. "There should be no schism in the body," writes Paul, "the members should have the same care for one another."[7]

Neither Jesus nor the early church were elitist. Jesus would bond with anyone who chose to follow Him. And He spent much of His time with people who didn't agree with Him, some of whom even hated Him. His disciples struggled with this. On one occasion when they came across a man who was healing people in the name of Jesus, they told him to stop because he wasn't a part of their group. Jesus saw the matter much differently. He told the disciples, "Do not forbid him, for no one who works a miracle in My name can soon afterward speak evil of Me. For he who is not against us is on our side."[8] Jesus' vision was fixed on the greater mission of reaching a needy world. If there were those who were achieving this end outside of His band of followers, that was fine. They should be allowed, even encouraged, to keep up the good work.

The early church followed Jesus' example. Though at first the early church had a hard time accepting the fact that Gentiles were being saved, once they realized it was a work of God, they threw their support behind it and marshaled more people to take advantage of this new evangelistic opportunity.

I simply don't see how we can be elitist in our attitude or approach and claim we're being Christian about it. Elitism, by its very nature, creates divisions, while within the Body of Christ unity is to prevail, not schism.

CAPITULATIONISM

Capitulationism is the ecumenism of political correctness. Rather than build alliances on genuine Christian orthodoxy, capitulationists look for politically correct causes or perspectives, parade them as at least closer to the spirit of Christianity than orthodoxy could ever claim, then try to "unite" Christians under the new banners. A perfect example of this occurred recently in Minneapolis.

An "ecumenical" conference of about 2,200 women convened in November 1993. The conference was billed as "A Global Theological Conference By Women; for Women and Men."[9] Participants included clergy and laity from the United Methodist Church, Presbyterian Church (U.S.A.), Evangelical Lutheran Church in America, and the American Baptist Church. The event was associated with the World Council of Churches' Decade of Churches in Solidarity. It was billed as a "Second Reformation." What happened there, however, was not church renewal but the revival of paganism. The Christian church and her historic faith were accused of being sources of the "oppression of women, racism, classism, violence in our cities, abuse of children, abusive rejection of gay and lesbian sexuality, and pollution of the environment."[10] Hardly any politically correct stone was left unturned.

The conference's leaders encouraged attendees during the first session of the four-day event to "dream wildly about who we are as people of God, and who we intend to be in the future through the power and guidance of the spirit of wisdom whom we name Sophia." Then throughout the conference, the following chorus was often repeated by participants: "Now Sophia, dream the vision, share the wisdom dwelling deep within."[11] Participants were told that Sophia was just another divine name that described God's feminine side. I believe, however, the Sophia praised at the conference had nothing to do with the God of Christianity. Sophia was the name of a pagan goddess who was being revived to exalt feminism and lesbianism and nature worship.

Conferees were given activities through which they were told to "re-imagine God through emotional images, and sing a song of blessing to Sophia, the goddess of Wisdom. . . . Melanie Morrison, co-founder of Christian Lesbians Out Together, . . . invited lesbian, bisexual, and transsexual women to join hands and encircle the stage." About one hundred women, many of them smiling, moved to the front. "One held high the rainbow flag, which has become a symbol for the diversity among lesbians and gay men. Many of the women remaining in the audience rose to their feet and began to applaud." According to the Reverend Kittredge Cherry, "a minister in the predominately homosexual Metropolitan Church, . . . the goal of the demonstration was to help people 're-imagine' the church as the embodiment of justice for everyone, including lesbians and homosexual men."[12]

A self-avowed lesbian clergywoman in the Presbyterian Church (U.S.A.) said in her presentation that "her theology is first of all informed by 'making love with Coni,' her lesbian partner." She then told the audience, "Sexuality and spirituality have to come together—and Church, we're going to teach you!" Echoing similar sentiments, a United Methodist clergywoman told conferees that "'The Church has always been blessed by gays and lesbians, . . . witches, . . . shamans.' She joked about the term 'practicing homosexual,' noting that her partner says she's not practicing, she's pretty good."[13]

With the promotion of immorality as the new ethical norm, other Christian teachings had to be modified or completely abandoned. For instance, hotly criticized was the biblical teaching that the Son of God freely obeyed His heavenly Father by giving up His life on the cross in payment for our sins. Rather than seeing this as a priceless act of incredible grace and mercy, Aruna Gnanadason of the World Council of Churches said it showed that the church "centered its faith around the cruel and violent death of Christ on the cross, [thereby] sanctioning violence against the powerless in society." The radical feminist theologian Virginia Mollenkott declared, "I can no longer worship in a theological context that depicts God as an abusive parent and Jesus as the obedient trusting child. This violent theology encourages the violence of our streets and our nations."[14]

A Chinese feminist denied Jesus' uniqueness as the world's Savior. She said, "We cannot have one savior—just like the Big Mac in McDonalds, prepackaged, shipped all over the world. It won't do. It's imperialistic."[15] Instead she recommended the 722 gods and goddesses of China as a good example of the inclusiveness modern faith should uphold and embrace.

With Jesus and salvation so totally redefined, God had to be "re-imagined" as well. Participants were told to be speculative about God because "there is no 'answer.' We can't imagine what God is like. Being together in our own images is the ultimate."[16] In support of this idea, Carla DeSola, a conference speaker, encouraged the women to "feel your being, this being is sacred like the earth. . . . When we really move in an integrated way of body and soul together we know who we are on a deeper level; and knowing who we are, we can garner that power and energy into our prayer. It becomes the full expression because we are in touch with our deep self and we release the spirit into the world. We become like Sophia, a tree of life for the healing of ourselves and the nations."[17] At one point in the conference, women put red dots on their foreheads to signify the divine within each of them, then they bowed to one another in acknowledgment of their divinity.

Toward the end of the conference, a profane counterfeit of the Eucharist was performed. Substituting milk and honey for bread and wine, and scriptural responsive readings for pseudosexual ones, the goddess Sophia was worshiped. Here's just a portion of the liturgy that was held:

> Our maker Sophia, we are women in your image: With the hot blood of our wombs we give form to new life. With the courage of our convictions we pour out lifeblood for justice. . . .
>
> . . . With nectar between our thighs we invite a lover, we birth a child; With our warm body fluids we remind the world of its pleasures and sensations. . . .
>
> . . . With our moist mouths we kiss away a tear, we smile encouragement. With honey of wisdom in our mouths, we prophesy a full humanity to all the peoples. . . .
>
> We celebrate the sensual life you give us. We celebrate the sweat that pours from us during our labors. We celebrate the fingertips vibrating upon the skin of a love. We celebrate the tongue which licks a wound or wets our lips. We celebrate our bodiliness, our physicality, the sensations of pleasure, our oneness with earth and water.[18]

There's no question that this expression of capitulationism has no relationship to orthodox Christianity. Numerous men and women, clergy and laity alike, from the denominations represented at this conference recognized this and clearly spoke out against what had happened there. Critics rightly pointed out that self was the idol of Sophia, and worship of self was a very modern yet pagan preoccupation. They lifted their voices in protest, stating that the "Re-Imagining" conference "made a mockery of Christian doctrine and morality," that it "applauded heresy and celebrated blasphemy." They added that it gave "'ecumenical dialogue' a bad name." In fact, "The character of 'Re-Imagining' was not that of dialogue, but rather of indoctrination in a feminist/womanist/lesbian agenda."[19]

Arguing along similar lines, another critic correctly noted: "The traditional understanding of ecumenical gatherings . . . demands that those present affirm their own faith but refrain from denigrating the beliefs of others. Also, ecumenical gatherings have historically been respectful and faithful to the parameters of orthodox Christian beliefs, as set forth in historic creeds and confessions. At the 'Re-Imagining' Conference, however, not one of the 34 major speakers represented orthodox Christian faith as expressed in the classical creeds or confessions. Rather than being ecumenically grounded in the Christian faith, this meeting was interreligious, with its major emphasis being nonchristian belief."[20]

And concerning attacking and redefining Christianity in an attempt to make room for women and their needs, William R. Cannon, a retired bishop of the United Methodist Church, insightfully wrote:

> It is pitiable that a group of feminist enthusiasts within the church find that the only way they can advance the cause of women . . . is to modify the doctrine of God to the degree that the feminine principle is made a part of the Godhead. If they only thought through carefully the teachings of Christianity, they would realize that this is unnecessary, even redundant. There is more than enough in the Bible that affirms the importance of women and gives them their opportunity of leadership and creativity in society alongside and equal to that of men. . . . Except for our divine Lord himself, there is no person in the Bible more significant than the Virgin Mary. It was through her, a woman, that the incarnation took place. It was Mary, a woman, who was the mother of the Incarnate God. Mary said of herself in the Magnificat, "All generations will call me blessed, for the mighty one has done great things for me" (Luke 1:48-19). It is not possible to conceive a position more noble than that of the Virgin Mary—a woman—mother of Christ.[21]

The Christian faith is rich with answers for the needs of women and men of all ages, nationalities, and races. Christians do not need to sacrifice the faith on the contemporary altars of political correctness or any other perspective that contradicts or undermines Christian orthodoxy.

The church's teachings have stood the test of time quite well. If modernists and postmodernists would just listen and come to grips with those teachings rather than caricature and recast them in light of their own agendas, they would find deeply satisfying answers to the problems they face.

Many Christians who capitulate to these agendas have legitimate concerns, but they have not adequately understood the great treasury they have in the historic Christian faith. My plea to them is to rediscover your faith's rich heritage. Fashioning a new pseudo-Christianity will not solve anything. It never has, and it never will. The solutions really are found in Christ and His church, and they work best at full strength, not in the watered-down form presented in capitulationist attempts at what is really Humpty Dumpty ecumenism.

POLITICIZING

Especially in the last twenty years, Christians of many persuasions have banded together to influence American society through the political process. In a number of ways, I have been a part of some of these efforts. I applaud believers who exercise their democratic rights and responsibilities in political activities. The early Christians couldn't elect their choice for Caesar; we can. We shouldn't treat that opportunity flippantly or apathetically.

On the other hand, perhaps the greatest danger in building alliances among Christians to engage the culture politically is falling prey to the Humpty Dumpty solution of politicizing. I've seen many Christians identify Christian orthodoxy with political parties or the platform of a political party or with certain politicians or with political labels such as "conservative" and "liberal." In the 1980s, numerous Christians did this with the Republican party and Ronald Reagan, and then with George Bush. They saw the Republicans' conservative moral values and commitments to certain pro-life and pro-family positions as very compatible with a "conservative" Christian understanding of these matters. So they worked hard to get Republicans elected, including their presidential candidate, former actor and state governor Ronald Reagan. When their candidates won and Christians captured some important political appointments, many of these Christian political activists looked upon Washington, D.C., almost as if it were the "New Jerusalem." All of a sudden, they were in power, or at least politicians they believed would truly represent their interests were the new resident authorities. That felt good. The "conservative" Christian version of JFK's Camelot had finally arrived.

All was not bliss, however. Some political appointments and legislative decisions were made that divided Christians of even conservative political persuasion. Although evangelical Protestants in particular enjoyed an unusual access to places of governmental power, their advice wasn't always heeded and practices they had hoped to halt, like abortion, continued. It was at times a troubled marriage that became somewhat rockier during George Bush's presidential reign.

When the Clinton ticket won and took office in 1993, Christians who had politicized their faith and alliance-building efforts felt betrayed and even went into shock. How could the Democratic party win such a victory? Hadn't the Reagan-Bush years shown the American people the many values of adhering to "conservative" Christian values and views? Why did they vote for a change? How could those in and on the "right" lose the political race and agenda to those in and on the "left"? It seemed as if evil had triumphed over good.

A large majority of Christians would certainly agree, me included, that many of the Clinton administration's policies are morally wrong and politically ill-advised. But I disagree with those Christians who claim that his policies are this way because his administration is politically liberal or Democrat. Sometimes political liberals have more compassion and concern for the disadvantaged and downtrodden in America than many political conservatives do. Sometimes "liberal" understandings of free speech and the relationship between church and state are more in tune with the Constitution's First Amendment than some "conservative" positions are. And on moral issues, one can find genuine and quite activist pro-life and pro-family groups among political liberals, not just among "conservatives." Indeed, as I said earlier in this book, the liberals of the nineteenth century would be appalled by some of the rhetoric and viewpoints being espoused by many self-proclaimed liberals today.

Political conservatism is not equivalent to Christianity any more than political liberalism is. Political posturing and policy making must adapt to the views of the electorate, otherwise parties lose the reins of power. Each party wants to be at the top, and each party knows that involves compromise, and sometimes calls for abandoning the agenda of one group in order to secure the support of another more powerful group. Power is the ultimate name of the game, and if winning the prize means cutting loose certain people or altering certain positions, then so be it. With this approach in the political arena, Christians can never be sure from political season to political season that their moral or public-policy convictions will be better represented by the Republican or the Democratic party. Neither can they be certain that once their candidates are in office, they will remain advocates of "Christian" viewpoints.

Along with these caveats, my good friend Charles Colson made some very astute observations in his article "Don't Wait for the Next Reagan Era." Commenting on "the flaw of the eighties," which he identified as Christians relying on "politics *alone*" to change the culture, he noted several ways in which "excessive politicization damaged us."[22] His comments boiled down to this critical point:

> The political obsession [of the eighties] blinded us to an elementary lesson of history: reforming a culture involves more than just changing leaders and laws. ... [P]olitics, while critically important, is not the *primary* means of cultural change. In a free society, political values rest on an underlying moral consensus formed by what Tocqueville called "the habits of the heart." ...
>
> ... *[B]eing precedes doing*. What we *do* must flow from *who we are*. ... Before we can bring a holy influence in society, we must first *be* holy people. And the institution by which we are equipped to be holy people is the church: the community whose identity, purpose, and mission transcends political agendas, and whose power comes from the presence of the Holy Spirit.
>
> ... The church must be the church: holy communities of men and women being equipped to *be* God's people in the world, witnessing his love and truth in society.
>
> This is the key to our influence. ...
>
> Christians apprehensive about Washington's new leadership should take heart from the Christians in Eastern Europe. Under a hostile government, they built communities of believers. They knew that the church is the one institution Jesus promised the gates of hell could not stand against. They clung to that truth in the face of persecution.
>
> They knew that real power was not in the bayonet—as in our democracy, real power is not in the ballot box. It is in the Cross, the supernatural might of Jesus Christ to transform individual hearts and minds—and thereby, to reform society at large.[23]

We dare not politicize the faith. Neither should we disengage politically. We need to stay involved in the political arena, especially to keep the marketplace of ideas open to people of faith. But we must always keep in mind that society's long-term transformation will never come about through the political process alone. It must be accompanied by the renewal of human minds and hearts in the Person of and truths about Christ. Only then will American society, or any society for that matter, become what God had intended it to be.

TAKING THE HIGH ROAD

We can and we must engage our culture, and I believe we can most effectively do this together—Protestant, Catholic, and Orthodox Christians jumping into the same foxholes and fighting up the same hillsides. But we must avoid Humpty Dumpty approaches to our alliance-building efforts. Yes, we're a broken Family, and yes, only God can truly reunite us in Christ. But healing the wounds brought about by our divorce must also begin with us. And I believe that as we join to change society on a solid ecumenical foundation, we will rediscover and gain a renewed appreciation for our common heritage, and we will influence our culture in ways we can hardly imagine. This fact was brought home to me in a dramatic way some years ago.

The Youngstown Forty-Seven
I was in Steubenville, Ohio, serving as general counsel to Franciscan University. The day was cold and dark, and I was the only major administrator in the campus office. Father Michael Scanlan, the university's president, was on a pastoral trip with the bishop of Steubenville. They were checking up on a group of Franciscan University students who had accompanied another group of peaceful pro-life demonstrators to Youngstown, Ohio. My phone rang and on the other end was Father Michael.

He told me that he, the bishop, and all the students they had gone to see had been arrested. While they were praying together outside of an abortion clinic, the police moved in and took them into custody. I was shocked. The man I dearly respected and loved as a brother in Christ and my own bishop, who was also a dear friend, were behind bars for praying! They had not gone to Youngstown to stir up trouble or land in jail. And yet, simply by raising their voices Heavenward on behalf of the unborn and the mothers who would be victimized as well, they had been treated as criminals. I had to do something, so I quickly made arrangements to have all of the administrative bases covered at the university, then I got in my car and drove straight to Youngstown.

When I arrived, I met with two courageous lawyers who had already begun to represent the people who would come to be known as the Youngstown Forty-Seven. One of the lawyers, David Betras, was a very successful criminal defense attorney who was passionately pro-life and a Greek Orthodox Christian. He was volunteering his time and talent. David filled me in on their experience with the court since the arrests. The judge had been brutal, slamming his fist on the table throughout the preliminary hearing. Himself an alumni of the civil-rights movement, he failed to see the analogy between the rights and values that undergirded and motivated that movement and those that did the same for the pro-life demonstrators who had appeared before him looking for justice. Consequently, the judge had sent Father Michael, Bishop Albert, and forty-five other peaceful pro-life protestors to jail.

One of the first steps I took was to "file an appearance" on behalf of Father Michael and the bishop. This let the court know that I was representing them as their lawyer. While I was in the judge's chambers, a very unusual event occurred: This hardened judge began opening up to me. Feeling more at ease with me because I was an attorney from outside his jurisdiction, the judge expressed the agony he experienced handling this case. As we talked, I told him that my clients' activity was protected speech under the First Amendment, and I argued that their standing in the community demanded they be released immediately. The judge accepted my first claim but rejected the second.

The next thing I knew, I was visiting my two friends and their companions "in crime" in the Youngstown Armory. Because so many arrests had been made that day, a makeshift jail had been set up at the armory. I will never forget the feeling I had when I walked in to find Father Michael, Bishop Albert, and so many others confined for trying to save the lives of unborn children by simply peacefully exercising their constitutional rights of freedom of speech and assembly. I had long been aware of social protest movements and had been socially active during the tumultuous sixties. I had also been an outspoken advocate of the pro-life view. But this was the first time I had witnessed for myself the willingness of people to lose their freedoms and reputations for what they knew was right. Their courage challenged me to the core of my being.

During the days that ensued, I traveled back and forth between Franciscan University and Youngstown. I was fascinated by what I saw transpire in that armory. Here were deeply dedicated pro-life people from various Christian confessions—evangelical Protestants, Pentecostals, nondenominational Christians, Roman Catholics. All of them were committed to the protection of life and to the same Savior, and all of them had been wrongfully incarcerated. They were also all committed to making the best of their situation.

Within just two days, their confinement activities became impeccably organized. They would arise together early each morning for a joint prayer, then break up into denominational tracks for specific worship services. This would be followed by classes offered on an impromptu basis by professors and scholars in their midst. These classes were on the Bible and theology, and they were taught from various Christian perspectives. It was not unusual to find Protestants in the Catholic classes and Catholics in the Protestant ones. At lunch, they would break bread together and have a rest period. That would be followed by everyone participating in physical exercise by marching around the armory singing songs of praise. Then they would gather for dinner, nightly recreation, and evening prayers. They had transformed prison life into a living, working, interceding, dynamic experience of genuine Christian community.

The hearts of the prison guards were changed by these pro-lifers and their living witness. My heart was changed too. They helped me see that even deprivation and difficulty could be effectively used to bring about social change. These women and men, like countless others who had gone before them, had put their lives on the line for a just cause. They deserved legal representation, and they inspired me to provide it in every way I could.

As the days wore on, I saw a hardened judge slowly soften. In his chambers, he shared with me his struggle to adjudicate between what he called the "laws of men" and the "law of God." I saw the Bible on his desk, and I watched him struggle deeply to find a resolution to what he was experiencing as a real dilemma, one unlike he had ever faced before.

As one week drew to a close, a final hearing was held on this case. The local press had gathered in the courtroom expecting sentencing. Peaceful protestors were also there looking for vindication. I was there hoping for a miracle. Everyone was tense.

As the judge entered the courtroom, we all rose. The judge asked us to be seated, then called for the bishop to step forward, which he did. The judge publicly stated how much he admired the bishop and Father Michael and all those who were willing to sacrifice so much for something in which they believed. Then the judge found them guilty, credited their time served, dismissed them from jail—in effect, set the Youngstown

Forty-Seven free. The courtroom erupted into sounds of rejoicing.

I firmly believe that God softened the heart of that judge as He had softened the heart of an Egyptian ruler so many centuries earlier.[24] In both cases, Heaven responded to the persistent prayers of people of faith, and God's people experienced freedom and vindication as a result.

The Youngstown event also changed my life. It spurred me on to become an even greater advocate for the pro-life movement. But little did I realize then that this renewed sense of mission would lead me to be called to form and serve as the executive director of a national public-interest law firm that would be dedicated exclusively to pro-life, pro-liberty, and pro-family work. The heroism and prayers of the Youngstown Forty-Seven continue to impact the lives of countless thousands of people, many of whom they have never met.

This was a movement of the Spirit of God. The church was being the church, protecting human life, and for that the church was persecuted. But even during persecution, these courageous believers rallied together on still deeper levels, further evidence of the Spirit's work in their midst. And in the end, a judge's decision and life were changed, prison guards were deeply moved, and a lawyer's life was further catapulted into alliance-building efforts for social transformation. This was no Humpty Dumpty ecumenical effort. No one denied their differences, but neither did anyone allow those differences to get in the way of accomplishing the church's mission with fellow believers.

In the chapters that remain, I will lay out some guidelines for building such alliances, and I will provide several examples of Family alliances at work. My prayer is that this material, through the Lord's movement in your life, will help provide you with either the impetus to build an alliance or join or support one, or the encouragement to stick with or perhaps reorient an alliance of which you may already be a part. We have much to do, and we need not fear any of it, for greater is He who is in us than he who is in the world.

PART V

Family Alliances
for the
Next Millennium

CHAPTER FOURTEEN

OUR FAMILY HERITAGE

Therefore, since we are surrounded
by such a great cloud of witnesses,
let us . . . run with perseverance
the race marked out for us.
Hebrews 12:1, NIV

Throughout our common Judeo-Christian history, a tremendous Family legacy has come to us, passed on from generation to generation. As we've seen, much of our heritage has nourished and strengthened our Family tree, while some of it has left lightninglike burns on our branches. By drawing from our roots and remaining firmly connected to our common trunk, however, we can continue to grow as the church and carry out our mission in a needy, searching world.

Here I'd like us to examine some of our Family tree together. We'll find our shared theology, mission, and experience, and we'll also get just a thumbnail sketch of some of the many heroes of the faith who served the church and reached out to the world. This collected and common insight, this shared heritage of belief and practice provide the evangelical foundation we need to come together to transform the culture for Christ.

COMMONALITIES AMONG DIFFERENCES

As I've said often, we have many differences between us in doctrine and practice. We should not ignore or make light of those differences in coming together, and even as we work together to make common cause, we can discuss those differences in an atmosphere of mutual respect and love for one another in Christ. We can do this realizing that none of us, individually or collectively, has a corner on truth. God is infinite, we are finite. As the Apostle Paul says, "we know in part and we prophesy in part" and "now we see in a mirror, dimly."[1] This means we're all searchers. The accord "Evangelicals and Catholics Together" understands this. I like the way the accord puts it:

> Together we search for a fuller and clearer understanding of God's revelation in Christ and his will for his disciples. Because of the limitations of human reason and language, which limitations are compounded by sin, we cannot understand completely the transcendent reality of God and his ways. Only in the End Time will we see face to face and know as we are known. (1 Corinthians 13) We now search together in confident reliance upon God's self-revelation in Jesus Christ, the sure testimony of Holy Scripture, and the promise of the Spirit to his church. In this search to understand the truth more fully and clearly, we need one another. We are both informed and limited by the histories of our communities and by our experiences. Across the divides of communities and experiences, we need to challenge one another, always speaking the truth in love, and in order to build up the Body.[2]

Fortunately, our common searching has led us to many common conclusions, which have given us a shared theology. And this Christian knowledge base has many facets, but those I would like to highlight here are these:

A Common Book

The Bible is the treasure chest of our common faith. Though we may disagree in our understanding of its origin and even perhaps its extent, evangelical Christians agree it is God's Holy Word given as a "measuring stick," a rule of love for all of life.

A Common History

All of our churches, groups, traditions, communions, and fellowships spring from one root—the root of Jesse, the root and offspring of David: Jesus Christ.[3] He is our Founder, our Savior, our Head, our Lord. We are His bride, His people, His flock, His Family.

We would all do well to study our Family history through all the centuries with an eye toward rediscovering our common heritage. We

could all rejoice in the victories, repent for the mistakes, and most importantly, grow through the lessons.

A Common Creed

Although our doctrines are grounded in Scripture, they have been
expressed and formalized in numerous creeds. Some of these creeds are
distinctively Catholic, some are definitely Protestant, and others are
explicitly Orthodox. Two creeds, however, have found acceptance among
almost all Christian churches: the Apostles' Creed and the Nicene Creed
(see chapter 1). These creedal formulas contain the essence of our common faith, "the faith that was once for all entrusted to the saints."[4]

A Common Savior

Perhaps most important to remember is that we have a common Savior.
There is not a Protestant Jesus, a Catholic Jesus, or an Orthodox Jesus.
Certainly each church communion has cherished important distinctives
in doctrine and practice arising from reflections upon Him, but He is the
same, as the author of Hebrews reminds us, "yesterday and today and
forever."[5]

In his correction of the Corinthian Christians, the Apostle Paul asked
a question we should ponder: "Is Christ divided?"[6] He cannot be and
He is not. But we can be and we are. Let's not confuse our state for His.
He is united and the same; we are divided and different. Different is
okay, even healthy and good. Divided is neither good nor healthy. Christ
longs for us to be united again under Him.

My friend Harald Bredesen spearheads an effort called The Prince
of Peace. He honored Mother Teresa with an award for her witness to the
world of Christ's love, and she accepted it. A truly ecumenical coalition, including Regent University and Franciscan University, came
together to plan the event. As Harald and I worked together on this award
ceremony, we looked to the Lord for a Scripture passage that would
express His deep longing for the unity of His people. We were drawn
to Paul's exhortation to the Ephesian Christians, who in their day were
struggling through some deep issues involving the coming together of
both Jewish and Gentile Christians in the Body of Christ. Paul's response
to their struggle has tremendous relevance for us. As you read his words,
hear them speak to your heart.

> For [Christ] himself is our peace, who has made the two
> [Gentile and Jew] one and has destroyed the barrier, the dividing

wall of hostility, by abolishing in his flesh the law with its commandments and regulations. His purpose was to create in himself one new man out of the two, thus making peace, and in this one body to reconcile both of them to God through the cross, by which he put to death their hostility. He came and preached peace to you who were far away and peace to those who were near. For through him we both have access to the Father by one Spirit.[7]

Our common Savior can destroy the wall of ignorance and hostility that has separated us and seriously hindered our missionary efforts. And when that divisive and derisive wall finally collapses, it will unleash a flood of grace that will soak the parched and abused souls of God's people, nourishing the seeds of peace and unity that long to grow. Until that occurs, and even in preparation for that event, we can and must cooperate together for the soul of our culture.

A Common Mission

Our common mission is the proclamation and teaching of the gospel of Christ, which impacts every aspect of human nature and human culture, and living it out in word and deed.

To effectively carry out our mission, we need to be fully empowered by the same Holy Spirit who has animated our Family from the day of Pentecost; we need to be fully faithful to our own convictions, those that flow out of our common faith and those that come from our distinctive church traditions; we need to be in communion with God's people and in submission to church authority; we need to make room for one another, building on our commonalities while respecting our differences. The harvest is indeed plentiful and the laborers are still few. Together, though, we are many. In cooperation, we can support one another to accomplish our common, divinely commanded agenda.

Within each of our churches, we need to preach an evangelical message to awaken dry bones and rouse sleeping warriors. To the nations who have never heard or who have turned a deaf ear to the One who fashioned them from dust, we need to "tell the old, old story of Jesus and His love." It's an old story that's ever new. It's our story . . . our Family history . . . and we must not rest until we see the members of our Family span the globe, locked arm in arm in the unifying love of our common Lord.

SHARED UNCOMMON HEROES

When we look to our past, as we did in chapter 10, we find numerous saints who lived uncommon lives in obedience to our common Savior and Lord. They demonstrate to us the walls we can scale when we submit to the Lord and move out in the power of the Holy Spirit.

The Evangelical Preachers

Let's first look at just a few of the evangelical preachers. Probably the greatest among them was the Apostle Paul. He stands as a prime example of a transformed life, a life that became a powerful tool for the Kingdom. Whether as a free man or as a prisoner, he was a messenger of liberation to unbelievers and a source of encouragement for Christians. He preached, defended, and struggled to live out the gospel message until his death. Christ's death and resurrection permeated his teaching and preaching; they were the strength and hope from which Paul moved. As a result of his commitment to our Lord, he has left us a written treasure of power, a storehouse of truth, and an encouraging portrait of perseverance.

Evangelical Christians since Paul have relied on his insight, his faithfulness, and his written word—the word that amazingly touches all of life. This is a wonderful testimony to the timelessness of the gospel message. The worldview of the first century was obviously quite different from our twentieth-century perspective, but even though the accidents of culture change, the substance of being human never alters. Paul's message was aimed at the heart of what it means to be human, at what it means to desire truth, at what it means to love. These basics are timeless and that is why Paul's words will never become outdated or obsolete.

Many of the well-known evangelists were and are power preachers, relying heavily on the words of sacred Scripture. John Chrysostom, one of the Eastern Fathers of the church, was most famous for his ministry of forceful, prophetic preaching. But we have sometimes forgotten that his ministry was partially motivated by his concern for the sinful state of the world. Listen to how he put it: "My work is like that of a man who is trying to clean a piece of ground into which a muddy stream is constantly flowing."[8] That's not despair—that's reality.

Later, in the thirteenth century, we see Dominic establishing the first group of church-sanctioned itinerant preachers. One of the charisms of this group of men was their ability to preach with so much zeal that when their religious order was formally established, they were called the "order of preachers." Dominic, one of the great preachers and defenders of the faith, converted many souls to the Savior.

Looking ahead to post-Reformation Protestant leaders, we discover such men as John Wesley, Charles Finney, and D. L. Moody, all men who relied solely on the power of the proclamation of the Word to evangelize. Wesley preached the fundamentals of Christianity, mainly the doctrines of justification (what God does for us) and the new birth (what God does in us). The Wesley brothers' ministry was itinerant. Fired by their own experience of saving grace, they traveled extensively, preaching the message of the gospel with unquenchable zeal. In fact, identified with these two preachers is the classic phrase, "I look upon all the world as my parish."[9]

In the early 1830s, another evangelical leader, Charles Finney, promoted the practice of revivals and toured many major cities in the United States, including New York, Philadelphia, and Boston. Due to his efforts, revivalism became a major force in Protestant evangelism. In fact, D. L. Moody transformed the technique of revivalism, changing it from one-night camp meetings and single church affairs to power-packed, nightly events that spanned several weeks and grew from the collaborative efforts of many denominations.

Such revivals were and still can be an experience of extended, intensive proclamation of the Word. The participants are drawn by powerful moments of praise and worship so key for openness to the voice of God. If the meeting begins in the power of the Holy Spirit, the effects of the preaching will be intensified. Moody fortunately knew how to organize these revivals and follow the inspirations of the Holy Spirit. Thank God he did. Thousands were brought to the Lord through the power of such approaches to revivalism.

Protestants, however, were not the only ones involved in revivals. Clarence Walworth, a nineteenth-century Catholic priest, was converted to Christianity in a revivalist meeting and became one of the most forceful parish mission preachers of his time. He adopted a revivalist style of preaching that was described this way: "First he would speak in a quiet, gentle manner, then he screamed out so that the walls of the Cathedral reechoed it back again; it reverberated and resounded. It was magnificent and terrible and the people cried, groaned, beat their breasts."[10] Another penned these observations about Walworth: "During his sermons he not only pointed to the mission cross, but he even clung to it, till it swayed back and forth with the weight of his body, whilst the people, conscience-stricken and pale with emotion, watched and listened with almost breathless silence."[11] That is anointed preaching, the kind that brings about conversion.

Not just individuals but entire religious communities in the Roman Catholic Church have also been known for dynamic mission preaching. In fact, the Passionists, a Catholic religious community founded by Paul of the Cross, another great hero of mine, were known for conducting crusadelike events. The early Jesuits did too.

In our own century, we can see many examples of wonderful missionary preachers, but perhaps none more obvious than our own twentieth-century Paul, Billy Graham. More than any other evangelical Christian, Dr. Graham is responsible for restructuring mass evangelism. Mass media and convenient means of travel have enabled Dr. Graham to reach almost every country in the world. He and those like him have engaged in a truly global mission of evangelization.

Another major mass-evangelization organization is FIRE, a Catholic alliance of Faith, Intercession, Repentance, and Evangelism based at Franciscan University. Working from Luke 12:49—"I have come to bring fire on the earth, and how I wish it were already kindled!" (NIV)— members of FIRE proclaim the gospel of salvation: the fire of judgment, the fire of the Holy Spirit, and the fire of God's love. Testimonies of conversions, restoration of relationships, physical and emotional healings, and spiritual rebirths are the fruit of this evangelistic ministry, a sign that the hearts of many who hear the gospel message are willing to receive it personally.

Charismatic-renewal conferences, much like revival meetings, have drawn thousands to a deeper experience of God and radically committed Christian lifestyles. For instance, the 1977 interdenominational charismatic conference in Kansas City was a good example of an evangelical event of magnitude. More than fifty thousand Christians attended, and the Word was preached in power and truth. Amid the praise, prayer, and teaching, Christians experienced the excitement of our common faith, the excitement of being Christian together.

The Social Activists
While Word-centered preachers and evangelists such as those we just scanned are desperately needed, we also need social activists, for evangelism entails social action as well as preaching. Take Jesus, for example. His ministry encompassed much more than preaching and teaching. He attended to the needs of the poor and hungry, the emotionally and

physically sick, the children, the lonely—in short, the profoundly help-less who needed the touch of love. He saw the interrelatedness of the gospel and social action so clearly that when He spoke of the Last Judgment, He revealed that social involvement was a prerequisite for entering the Kingdom: "'Come, you who are blessed by my Father; take your inheritance, the kingdom prepared for you since the creation of the world. For I was hungry and you gave me something to drink, I was a stranger and you invited me in, I needed clothes and you clothed me, I was sick and you looked after me, I was in prison and you came to visit me."[12]

Charity permeates the record of Jesus' life. In His teachings (par-ticularly the parables) and His actions, He demonstrated the significance of reaching out in genuine love and concern for others. In the story of the good Samaritan, for instance, Jesus illustrated the importance of com-passion. He told of a Jewish man who was badly beaten and left on the side of the road to die, visible to all who passed. Two men, a priest and a Levite, passed by without helping this half-dead man. The third indi-vidual, a Samaritan, saw him and was moved with pity. He approached him and dressed his wounds, "pouring on oil and wine. Then he put the man on his own donkey, took him to an inn and took care of him. The next day he took out two silver coins and gave them to the innkeeper. 'Look after him,' he said, 'and when I return, I will reimburse you for any extra expense you may have.'"

Jesus then asked His listener, "'Which of these three [the priest, Levite, or Samaritan] . . . was a neighbor to the man who fell into the hands of robbers?' The expert in the law replied, 'The one who had mercy on him.' Jesus told him, 'Go and do likewise.'"[13] Go and be com-passionate.

Jesus was the greatest social activist of all time, and many after Him followed in His tradition, including the apostles, who were often involved in the ministry of healing and deliverance. Moreover, the apostolate of all of the great saints of history has always entailed compassion for the poor and suffering.

I immediately think of Francis of Assisi and his ongoing ministry to and love for the lepers. Originally, Francis was so repulsed by their physical appearance that he was unable to even look at their oozing sores. But when the love of Jesus overcame him, Francis no longer saw the sores of a leper—he saw the wounds of Christ. He saw pain that needed relief; he saw people in need; he saw the alienation of being marked, of being different, of being cast down. He saw all things through the eyes of Love, through the eyes of Christ.

Leprosy finds its modern counterpart in the tragedy of AIDS. How compassionate are we to the victims of this disease? Do we try to find ways to help them, or do we reinforce the alienation that is heaped upon them, or worse, do we judge them? Do we have a desire to serve God by serving His creatures? Francis and the brothers did not run when service was difficult. Embracing the difficulty for the sake of Christ, they chose to love.

Developing social conscience and acting on it are necessary to a truly Christian life, but they are only authentic when they flow out of the gospel values of love and service. Social action should never be a substitute for evangelism; rather, it's a handmaid. Charity in the form of social awareness should flow from a love affair with Jesus and a desire to help others enter into a personal relationship with Him by bringing them into relationship with His presence in each of us.

Probably the most well-known examples of twentieth-century Christians committed to social action are Mother Teresa and the Sisters of Charity. These sisters have a specific apostolate to the forgotten, the homeless, the dying. They spend the entire day walking around the streets of Calcutta (or any other city with a branch of the order), picking up people on the brink of death. They help them all, even if all they can do is provide an opportunity for them to die with dignity and in peace. To die in peace is a key concept here. Not only do the sisters clean these people and provide for them humane conditions in which to die, but they also introduce them to the Lord. After all, no one can truly die in peace without coming to terms with the Savior.

Mother Teresa walks with spiritual eyes; when she looks, she sees only Christ and the things of Christ. She therefore radiates Christ in all she says and does, and her fruit shows it.

The Literary Giants

A whole other branch of the Christian Family tree is remote from the physical pain of the poor and the desperate. Pain of a different type exists in this branch, though, and it needs to be healed and redeemed as well. I'm talking about the world of letters, the world of the intellectual. Faith is often very difficult for those who insist on reasonable, objective proof of the existence, nature, and work of God. Consequently, they need to be approached with the claims of faith in a way that will appeal to the intellect, not just the heart.

Through the ages, our Christian Family has been blessed with many profoundly faith-filled intellectuals. The early church Fathers were some of the finest scholars and apologists the church has ever had. During the Middle Ages, the Benedictine monks, Augustine, and other scholastics and scholars continued to protect and preserve the faith. Some of the most profound theology as well as some of the great spiritual classics emerged during this historical period.

Probably the greatest medieval mind and arguably one of the great minds ever was the Dominican scholar Thomas Aquinas. Many scholars consider his *Summa Theologica* to be his finest contribution to Christian thought. It is a theological masterpiece in which Aquinas treats almost every imaginable issue of our human experience. Not only does he show how incredibly reasonable it is to believe in God, but he also explores such themes as love, hate, sin, virtue, justice, mercy, emotions, nature, grace, angels, Heaven, and hell. The reasonableness of his positions makes him appealing to the scholar. He addresses the possible difficulties with his viewpoint and systematically refutes them. Moreover, he validates his arguments with numerous sources, including the Bible and the writings of Aristotle and Augustine. Thomas Aquinas is the premier doctor of the church, and to this day, scholarly members of the Christian Family study his works to break open his timeless insight and wisdom.

Another wonderful doctor of the church in the 1300s was Catherine of Siena, another Dominican. Catherine, along with Teresa of Avila, was one of only two women doctors of the church. She was a defender of the faith in a critical time for the church and was instrumental in the pope's return to Rome from Avignon.

One hundred or so years after Catherine and immediately before the Reformation stands one of the great scholars of all time, Ignatius of Loyola. Ignatius founded the Society of Jesus (the Jesuits), which is still recognized as the great priestly order of scholars, thinkers, and writers. Many Christians have found the *Spiritual Exercises* of Ignatius tremendously helpful for growth in holiness.

In the twentieth century, one of the finest Christian thinkers and imaginative writers is C. S. Lewis. His books include *Mere Christianity*, *The Screwtape Letters*, *The Great Divorce*, *The Abolition of Man*, *The Four Loves*, and *The Problem of Pain*. Lewis has a unique ability to draw the reader into a fantasy world that is all too real. The reader emerges from that world somewhat uncomfortably challenged in his or her Christian walk.

The Screwtape Letters, for instance, is a fictional collection of correspondence between Screwtape, an agent for the Devil, and his nephew,

Wormwood. The letters outline the plan of destruction for the individual human soul to whom Wormwood is assigned. Lewis chillingly awakens us to the possibility that, just as we all have a personal guardian angel, we may all have a personal angel of darkness whose entire function is to lead us to destruction. Lewis reveals gospel truth subtly, pointing to the temptations that we face and also to the ways in which we cleverly rationalize our sin until we finally become desensitized to it altogether. Provocative and full of cryptic messages, his writing commands the reader's attention.

Those more drawn to the genre of literature can find their fill of the Christian worldview in many writers who have nourished the Christian Family tree. Many have found consolation and challenge in the writings of Dante, John Milton, and John Donne; the poetry of John of the Cross and Teresa of Avila; and in our own century, the works of Graham Greene, T. S. Eliot, and G. K. Chesterton. Chesterton and Eliot are particularly intriguing because of their personal styles and their insight into the twentieth century.

Through the power of great writing and sound scholarship, these Christians, and many others like them, have provided a medium for evangelization and apologetics that has impacted untold numbers who may never have come to the Cross otherwise.

We need a new generation of men and women who can carry this great heritage forward and ensure that the next century is filled with the truths of the Christian faith.

THE PAST FOR TODAY

I find it wonderful and encouraging to look at our evangelical heritage from such different approaches over many generations. It helps us see that God has created each and every human being uniquely with different needs, different gifts and talents, and with different approaches to a faith experience. The rich and varied heritage of our Christian Family tree acknowledges our individual uniquenesses as it preserves and proclaims our unity in Christ.

Given our human uniquenesses and divinely bestowed and various gifts, it's vital that we who know the truth reach out to others who need the truth. We need to appeal to the people who need an evangelical fervor behind the Word of God, to the people who need to be ministered to by action, and to the intellectuals who need to exercise the gift of reason even more actively in their search for faith and in their faith in Christ.

God knows our needs, and He has faithfully provided men and women who, imbued with the Spirit of the gospel, have gone out in the world and worked for the Kingdom, taken chances, risked, fought, been persecuted, trusted in God, acted on their convictions, and loved. Looking at their lives is rather convicting because they are just ordinary human beings like you and me who chose to respond to God's supernatural grace and call. What if some of these Christians had ignored the call that God placed on their hearts? Christianity would have a different face today.

God wants to use all of us in a mighty way. And one of those ways is in cooperation to impact the social order. Building on our common Family heritage, we can do just that.

CHAPTER FIFTEEN

A COMMON AGENDA

America is great because she is good,
and if America ever ceases to be good,
America will cease to be great.
Alexis de Tocqueville

In the 1830s, the great French jurist and historian Alexis de Tocqueville traveled around America. His journey resulted in a two-volume study entitled *Democracy in America*. His observations on the effects of religious faith on the American experiment seem incredibly distant to those of us struggling in a secularized America. Tocqueville wrote: "There is no country in the world where the Christian religion retains a greater influence over the souls of men than in America. . . . For the Americans, the ideas of Christianity and liberty are so completely mingled that it is almost impossible to get them to conceive of one without the other; it is not a question with them of sterile beliefs bequeathed by the past and vegetating rather than living in the depths of the soul."[1]

His words are inspiring, but given the current trends in our country, they are also frightening. In 150 years, we have gone from a country in which people of faith, especially Christians, were honored and extremely influential, to a nation that has even instituted laws and supported public policies to silence and quarantine religious people, particularly Christians, whenever they want to bring their faith to bear in the public arena.

As a French American, I have a particular interest in Tocqueville's observations. He, of course, understood that America became independent through revolution. His native land, France, had also experienced revolution. But the French Revolution had rocked his nation much differently than the American Revolution affected the colonies. The French Revolution was antitheist and antichurch. It was an effort to thrust God out of the human equation. Consequently it resulted in tyranny, persecution, and the unleashing of ideological principles that many say led to Marxism, utilitarianism, and the moral relativism that would later enslave millions.

What Tocqueville found in America was very different. He discovered the fruit of a theistic, pro-church revolution. Americans had fought for their independence, but for most of them God was active in human history, and He would one day judge every person for his or her deeds.

Today many people squabble over who among the founding fathers was a Christian. Regardless of the outcome of that debate, no knowledgeable historian of early American history would deny the fact that the concept of a Creator God who endowed His creation with inalienable rights was an essential underpinning of the American proposition. These rights were derived, not from a government that was transitory, but from a Governor who was eternal. It was the role of government to defend these rights and not dilute or remove them.

There is no question either that the Judeo-Christian heritage had a profound impact on the founding of America and the structuring of her understanding of her experiment in "ordered liberty," the role and primacy of the family as the first mediating institution, the respect for life, and the "pursuit of happiness," which of necessity involved the right to private property. All of these principles embodied in America's enabling documents and proclaimed by the founders made this new nation unique among the nations. They still do.

Tocqueville came to America to try to better understand the uniqueness of the American experiment: "I sought for the greatness and genius of America in her commodious harbors and her ample rivers—and it was not there. . . . in her fertile fields and boundless forests—and it was not there. . . . in her rich mines and her vast world commerce—and it was not there. . . . in her democratic congress and her matchless Constitution—and it was not there. Not until I went into the churches of America and heard her pulpits flame with righteousness did I understand the secret of her genius and power."[2]

When one strips the religious influence from our foundational documents and culture, what is left is no longer America. Yet, that is exactly what is occurring to our nation. We are undergoing the secularization of our soul, and it is stripping us bare of our inherent dignity and value as creatures made in God's image. It is tearing apart marriages and families, undermining our schools, and creating tyranny in our public policies. Its impact has already been staggering, but if it continues it will eventually kill the American experiment and perhaps usher in something much closer to that beast created by the French Revolution.

If you doubt this, consider the insights of one of my great contemporary heroes, Richard John Neuhaus. While reflecting on America's deeply religious past in light of the rise of secularism, he made a telling observation: "'We hold these truths' was the beginning of the conversation that launched this experiment, and it should now be obvious to all that the experiment cannot be sustained by a secular liberalism that divorced the cause of freedom from the claims of truth. Those who now fear publicly resurgent religion will in time, one hopes, come to recognize that freedom grounded in moral truth provides a greater security for virtues cherished by old fashioned liberals—openness, rationality, tolerance, and mutual respect. But that may take a long time."[3]

I agree with Father Neuhaus. It may take a long time, for secularism is becoming more firmly entrenched in the nation's psyche and policies with each passing day. But I'm convinced the tide of moral and religious demise will not be turned back unless Christians come together to block and reverse it. We must work to restore in America the great influence of truth; we must strive to restore an understanding that true freedom has to be grounded in objective moral truth. Ultimately, this is our common task worldwide as well.

Not only Christians recognize the declining state of America and the need for the inculcation of Judeo-Christian values and truths. Rabbi Daniel Lapin is part of the Pacific Jewish Center and president of the Seattle-based organization Toward Tradition. He is a prolific writer and an inspiring speaker. He is not a Christian but an orthodox Jew. He, too, recognizes the incredible importance of the Judeo-Christian heritage in America. In a recent article in *Crisis*, a journal of lay Catholic opinion, Rabbi Lapin made these comments on the breakdown of the family:

> The fight waged in our culture over the past 30 years has chiefly been over whether the Bible's model of marriage and family life is still correct for America. The traditional view is that humans will be happiest, they will feel most fulfilled, and their society will best flourish when conventional family life is widely practiced.
>
> The opposing viewpoint, which has increasingly insinuated itself into our laws, schools, and public policy, argues that

anything endorsed by the Bible is bad. This approach has bequeathed bitterness to those who bought its animalistic message; its legacy consists of the dangerous streets and squalid neighborhoods that altogether appropriately are referred to as the urban jungle. The cure is the Judaeo-Christian marriage model, which turns animals into men and jungles into shining cities.[4]

In a very sobering sense, we should not be surprised that we are witnessing the breakdown of the family, a resurgence of heinous crime in our streets, and a cheapening of life itself. These are all symptoms of the very dangerous disease of secularism. This malady strips religious principle out of the human community, leaving it extremely vulnerable to destruction. Men and women are left to their own designs. No longer inspired to follow what Abraham Lincoln called their "higher angels," to aspire to virtue, charity, selflessness, and community, they degenerate individually and corporately.

Nevertheless, Christians can change the course of history. The great church historian Eusebius, writing around AD 320, recorded how Christians took the gospel of Christ from Jerusalem to Samaria, and then to the outermost ends of the earth. He exposes the hostile world Christians faced and documents how, out of faithfulness to the Lord, they advanced into the corruption of the Roman Empire and accomplished the unbelievable. Eusebius wrote: "Persians, when they have become pupils of the Savior, no longer marry their own mothers. Neither do the Scythians, since the word of Christ has penetrated their lands, any longer feed on human flesh. Other tribes of barbarians no longer have unlawful relations with their daughters and sisters; nor do men fall madly in love with men and indulge those pleasures which are contrary to nature."[5]

Because of their courage and willingness to engage and transform the culture of their day, these early Christians altered the course of history. Indeed, we exist today as a Christian people because of what our ancestors accomplished. We can derive courage and vision from them as we confront secularism and the many resurging forms of paganism.

Paganism is coming back, and it's finding fertile ground in North America. Many contemporary immoral behaviors are simply the fruit of a vibrant and growing rebirth of paganism, a cultural return to pre-Judeo-Christian ideologies and practices. Like the pagans of yesterday, many people today are sacrificing their children, killing their spouses, engaging in illicit sexual unions, and worshiping pagan gods and goddesses, such as Sophia. The description of sins listed by the Apostle Paul in Romans 1 has a frightening ring of contemporary relevance. Just a generation ago, as a culture we would have found such activities quite unthinkable, at least unmentionable in public conversation. Yet these activities are now a standard topic on the nightly news, television talk shows, and in every sort of print media imaginable.

What are we to do about all this? We are to do what Christian people have always done: serve, fight, work, and lead as we seek to reassert the influence of our faith on our culture. And we must do this together. The barbarians are scaling the walls. The Axis and ancient Roman ideologies are at work among us. Will we wake up to their threat and align our combined forces against them? Or will we allow the petty quarreling within our camp to render us immobile?

"EVANGELICALS AND CATHOLICS TOGETHER"

At least some Christians are calling for a truce and a new pact of cooperation. These Christians are combining forces to make common cause to engage and transform our culture for the Lord. The history-making accord, "Evangelicals and Catholics Together," provides, I believe, a profound and concise statement regarding the need and parameters for just such an alliance-building "war effort." It lays the theological and sociological foundation for how we can unite in common cause for Christ Jesus, as well as face our common cultural threats and foes.

Because I believe this accord is so important and relevant to our current age, I have chosen to shape much of this chapter around it, especially focusing in on one of its main sections. The accord is divided into six segments: an Introduction followed by five sections. The first section, "We Affirm Together," is a short yet brilliant statement of what we have in common as Christians, the basic foundation of our faith. The remaining four sections—"We Hope Together," "We Search Together," "We Contend Together," and "We Witness Together"—set forth a fuller rationale for our cooperation and convergence, including an agenda we should all be able to embrace. I believe that section 4, "We Contend Together," provides us with the most concise summary of a common *social* agenda for our time, and it's this I want to concentrate on here.

Before I do, though, I'd like to briefly raise the issue of evangelism.

A Word About Evangelism

All evangelical Christians are committed to the proclamation of the *kerygma*, the good news about the reconciliation between a Holy God and unholy people made possible by the life, death, and resurrection of Jesus Christ. We all agree that this reconciliation has come because of God's undeserved, gratuitous grace and that any human being can receive its incredible benefits by faith. Between our various traditions and confessions, there are numerous differences over God's role and humanity's role in the salvation process, but these are Family differences. They are not disagreements between nonChristians and Christians but between committed Christians with different theological and biblical understandings. Our differences are important, but they do not mean some of us are going to hell while those who are "right" among us are going to Heaven. We are brothers and sisters in Christ, not only by name but by conversion in, through, and by Him.

Consequently, all of us can and should tell others about the gospel. And I pray for the day when more of us will evangelize together. The authors of the accord certainly envisioned this day as well. In the section "We Contend Together," they rightly acknowledged:

> The cause of Christ is the cause and mission of the church, which is, first of all, to proclaim the Good News that "God was in Christ reconciling the world to himself, not counting their trespasses against them, and entrusting to us the message of reconciliation." (2 Corinthians 5) To proclaim this Gospel and to sustain the community of faith, worship, and discipleship that is gathered by this Gospel is the first and chief responsibility of the church. All other tasks and responsibilities of the church are derived from and directed toward the mission of the Gospel.[6]

In my first book, *Evangelical Catholics*, I talked a lot about Christians cooperating to evangelize. Evangelism is one of my passions. It's a task I have engaged in for years, as have many of my Catholic brethren. I'm delighted that evangelists such as Billy Graham have seen fit to link his efforts with Christians from across the theological spectrum, including those who count themselves as Roman Catholic Christians. I would even contend that one of the reasons his evangelistic efforts have been so divinely blessed worldwide is because of the broad Christian alliance he has courageously and faithfully developed.

However, I also realize that for many Christians the thought of building alliances for the purpose of evangelizing is simply too much to consider right now. This is as true in Protestant circles as it is in Catholic circles. Some Protestants feel Catholics believe a different gospel, and some Catholics feel the same way about Protestants.

Over my years of study, dialogue, and alliance building with Christians from across the confessional spectrum, I have come to the conclusion that neither evangelical Protestants nor evangelical Catholics nor evangelical Orthodox believers embrace a false gospel. But it can appear that way because we understand certain terms and interpret various biblical texts differently. So when we talk to one another, our words are often misconstrued, hence our doctrine becomes suspect. Of course, our different practices also generate misunderstandings and frequently uninformed criticism.

For reasons such as these, I have not focused my attention in this book on cooperative evangelistic efforts. I hope one day we will preach the basic gospel message together to a dying world. And I think that will happen if we commit ourselves to listen more closely to each other, to ask questions that seek understanding rather than entrapment, to clarify terms and support friendly, reasoned dialogue rather than hostile, ill-reasoned diatribes. I also believe that as we work together on social issues, we will discover how much we really do have in common. Our activist efforts will also open much-needed dialogue among us over our differences, and I pray that will eventually lead to the end of much, if not all, of the current suspicion, misunderstandings, and ill feelings between all too many of us. Then, perhaps, we will carry the gospel throughout the world as a single Body.

Until then, I will continue to plead for us to work together to redeem the culture. There is more than enough for us to do together in the social arena. So let's turn our attention to that.

Principles for Allied Social Action

Throughout the context of the accord, two important principles are repeated—convergence and cooperation. In one place the accord reminds us, "Our cooperation as citizens is animated by our convergence as Christians. We promise one another that we will work to deepen, build upon, and expand this pattern of convergence and cooperation."[7] I fully agree with these principles as a vehicle toward jointly achieving our goals in the twenty-first century and beyond. We need to learn to cooperate together, to make common cause. It is in that very cooperation that we will find our convergence—the numerous intersections of commonality that link us together as followers of Jesus Christ.

This document also calls on us to reassert the influence of what we hold in common upon contemporary America and beyond her borders to the entire world. The accord correctly understands that this is the essence of the function of the church.

Christ seeks the redemption of the whole of humankind, which includes the body and the soul, and all temporal and eternal relationships. The Fall affected everything; redemption restores and transforms everything. This includes the social order. The authors of the accord understand this, and they also agree that our cooperation in the redemption mandate carries a sociopolitical limitation.

> Christians individually and the church corporately also have a responsibility for the right ordering of civil society. We embrace this task soberly: knowing the consequences of human sinfulness, we resist the utopian conceit that it is within our powers to build the Kingdom of God on earth. We embrace this task hopefully: knowing that God has called us to love our neighbor, we seek to secure for all a greater measure of civil righteousness and justice, confident that he will crown our efforts when he rightly orders all things in the coming of his Kingdom.[8]

We cannot do what only God can do. Only He can establish a theocracy, a sociopolitical order in which He rules all the affairs of humankind. And this He will do at the end of the age, in the new heavens and the new earth.

At the same token, we must do what He calls us to do. We must seek to influence every facet of human society with the Judeo-Christian worldview. We should not look to wed church and state; neither should we tolerate the state's efforts to remove the church's influence from the social order.

For what, then, should we contend together? The accord sets forth a mandate that I believe and hope all of us will adopt and strive to achieve as allies. It begins with truth.

Contending for the Truth
America's birth certificate is the Declaration of Independence. That wonderful document begins with the words, "We hold these truths. . . ." Our nation's founders understood there were truths to be held, and these truths were "inalienable." These truths were grounded in our common Creator, and they were true of all humankind, even if some people didn't believe them or even know about them. In short, these truths were absolute—they applied to all people at all times and in all places. They

were universal. They transcended culture and the different religions and individual human experience. And yet these truths were applicable to every aspect of human life.

In an age of relativism and skepticism, the clarity of that proclamation is refreshing. It is also the place where we must begin as we embark upon a common agenda. We must contend together for absolute truth. The accord tells us, "As we are bound together by Christ and his cause, so we are bound together in contending against all that opposes Christ and his cause. We are emboldened not by illusions of easy triumph but by faith in his certain triumph. Our Lord wept over Jerusalem, and he now weeps over a world that does not know the time of its visitation. The raging of the principalities and powers may increase as the End Time nears, but the outcome of the contest is assured."[9] Truth will prevail; God has assured us of that. But our task is to fight for it, for the church has been enlisted to contend for the truth.

Why is this so important? Because the first and most fundamental right of every human person is to hear the truth and the truth's greatest affirmation, the gospel. That is why religious freedom is the first freedom. That is why it is so essential that we oppose all efforts to censor faith out of the marketplace. For it's in the marketplace, the public square, that most people will hear the truth when it's presented. This is also the place where error is sold and bought.

We live in an age of falsehood. The best antidote for what is false is the proclamation and demonstration of the truth. And truth is best demonstrated in the moral sphere of our lives. As the accord so clearly states:

> Together we contend for the truth that politics, law, and culture must be secured by moral truth. With the Founders of the American experiment, ... we hold that this constitutional order is composed not just of rules and procedures but is most essentially a moral experiment. With them, we hold that only a virtuous people can be free and just, and that virtue is secured by religion. ...
>
> Americans are drifting away from, are often explicitly defying, the constituting truths of this experiment in ordered liberty. Influential sectors of the culture are laid waste by relativism, anti-intellectualism, and nihilism that deny the very area of truth. Against such influences in both the elite and popular culture, we appeal to reason and religion in contending for the foundational truths of our constitutional order.[10]

Together we must defend, demonstrate, and proclaim the truth in every segment of our society. We must fight in the courts, the legislatures, the classrooms, the marketplace, the media, and our homes. We must reassert the truths to which our founders referred when they uttered those now historic words, "We hold these truths." They're *our* truths. In an age of relativism and subjectivity, it is only when people of faith reassert these fundamental truths that we will begin to see positive change.

Contending for Religious Freedom

The accord also addresses the relationship of religious freedom to truth and challenges us to stand together to defend religious freedom:

> We contend together for religious freedom. We do so for the sake of religion, but also because religious freedom is the first freedom, the source and shield of all human freedoms. In their relationship to God, persons have a dignity and responsibility that transcends, and thereby limits, the authority of the state and of every other merely human institution.
>
> Religious freedom is itself grounded in and is a product of religious faith, as is evident in the history of Baptists and others in this country. Today we rejoice together that the Roman Catholic Church—as affirmed by the Second Vatican Council and boldly exemplified in the ministry of John Paul II—is strongly committed to religious freedom and, consequently, to the defense of all human rights. Where Evangelicals and Catholics are in severe and sometimes violent conflict, such as parts of Latin America, we urge Christians to embrace and act upon the imperative of religious freedom. Religious freedom will not be respected by the state if it is not respected by Christians or, even worse, if Christians attempt to recruit the state in repressing religious freedom.[11]

In any discussion of religious freedom, the issue of what has come to be called the "separation of church and state" always comes into play. Though I affirm the separation of church and state, I strongly oppose the growing effort to separate religion from public life. It is an ominous step toward religious cleansing.

Over the last twenty-five years, the concept of separation has devolved from the founders' intent. The U.S. Constitution's First Amendment contains what's called the Establishment Clause, which states, "Congress shall make no law respecting an establishment of religion, or prohibiting the free exercise thereof." This clause was originally designed to prevent the federal government from establishing one religion above all others—in other words, from setting up a national religion. People were to be free to worship according to their faith and to practice their faith as conscience led. The state could, and often did, support religious practice, but it could not select or create one particular religious expression and foist it upon the American people.

This understanding of the Establishment Clause seems tragically foreign in the current atmosphere of judicial debate and practice. Many of today's constitutional interpreters have virtually ignored the original intent of this clause and have twisted it into a club to be used against the individual and corporate free exercise of religion, religious speech, and civil protest inspired by deeply held religious beliefs.

We need a rebirth of liberty in the United States. The fall of the Berlin Wall helped democracy take a giant step forward throughout the world. Now the wall that has been thrown up to keep religion out of American public life must be demolished so democracy can once again flourish in the United States.

Consider just a few of the chilling effects that the current abuse of the Establishment Clause has brought to our nation:

◆ Religious speech is discriminated against in every part of public life.
◆ Our rich religious heritage is being systematically stripped from public buildings and education.
◆ Hostility to religion has replaced the Constitution's original staunch protection of religious freedom.

Through my work with the ACLJ, I have become even more familiar with the devastating effects caused by America's wall against religious freedom.

For instance, in a case before the Georgia Supreme Court, we helped secure the right of citizens to share their faith at the 1996 Olympic Games in Atlanta.

We also argued successfully before the U.S. Supreme Court on behalf of Lamb's Chapel, a Christian church which had been denied equal access to the after-hours use of a public auditorium to show a film on family life to the public. The state of New York sought to censor the film because it was perceived as "religious." We consider this kind of state-sponsored censorship to be a form of religious apartheid.[12]

Along with our legal work in the courts, we also aggressively defend religious freedom at all other levels of our society, including in administrative and school-board meetings. And the victories we achieve for people of faith have tremendous benefits for all American citizens, even those who profess no religious faith at all. For if religious speech can be censored because of its content, so could political speech or scientific speech or literary speech or any other kind of speech. In fact, isn't that the intent of politically correct speech—to control the language and thereby control the public debate and public conclusions? Isn't that kind of control coercive? We at the ACLJ certainly think so.

Many secularists would have the nation believe that Christians actually oppose the separation of church and state and wish to force our religious convictions on the American people rather than win them through public debate on the issues. Here the accord does an outstanding job of clarifying a position upon which we can all find common ground:

> In this country, . . . freedom of religion cannot be taken for granted but requires constant attention. We strongly affirm the separation of church and state, and just as strongly protest the distortion of that principle to mean the separation of religion from public life. We are deeply concerned about the courts' narrowing of the protections provided by the "free exercise" provision of the First Amendment and by an obsession with "no establishment" that stifles the necessary role of religion in American life. As a consequence of such distortions, it is increasingly the case that wherever government goes religion must retreat, and government increasingly goes almost everywhere. Religion, which was privileged and foundational in our legal order, has in recent years been penalized and made marginal. We contend together for a renewal of the constituting vision of the place of religion in the American experiment.
>
> Religion and religiously grounded moral conviction is not an alien or threatening force in our public life. For the great majority of Americans, morality is derived, however variously and confusedly, from religion. The argument, increasingly voiced in sectors of our political culture, that religion should be excluded from the public square must be recognized as an assault upon the most elementary principles of democratic governance. That argument needs to be exposed and countered by

leaders, religious and other, who care about the integrity of our constitutional order.[13]

We must unify in our effort to oppose the radical, rabid, and unconstitutional trend to remove all religion from the public square. We should stand together on the proposition that God and country are complementary in America. This is our history and this is our heritage. Our first president, George Washington, stated as much: "It is the duty of all nations to acknowledge the providence of almighty God, to obey His Will, to be grateful for His benefits, and to humbly implore His protection and favor."[14] We stand united to be good citizens and keep religion where it belongs, as perhaps the primary influence of public life in America, not a side concern locked away in the church sanctuary or hidden behind the front doors of our homes.

When Alexis de Tocqueville traveled America, he concluded, "America is great because she is good, and if America ever ceases to be good, America will cease to be great."[15] America's greatness is slipping fast, and she will only regain it when religion—particularly the Judeo-Christian faith—takes its proper place, especially as America's guiding moral light. And that takes Christians being that light at every level of American society.

Contending for Life

The next area where we have a common agenda is the litmus test of any civilization: the way life is viewed and treated. The architects of our new cultural order have a very low view of human life, which is why they can sanction the killing of the unborn, the newborn, the gravely ill, the differently abled, and many other vulnerable people in our society. When Christians stand up for life and defend the right of the vulnerable to live, the promoters of death rise up and "rail against the 'religious right' and evoke the 'separation of church and state' by which they mean the separation of religion and religiously based moral judgements [sic] from public life."[16] They want us to take our religious convictions and moral judgments and go away. This is clearly evident on the most controversial issue of life in our country today: the question of abortion.

We must contend together for life. To be pro-life is to be pro-human. It is to believe that every human person from conception to the moment before death deserves life because the Giver of all life has endowed each of us with a right to life. My experience with the pro-life movement has inspired my conviction that alliance building between Christians on this issue is not only possible but essential. To me, pro-life efforts are the greatest example of how convergence and cooperation can effectively take place among Christians of very different theological perspectives. The accord shows an unequivocal understanding of this as well:

> The pattern of convergence and cooperation between Evangelicals and Catholics is, in large part, a result of common effort to protect human life, especially the lives of the most vulnerable among us. With the Founders, we hold that all human beings are endowed by their Creator with the right to life, liberty, and the pursuit of happiness. The statement that the unborn child is a human life that—barring natural misfortune or lethal intervention—will become what everyone recognizes as a human baby is not a religious assertion. It is a statement of simple biological fact. That the unborn child has a right to protection, including the protection of law, is a moral statement supported by moral reason and Biblical truth.
>
> We, therefore, will persist in contending—we will not be discouraged but will multiply every effort—in order to secure the legal protection of the unborn. Our goals are: to secure due process of law for the unborn, to enact the most protective laws and public policies that are politically possible, and to reduce dramatically the incidence of abortion. We warmly commend those who have established thousands of crisis pregnancy and post-natal care centers across the country, and urge that such efforts be multiplied. As the unborn must be protected, so also must women be protected from their current rampant exploitation by the abortion industry and by fathers who refuse to accept responsibility for women and children. Abortion on demand, which is the current rule in America, must be recognized as a massive attack on the dignity, rights, and needs of women.
>
> Abortion is the leading edge of an encroaching culture of death. The helpless-old, the radically handicapped, and others who cannot effectively assert their rights are increasingly treated as though they have no rights. These are the powerless who are exposed to the will and whim of those who have power over them. We will do all in our power to resist proposals for euthanasia, eugenics, and population control that exploit the vulnerable, corrupt the integrity of medicine, deprave our culture, and betray the moral truths of our constitutional order.[17]

We must redouble our efforts to secure the legal protection of the unborn. We currently have a president and an administration who violently disagree with our pro-life goals. In fact, in a medical nightmare every bit as horrible as Eusebius's recounting of the pagan Scythians' eating of human flesh, the National Institute of Health wants to engage in tax-funded ghoulish experimentation on babies harvested in the wombs of their abortion-bound mothers. The modern pagans will plead for mercy for rabbits subjected to Revlon makeup testing, only to clamor for the medical right to harvest brains from preborn humans. We must stand together, unified, and cry, "NO!"

But the abortion issue is only the tip of the iceberg. It is one small part of the culture of death. Euthanasia is here. Frighteningly enough, the very court precedent secured by *Roe v. Wade* is now being applied in federal courts as the legal strategists seek to bring euthanasia into the forefront of the culture of death. After all, if personal bodily autonomy is the most cherished right; if there is no protection for unborn children; if there is no recognition of the sanctity of life; if there is no longer a claim that it is more compassionate to preserve life; is it not in a profane way consistent to make it a right to kill people who are ill, in pain, or somehow no longer as productive as they once were?

On Tuesday, May 3, 1994, Judge Rothstein, a federal judge in Washington State, held that the Constitution's Fourteenth Amendment guarantees that Americans can kill themselves and are even entitled to assistance to carry out their wishes. She based her decision on *Roe v. Wade*, which had also found its legal foothold in the Fourteenth Amendment through what even some pro-abortion proponents realize was imaginative and irrational legal "reasoning." In Judge Rothstein's own words, "Like the abortion decision, the decision of a . . . person to end his or her life involves the most intimate and personal choices a person may make in a lifetime and constitutes a 'choice central to personal dignity and autonomy.'"[18]

Using this reasoning, Judge Rothstein would likely have a problem with what the state of California did recently. To help reduce the number of suicides on the Golden Gate Bridge, the state installed telephones on the bridge so would-be jumpers could call for counseling help. In light of Judge Rothstein's decision, the state should have probably built diving boards.

Some years ago, I remember seeing a movie called *Soylent Green.* It was a science fiction movie about a futuristic time when people began eating a new food that was touted as the solution to starvation. Toward the middle of the movie, someone discovers that this food, called "Soylent Green," is really human bodies that have been processed for consumption. Farfetched? Of course it is. Impossible? Not at all. As ancient pagans ate one another because they saw human beings simply as animals, so moderns see the human person as a mere machine to be used until it wears down and becomes "useless" or a "burden" to the social order. Then the human machine can be dismantled and its parts reused or sold.[19]

Emboldened by his court victories in Michigan, Jack "Dr. Death" Kevorkian has called for the establishment of suicide clinics across the nation. Just as abortion clinics have franchised death for the unborn, so Kevorkian wants to do the same for those despairing of life. Rather than exercise compassion by giving hope, Kevorkian and his ilk want to capitalize on hopelessness. Pagan morality is reawakening from its long centuries of sleep and finding partners for its death dance and all else that opposes God in contemporary America. Dr. Kevorkian has joined the dance. His step is called "medicide," and its practitioners want to kill people with impunity.

Against this death cult, Christians stand together on the infallible Holy Scriptures, which tell us that God's way is one of life, not death. We are told not to murder each other. This is given not as a suggestion or as an option or as an opinion but as a divine commandment: "You shall not murder."[20]

Contending for Education

Notre Dame, Princeton, Harvard, Yale, and Dartmouth are just a few of the many universities begun by people of faith—in this case, Christians—to perpetuate moral values, excellence in scholarship, and absolute truth. Numerous colleges and seminaries, as well as preschools through high schools, have had similar beginnings. Even today, many schools—most of which are private religious schools—are continuing this great tradition.

But as all of us know, most of our current educational system is devoid of moral instruction. Belief in the absolute nature of truth has been replaced by adherence to the alleged relativity of evolving truths. And the acknowledgment, much less acceptance, of religion as a viable source of knowledge is virtually nonexistent. The secularization of our culture has certainly played a large role in this desperate state of affairs, but so has the retreat of many people of faith, particularly Christians, from the public and even the private school systems. With the light of faith withdrawn, darkness will certainly fill the void.

Therefore, I propose we take a two-pronged approach to reclaim our schools from secularism. First, many of us need to return to the secularized public and private schools and work to transform them. Second, others of us need to begin new schools, and even new universities, that are dedicated to the advancement of a worldview that promotes life, liberty, faith, and family. Both tasks will require the tireless dedication of teachers, administrators, parents, and philanthropists. We can restore American education to its rich religious heritage, but we must begin now and work with a vision commensurate with the greatness of the God in whose image we have been created.

A page from the American history of public education reminds us that two hundred years ago, Dr. Benjamin Rush, one of the leading physicians of his day and hailed as the "Hippocrates of Pennsylvania," championed the burgeoning movement toward public education. Dr. Rush was well known in the medical circles of Europe for establishing a postgraduate scholarship at the University of Edinburgh after his graduation from Princeton. Beyond his commitment to medicine, however, Dr. Rush was dedicated to the idea of an independent United States of America. This learned professional pledged his life, fortune, and sacred honor to the cause of freedom on July 4, 1776, by signing the Declaration of Independence. Dr. Rush was a patriot.

After the American Revolution, Dr. Rush gave himself to the cause of public education. He believed that only an educated citizenry could build a vibrant and free nation. In his most impassioned essay on establishing an American public school system, he placed as the number one priority the teaching of religion and its natural result, the infusing of morals. He wrote, "Next to the duty which young men owe to their Creator, I wish to see a regard to their country inculcated upon them."[21] A love for country was the number two priority.

When the suggestion was made that the public schools should perhaps be secular institutions, as was being done in revolutionary France, Dr. Rush firmly rejected the idea as unworkable and undesirable: "I beg leave to remark that the only foundation for a useful education in a republic is to be laid in religion. Without this there can be no virtue, and without virtue there can be no liberty, and liberty is the object and life of all republican governments."[22]

The new accord again gives us an area in which we can find a common agenda.

In public education, we contend together for schools that transmit to coming generations our cultural heritage, which is inseparable from the formative influence of religion, especially Judaism and Christianity. Education for responsible citizenship and social behavior is inescapably moral education. Every effort must be made to cultivate the morality of honesty, law observance, work, caring, chastity, mutual respect between sexes, and readiness for marriage, parenthood, and family. We reject the claim that, in any or all of these areas, "tolerance" requires the promotion of moral equivalence between the normative and the deviant. In a democratic society that recognizes that parents have the primary responsibility for the formation of their children, schools are to assist and support, not oppose and undermine, parents in the exercise of their responsibility.

We contend together for a comprehensive policy of parental choice in education. This is a moral question of simple justice. Parents are the primary educators of their children; the state and other institutions should be supportive of their exercise of that responsibility. We affirm policies that enable parents to effectively exercise their right and responsibility to choose the schooling that they consider best for their children.[23]

There is a lot of disagreement within the Christian community about public education. Some Christians oppose it entirely as an unconstitutional intrusion of the government. I do not share that approach. Though I certainly recognize the constitutional arguments in its favor, in my opinion, they are virtually a moot issue. Public education is here and it won't go away. It is thoroughly entrenched in the American way of life. Therefore, the issue isn't whether there will be public education, but what kind of public education it will be. The idea that we as a nation should be pushing condoms over character is frightening. It is also a symptom of the secularization of America. Christians need to band together to desecularize the public schools, to make positive instruction in moral values a viable part of every child's education, not to disparage or purge religion from the public education arena but to support it as a vital aspect of life.

William J. Bennett, the former secretary of education under President Ronald Reagan, provides his answer to the question, What is the purpose of school? "My view, to put it simply, is that the purpose of school is to make students both smarter and better, to develop intellect and moral character. When the American people are asked what they want from our schools, they consistently put two tasks at the top of their list: First, teach our children how to speak, write, read, think and count correctly; and second, help them to develop reliable standards of right and wrong that will guide them through life."[24]

Education must be designed to transmit the values and great truths that set America apart from all other nations on the stage of history, and this must be done with great respect for the two most important institutions in America: the family and the church.

The inability of Protestants, Catholics, and Orthodox to recognize our common goals in the educational arena have set us back and even opened the door for secularism to enter in and set up shop. It is an unfortunate fact of history that the squabbling between Protestants and Catholics in the early 1900s helped, if indirectly, lead to our current crisis. The suspicions between these two Christian communities oftentimes precluded their working together to ensure that private, parochial, and public schools accomplished their respective goals.

Today, as Protestants and Catholics recognize religious cleansing in the school system, we are beginning once again to rediscover our common ground. As we do, we need to agree together to support private, parochial, and public education. We need to reform public education to ensure that it is fruitful for the students and for the culture. But most importantly, we need to work to return decisions about education to parents.

The family is the first school. The birth of public schools itself was attributable to an effort to assist, not supplant, families in educating their children. Many of the ancient legal doctrines that have, unfortunately, been stripped away by the new legal engineers reinforced the subservient role of government in the public educational system. The Latin phrase *in loco parentis* stood for an extremely important principle. The government stood in the place of parents. The government did the bidding of parents. Unfortunately, in the last twenty years, we have seen the government become the parent.

Whose children are they? Who will determine how they are educated? It is essential that parents of students, especially in public schools, get involved in the decision-making process. That is why the entry of Christians into school boards throughout this country, though often impugned by the new secularists, is one of the greatest signs of hope for the restoration of sanity in public education.

Putting the power back into the hands of the parents is, as the accord says, "A moral question of simple justice." Joining together for parental choice in education is a vital area in which Catholics, Protestants, and Orthodox Christians can cooperate with one another as well as with other people of faith and all people of good will.

Contending for the Media and the Arts

Another meeting ground for cooperation involves launching a joint effort against the forces of the media elites. We have witnessed a growing hostility toward people of faith, especially Christians, in the media. Just recently a television commentator referred to the "threat" posed by the "Christian Right's" involvement in the political process and said they were engaging in a "jihad" (the Arabic term for holy war) and were no different from Islamic extremists. This kind of caricaturizing has become commonplace. The movie and television industries often portray religious people, especially Christians, as either bungling morons, or naive and ill-equipped counselors, or con men ready to pounce on innocent victims.

Cartoonists often do the same, and one, Pat Oliphant, went so far as to depict Christians as rats, dragging the Republican party into the "Fundamentalist Christian Mission" in order to save it. This particular portrayal is all the more disturbing when we recall that Nazi propaganda films and cartoons once depicted Jews as rats. The reason was frighteningly clear, as Sam Keen, author of *Faces of the Enemy*, explains:

> The anti-semitic propaganda that reduced the Jew to louse or rat was an integral part of the creation of the extermination camps. When Franz Stangl, the commandant of Treblinka, was asked why the killing of the Jews was organized in such a way as to achieve the maximum humiliation and dehumanization of the victims, he replied, "To condition those who actually had to carry out the policies. To make it possible for them to do what they did." The Jew was reduced to "cargo" by being shipped in cattle cars, to contaminated pest that should be exterminated by poison gasses originally designed as pesticides.[25]

We cannot allow this kind of misuse of the media to further undermine our ability to influence the culture.

Furthermore, we must stand together against the cheapening of human life, the family, sexuality, and male and female identity that is also promulgated through much of the media. In this regard, the accord says:

> We contend together against the widespread pornography in our society, along with the celebration of violence, sexual depravity, and anti-religious bigotry in the entertainment media. In resisting

such cultural and moral debasement, we recognize the legitimacy
of boycotts and other consumer actions, and urge the enforcement of existing laws against obscenity. We reject the self-serving claim of the peddlers of depravity that this constitutes illegitimate censorship. We reject the assertion of the unimaginative that
artistic creativity is to be measured by the capacity to shock or
outrage. A people incapable of defending decency invites the rule
of viciousness, both public and personal.[26]

The so-called entertainment media is anything but entertaining much
of the time. However, its current abuses should not lead us to abandon
it. Some of the greatest artistic contributions the world has ever seen
have been, and continue to be, inspired by faith. From the walls of the
Sistine Chapel to theaters and libraries throughout the world, Christians
have taken their place in creating beauty. Art, theater, and culture are
not avenues of expression Christians should leave completely in the
hands of others. We must involve ourselves much more in the entire
arena of the media and the arts.

Our efforts to transform this aspect of society should be twofold.
First, we must stand against the cheapening of life demonstrated in many
of today's "entertainment" offerings. We should oppose the "peddlers
of depravity" and stand against religious cleansing. Second, we must
reclaim our place at the palette, on the stage, on the screen, in literature,
and on television. We must get involved in the media and arts industries
and work to change them from the inside out. I realize this is easier said
than done in the current climate of religious hostility. Many Christians
have been kept out or immobilized by media and art moguls because of
their religious convictions. But these censoring tactics will not succeed
over the long haul as long as believers remain persistent and continue to
strive to be the best craftspeople in their chosen professions within the
media and art communities.

Father Neuhaus recounts the results of a far-reaching Gallup Poll
on the question of religiosity. "Among the nations of the world—measured by belief and behavior—India is the most pervasively religious
society. Very close to India is the United States. At the very bottom of
the list is the most thoroughly secularized society, Sweden. Peter Berger,
the distinguished sociologist, has drawn from these findings a memo-
rable apothegm: 'America is a nation of Indians ruled by an elite of
Swedes.'"[27]

In reviewing Michael Medved's 1992 documentary work *Hollywood vs. America*, actor and comedian Steve Allen astutely states, "Everyone—left, right, and middle—is perfectly aware that we are in a period of cultural and moral collapse. But some people don't want to concede that the popular media bear part of the responsibility. Michael Medved's book should convince them that it does."[28] Medved names the names and documents the programming that have helped bring about the unraveling of America's moral fabric.

Now it is up to Christians to reverse this destructive trend. United we can bring the pressure to bear to rein in the rampant sickness, perversion, and blasphemy. United we can call the cultural elites to task and reclaim entertainment, art, theater, and film for beauty, joy, and a true celebration of the best of humanity.

Contending for Equality of Opportunity and Responsibility

The accord also calls on Christians to contend

> for a renewed spirit of acceptance, understanding, and cooperation across lines of religion, race, ethnicity, sex, and class. We are all created in the image of God and are accountable to him. That truth is the basis of individual responsibility and equality before the law. The abandonment of that truth has resulted in a society at war with itself, pitting citizens against one another in bitter conflicts of group grievances and claims to entitlement. Justice and social amity require a redirection of public attitudes and policies so that rights are joined to duties and people are rewarded according to their character and competence.[29]

We are witnessing in our age a reexamination of the social compact of this nation. All of the efforts to reform the welfare state and somehow reexamine the promise of the "great society" point to failures in public policy. Moreover, our efforts at government action to break down the walls that separate us by religion, race, ethnicity, sex, and class have all too often come up short. This is where Christians have the most to offer. In fact, the entire premise of the equality of all human beings that is at the heart of the American experiment is rooted in the Judeo-Christian understanding of the intrinsic dignity and value of the human person.

From the very beginning, the American experience has had deep religious roots. From Columbus's discovery, to the later Spanish explorations, to the landings of the Pilgrims and the writing of the Declaration of Independence and the U.S. Constitution, the belief in a sovereign

Creator who had revealed Himself and His moral will in nature and Scripture and was involved in the affairs of humanity was branded on the American conscience. And the Judeo-Christian perspective was the dominant (though admittedly not only) worldview in which this belief in a creator was understood. In many respects, the America of the seventeenth and eighteenth centuries was a Christian culture. Addressing himself to the late 1700s, one historian rightly states: "The consensus of the overwhelming majority of the American people in 1776 and 1789 [was] that the state indeed has an obligation to worship God or perish. The Declaration of Independence and the Federal Constitution, as well as the state constitutions . . . were seen at the same time as having meaning only within the much larger 'oral constitution' of what was a Christian culture—not an Enlightenment culture! . . . The point is, that for practically everyone in that generation, it was still their Christian culture that endowed documents with meaning."[30] America's early charters and founding documents were interpreted—indeed, only made full sense—within this religious perspective.

When we read in these documents such concepts as "inalienable rights" and being "endowed by a Creator," we will not grasp their full meaning unless we understand them in their primary religious context, which is the Judeo-Christian worldview. And it's this worldview that informs us of the inherent dignity of the human person as a special creation of the divine Creator. Human beings are gloriously distinct from the rest of creation since they have been made God's image-bearers. All of creation certainly exhibits God's handiwork, but only humanity has been imprinted with God's "image."

The biblical word translated "image" comes from the Hebrew word *eikon,* from which we get our word *icon.* Just as icons of Joseph, Mary, and the Apostle Peter stand for them without being identical with them, so we stand for God without being deity ourselves. But unlike statues or paintings, we are living, breathing icons. We are visible, physical representations of the invisible, spiritual God. We reflect, reveal, and represent His character and His work in the created order.

The civil-rights movement led by deeply committed Christians such as Martin Luther King, Jr., was inspired by this understanding of the inherent dignity of the human person. Dr. King's speeches are filled with imagery from the Scriptures and the teaching of the Christian faith. His now-famous request that we not judge one another by the color of our skin but by the content of our character is rooted as well in this understanding that all of us are created in the image of God.

Christians, of all people, should be the ones joining together to reclaim the high moral ground of opposing racism, sexism, religious bigotry, and class oppression. None of these social problems can be fully dealt with without the influence of faith, because at the root of each of them is the problem of sin.

Unfortunately, I have seen in many "conservative" circles an unwillingness to deal with sins such as these. But some of the greatest champions of true civil rights have been and will continue to be dedicated Christians. Men and women like William Wilberforce in Britain; the great champions of American history such as Abraham Lincoln and Martin Luther King, Jr.; and even, yes, the early feminists in American history. Many of the first feminists were Christians, and they were overwhelmingly against abortion.

Stripping the influence of religion from American life will not end discrimination; it will only make it worse. We will end up Balkanizing America, polarizing society into small warring camps. Rather than "e pluribus unum" (out of many one), we will see the fracturing of the great American social experiment, the meltdown of the melting pot. This, of course, is the danger of misguided approaches to multiculturalism.

We must contend against racism and all social sins, but we must do so equipped with the only force that can truly make a difference—the understanding, rooted in faith, that all men and women are equal and are created in the image of God.

Contending for Economic Freedom and Cultural Integrity

On the issues of economics and cultural integrity, the accord also finds common ground on which Christians can cooperate:

> We contend for a free society with a vibrant market economy. A free society requires a careful balancing between economics, politics, and culture. Christianity is not an ideology and therefore does not prescribe precisely how that balance is to be achieved in every circumstance. We affirm the importance of a free economy not only because it is more efficient but because it accords with a Christian understanding of human freedom. Economic freedom, while subject to grave abuse, makes possible the patterns of creativity, cooperation, and accountability that contribute to the common good.
>
> We contend together for a renewed appreciation of Western culture. In its history and missionary reach, Christianity engages

all cultures while being captive to none. We are keenly aware of, and grateful for, the role of Christianity in shaping and sustaining the Western culture of which we are part. As with all of history, that culture is marred by human sinfulness. Alone among world cultures, however, the West has cultivated an attitude of self-criticism and of eagerness to learn from other cultures. What is called multiculturalism can mean respectful attention to human differences. More commonly today, however, multiculturalism means affirming all cultures but our own. Welcoming the contributions of other cultures and being ever alert to the limitations of our own, we receive Western culture as our legacy and embrace it as our task in order to transmit it as a gift to future generations.[31]

Bill Bennett documents that in 1987, the Reverend Jesse Jackson, marking the birthday of Martin Luther King, Jr., on the campus of Stanford University, led students in the chant "Hey, hey, ho, ho, Western culture's got to go." The claim was that Western culture was sexist, racist, and imperialistic. A campus paper editorial caught the mood of the university when it quipped, "We're tired of reading books by dead white guys."

This is a dangerous precedent. As education-expert Bennett points out, "The fact that they were white is irrelevant as is the fact that they're dead. If the books are important, they should be read."[32]

That is exactly right. Many of the critics of Western civilization are devaluing our heritage under the guise of multiculturalism and pluralism. They portray Western culture as the seed bed for all things evil and oppressive. While our Western heritage is far from perfect, it's also true that it's the foundation for much that is very good.

In 1990, the State University of New York published a provocative work by Bruce Wilshire on the philosophy of education. The book was entitled *The Moral Collapse of the University*. Wilshire simply accepted as fact that revelation as a source for truth in the modern university was dead and buried. What concerned him was how to set the university free to explore new horizons. His answer? Look to the ancient goddess myths and mysticism of pre-Christian Europe. Wilshire called for "think tank" elites to draw from the well of paganism and use its resources to water the course offerings of alternative, women's, and minority programs. Through those, he argued, the university could be reordered and society's identity, concept of gender, and understanding of knowledge redefined. Wilshire also contended that this would provide the foundation for a new ethic, one that would help modern man make the hard decisions, such as how to save himself from extinction and what to do with human life created via genetic engineering in the labs of the brave new future.

Eusebius would likely recognize Wilshire and the other academic elites of his persuasion as the high priests of an age Christianity had once defeated and reformed. They may not be eating human flesh as the Scythians did, but their answers to human problems are no better.

If Western civilization does disappear from America's educational curriculum, something sinister will fill the void. G. K. Chesterton was right: "The trouble when people stop believing in God is not that they thereafter believe in nothing, it is that they thereafter believe in anything."[33] Our schools have abandoned the Judeo-Christian God, and they are leaving behind study of the culture that was built on belief in that concept of God. In its place is coming paganism. The barbarians are returning with a vengeance.

We must join together with one voice and witness to the truth that Western civilization is the only foundation for a stable social order and the only path to social sanity because it is rooted in the great Judeo-Christian heritage. Once unified, we have a much better chance of recapturing our heritage for the benefit of future generations. But only if we are unified. Given the forces raging against us, we have no other choice but to hang together. If we don't, we will surely hang separately! As our Lord said, if the salt loses its saltiness, it is good for nothing except to be thrown out and trampled under foot. I ask you, could those be the jackboots of history I hear goose-stepping our way?

One of the unique contributions of Western culture is America's approach to democratic capitalism. History has proven its effectiveness. The planned, state-controlled economies of the former Soviet bloc have failed. A free economy is clearly more efficient, but also is much more in keeping with the Christian understanding of human freedom. And due to America's Judeo-Christian heritage, her approach to a free market has been tempered with an understanding of compassion and a concern for the poor. The balance between profits and people hasn't always been maintained well, but America's attempt to make it work has been healthy. And for the most part, it has produced the greatest economy and social structure the world has yet seen.

As America flirts with abandoning economic freedom, she runs the risk of losing her capitalistic success. Together as Christians, we must reject the application of totalitarian and atheistic ideologies that have given the world such failed systems as communism and socialism. Yet at the same time we must uphold the right role of compassion in a capitalist economy. There is a just hierarchy of values that should be considered in economic activity and social justice.[34]

Contending for a Sane Public Policy at Home and Abroad

The last social-activist portion of the accord deals with the role of mediating structures and America's international responsibility:

> We contend for public policies that demonstrate renewed respect for the irreplaceable role of mediating structures in society—notably the family, churches, and myriad voluntary associations. The state is not the society, and many of the most important functions of society are best addressed in independence from the state. The role of churches in responding to a wide variety of human needs, especially among the poor and marginal, needs to be protected and strengthened. Moreover, society is not the aggregate of isolated individuals bearing rights but is composed of communities that inculcate responsibility, sustain shared memory, provide mutual aid, and nurture the habits that contribute to both personal well-being and the common good. Most basic among such communities is the community of the family. Laws and social policies should be designed with particular care for the stability and flourishing of families. While the crisis of the family in America is by no means limited to the poor or to the underclass, heightened attention must be paid those who have become, as a result of well intended but misguided statist policies, virtual wards of the government.
>
> Finally, we contend for a realistic and responsible understanding of America's part in world affairs. Realism and responsibility require that we avoid both the illusions of unlimited power and righteousness, on the one hand, and the timidity and selfishness of isolationism, on the other. U.S. foreign policy should reflect a concern for the defense of democracy and, wherever prudent and possible, the protection and advancement of human rights, including religious freedom.[35]

American domestic policy must favor the family with no apologies or subterfuge. The nuclear family has been clearly understood throughout human history, especially in Holy Writ, as heterosexual parents and their offspring. This has been the normative definition of family. It was rightly extended to cover aunts, uncles, grandparents, adopted children, widows, orphans, and the like, but it has not meant what many militant feminists and homosexuals are stretching it to cover.

For example, homosexual activist attorney Beatrice Dohrn, while addressing a symposium on the family on the campus of William and Mary, recently asked why the government should be involved in defining families at all. She believes that no higher authority exists to define the family than those living together calling themselves a family. If that's so, then the concept of family would have to include homosexual marriages, children divorcing parents, even children marrying their mothers, as Eusebius reports the pre-Christian Persians were doing. Are these really families or perversions? No doubt Dohrn would have concurred with a California school district's recent use of tax dollars to throw a prom for homosexual high schoolers.

American domestic policy is sinking to new lows, depths unheard of since the Christian faith triumphed over paganism seventeen hundred years ago. Jim Dobson and many others have documented the family's demise well. We are in a war for the family, and so far the good guys are taking a beating. We must move boldly and decisively to uphold the family as the very building block of all culture, as the domestic church. If we don't, the normative family will soon be an abnormal phenomenon in American culture.

Moving from the domestic stage to the international one, we find that challenges abound there as well. Somalia, North Korea, Haiti, Cuba, Rwanda, Bosnia—the list of hot spots is expanding faster than the current administration can keep up.

Do we have a consistent foreign policy? Thirty years ago it seemed as if America's reason for existence was to contain, even defeat, godless communism. Now to even talk about communism this way will bring chastisement in many circles, especially in our educational institutions of higher learning. The atheists ran socialism aground on the shores of hard economic reality, but they managed to come back into vogue by highjacking the American education system as their new ship. And they have successfully sailed it into the harbor of American politics. There they have attempted to reduce the battle of ideologies from pro-God or anti-God to a mere question of economics. Human rights, morality, justice, leadership, courage—all have taken a back seat to promoting economic well-being. We now have no focus for our foreign policy, no philosophy save consumerism to export.

America has lost her soul. We must help her rediscover it. United we can bring about a rebirth of freedom and a rebirth of national purpose. United we can help restore America as a light of responsible democracy to the nations instead of a curse of amoral profiteers.

We face severe obstacles on the path to achieving this goal. For instance, President Clinton has made worldwide abortion and contraception a national priority. By the time you read this, the United States will have already had representatives attend the Cairo Conference on World Population in September 1994, where they are expected to pledge billions of dollars toward the goal of ensuring that fewer people live on planet earth. Almost two thousand years of church history have testified to the church's stance against halting the bearing of children.

Creating families is one of God's greatest blessings to humankind. We must stand with our Christian forefathers and challenge a U.S. foreign policy dedicated to denying the right to bear children to other nations. We must stand against the plans to make abortion a leading export and byproduct of the United States. The very future of the human race is at stake.

A GREAT BEGINNING

When you think about it, we have much we can work on together, even when we consider just the social arena. The accord gives us several great places to begin cooperating with one another for the transformation of our culture. If we will only start working together, I know we will find numerous points of convergence.

Alliance building will not be easy. I have found in my own work over the years that alliance building among Christians is challenging, difficult, and painful. But I can also tell you in the same breath that it has been thoroughly enjoyable. We can make common cause, and as we do, we will make a difference in the course of history that only Christ's church can ever make.

CHAPTER SIXTEEN

ALLIANCE BUILDING: THE ROAD HOME

We have found ourselves in the same foxhole.
Tommy Lea

In June 1994, the Southern Baptist Convention convened what became a truly historic gathering. On the final day of the 137th annual meeting, the dean of Beesom Divinity School in Montgomery, Alabama, addressed the convention: "We live in a land where there is a demonic onslaught against the forces of decency and righteousness, and we need to stand with good people together."[1] That began a host of other statements that led to the convention officially encouraging joint cooperation between Catholics and Baptists. Seventy-five hundred convention delegates overwhelmingly approved a resolution that affirmed the central tenants of the Christian faith as shared beliefs between Catholics and Baptists. The resolution also strongly encouraged Baptists and Catholics to work together on social issues such as abortion, pornography, racism, and the many other cultural ills.

In support of these historic moves, a member of the Baptist Mission Board said, "As Christians we have to be in communication with all those we walk this earth with, and it's especially important with all those who acknowledge the Lordship of Christ."[2]

In my opinion, though, perhaps the most telling statement to come out of the convention was made by Tommy Lea, the chairman of the Convention's Resolution Committee: "We [Baptists and Catholics] have found ourselves in the same foxhole."[3] And so we have.

In a letter to Richard Burke in 1793, Edmund Burke, long heralded as a great Christian leader and known particularly for his famous quote "Evil will only triumph when good men do nothing," reflected on the struggles then facing the British. His insight was tremendously astute, not only for his time, but for ours as well, especially as we examine the right role of alliance building for transforming contemporary culture. Consider what Burke wrote:

> I do readily admit that a great deal of the wars, mediations, and troubles of the world did formerly turn upon the contention between *interests* that went by the names of Protestant and Catholic. . . . [But] if ever the church and the Constitution of England should fall in these islands (and they will fall together), it is not Presbyterian discipline nor Popish hierarchy that will rise upon their ruins. It will not be the Church of Rome nor the Church of Scotland, not the Church of Luther nor the Church of Calvin. On the contrary, all these churches are menaced, and menaced alike. It is the new fanatical religion, now in the heal of its first ferment, of the Rights of Man, which rejects all establishments, all discipline, all ecclesiastical, and in truth all civil order, which will triumph, and which will lay prostrate your Church, which will destroy your distinctions, and which will put all your properties to auction, and disperse you over the earth. If the present establishment should fall, it is this religion which will triumph in Ireland and in England, as it has triumphed in France. This religion, which laughs at creeds and dogmas and confessions of faith, may be fomented equally amongst all descriptions and all sects—amongst nominal Catholics, and amongst nominal Churchmen, and amongst those Dissenters who know little and care less about a presbytery, or any of its discipline, or any of its doctrine. Against this new, this growing, this exterminatory system, all these churches have a common concern to defend themselves.[4]

I wish Burke's comments had been taken more seriously in his day, two hundred years ago. Unfortunately, history took a different course. Burke's insights and counsel, however, need not go unheeded today, not among Christians at any rate. We all know the barbarians are at the door—indeed, they have already crashed through and are setting up camp in our midst. Will we rise up and defend ourselves and Western civilization together? If not, history will show a legacy of destitution left by the one entity that should be passing on the abundant resources of God—the church. We've already given up much ground due to five hundred years of bickering. How much more will have to be lost before we recognize each other as Christians fighting from the same foxhole?

Southern Baptists have taken a courageous and critical stand on this issue. I hope other Christian traditions and confessions will soon do the same, for principled alliance building really is the road back home. But it is not an easy road. Very little worthwhile in life ever is.

BECOMING A FAMILIAR CALL

Throughout my adult life, I have sought to build principled alliances among Christians. I've shared several of my efforts earlier in this book. My approach to alliance building has been forged from my own experience in ecumenical efforts and from my own thinking about the true nature of ecumenism.

I'm grateful that I have not been a voice crying in the wilderness for Christians to come together as allies. Many others in and outside my tradition have lifted their voices as well. Some, even, who have been Christian in more than one tradition.

When Richard John Neuhaus was still a Lutheran pastor, he addressed graduate theology students at Franciscan University in 1989. He warned against what I call "Humpty Dumpty" solutions, then he called for an unrelenting pursuit of alliance building based on what he referred to as "reconfessionalized ecumenism." Christians should avoid that . . .

> kind of pseudo-ecumenism that was not premised upon the Spirit-given imperative in the divine gift of unity that is prior to our efforts to actualize that unity, but premised rather upon a kind of superficial 'let's all be nice to one another and pretend that our deepest differences make no difference.' That is pseudo-ecumenism. It has a terribly well-intended but terribly superficial understanding of Christian unity.
>
> Reconfessionalized ecumenism is the ecumenism in which we each go deeper into the various traditions of theology, piety, liturgy, Christian experience, and encounter one another precisely with our differences unfurled—if you wish. Because the only way you can, in your Christian life and your community and its communal life, enrich other persons and other communities is to

be bringing your differences. If we say from the beginning that we are all alike, if we don't have much to give to each other, if you're just like I am, I already 'got by definition everything you got,' then I don't need you that much. It is in your difference and I in mine, and our communities and theirs that we engage in genuine ecumenism.[5]

As I look back on that talk, I have often recalled the responses of some of the listeners. Several faculty members, who were deeply admired and still are, did not like Neuhaus's comments. I believe in their own mind they had concluded that because he was a Protestant, he didn't understand the fullness of theological reflection. Therefore, no matter what he said, it would always not be good enough and thus not truly worthy of serious consideration by fully orthodox Catholics. In my opinion, their reaction was haughty. Their response annoyed me, but it also helped me understand some of the obstacles we all face in alliance-building efforts.

The irony, of course, is that Lutheran Pastor Neuhaus is now Catholic Father Neuhaus. Some time after he spoke at Franciscan University, he made what he described as a very heart-wrenching, soul-searching decision to come into full communion with the Roman Catholic Church. What led him to make this switch? According to Neuhaus, he was simply being faithful to the Reformation. Many of the original reformers had never intended on leaving the Catholic Church; they simply wanted her to address the abuses that had gained a foothold in her midst. Neuhaus came to the conclusion that she had done that, so, as he put it, he returned home.[6]

When the news of Neuhaus entering the Roman Catholic Church reached those faculty members who had received his words with such critical scrutiny on that important day at Franciscan University, I wonder if they felt the need to reflect on their own judgmentalism.

Neuhaus was right when he spoke those words as a Lutheran. We really do need to adopt a "reconfessionalized ecumenism." Indeed, it is that kind of ecumenism that has now become the framework for much of my ecumenical work.

SHATTERING THE WALL

The opposition to alliance building, while waning somewhat, is still very much alive and kicking. And in some ways, it will grow more vocal and even hostile as more and more Christians turn their weapons batteries away from Christians of other traditions. Be that as it may, warmongering among believers must stop, and the more believers who rise up to oppose it, the better off all of us will be. Ironically enough, alliance-building efforts themselves can be the very means for turning enemies into friends. Years ago I had two experiences that gave me great hope that alliance building among Christians could help crack the wall of hostility between them and accomplish a great deal of good in the contemporary age.

The first experience involved an ongoing dialogue that I was engaged in with a major evangelical Protestant leader. This man is a close personal friend and an individual whom I greatly respect. Even back then, he had the courage to have personal and public relationships with Catholics. Those relationships cost him popularity among some of his constituents, but thankfully those relationships have continued and grown. They still cause him difficulty, but he has not backed off from further developing them.

I remember in one conversation on the telephone he said, "Keith, the leaders of your church are shaming us all in the evangelical Protestant world with their courage in the fight for life. They have become our conscience. Thank God for great churchmen like Cardinal O'Connor."

I accepted this backdoor compliment because I knew it knocked a chip in the wall. That's how it began in Berlin, and before long whole segments of the wall were being torn down by the people it had so long divided.

The second incident happened during a meeting I attended of what was then called the American Congress of Christian Citizens. The congress became the precursor for what later came to be known as the Christian Coalition. Both were founded by Pat Robertson out of a desire to build an alliance among Protestants and Roman Catholics that would confront the rising tide of anti-Christian bigotry in the media and in the political process. I attended the congress on behalf of Father Michael Scanlan and Franciscan University.

I will never forget my experience sitting in a meeting room with major evangelical leaders I had admired for years—men such as Dr. Charles Stanley, Dr. Jerry Falwell, Dr. D. James Kennedy, Dr. Pat Robertson, and many others. I found not only a tremendous openness to my presence but also a growing respect for my church and a thawing in what had been hard ice in the past. Perhaps the comments by Dr. Falwell were most illustrative. With a sincerity born of battle fatigue, he told the whole group not even to consider trying to affect public policy with only a narrow evangelical Protestant church coalition. He said that from its inception any such effort must include Catholics and consultation with great churchmen such as Cardinal Law and Cardinal O'Connor. Clearly not backing off one bit from his self-described "narrowness of doctrine," Dr. Falwell showed a refreshing openness.

Bringing the good news to the darkness of our time will be difficult, but none of us has to do it alone. The West can be turned from its collision course with disaster, but it will not be accomplished without an allied effort. The task is too great and the enemy too strong. The reclamation of the West will require a missionary strategy that builds on the foundational methodological approach so well enunciated by Paul himself: "I have become all things to all men, so that by all possible means I might save some."[7]

The way to best achieve this is by building active, effective, and principled alliances, true ecumenism at work.

PRINCIPLES OF GENUINE ALLIANCE BUILDING

As I've said, I am a loyal, evangelical Roman Catholic Christian. As such, I am committed to what my church tradition teaches about ecumenism. In the newly released *Catechism of the Catholic Church*, Catholics are strongly encouraged to engage in efforts toward promoting unity among Christians. At the same time, they are reminded "that the desire to recover the unity of all Christians is a gift of Christ and a call of the Holy Spirit."[8] The catechism lists seven things that are "required in order to respond adequately to this call":

- ◆ a permanent *renewal* of the church in greater fidelity to her vocation; such renewal is the driving force of the movement toward unity;
- ◆ *conversion of heart* as the faithful "try to live holier lives according to the Gospel," for it is the unfaithfulness of the members to Christ's gifts that causes divisions;
- ◆ *prayer in common*, because "change of heart and holiness of life, along with public and private prayer for the unity of Christians, should be regarded as the soul of the whole ecumenical movement, and merits the name spiritual ecumenism;
- ◆ *fraternal knowledge of each other;*
- ◆ *ecumenical formation* of the faithful and especially of priests;
- ◆ *dialogue* among theologians and meetings among Christians of the different churches and communities; and
- ◆ *collaboration* among Christians in various areas of service to humankind. "Human service" is the idiomatic phrase.[9]

In the last chapter especially, I focused my discussion on the human-services aspect of ecumenical efforts, or what I call making common cause for the transformation of the culture. But as the catechism notes, there are many other facets to the ecumenical task. What I've said is in concert with the catechism's insights on this matter. What I'd like to say in this chapter is also. I am speaking out of my tradition, a fact I wish not to hide but highlight in the spirit of genuine ecumenism. If you take issue with me, I ask that you not do so simply because I'm Catholic or what I say flows out of my tradition. I hope that if you disagree at all it will be out of a truly informed and respectful understanding of Scripture, church history, Christian teaching, and what I've tried to communicate and the spirit in which I've done so. Our common brotherhood in Christ demands nothing less.

Some Important Reminders

Authentic ecumenism seeks unity in the Body of Christ, striving for all Christians to become part of the restored universal church. It strives for unity in the scope of the whole truth. Persons involved in ecumenical dialogue should seek and be open to the full revelation of truth. Ecumenism is not another label for a negative form of compromise that dilutes or ignores the truths of the faith. Rather, true ecumenism is rooted in:

◆ An acknowledgment that Christians from all Christian traditions and confessions are members of the same Family.

◆ An ability to grieve over our Family's separation and longing for its full restoration to unity.

◆ A recognition of the challenges we face in the contemporary mission field.

◆ A willingness to embrace our own traditions with confidence and humility.

◆ The humility to learn from one another and allow one another to operate freely in our respective parts of the Family.

◆ The desire to work together for the sake of the gospel and its application to every facet of human life.

Firm adherence to these principles should allow Catholic believers to rejoice at the sight of a thriving Romanian Baptist church and permit Protestant believers to rejoice at the swelling crowds present in a Polish cathedral. Why? Because believers from both traditions are meeting our common Father, being saved through the merits of our common Savior, and being led and gifted by the same Spirit. They may express their Christian convictions differently as the result of their cultural differences and differing doctrinal and liturgical understandings. But they are all in the Family, and that's more than enough reason for us to turn our voices Heavenward in praise of our common Triune God.

Far too often the ingredient most lacking in our missionary efforts is humility. The Apostle Paul reminded the Philippians, "Your attitude should be the same as that of Christ Jesus: Who ... made himself nothing ... [and] humbled himself."[10] We need to empty ourselves of pride and serve one another.

Years ago, pastor John Wimber pierced my heart. He told a capacity crowd of leaders, "The Lord is looking for a generation of faceless leaders." I believe He is. The Lord is seeking men and women who care more about Jesus Christ being exalted than they do about their own names or versions of Family living.

Tom and Marie Pucci are good friends of my family. They have successfully raised wonderful children and are now enjoying their "children's children."[11] They have a lot of wisdom about in-law relationships that came about, they explained, because they first felt like outlaws. When their sons and daughters married, the Puccis had to develop a whole new holiday pattern that acknowledged that to marry a spouse means marrying a family. No longer could they just adhere to their own family's traditions. They also had to make time and space for the traditions of another family. By choice and desire, they became flexible enough about long-held family traditions to hold the entire family together.

Their wisdom about the natural family recurred to me several years back when I read an intriguing report in *Christianity Today* on English evangelicalism. The headline read, "Roman Catholics No Longer Outlaws."[12] Well, at least it signaled a step in the right direction—maybe not that far away from being rediscovered as in-laws, as part of the Family of families, by our Protestant brethren.

In many regions of the world, Christians are fighting one another to influence the resident culture with their own respective values. These Christians might benefit from the Puccis' recognition that to move our whole Family into the future they need to exercise some flexibility. Global efforts will only be helped if our warring against one another is replaced with a willingness to negotiate both our space and our togetherness.

I hope we will move toward a missiology that seeks to find Family members and strengthen them. Where Catholic, Orthodox, or Protestant churches are alive and thriving, we can support them with the message of evangelical faith in Jesus Christ as personal Savior and Lord without prejudice toward or intolerance of their respective traditions and essential theological distinctives.

Let me repeat once again: I am not calling for a least-common-denominator ecumenism. I've experienced that and it doesn't work. I firmly believe in what the Catholic Church teaches (though I must admit it isn't perfectly lived). I welcome inquiries from Christians of other churches about my convictions. But other Christian churches are not my primary mission field. As long as many people have never heard the gospel and many in my own church have allowed it to fall on rocky ground, my work is there.

Some Overall Guidelines

So where do we begin in our alliance-building efforts? At the beginning. One person, one relationship at a time. If each of us would examine how the great divorce has affected our opinions of one another and if each of us would resolve to rediscover one another's gifts, we would make a great deal of progress. If we could admit we are Family—separated brethren—we could begin rediscovering our common history and mission and thus resecure the foundation necessary for genuine alliance building.

I can't lay out a manual for common allied efforts. Even if I could, it would be presumptuous because I don't have the jurisdiction to speak to all the churches, nor do I have the ability or understanding to design a global alliance-building strategy. I can only suggest some things I've experienced and come to learn that might help. Among the principles I try to adhere to in my alliance-building efforts, I propose the following as a general and central guide:

1. Alliance-building efforts are part of God's plan for this generation. They can and must stand as a prophetic call and resource for Christian unity. But alliance groups must respect individual church memberships and convictions above the common purpose for which they've come together. Communities of purpose that gather around common goals (pro-life groups, grass-roots political groups, common cultural engagement, issues groups, etc.) cannot replace church. They should be viewed as supplementary. If membership in such groups becomes primary, the group takes on the indicia of church and ultimately, indifference toward church affiliation grows. In so doing, the group makes major mistakes pastorally, spiritually, juridically, and historically. Enough of these mistakes have been made already. We don't need to keep repeating them.

2. Long-term evangelization must be seen as a process. Evangelism is never finished, not on this side of Heaven. Consequently, though there is room for cooperation between Protestants and Catholics in personal evangelism, long-term evangelization should be pursued according to individual church conviction and tradition. It must of necessity be directed to church life and have as its primary goal the full embrace of the Christian life in a church communion. Ecumenical communities can certainly help in the evangelistic mission, but incorporation into those communities should not be the focus. Rather, these ecumenical efforts should encourage the promotion of deeper church life in the respective church bodies of those individuals they evangelize.

3. Efforts at building allied groups and communities of purpose should not avoid but rather openly acknowledge distinctives in church tradition and practice. For example, the primary pastoral care for members of allied groups should come from members of their own church. Furthermore, individuals within these groups should not act without proper ecclesiastical authority. They should respect and submit to appropriate church authorities within their respective traditions.

4. Though allied groups and communities can develop elements of a common Christian culture, the individual's church culture must be primary. Catholics participating in alliance-group activities should know their Catholic identity, tradition, and culture, and should be able to live them out. Christians in a Reformed Protestant tradition should be able to do likewise, and so on across the confessional spectrum.

5. When church groups and communities participate as a whole in alliance activities, their primary commitment and allegiance must be to their church in substance, not just form. Although we embrace a common creed on the faith's essentials, we have differing beliefs about other important beliefs and practices. A genuine alliance effort will allow, even encourage, its participants to embrace fully the doctrinal, ecclesiastical, and liturgical convictions of their distinctive traditions. Indeed, it's these differences that can help us all come to a fuller understanding of the whole counsel of God.

We misuse our differences, however, when we raise them as divisive barriers rather than sharing them with one another in honest, humble dialogue. We have much to learn from each other, but we won't learn anything if we cover up our differences or ignore them or refuse to listen to each other when we try to express those differences.

If we adhere to these principles, I believe we will find that the whole

Christian Family is like a very large, multifaceted jewel. We may not
see the beauty of it all at once, but if we're honest, flexible, and humble,
we will see her more as God does: the precious bride of the Lamb who
was slain, resurrected, and exalted for the sake of the world.

KEY TRAITS OF ECUMENICAL RELATIONSHIPS

With these general guidelines in mind, let's take a closer look at the kind
of relationships needed to establish and promote genuine alliances that
can make a radical difference in the social order, especially as we look
forward to the twenty-first century.

Informed

Much of the counseling and support philosophy that accompanies recovery from dysfunctional families applies to us, the children of the great
divorce of God's Family. Recovery groups are often refreshingly honest. We must be so as well in our work together. If we are, in time we will
come to understand that the greatest antidote to fear is faith; to confusion,
understanding; and to suspicion, trust. As Christians, we must make it our
business to learn about our whole Family history and heritage. There is
a world of difference between informed disagreement and uninformed
quarreling.

As I've read, listened, watched, and spoken with Christians all over
the country, I've been startled to discover how little we know about one
another's beliefs, culture, and practices. It's sadly amazing how much of
our antagonism and distrust is built on misinformation we pass along
generationally. Careful study of all Christian traditions is important.
How can we agree or disagree with anyone whose beliefs we don't know?
Each person has arrived at his relationship with God for a reason, and only
through sensitive discussion can we understand his or her reasoning.
Then, and only then, may we be able to offer them a portion of the truth
that may still elude their grasp, or they do the same for us.

Alan Schreck, a professor in the theology department at Franciscan
University, provides solid, clear, popularized teaching about Catholic
Christianity. The Lord has raised up other men and women in other
Christian traditions who are performing similar services. In his mar-
velous book *Catholic and Christian: An Explanation of Commonly
Misunderstood Catholic Beliefs and Practices*, Dr. Schreck explains
Catholic doctrine in a fresh and readable way. I highly recommend this
book to my Christian friends of other traditions, not as a polemic but as

a bridge toward understanding Catholicism.

I also recommend the *Catechism of the Catholic Church*, which was first released on June 22, 1994. It now is the greatest resource on what the Roman Catholic Church teaches. The first compendium of Catholic Christian teaching in four hundred years, the catechism sets forth a clear, concise, readable presentation of Catholic beliefs and practices. For Catholics who struggle with the current aberrations of heretical theology that seek to undermine their own church, the catechism has been welcomed with great relief. For Christians in other churches, the catechism provides a place where they can find what the Catholic Church really teaches. If they want to dialogue, disagree, or criticize, they must do so on the basis of what the catechism says and not on the grounds of suspicion, misunderstanding, or inherited hurt from the past.

In addition to studying carefully other traditions, our work together calls for a keen understanding of one's personal faith. If you have trouble understanding your beliefs, you will obviously have difficulty explaining them to others. We need to become educated and firm in our own positions. At the same time, we also need to be prayerfully open to the truth that may yet be beyond us. The truth will always prevail if the channels are open. We can't have a dialogue if we already think we know all the truth before we begin discussion. Dialogue is the interchange of ideas, not two sides talking at each other.

One-to-one exchange among friends and brothers and sisters in Christ is critical to any move toward unity, let alone cooperative action. Effective alliances build and grow on the ground level, among the people, not just among theologians, clergy, and scholars. All Christians are responsible for seeking unity within the Body. This critical position has been clearly stated by leaders of the Catholic Church: "The concern for restoring unity involves the whole church, faithful and clergy alike. It extends to everyone, according to the talent of each, whether it be exercised in daily Christian living or in theological and historical studies. This concern itself already reveals to some extent the bond of brotherhood existing among all Christians. It leads toward full and perfect unity, in accordance with what God and His kindness wills."[13]

Much contemporary missiology is built on the concept of *contextualization*, which simply recognizes the reality of culture and seeks to insert the gospel into it without diluting the gospel message or violating important cultural distinctives. While it's true some efforts in adapting the gospel have gone awry, the concept of contextualization is as ancient as Paul's missionary strategy and the conclusion reached by the first council of Jerusalem.[14] I propose we adopt it as we learn more about one another.

I am a Catholic Christian, and as such I have embraced a culture, a context for living out my faith. This church culture has much in common with other Christian cultures, but it also has its own signs, symbols, language, heritage, and tradition. I find it rich and fulfilling. You may be a Lutheran or an Episcopalian or a Baptist or a Mennonite. No matter. Whatever your church culture, it has elements in it that are common with others, and other elements that are distinctively its own. I will only really understand you and you understand me if we attempt to understand each other within the context of each other's church culture.

If you consider yourself "nondenominational," I believe you apply a term to yourself that is a misnomer. Belonging to Christ has immediate corporate connections to the invisible and visible expressions of the Body. You can't have the Head without the Body; you can't live a bodiless, disjointed Christianity. Whether you realize it or not, you live within a church cultural framework that draws from a heritage much older and richer than the local expression of your church.

It's time we learned one another's church cultures and discovered the richness of our whole Family. We have much to learn from one another and a whole lot of lost ground to reclaim.

Loving and Trusting

All our efforts must be rooted in sincere love that seeks only the best for one another. We want to strive for unity, not simply for the sake of togetherness, but because unity in the truth is the call of every Christian.[15] Our bond as children of God should move us to find the shared tenets of our faith and love each other in them. For instance, as Christians we embrace a common belief that the Father sent Jesus Christ who died for us as the Savior of the world. Christians also agree that the Word of God was inspired by Him; that Jesus will one day return; that the Holy Spirit makes possible godly living; that the virtues of faith, hope, and love are foundational to the Christian life. We can love one another as fellow believers in these shared truths.

Humble charity must be the impetus behind all our activities together. Our goal is not to get everyone to be like me or you, but to move everyone into the fullness of truth, the deepest possible relationship with the Lord. Arrogance and pride in a particular tradition don't belong in a loving exchange among Christians. Our mutual work should not be approached with the attitude of "I have the truth and you don't, so listen to me." That attitude has already failed miserably for hundreds of years.

While I can say and affirm all this, I also embrace the fact that as a Catholic Christian I believe I am following the Lord's plan for me and for His church. I am more deeply and freely Catholic today than I was ten years ago. I am also more dedicated to alliance building.

These affirmations are not contradictory but complementary. I cannot be fully Catholic without being committed to working with other Christians. I think the same should be true for any Protestant or Orthodox Christian. One Protestant friend who shares this conviction is Harald Bredesen.

Harald Bredesen, whom I believe is one of the greatest apostles of the Spirit and Christian unity today, is deeply and proudly Pentecostal. He acts out of his Lutheran convictions with a wonderful grasp of grace, but he couples this with a freewheeling, refreshing approach to following the Holy Spirit. In each of these areas, we express ourselves quite differently, and yet despite our cultural and theological differences, we work together because we both see the urgency of the times and know that only the gospel of Jesus Christ can save.

In 1989, Franciscan University conferred an honorary doctorate upon Harald for his apostolic endeavors toward true unity. He attended the baccalaureate liturgy at which our local bishop presided. For me it was an experience of "the best of the old and the best of the new," as Jesus says in Matthew 13:52. The liturgy was filled with spontaneous worship expressed at appropriate moments; the spiritual gifts came alive but with a solemnity and deep reverence appropriate to just such a liturgy. Because it was a special event, we also used sacramentals, such as incense, and we blended traditional church hymns with newer musical expressions of praise and worship that have grown up on that campus. In the middle of all this, Harald turned to me and said, "Brother, this is the kind of worship that is fitting and proper for a holy God. We led you Catholics into a deeper experience of the Holy Spirit; now you need to lead us into a deeper encounter with worship." This was greatly inspiring to me.

Harald is one of the original board members of the CBN ministry. Now, in my work at the ACLJ, I have the privilege of having him serve as one of our spiritual advisors while he also plays a vital role in our Nehemiah Wall Project. Along with Southern Baptist pastor Dr. Millard Box, a wonderful man who has served Christ faithfully for over sixty years, and Paul Chaim Schenck, a great hero of the pro-life movement who now serves the ACLJ as our director of special projects, Harald provides spiritual leadership to a national network of intercessors who pray twenty-four hours a day for our work. That's love at work for the benefit of the entire Body of Christ.

Evangelistic

Before any substantial progress toward Christian unity in the Family can occur, it needs to be a burden on the hearts of Christ's people. In my tradition, we have seen this burden grow, particularly since the Second Vatican Council.

But proclamation alone is never enough. You and I and the rest of Christ's followers must openly demonstrate our faith. When we fail to witness to the truth with our lives, we rob those without faith of tangible access to it. The bishops of the Second Vatican Council told Catholics, "Their primary duty is to make a careful and honest appraisal of whatever needs to be renewed and done in the Catholic household itself, in order that its life may bear witness more clearly and faithfully to the teachings and institutions which have been handed down from Christ through the apostles."[16]

There can be no effective cooperation between Christians without the interior conversion of the individual Christians involved. We need to have the Holy Spirit as our guide and let Him take actual leadership of our lives. The key is allowing the Holy Spirit to animate our thoughts and actions, but that will not happen apart from a personal relationship with Jesus Christ. This kind of evangelical renewal needs to be the energy that motivates individual Christians involved in alliance-building efforts.

This also entails that all Christians seek to ensure—not simply presume—that those who occupy our churches have been actually evangelized. For some of us that involves reaffirming our baptism as children; for others it involves an experience at an altar call or in the privacy of a pastor's study. No matter the means, it must involve a deep, abiding encounter, not simply with doctrine (though I believe doctrine is critically important) but with a Person, Jesus Christ. The heart of the Christian faith is not doctrine, sacraments, church government, or missionary efforts. The source of the Christian faith is the Person of Jesus Christ.

As a Catholic, I deeply believe that these many elements are important, but many Christians have, to some degree, fallen prey to perhaps the greatest single presumption the world has ever seen: We presume people have a personal, abiding relationship with the Lord Jesus Christ because they've been "through the system." That is simply and dangerously a false presumption. We can have sacramentalized but unevangelized Catholics. We can also have unevangelized Baptists, no matter how many times they have responded to altar calls. We must be dedicated to evangelizing and reevangelizing those in our own church communities. If we don't keep that as primary, we will fall short in our mission to the world.

Moreover, we dare not assume or teach that once we have encountered Christ personally, that is enough. It isn't. Coming to know Christ personally has a beginning but no end. Our initial act of faith begins an enduring relationship. We must meet Jesus over and over and over again, deepening our ties to Him, seeking to serve Him more faithfully and fully.

When I was a boy, I looked forward to Easter morning. Though we were very poor, my father made sure we experienced the lavishness of love when we celebrated Christmas and Easter. On Easter morning, we always woke up to a packed Easter basket and a chocolate bunny. We certainly knew that Easter was not about bunnies, but I sure looked forward to eating that delicious rabbit. Every Easter morning I scurried down the stairs eager to find out just how big my bunny would be. Of course, size wasn't the only issue. I also wanted to know if the bunny was solid or hollow. You really can't tell by looking at an Easter bunny whether it's filled with chocolate or air, but I sure could tell when I bit into it.

Sometimes Christians are like those candy bunnies. They may appear similar on the outside, but on the inside they are either hollow or solid. I have met many hollow Christians, and their presence spans all ecclesiastical boundaries. I'm not saying they don't look like Christians; I'm not even presuming that I can usually tell whether they are empty inside or not. I am saying, however, that the solid core—a vibrant, personal, ongoing relationship with Jesus Christ—has too often been lacking in Christians. They may have at one time given themselves to the Savior, but they have not continued to pursue a love relationship with Him.

We must rediscover and proclaim the full gospel in all of our church traditions and within our own jurisdictions. And that full gospel includes an ongoing, personal, ever-deepening relationship with the Lord of our salvation. This message is the essence of the Christian mission.

Earlier I shared with you about my experience at Franciscan University and the renewal it has undergone, but there are many other examples of true renewal throughout the churches in these days. Nevertheless, the job is far from over. All of our churches are ever in need of revival. By that I don't mean simply a planned event (though it may include some planning) but a renewal movement of God in our midst. Such events are usually precipitated by repentance, and their effects are furthered by the holiness and conversion demonstrated by the church. How much we need a lifestyle of renewal, individually and corporately. We need to recognize that these times demand holy living and sacrifice, the hallmarks of a truly evangelical Christianity. Some would say of a radical Christianity.

Radical is one of those great words that needs redemption. We have lost sight of its etymology. *Radical* simply means "a return to the root." Radical Christianity involves Christians getting back to the root of all Christian efforts, the cross of Jesus Christ. Without the cross of Christ, there is no salvation, no hope, no historic Christianity.

Many years ago, I received a phone call from a man in Moundsville, West Virginia. At the time I was working with Franciscan University. This man regularly listened to my radio program "Purpose for Living," and he called with a desire to discuss some of my comments. During the course of the conversation, I learned that he was a member of the Hare Krishna temple outside of Moundsville.

I said to him, "I find it interesting that you, a Hindu, are listening to a Catholic layman share the gospel."

He told me that several members of his religious community were listening. Well, my evangelical blood began running faster. Here was an occasion to share the gospel. And so I did. I began a telephone relationship with this man that continued for a year.

Although he never indicated that he had accepted the claims of Jesus Christ, our conversations were stimulating and challenging. At one point he said, "I believe in Jesus. After all, isn't the teaching of Jesus really what's most important, what He said and did? Why all this talk about His death?"

He obviously didn't understand that it's in Christ's death that the real issue lies. I said to him, "Duane, without the Cross of Jesus Christ, there is no Christianity. Unlike every other religion that sees man attempting to climb the mountain of salvation on his own, in Christianity God came among us in the Person of Jesus Christ and climbed that mountain for us. The mountain was Calvary. There He died for you and me. Unlike the teaching of your religion which indicates that you are bound by the *karma* of sin, Christianity proclaims that you have been set free if you will embrace the sacrifice for sin, the life of the incarnate Son of God on the Cross of Calvary. There God's justice and mercy met. The

Cross is the bridge to Heaven, the way out for you, for me, and for the whole human race."

I still pray that this man finds freedom in Jesus Christ. But if he does, it won't come through admiring Jesus' teaching and good deeds, though that can be a good beginning. A crossless Christianity will not save. The Cross is the only bridge to God, and thereby to reconciliation and life everlasting.

Furthermore, through Christ's resurrection, we can be raised to a new life and be born anew into the Family in which Jesus Christ is the firstborn Son. That Family, of course, is the church. That church will one day reign with Him in a new heaven and a new earth.

This is the good news entrusted to us, and we are called to bring it to the nations. This is the evangelical agenda all Christians hold in common.

I believe there are practical ways we can even express this agenda together. One way is through common evangelical efforts. As a Catholic, I understand evangelization to be a process involving both the proclamation of the faith and the eventual implantation of believers into the church. It is not my intention at this point to explain more fully this concept of conversion. Suffice it to say that the kind of evangelical cooperative effort I am speaking of involves the first phase of this understanding, namely, the proclamation of the gospel message.

The task facing believers as we approach the threshold of the twenty-first century is not only bringing those who do not yet know Christ to faith in Him but reevangelizing the Christian church and the peoples she once inspired. This work must continue until every Christian sees himself or herself as a missionary. Moreover, our common bond in Christ mandates our cooperation in this vital area of the Christian mission.

Moral Integrity
As I've articulated and demonstrated, our world is slowly deteriorating into a new pagan society. It needs people to fight the onslaught of darkness. In his work *The Waste Land*, T. S. Eliot described the spiritual aridity and desolation of the 1920s' society of wasted souls. Eliot's frighteningly bleak but realistic portrait of sexual license, manipulation, idolatry, escapism, occultism, numbed consciences, broken marriages, and fragmented lives was also a rather prophetic vision. If the world was a wasteland in 1922 when he published this poem, what is it now? Over seventy years later, we have fulfilled Eliot's worst-case scenario in our mechanized, human-centered society. After his conversion to the

Christian faith, Eliot asserted that "the choice for the future was between the Christian culture and the acceptance of a pagan one."[17] At least for now, the pagan choice is winning out.

The darkness is hungry. Not satiated by the secular world, it has begun to consume even the church. Chuck Colson cites an example of an Episcopalian bishop who not only condones but "celebrate[s] and welcome[s] the presence of our gay and lesbian fellow human beings." This bishop calls on the church to express its "willingness and eager desire to bless and affirm the love that binds two persons of the same gender into a life-giving relationship of mutual commitment."[18] These are the words of a leader of the church leading the faithful down dangerous paths.

The Christian church has long affirmed Saint Paul's admonition: "Do not be deceived: Neither the sexually immoral nor idolaters nor adulterers nor male prostitutes nor homosexual offenders . . . will inherit the kingdom of God."[19] If we believe the Word of God is the same yesterday, today, and forever, we believe that active homosexual practice is sin. It is not to be tolerated, much less celebrated. This doesn't mean we turn our backs on male or female homosexuals. On the contrary, it's through the church's longstanding teachings on temptation and sexual orientation that those struggling with sexual confusion can find hope. On the other hand, condoning objectively sinful lifestyles doesn't help anyone. It certainly cannot bring the good news of liberation from deviant and compulsive behavior.

Of course, not only active homosexual practice but also all kinds of sexual promiscuity, drug and alcohol abuse, abortion, and euthanasia are presented as morally viable choices in the current cultural climate and even in many churches. The Episcopalian bishop certainly has a good deal of support.

Those of us who follow Christ cannot continue accepting or tolerating amoral or immoral positions on issues that radically affect the moral face of our world and the lives of so many. Jesus was never morally neutral. In fact, He directed several warnings to the middle-of-the-road, fence-sitting, lukewarm believers of the first century. The Lord's stern warning to the church in Laodicea should be echoed throughout our churches today: "I know your deeds; I know you are neither hot nor cold. How I wish you were one or the other—hot or cold! But because you are lukewarm, neither hot nor cold, I will spew you out of my mouth!"[20]

I am not trying to project a hopeless worldview. Nor do I mean to be wrongly critical. I simply believe it's important that we understand the reality of what is happening to our world and within our churches. Foundations are crumbling and desperately need to be rebuilt. The sense of urgency is gripping. Thanks be to God that we can do all things through Christ who is our strength,[21] but we need to pull together in Christ if we are going to enter the battle full force. At the moment, the forces of evil seem to have the upper hand, but we have the advantage of appealing to the human heart and satisfying the human mind. Both have been created and designed by divine grace to receive the light and the truth. "Today the Christian people—and all people—are searching with a lamp for persons who radiate something of the light, something of nearness to the source."[22]

By building alliances we demonstrate an eternal flame that is the only antidote to the consuming darkness in our current age. We can reclaim our culture working hand in hand. Some of us are doing it. Many more of us must. The world is waiting—and it's growing darker every day we wait.

Sacrificial

In World War II, the Allies were a mixed bag of nationalities, customs, and beliefs. The French did not pretend to be English, nor did the English pretend to be American. Poles remained fully Polish, and Belgians fully Belgian. But they all stood together in the trenches fighting the same impending darkness. They recognized that the world of their time was being swept up in a movement, an ideology, which was attempting to unleash its fury and its lies throughout the world.

Looming before us is that kind of hungry darkness. As Chuck Colson has observed, we are in a new dark age. But Christians have been through dark ages before. Indeed, God gave us the light of Christ so we would reflect and magnify His brilliance and thereby dispel the darkness. We need not fear the dark. We can dispel it with the light of the gospel. The gospel is bright, but we are its lamps. If we combine our illuminary resources, we can push back the night. If we don't, small pockets of the darkness may recede, but it will envelop far more life with death than we can likely imagine.

Perhaps the area of common action in which we can bring our lights together most effectively is in the fight for life. How society treats unborn children, the elderly, and the infirm is a barometer of its heart. The heart of America has waxed cold. The pro-life movement is perhaps the best place for us to start action-oriented, sacrificial, alliance-building efforts. Life is the primary issue of our day, the litmus test of our moral and spiritual convictions. How we respond to this test will determine much in the next millennium.

We simply cannot compromise on the issue of life. Our view of life reveals our worldview. Remember, the Son of God occupied the womb of a holy woman, and the Father kept Him safe from infanticide.[23] The unbroken teaching of all the Christian churches for almost two thousand years is clearly pro-life. Contemporary attempts to justify the killing of children in the womb simply must not receive any credence from any Christian or Christian church. The attack on unborn children is an attack on family, on life, and on the nature of God and the truth of the gospel. Life is precious from conception to natural death and beyond. To embrace anything less is heresy. If we cannot join forces on this issue, on what can we?

Here we must give our all, even if it means engaging in peaceful acts of civil disobedience and spending some jail time and becoming social outcasts in the process. We can all play a vital part to stem the ever-encroaching tide of death in the culture. It may involve temporal sacrifice, but the eternal rewards will be well worth the effort.

RETURNING HOME

It is still the burden of God's heart and the commission of the whole Christian people to go into all the world and proclaim the good news. In order to respond today, we must now, in our own way, through our relationships with one another, fulfill the great prophecy of Isaiah and "beat [our] swords into plowshares, and [our] spears into pruning hooks."[24] As Jesus said, "The harvest truly is great, but the laborers are few."[25] We have a common mission, and we are part of the same Family. We are allies in a cause far more important than any humankind has ever fought for. But like the Allies of World War II, we must recognize our common mission and common need and join forces in alliances that are informed, loving, trusting, evangelistic, moral, and sacrificial.

What would such an effort look like? In the next chapter, we'll examine several groups and individuals that display many, if not all, of the characteristics of this kind of alliance building. They are traveling the road back home, and by following their lead, we can return home as well.

CHAPTER SEVENTEEN

FAMILY ALLIANCES AT WORK

*As Christ is one,
so the Christian mission is one.
That one mission can be and should be
advanced in diverse ways.*
"Evangelicals and Catholics Together"

The challenges of the twenty-first century compel us to come to the foot of the cross together based on the rich heritage we hold in common. The next millennium can be a Christian one. Whether it is or not depends in part on what we Family members do at the end of our current millennium.

This is a tall order given the huge gaps to be bridged in and outside our Family communities, but I'm convinced that Family alliance efforts are our only way to fill the order. Fortunately, we already have many models of groups and individuals who have shared the burden of reclaiming our churches and our culture. Some I will mention here. These models are not perfect. But these groups and individuals have had the courage and vision to try to work with Christians from different traditions and confessions, and they have succeeded. Yes, they have made mistakes, and they have also reevaluated and modified their action plans. But that is all part of any human endeavor. Therefore, we have good reason to admire, imitate, and be inspired by their example. After all, even in their mistakes and through many persecutions, these are some of the courageous few who have made an inner decision that working together is not an option but a gospel mandate.

PERSONAL CONVERSION

Two movements within the Catholic Church have dramatically affected thousands of people, helping them come into a deeper relationship with Jesus Christ. The focus of both movements is personal evangelism. In some instances they have helped people find Christ for the first time; in many more they have awakened a dormant spiritual walk. At times they have even positively impacted other parts of Christ's church Family. The movements are the Cursillo movement and the Catholic charismatic-renewal movement.

Cursillo

Cursillo originated in Spain in 1949. Gerry Hughes, executive director of the National Cursillo Center, defines Cursillo as "a movement of the church with its own method that makes it possible to live what is fundamental for being a Christian in order to create small groups of Christians who would evangelize their environment with the gospel and help structure Christianity."[1] The idea of small groups comes from the Spanish word *cursillo*, which means little or short course. The actual full title of the movement, *Los Cursillos de Christianded*, means "the little course in living Christianity."

Cursillo is best known for its special ministry weekends, a community experience in which the participants live and work together—listening to talks, discussing them, and making practical applications. In a Catholic Cursillo they also celebrate the Eucharistic liturgy. In all Cursillos they hold group prayer together, which is an essential part of the experience. But one of the most interesting and sustaining things about Cursillo is the follow-up program: in small weekly reunions, participants share experiences and insights from their prayer lives, studies, and outreaches.

The long-range goal of the movement is that Christ become the preeminent influence in society. The primary objective is twofold: (1) develop in its members a consciousness of their power and mission to become leaders in the work of Christian renewal, and (2) sustain them as they provide a Christian witness to the world. Gerry Hughes states:

> We challenge men and women to really do what they are supposed to do as Christians and help them to discover that. . . . We tell people, "If you want to live your Christianity in the world, find a group of friends, meet with them regularly, share your

Christianity with them, your living union with the Lord, how you are reforming your mentality to be more in line with the gospel, and what you are doing to build the kingdom in your family, your neighborhood, your place of work, or wherever.[2]

Cursillo has certainly affected many families, neighborhoods, work places, and indeed churches. It has even affected my own family.

My wife Laurine can attribute her own personal conversion to Jesus Christ to the Cursillo movement. When she went on a Cursillo weekend in the diocese of Peoria, Illinois, she was not a believer but more of an agnostic. She was definitely not a Catholic. In fact, she had been raised in a home that was at least cold toward Catholics, if not directly anti-Catholic. The experience of that weekend confirmed a process within her that began through the witness of a friend named Marge Helgoth. Marge had a deep and personal relationship with Jesus Christ. She was also Catholic. Her witness affected Laurine as did the witness of a customer in Marge's beauty business. Fortunately, a wonderful priest in the Peoria diocese responded to Laurine in her point of need. On that Cursillo weekend, Laurine came face to face with Jesus Christ. It was an evangelical moment that led to a vibrant relationship that has endured. Shortly thereafter, Laurine sought admission to the Catholic Church. Within six months from that we met, and the rest is a wonderful history.

Laurine's father, Mac, was also changed through a Cursillo weekend. Years after Laurine's initial confession of faith, Mac, too, encountered the saving power of Jesus Christ in a new way. He attended a Cursillo weekend sponsored by the Upper Room, a Methodist outreach. There he got in touch with the One who has been his constant companion ever since.

Cursillo has opened the door for great renewal in our time due to its direct and indirect influence on all the subsequent renewal movements.

Because of my personal experience and understanding of the Cursillo movement, I was deeply distressed to read Dave Hunt's comments in his newsletter *The Berean Call.* Under the heading "The Gospel Betrayed," Hunt said:

> I have been in contact with thousands of Catholics who were saved and left that Church. *Not one* ever heard the true gospel preached there. *Not one* was saved by being a Catholic, but by believing a gospel which is anathema to Catholics. In a recent

survey of 2,000 homes in Spain only two Protestants knew the gospel, while 1,998 Catholics thought good works, church attendance, etc. would get them to heaven. In their 15 years of evangelizing in Spain, missionaries with whom I spoke had *never met one* Catholic who was saved or who knew how to be saved. Knowing that these millions of Catholics are lost causes evangelicals there to work day and night to bring them the gospel![3]

Contrary to Mr. Hunt, the reality is that if it were not for the faith of dedicated evangelical Spanish Catholics, my wife, Laurine, would not know Jesus Christ as her personal Savior and would not now some twenty-one years later be standing faithfully for Him as the mother of our children and copastor of our domestic church, our family. I, and I'm sure many other saved Catholics in Spain and elsewhere around the world, resent Mr. Hunt's comments. I believe they are mean-spirited, but most importantly, I know they are absolutely wrong. The Cursillo movement alone is ample testimony to that fact.

Catholics are actively reevangelizing professing Catholics as well as evangelizing people who have no church affiliation and do not know Jesus Christ as their Savior and Lord. Catholics are also working with Protestants to reach out with the gospel message to a lost world. Simply because Catholics may not use the same lingo and draw on the same "formulas" to express their beliefs does not mean they are unsaved. The Hunts of the world need to come to grips with this before they point their critical guns at fellow brothers and sisters in Christ.

The Catholic Charismatic Renewal

The Catholic expression of the charismatic renewal began at Duquesne University in 1967 during a retreat weekend for students and faculty. As the weekend progressed, many participants knew they were being confronted with what it would mean to surrender fully to the Lord. Patty Mansfield, then a student, says, "Jesus was asking us to let Him reign, not simply to acknowledge Him as an important person, but to allow Him into the very center of our lives."[4] That statement may seem quite ordinary today, but in 1967 it was fresh and radical. Think about what that meant to people at the very beginning of a new movement of God, before it became common to say, "Jesus is Lord." The Holy Spirit was working mightily.

While these Christian men and women had loved the Lord, prayed, and desired to serve Him, they realized in retrospect that loving Him and being fully surrendered to Him were two different things. And they realized that prayer under our willpower and with the best of intentions was still vastly different from prayer in the conscious, experienced power of the Holy Spirit.

The charismatic renewal has spread like fire and had a global impact on Catholics. The experience referred to in the charismatic-renewal movement as baptism in the Spirit is a deeper conversion and encounter with God—it is an evangelical moment. Catholics are in a sense Johnny-come-latelies to this experience. In fact, the experience came to Catholics through the generosity and affection of Protestant brethren. Great men and women of God who suffered persecution as the result of their walk in the Spirit were not afraid to bring the treasure they had unearthed to these Catholic students at Duquesne. We are so thankful for individuals such as David DuPlessis and Harald Bredesen who understood that the work of the Holy Spirit is for the whole Christian Family, not just for Protestants.

Both of these movements focus on a particular dimension of conversion—encountering Jesus Christ personally. Their effect has been like a pebble thrown into the middle of a still pond. Ripples have gone out and positively affected the whole Christian Family for the Savior.

COMMUNITY LIFE

Another vital part of the Christian life is the rediscovery that to belong to Christ is to belong to His people. The Cursillo movement and the charismatic renewal only deepened the hunger of many Catholics and Christians of other traditions to respond to the call of community. Many groups seeking closer relationships with the Lord and His people have joined together.

One expression of such community life is what has been called covenant communities. The name derives from the fact that the members of these groups make an agreement with the Lord and one another to be committed to a way of living that often provides a tremendous model of the evangelical counsels (poverty, chastity, and obedience) and a truly evangelical lifestyle. Many of these communities still exist today and present a refreshing and vital example of how Christians can come together in a visible sign of dedicated fraternal and sororal life for the purpose of missionary activity.

Unfortunately, some of the early efforts at covenant community have also failed. In their wake they have left broken relationships, pain, and disillusionment. Nevertheless, the experience of community is an essential part of the gospel and church life, therefore they should not be abandoned. Even in the light of their mistakes, efforts at building covenant communities have served as heroic attempts at alliance building. It is a very difficult lesson to learn, but the fact of the matter is that mistakes, problems, and pain can become the tutors of tomorrow. Covenant communities are learning this lesson.

These communities traverse the globe. Efforts at connecting them have produced mixed results. However, their existence and impact is a breath of fresh air and an inspiration for all believers who call themselves evangelical Christians.

The covenant community I had been closely associated with is called the Servants of Christ the King, which was located in Steubenville, Ohio. For a while it was linked with many international associations of communities that emerged in the 1970s and 1980s. One of these was the Sword of the Spirit. In my experience years ago with the Sword of the Spirit movement, the least-common-denominator approach to ecumenism characterized our early days. It did eventually evolve into a mutuality of respect toward our differences. Though I left the movement long ago, I understand that the leaders of the Sword of the Spirit have made adjustments in structure, leadership, mission, and most importantly, relationships. I don't know what the result will be. I do believe, however, that the years of efforts at bringing Christians together bore some good fruit. Mistakes were made, but risks are a part of all advancement in Christian work. I am proud to have at least tried with brothers like Ralph Martin, Father Mike Scanlan, Randy Cirner, and so many others in years of struggle.

The Word of God is another covenant community in Ann Arbor, Michigan. Under the courageous leadership of men like Ralph Martin, the Word of God has provided perhaps the greatest model of alliance building. Its many outreaches and efforts over almost thirty years have touched thousands upon thousands of lives throughout the world. It has also promoted church-based communities like the one I formerly served in Steubenville.

Throughout the history of covenant communities, there has been an ongoing need to readjust their expressions and understanding of ecumenism in order to comply with the teaching authority of the churches their members belong to. Like individuals, communities go through a process of maturation. That process has brought a clear and deeper revelation for many members of covenant communities as to what it really means to be fully Catholic or fully Lutheran or fully Presbyterian. What has emerged in recent years, at least among some of these communities, is a realization that memberships in the individual church body must be primary. Missionary alliances and communities of purpose cannot be a substitute for church. They must continue to seek to demonstrate a genuine submission to appropriate church authorities while they join with that a prophetic conviction about Christian unity. That's one tough but rewarding task.

Hopefully, the struggles, mistakes, failures, and readjustments in understanding leadership structures and relationships among these communities, though often difficult, will in the long run produce an even sounder model of Family life for the next millennium of Christianity.

STRENGTHENING FAMILY LIFE

A fruit of understanding the challenge of our times is the full recognition that a relationship with Jesus Christ is not simply personal. It must also affect family living—how we relate to our parents, spouses, children, cousins, and so on. After all, the natural family is the first cell of the church and even the domestic church. Without a genuine renewal of Christian family life, there will be no true renewal of Christian churches.

In our day we have been truly fortunate to have family movements that have directly affected thousands. Two Catholic movements have moved beyond their own church Family to impact the broader Christian church. They are Couples for Christ and Worldwide Marriage Encounter. Among the many evangelical Protestant groups, Focus on the Family has had the greatest impact and reached beyond church and confessional lines, providing sound spiritual and psychological counsel to families everywhere.

Couples for Christ

Couples for Christ (CFC) began in 1981 when members of a Christian community in the Philippines called the Joy of the Lord realized the need for family outreach and began bringing couples into private homes on a weekly basis to share the power of God in their lives. CFC's primary goal is the renewal and strengthening of the natural family as the basic unit of society. CFC members provide support, guidance, and Spirit-directed strength to many families trying to live gospel values in the contemporary world. They help one another grow into maturity as men and women of God, showing them how to fulfill their primary vocation of raising families under the lordship of Jesus Christ and for the service of His Kingdom. CFC moves toward this goal step by step, beginning first with each individual's personal encounter with Christ. After each partner renews his or her commitment to God and becomes open to a fuller working of the Holy Spirit, he or she can then recommit to each other in a vital way. When the parents are strong in the Lord, their example touches the entire family; then once united, the family can become an example and a source of evangelism to the church at large.

Before becoming a member of CFC, a person must attend what's called the Christian Life Program, a series of introductory teachings, sharings, and fellowships. Twelve weekly sessions focus mainly on the basics of the Christian life; on the call of each Christian, with particular emphasis on family; and finally on what it means to be totally committed to Christ. These sessions pave the way for an initial encounter with Christ and offer a basis for continuing spiritual growth. If couples wish to dig deeper, they are placed in a small group of five to seven couples who meet weekly for support, encouragement, and prayer.

The model developed by CFC is an effective example of how family ministry can happen effectively through cooperative efforts among Christians. It can be readily adapted in any Christian confession as well as interconfessionally.

Worldwide Marriage Encounter
Worldwide Marriage Encounter (WME) ministers to married couples, priests in the Catholic Church, and Christians of most major traditions within Protestant Christianity. WME leaders realize that all God's people share a common thread in their relationship with and in the Lord. Their vision is of a new world—a world made new by the power of love, which is a vision that comes from Jesus Himself and has been handed down by His church for generations.

Married couples and priests have a call beyond baptism to the special gifts and graces appropriate to their respective sacraments. The lives of married couples uniquely reveal the mystery of the Trinity wherein, as Augustine once said, you find a Lover (the Father), a Loved One (the Son), and a Spirit of Love (the Holy Spirit). Their lives also stand as illuminating examples of Christ's special love for His church.[5] And the priest's loving service to his people tangibly reveals the depth and power of Christ's own love for them. So on a practical level, WME encourages the renewal of the sacraments of marriage and priesthood for the renewal of the church that will ultimately impact the whole world.

WME does this in a weekend encounter that challenges participants to live a new way of life in full, intimate relationship—a radical lifestyle of reevaluation and intimacy through dialogue. They teach that pursuing values such as responsible relationship, intimate communication, and sacramental living will produce dynamic growth in and for Christ. During the weekend, couples share marriage values, weaknesses, and strengths. WME encourages couples to see marital encounters as a way of life, for as their mission statement says, "It is through awakening in couples an awareness of the gift that they are as the Sacrament of Matrimony, that we will assist in strengthening and renewing the Church and aid in its work of changing the world."

Focus on the Family
Of course, any treatment of evangelical renewal and family life would be incomplete without mentioning the wonderful work of Dr. James Dobson and Focus on the Family. I was privileged years ago to participate in honoring Dr. Dobson and Focus on the Family at Franciscan University. The university bestowed on him an honorary doctorate as a statement of its support for him and his work. During the summer of '94, the ACLJ proudly gave Dr. Dobson our prestigious Defender of the Family Award. God has certainly used him as a healing balm to countless numbers of families over the many years he has faithfully served in this ministry. Through numerous avenues, including radio, magazines, and books, Dr. Dobson has faithfully brought effective and practical help to the fractured homes of Christian families from virtually all church traditions. My own family life has been sustained through the rearing of five children in twenty years of the ins and outs of practical daily living by Jim Dobson's practical counsel on raising a family.

The Family Research Council
The Family Research Council (FRC) is unashamedly and unabashedly dedicated to defending the normative family. Their literature and other efforts reflect their belief that "rebuilding the family must become a national priority—we would say the national priority." Formed in an alliance with Dr. James Dobson's Focus on the Family, the FRC is a public-policy think tank that actively lobbies the government, in their words, to remind "legislators, judges and administrators of these traditional ideas—and buttressing them with fresh research and legislative initiatives."[6]

The FRC documents the war being waged against the American

family and proposes winning strategies to prevail in these conflicts. A four-page monthly newsletter, *Washington Watch*, serves a watchdog function, alerting readers to the legislative threats against the family. A bimonthly publication entitled *Family Policy* probes major concerns affecting the family. This publication goes to all members of Congress and to key players in the media. It is also offered to the public on a subscription basis. Another publication, *Insight and in Focus*, sets forth policy positions in response to binding legislation affecting family values. These "as needed" releases are designed to facilitate grass-roots responses to legislative efforts, either to beat back advances by those opposed to time-tested family values or to support those moving to protect the normative family.

Gary Bauer, the president of FRC, is a frequent guest on Dr. Dobson's worldwide radio programs "Focus on the Family" and "Family News in Focus." Bauer is also a regular contributor to Dobson's monthly *Citizen* magazine. The FRC serves the Dobson ministry as an expert resource in the areas of family law, legislation, and social science. This is in keeping with FRC's mission, which is "to identify the family factor in social policy, whether the issue is taxes, welfare, education or crime. The Council has devoted its energies to gathering and publishing data about the family, and to promoting policies and legislation that strengthen the legal and economic status of the family unit."[7]

These are just a few of the many groups addressing the crucial problems facing today's families. Many of these groups are alliance-building efforts dedicated to helping families make vows to one another in Christ, to strengthen those vows, to grow together in holiness, to work through their salvation in the context of family life. We need these bold, courageous efforts. The fury of hell has been unleashed against the modern family. The Devil knows that where the family goes, so will civilization. We must preserve and defend the divinely instituted family. If we don't, all of humankind will pay the horrible price.

FIGHTING FOR SOCIAL JUSTICE

Social justice is one of the greatest arenas where we can build effective alliances among fellow Christians. Some organizations have taken this challenge very seriously. For instance, among the many works of mercy that manifest Jesus among the materially destitute, I have been particularly impressed with Love Incorporated, Ferdinand Mahfood's Food for the Poor, The Salvation Army, Goodwill, and Mother Teresa's

Missionaries of Charity. Below are a number of other social-justice ecumenical efforts I would like to highlight.

Prison Fellowship Ministries

Prison Fellowship Ministries (PFM) was founded in 1976 by former presidential aide Charles Colson after he had served prison time for his involvement in the Watergate scandal. While in prison, Chuck experienced firsthand the loneliness, bitterness, fear, and pain of men and women who live behind bars without hope for the future. Fortunately, through the care and ministry of others, Chuck became a committed Christian during his confinement.

After his release, Chuck was unable to ignore the pain he had witnessed in the hearts of many prisoners. Now convicted by God, he began a small discipleship program for inmates with just two staff members and three volunteers. God blessed his outreach.

Today, PFM is a worldwide ministry with branches in thirty-four countries. In the United States alone, twenty-two thousand PFM volunteers minister to inmates in 550 prisons. The ministry also extends to former inmates and to families that have been touched by prison experience.

PFM is a fellowship of men and women who, motivated by their love for the Lord Jesus Christ and in obedience to His commands, have joined together to exhort and assist His church in the prisons and in local communities. Much of their ministry work is focused on prisoners, ex-prisoners, and their families. But PFM also seeks to promote biblical standards of justice in the criminal-justice system. The ministry includes in-prison seminars, discipleship seminars, Bible studies, marriage seminars, one-to-one visitation, correspondence with inmates (pen pals), community service projects, family assistance, aftercare for released inmates, and Project Angel Tree—a program that supplies Christmas gifts for the children of indigent inmates. Gifts are given in the name of Jesus on behalf of the parent.

Justice Fellowship, a subdivision of PFM, promotes reforms that hold offenders responsible for their crimes, restores victims, and protects the public. It advocates biblically based concepts such as restitution and community-service punishments for appropriate offenders, victim assistance and compensation programs, and reconciliation opportunities for victims and offenders. It also promotes the fair and effective use of prisons for offenders who must be imprisoned.

PFM is exploding with outreach opportunities, and because their focus is reaching out with Christ's love, one's church tradition and identification scarcely become issues. The PFM staff and volunteers simply want to touch unbelievers and fellow Christians with the love of Christ. So when their work takes them to predominantly Catholic countries and Catholic environments, they strive to work with Catholic Christians. When they minister in predominantly Baptist environments, they try to work with and through Baptist Christians. A Prison Fellowship chapter has even been started on the campus of Franciscan University.

Undoubtedly, PFM is a model for alliance building that is forward-thinking, prophetic, and definitely worth following. It demonstrates the mutuality of respect for different church communions that is the message of this book.

I've been honored to have Chuck Colson, whom I consider a prophet for our time, as a dear friend. I still remember with joy my opportunity to address Prison Fellowship's morning devotions years ago. There I stood, a lay Catholic, in the midst of a group of Protestant brethren engaged in a beautiful evangelical work of mercy and true Christian social action. I shared our common gospel and read an excerpt from Bernard of Clairvaux, a member of our common Family heritage. These dear believers received me as a fellow follower of Christ.

We need more works that exhibit the depth of cooperation and convergence of Charles Colson and Prison Fellowship Ministries.

The Rescue Movement

In 1988, Randall Terry and the group known as Operation Rescue burst onto the nightly news. They quickly became famous for blocking abortion clinics, first on the east coast, then almost anywhere an abortion clinic could be found. Many times thousands of people would participate in these rescue efforts. Among Operation Rescue's rank and file as well as its leadership are Catholics and Protestants who have learned to live, worship, and stand up for life together.

Of course, Operation Rescue was not the first pro-life group to physically blockade aborturaries. For years a courageous cadre of men and women scattered in cities across America acted in faith and out of conscience to nonviolently intervene between the child-killer's scalpel and the preborn child. In fact, most of the early rescuers were dedicated Roman Catholic Christians.

As the rescue movement grew, unity became one of its major byproducts. Randy Terry himself often stressed the need for unity while poking fun at all denominations equally and exposing the minimal nature of their differences in light of the great need to save children from the abortion industry. When asked his own creed, Terry would characteristically and openly reply, "I am Presbyterian in my doctrine, charismatic in my expression, and Catholic in my heart." This same spirit was conveyed by another rescue leader who wrote in a newsletter:

> The greatest contribution of pro-life activism to our nation may be the healing of a shattered church. Together as one body we act in love to save children and warn women, acknowledging that Jesus is Lord, that His law is to be the law. In the heat of this battle with the fallen world system (our common enemy) the "great distinctions" in modes of baptism, local church government and theological terms suddenly come into a focus never before clear—we are to forbear with one another in love, not build walls of separation from each other. What matters most is that the person marching (or sitting) next to you is sworn in loyal obedience to the King of kings and is stumbling forward in love. . . . Everything else can be worked through in the "peace that passes all understanding."[8]

The rescue movement has indeed resulted in a greater understanding and unity among Protestant, Catholic, and Orthodox Christians, while also saving the precious lives of little ones. Such are the incredible benefits accrued when Christians struggle together in the common cause of serving the Lord.

Operation Blessing
No description of genuine social-justice movements would be complete without mentioning Operation Blessing (OB), which was founded by Dr. Pat Robertson. It is an absolutely wonderful example of Christianity in action.

In response to the biblical teaching that the church should care for the poor and needy, as well as the conservative belief that the private sector should be about the work of charity, Pat Robertson launched OB in the early 1980s. Through this organization, funds and goods are gathered at locations nationwide, donated by the faithful who heed the call to charity broadcast on the television program "The 700 Club." From these decentralized locations, volunteers distribute the goods to poor and needy families.

This grass-roots charity organization is run with very little overhead cost, quite unlike the federal and state programs of similar size and mission. In a 1985 interview with Pat, he stated, "We just allocate money from our general revenue and we take that into an inner city and tell a church there, 'If you are really concerned about helping your people, we will match what you give.' We go to a private business and say, 'If you've got some surplus rice, beans, or flour, we will facilitate the transportation and distribution.'"[9]

Inner-city schoolchildren are a special burden to those who run the OB network. In 1991, OB gave more than $1.7 million worth of new clothes and school supplies to nearly sixty thousand children nationwide. At that time, OB had programs active in twenty-one states and the District of Columbia. In 1992, OB launched its Hunger Strike Force, a program designed to distribute surplus farm crops to the needy. At the March 17, 1992, news conference kicking off this battle against inner-city hunger, OB distributed over three hundred thousand pounds of potatoes, cabbages, and assorted produce to Washington, D.C., charities. They also handed out one thousand food baskets in a southeast D.C. neighborhood.

Operation Blessing is also active in humanitarian efforts overseas. The organization took a good deal of flak from some portions of the media in the mid-1980s for sending blankets and medicine to refugee camps made up of people fleeing Nicaraguan communism.

This politically incorrect yet faithful-to-the-gospel food and clothing network continues to grow, spurred on by Pat Robertson's televised pleas for Christians of all persuasions to come to the aid of the poor. The generosity of Christians worldwide has been incredible, a true testimony to Christ's love for the nations.

GLOBAL EVANGELISM

In respect to the proclamation of the gospel worldwide, Christians from across the confessional spectrum are linking up and making great strides for the Kingdom.

Teen Evangelism
Teenagers throughout the world are reached for Christ through national evangelization teams begun and supported by the Roman Catholic Church.

One project that has particularly impressed me is Youth with a Mission. Leland Paris, one of its key leaders, is a man on fire with a desire to see the nations come to Christ through the next generation.

And that fire has enough burning embers to light Christians of all traditions. Although Leland is a Protestant, he carries on the work of Youth with a Mission in Catholic areas, using the talents of Catholic youth to reach other teenagers. He and Youth with a Mission understand that the Spirit of God knows no boundaries in the work of revival.

Just this past June, the ACLJ's chief counsel, Jay Sekulow, led a SWAT team of lawyers to Albany, New York. One of the Youth with a Mission ships used to sail around the world to feed the spiritually needy with the gospel was almost refused permission to dock in New York. The state of New York seems bent on bearing incredible hostility toward people of faith. Representing Youth with a Mission, Jay managed to convince state officials to allow the ship to dock.

The story, however, didn't end there. In another act of religious bigotry, state officials turned around and refused to allow Peter Whitehouse, the director of missions and evangelism for Our Savior Lutheran Church in Albany, permission to use Capitol Park in downtown Albany to conduct a public preaching and music ministry as well as distribute Christian literature to passersby. Whitehouse was working with Youth with a Mission in this activity.

The ACLJ filed suit on behalf of Whitehouse, charging that his federal civil rights had been violated and that the state's action was unconstitutional. With the effective and dynamic skills of Jay Sekulow, a federal judge ordered the state of New York to cease its prejudicial treatment of Christians. A restraining order was granted and the proclamation of the gospel proceeded.

This was a great example of what can happen when Christians come together as allies rather than stay at arm's length and criticize each other.

Lausanne

Another powerful example of Christians coming together emerged in Lausanne, Switzerland, in 1974. This city hosted the First International Congress on World Evangelization, which was possibly the widest-ranging meeting of Christians ever. Twenty-seven hundred evangelical leaders from all confessional persuasions gathered at this congress to consider how to carry on the task of winning the world for Christ. They worked to draft a document that any church could adopt to help launch evangelistic efforts. After much discussion and debate, delegates to the congress drafted the Lausanne Covenant, which affirmed their commitment to pray, study, plan, and work together to fulfill the mission of spreading the good news commanded by Christ in the Great Commission.

As a result of this ecumenical conference, significant cooperative evangelistic efforts began. Eventually, however, many leaders made an urgent plea for a second congress. So in July 1989, Lausanne II was held in the city of Manila in the Philippines. Numerous participants and observers believe that this congress was the twentieth century's most strategic gathering of Christians committed to world evangelism. We will undoubtedly see the wonderful fruit of this ecumenical conference for decades, even centuries to come.

The Lausanne Covenant speaks to many issues, all of them rooted in a central mission: "We [the participants] are deeply stirred by what God is doing in our day, moved to penitence by our failures and challenged by the unfinished task of evangelization. We believe the gospel is God's good news for the whole world, and we are determined by his grace to obey Christ's commission to proclaim it to all mankind and to make disciples of every nation."[10]

One leader of the congress simply and clearly expressed the spirit of Lausanne: "It is only when we meet face to face, and struggle to hear and understand each other, that our type-cast images of each other (developed in separation) are modified, and we grow in mutual respect and shared conviction. This is the 'spirit of Lausanne'—a spirit of openness, integrity, and love."[11]

Lausanne has reached out to Christians of every church communion. The delegates' efforts to bring Catholics, Protestants, and Orthodox together are being carefully scrutinized by different church authorities, but this should not be feared. If there is need for readjustment, it should be welcomed, and I believe Lausanne leaders and participants will accept such a challenge. They are committed to a genuinely evangelical, ecumenical global outreach.

Efforts Aimed at AD 2000

In the hearts of God's people, a prophetic urgency is growing as we near the year 2000. Responding to that urgency have been groups like Evangelization 2000.

Evangelization 2000, under the leadership of Father Tom Forrest, is dedicated to rallying Catholics to the challenge of global evangelism within the next decade. It is accomplishing its agenda by joining ranks with other church efforts at worldwide evangelism. Service committees, such as the North American Renewal Service Committee, which is under the dynamic leadership of Dr. Vinson Synan, are giving birth to efforts such as *A.D. 2000*, which is a magazine geared toward networking these committees. The North America Renewal Service Committee is one of the many organizations that has grown out of the Catholic renewal movement. I have had the privilege of serving as a member of that organization's board for a number of years.[12]

The common denominator of all such groups is simple: They want to give a special birthday gift to Jesus Christ in the year 2000—a more Christian world.

MODERN-DAY PROPHETIC LEADERS

In John Paul II's exhortation to the lay faithful entitled *The Lay Members of Christ's Faithful People (Christifideles Laici)*, he gives a compelling call to all of us to reevangelize the church. Some Christians question John Paul's position as successor to Saint Peter—I do not. Others question his theology—I do not. But no one can question his love for Jesus Christ and deep commitment to proclaiming the gospel. His courage has opened doors that have long been shut. His visits to Eastern bloc countries and Latin America prophetically preceded and affected many of the events of liberation and spiritual and civil renewal that have occurred there.

Dr. Billy Graham is another prophetic leader in our century. A beautiful exception to the problem of arrogant Western presumptions, he has long worked with native churches and, though criticized by some, was proclaiming the gospel behind the Iron Curtain long before the Berlin Wall showed any cracks. He readily acknowledges that God is in the midst of Eastern Orthodoxy and Roman Catholicism, not just Protestantism.

One other prophetic voice is Chuck Colson. Through his numerous writings, ministry outreaches, talks, and other commitments, he has scaled the walls separating believers and courageously stood with Christians of all traditions to confront the darkness of our age. He and his work embody the spirit of charity and love of Christ that should characterize all believers. He is so committed to alliance building within the Body of Christ that he took the risk of asking faculty members and students at Franciscan University what they thought of the statement of faith of Prison Fellowship Ministries. When some concerns were raised about the statement's terminology (not so much about its content), Chuck immediately began reworking the statement to alleviate the stated concerns. That took a great act of humility and courage. It always takes leaders such as Chuck who are willing to change and be misunderstood to move the rest of us on to higher ground. It is no surprise that the Lord used him, along with Father Neuhaus, to draft the historic accord

"Evangelicals and Catholics Together."

Several years ago, while I was still at Franciscan University, the school honored Chuck with its Poverello Medal, the highest award given annually to the man, woman, or organization that most reflects the spirit of Saint Francis in a simple love for Jesus Christ. The university honored Chuck for his work with PFM and his prophetic ministry in a desperate world. I am delighted he and his ministry are continuing with such profound success.

Dr. James Dobson and Harald Bredesen, both also mentioned earlier, are great evangelical believers who are speaking prophetically to our time: Dr. Dobson, to the Christian family and beyond to our Western culture; Harald, to the churches, with a clarion call for their renewal and reunification.

I also believe Ralph Martin is a significant prophetic voice for our day. A Catholic layman, Ralph has long been active in renewal movements such as Cursillo and the charismatic renewal. He is also a founder of the Word of God community and a leader in other community movements. An ardent pro-lifer, he has been arrested for saving children from abortionists. He has consistently and clearly proclaimed a message of Christian unity, and through his work in Renewal Ministries, his many books, and his television and radio program "Choices We Face," he delivers a strong evangelical message of repentance and conversion.

Another prophetic voice that I deeply admire is Mother Angelica. She is a Franciscan nun with a big vision who has presided over a modern-day miracle, the Eternal Word Television Network. EWTN is a Catholic television network proclaiming the gospel twenty-four hours a day. The story of Mother Angelica and the sisters who have joined her, and the work of the network, are chronicled in numerous books about her life. She demonstrates the kind of evangelical fervor, courage, and conviction for which this book calls.

Yet another voice crying in the wilderness is Pat Robertson. His Christian Broadcasting Network has brought hope to Christian people for many years. His clear teaching, personal example, and founding of Regent University have been an inspiration to Christians of all churches, including me.

OUR FAMILY CONTINUITY

Did you notice the threads of continuity woven between all of these groups, movements, and prophetic leaders? All are sharply focused on

Jesus Christ as personal Lord. All seek ways to share His lordship among themselves and with others. And all desire cooperation and convergence toward the goal of unity. They sense the urgency of our mission under the call and example of Christ, and they realize we cannot ultimately achieve it as separated brethren going in separate directions.

In these movements and numerous others, hundreds of thousands of Christians have found access to renewal. And as these movements grow, their fruit will become even more widespread and apparent. Their testimonies to personal encounters with the Lord Jesus verify their readiness to transform the culture for Him. They also understand that our common mission requires the ongoing conversion of all Family members, that renewal must begin and continue within the Body of Christ even as she strives to expel the darkness beyond.

Although their practices have not always measured up to a perfect theology of community or ecumenism, their very existence testifies to a common conviction that to belong to Christ is to belong to His Body and to do what He commanded. The groups and individuals discussed here understand that community is a necessary dimension of church life and that as a community we have a mission to equip Christians to share their faith in Jesus Christ and live lives motivated by His love for all peoples. These movements and leaders call us back to the roots, back to the real meaning of the word *radical*, back to the Cross of Jesus Christ.

At the foot of the Cross, Christians are all equal. There we see we are all sinners in need of Christ's righteousness. There we see we are all loved by Him who gave Himself for us. There we can truly see each other as fellow sinners saved by His love, His grace, His mercy. There we can see what it really means to follow God, to give Him our all. There we can all see how foolish it is for us to stand before His profound love for us while we bicker among ourselves.

The Family can work together. As Family we must work together. As we look upon Christ crucified, Christ resurrected, Christ ascended, how can we fail to come together in service to Him?

CHAPTER EIGHTEEN

RESTORATION BEGINS AT HOME

*If God still loveth us,
we ought also to love one another.
We provoke one another to love and to good works.
Let the points wherein we differ stand aside:
here are enough wherein we agree,
enough to be the ground of every Christian
temper and of every Christian action.*
John Wesley

Alliance building among Christians will always face opposition, regardless of who favors it or gets involved doing it. Christians will fight against it for a number of reasons, some fairly well thought out and others poorly reasoned by anyone's standards. I hope this book will generate dialogue, even heated discussion among friends and foes alike of genuine ecumenical efforts. We need to work out our differences.

At the same time, I realize that some of the opposition to alliance building has and will come from Christians who see it as a monumental threat to the purity of the faith they hold dear. Many of these believers, no matter how sincere they may be, will not calmly sit down and engage those who disagree with them in humble discussion; rather, they will stand up and practically shout at them dire pronouncements of impending, even everlasting doom if they don't repent of their ecumenical desires and efforts. Some of these folks have seemingly made it their life's ambition to oppose any efforts at Christian cooperation. Without impugning their motives, I abhor their tactics.

Dave Hunt is one of these doomsayers. While he attempts to take a high moral ground in unequivocally opposing any form of cooperation between what he considers to be evangelical Protestants and anyone else, he practically anathematizes those Christians who disagree with him. In response to the ecumenical accord "Evangelicals and Catholics Together,"

Hunt writes, "The document overturns the Reformation and does incalculable damage to the cause of Christ." Right after he says he does not "impugn the motives nor question the salvation of the evangelical signers," he adds, "yet I believe the document represents the most devastating blow against the gospel in at least 1,000 years." Throughout the rest of the article, Hunt hurls vitriolic accusations against Catholics, their tradition, and their leaders. Claiming to be citing just the facts, he really distorts the truth as he spews out bigotry. He also attacks the intellectual and moral integrity of the signers of the accord. For if they only knew what he did about Catholicism or had been honest with the "facts," they would not have sought "to prevent the gospel from being presented to lost millions who have now been wrongly reclassified by evangelical leaders [notably, those who attached their names to the accord] as Christians."[1]

Are Protestants as astute in their understanding of theology, history, and culture as J. I. Packer, Charles Colson, Os Guinness, Richard Land, Pat Robertson, John White, and Thomas Oden really that far off base? Are Catholics as devoutly committed to Jesus Christ as Richard John Neuhaus, William Bentley Ball, John Cardinal O'Connor, James Hitchcock, Peter Kreeft, and Ralph Martin really unsaved and deceivers of the faithful? Granted, no Christian is always right and many can be sincerely wrong, but does it stand to reason that Christians of this stature coming from across the confessional spectrum have been conned and are conning others?

I don't think so, and neither do numerous other believers. People such as Hunt in effect set themselves up as their own magisterium, then they try to make all other Christians heed their pronouncements of what's orthodox and what's not. In the process, whether they intend to or not, they wound the Body of Christ. Rather than strive for unity, they perpetuate schism and thereby deepen the scars created by the great divorce.

Fortunately for the Body of Christ, I do not believe the naysayers of genuine alliance building and unity will ultimately prevail. God is at work. By grace He is healing His church and moving it toward its intended end. Contrary to Hunt's pronouncements, I believe one of those moves of God is the signing of the accord "Evangelicals and Catholics Together."

This document does not embrace Humpty Dumpty solutions, and neither does it sound the death knell to alliance-building efforts. It takes a sound, honest, and inspiring stand for Christians of all confessions and traditions to become allies for the sake of the church and the culture. As it proclaims, I also believe:

As Evangelicals and Catholics, we pray that our unity in the love of Christ will become ever more evident as a sign to the world of God's reconciling power. Our communal and ecclesial separations are deep and long standing. We acknowledge that we do not know the schedule nor do we know the way to the greater visible unity for which we hope. We do know that existing patterns of distrustful polemic and conflict are not the way. We do know that Christ is the way, the truth, and the life (John 14) and as we are drawn close to him—walking in that way, obeying that truth, living that life—we are drawn closer to one another.

Whatever may be the future form of the relationship between our communities, we can, we must, and we will begin now the work required to remedy what we know to be wrong in that relationship. Such work requires trust and understanding, and trust and understanding require an assiduous attention to truth. We do not deny but clearly assert that there are disagreements between us. Misunderstandings, misrepresentations, and caricatures of one another, however, are not disagreements. These distortions must be cleared away if we are to search through our honest differences in a manner consistent with what we affirm and hope together on the basis of God's Word.[2]

AN UNCOMMON PLEA

You have heard my plea to all Christians to lay down their weapons, scale the great wall of division, embrace each other once more as fellow members of the same church Family, and together penetrate the stronghold of our common foe with the reconciling sword of the Christian worldview. You have heard about other individuals, groups, communities, churches, and fellowships that are fighting the good fight from a solid ecumenical base and calling for fresh recruits from every corner of the Christian camp. Encouraging? Yes. Tragic? That too, because all these voices are too few. They are still lonely cries echoing across the battlefields of secularism, relativism, atheism, New Age-ism, resurgent paganism, and all the other *isms* threatening to kill and bury believers and unbelievers alike. Our plea is still rarely voiced, but I'm grateful it is beginning to gain a greater hearing. Even so, it still seems insane to me that given all we have in common, the plea for peace in our Family is still uncommon.

But once again, when we turn back the pages of our common history, we find how old this uncommon plea really is. As far back as 1749, we discover a great evangelical Protestant hero of mine, John Wesley, writing a letter to a Catholic friend. This lengthy piece of correspondence later became a tract that was distributed in Ireland, where great bitterness existed between Catholics and Protestants (and tragically still does). But before that it was placed into the hands of one Catholic, given as a vehicle to foster unity, not divisiveness, in a personal relationship.

From this letter we can see the heart of a man on fire for the gospel and true ecumenism. It is too long to quote in its entirety, but if we would only hear Wesley's uncommon plea, perhaps more of us would take it as our own, and perhaps in time, it would reverberate throughout the world, carried on every tongue that confesses Jesus Christ as Lord.

> 1. You have heard ten thousand stories of us who are commonly called Protestants, of which, if you believe only one in a thousand, you must think very hardly of us. But this is quite contrary to our Lord's rule, "judge not, that ye be not judged" (Matt. 7:1), and has many ill consequences, particularly this: it inclines us to think as hardly of you. Hence, we are on both sides less willing to help one another and more ready to hurt each other. Hence brotherly love is utterly destroyed and each side, looking on the other as monsters, gives way to anger, hatred, malice, to every unkind affection—which have frequently broken out in such inhuman barbarities as are scarce named even among the heathens.
>
> 2. Now can nothing be done, even allowing us on both sides to retain our own opinions, for the softening our hearts towards each other, the giving a check to this flood of unkindness and restoring at least some small degree of love among our neighbours and countrymen? Do not you wish for this? Are you not fully convinced that malice, hatred, revenge, bitterness (whether in us or in you, in our hearts or yours) are an abomination to the Lord (Prov. 15:26, 16:5)? Be our opinions right or be they wrong, these tempers are undeniably wrong. They are the broad road that leads to destruction, to the nethermost hell.
>
> 3. I do not suppose all the bitterness is on your side. I know there is too much on our side also. So much that I fear many Protestants (so-called) will be angry at me, too, for writing to you in this manner, and will say, "Tis showing you too much favour; you deserve no such treatment at our hands."

4. But I think you do. I think you deserve the tenderest regard I can show, were it only because the same God hath raised you and me from the dust of the earth and has made us both capable of loving and enjoying him to eternity; were it only because the Son of God has bought you and me with his own blood. How much more, if you are a person fearing God (as without question many of you are) and studying to have a conscience void of offence towards God and towards man?

5. I shall therefore endeavour, as mildly and inoffensively as I can, to remove in some measure the ground of your unkindness by plainly declaring what our belief and what our practice is: that you may see we are not altogether such monsters as perhaps you imagined us to be.

After describing the essentials of Protestant belief, Wesley made an appeal Christians of all traditions should accept. Indeed, his four closing exhortations could still serve as the basis for a genuine ecumenism and genuinely evangelical agenda.

16. Are we not thus far agreed? Let us thank God for this, and receive it as a fresh token of his love. But if God still loveth us, we ought also to love one another. We provoke one another to love and to good works. Let the points wherein we differ stand aside: here are enough wherein we agree, enough to be the ground of every Christian temper and of every Christian action.

O brethren, let us not still fall out by the way. I hope to see you in heaven. And if I practise the religion above described, you dare not say I shall go to hell. You cannot think so. None can persuade you to it. Your own conscience tells you the contrary. Then if we cannot as yet think alike in all things, at least we may love alike. Herein we cannot possibly go amiss. For of one point none can doubt a moment: God is love; and he that dwelleth in love, dwelleth in God, and God in him (1 John 4:16).

17. In the name, then, and in the strength of God, *let us resolve, first, not to hurt one another*, to do nothing unkind or unfriendly to each other, nothing which we would not have done to ourselves. Rather let us endeavour after every instance of a kind, friendly and Christian behaviour towards each other.

Let us resolve, secondly, God being our helper, to speak nothing harsh or unkind of each other. The sure way to avoid this is to say all the good we can, both of and to one another; in all our conversation, either with or concerning each other, to use only the language of love; to speak with all softness and tenderness, with the most endearing expression which is consistent with truth and sincerity.

Let us thirdly, resolve to harbour no unkind thought, no unfriendly temper towards each other. Let us lay the axe to the root of the tree (Matt. 3:10), let us examine all that rises in our heart and suffer no disposition there which is contrary to the tender affection. Then shall we easily refrain from unkind actions and words, when the very root of bitterness is cut up (Heb. 12:15).

Let us, fourthly, endeavour to help each other on in whatever we are agreed leads to the Kingdom. So far as we can, let us always rejoice to strengthen each other's hands in God. Above all, let us each take heed unto himself (since each must give an account of himself to God) that he fall not short of the religion of love; that he be not condemned in that he himself approveth. O let you and me (whatever others do) press on to the prize of our high calling—that, being justified by faith, we may have peace with God through our Lord Jesus Christ; that we may rejoice in God through Jesus Christ, by whom we have received the atonement (Rom. 5:1-2); that the love of God may be shed abroad in our hearts by the Holy Ghost which is given unto us (Rom. 5:5).[3]

SIGNS OF RESTORATION

The good news for the Body of Christ is that the spirit of Wesley's courageous and visionary words lives on. Christians, individually and corporately, are making peace with one another and treating one another with the love and respect that should characterize fellow Family members. For example, since 1966, Anglican and Catholic leaders have been working to resolve differences between them that date back to the Protestant Reformation period. To date they have come to important agreements on such matters as the Eucharist, the ministry, and the role and authority of the pope. They have even resolved many of the issues on justification by faith that have kept the two churches apart for centuries. Still a serious matter left to resolve is that of the ordination of women, but both confessions are committed to achieving a greater unity between them, with both acknowledging the other's Family position in

Christ. So the channels of honest, truth-seeking dialogue remain open.[4]

The same search for healing old wounds and creating new bonds of cooperation and unity has been occurring between Catholics and Lutherans in recent years. Since 1963, leaders from both confessions have been wrestling together through issues such as tradition and Scripture, the doctrine of justification, the gospel and the world, the ordained ministry, and the papacy. Recognizing one another as brothers and sisters in Christ, they have made great strides toward reconciliation, including on one of the central issues that had led to their separation during the Reformation—justification by faith.[5]

An incredible sign of their progress toward reconciliation occurred in October 1991. Pope John Paul II presided at the first joint prayer service with Lutherans inside St. Peter's Basilica in Rome, Italy. Among those in attendance were the king of Finland and the queen of Sweden, both of whom are Lutheran archbishops. This was the first time since the sixteenth-century Reformation that such a service was held. Bertil Werkstrom, the Lutheran archbishop of Uppsala said, "It grieves us that we cannot share the Holy Supper today . . . the purpose of the Reformation was not to lead us away from each other or to break the eucharistic communion." Echoing the archbishop's sentiments, Pope John Paul II stated, "We can rightly say that their (Lutherans and Catholics) centuries-old mutual distrust has faded away and is being replaced by ever more tangible signs of trust and hope. . . . With courage and confidence let us continue to draw closer to one another."[6]

Catholics, Protestants, and Orthodox can come together, must come together, and are coming together. The wall of separation is cracking; portions of the wall are beginning to fall away. Christians are waking up and starting to see one another as allies in a common war effort. They are even beginning to see each other as Family. We still have a long, tough road ahead of us. But it's a road we need to travel together—with courage and confidence.

One day we will see the true Family unity all of us should desire— the unity Wesley so much wanted with his Catholic brother in Christ. Until then, we can build cooperative alliances together and through them begin to rediscover all the lines of convergence that are ours in our common Savior and Lord, Jesus Christ. May the "grace of the Lord Jesus be with God's people" in this effort.[7]

APPENDIX

EVANGELICALS AND CATHOLICS TOGETHER:
THE CHRISTIAN MISSION IN THE THIRD MILLENNIUM[1]

The following statement is the product of consultation, beginning in September 1992, between Evangelical Protestant and Roman Catholic Christians. Appended to the text is a list of participants in the consultation and of others who have given their support to this declaration.[1]

Introduction
1. We are Evangelical Protestants and Roman Catholics who have been led through prayer, study, and discussion to common convictions about Christian faith and mission. This statement cannot speak officially for our communities. It does intend to speak responsibly from our communities and to our communities. In this statement we address what we have discovered both about our unity and about our differences. We are aware that our experience reflects the distinctive circumstances and opportunities of Evangelicals and Catholics living together in North America. At the same time, we believe that what we have discovered and resolved is pertinent to the relationship between Evangelicals and Catholics in other parts of the world. We therefore commend this statement to their prayerful consideration.

2. As the Second Millennium draws to a close, the Christian mission in world history faces a moment of daunting opportunity and responsibility. If in the merciful and mysterious ways of God the Second Coming is delayed, we enter upon a Third Millennium that could be, in the words of John Paul II, "a springtime of world missions." (*Redemptoris Missio*)

3. As Christ is one, so the Christian mission is one. That one mission can be and should be advanced in diverse ways. Legitimate diversity, however, should not be confused with existing divisions between Christians that obscure the one Christ

337

and hinder the one mission. There is a necessary connection between the visible unity of Christians and the mission of the one Christ. We together pray for the fulfillment of the prayer of Our Lord: "May they all be one; as you, Father, are in me and I in you, so also may they be in us, that the world may believe that you sent me." (John 17) We together, Evangelicals and Catholics, confess our sins against the unity that Christ intends for all his disciples.

4. The one Christ and one mission includes many other Christians, notably the Eastern Orthodox and those Protestants not commonly identified as Evangelical. All Christians are encompassed in the prayer, "May they all be one." Our present statement attends to the specific problems and opportunities in the relationship between Roman Catholics and Evangelical Protestants.

5. As we near the Third Millennium, there are approximately 1.7 billion Christians in the world. About a billion of these are Catholics and more than 300 million are Evangelical Protestants. The century now drawing to a close has been the greatest century of missionary expansion in Christian history. We pray and we believe that this expansion has prepared the way for yet greater missionary endeavor in the first century of the Third Millennium.

6. The two communities in world Christianity that are most evangelistically assertive and most rapidly growing are Evangelicals and Catholics. In many parts of the world, the relationship between these communities is marked more by conflict than by cooperation, more by animosity than by love, more by suspicion than by trust, more by propaganda and ignorance than by respect for the truth. This is alarmingly the case in Latin America, increasingly the case in Eastern Europe, and too often the case in our own country.

7. Without ignoring conflicts between and within other Christian communities, we address ourselves to the relationship between Evangelicals and Catholics, who constitute the growing edge of missionary expansion at present and, most likely, in the century ahead. In doing so, we hope that what we have discovered and resolved may be of help in other situations of conflict, such as that among Orthodox, Evangelicals, and Catholics in Eastern Europe. While we are gratefully aware of ongoing efforts to address tensions among these communities, the shameful reality is that, in many places around the world, the scandal of conflict between Christians obscures the scandal of the cross, thus crippling the one mission of the one Christ.

8. As in times past, so also today and in the future, the Christian mission, which is directed to the entire human community, must be advanced against formidable opposition. In some cultures, that mission encounters resurgent spiritualities and religions that are explicitly hostile to the claims of the Christ. Islam, which in many instances denies the freedom to witness to the Gospel, must be of increasing concern to those who care about religious freedom and the Christian mission. Mutually respectful conversation between Muslims and Christians should be encouraged in the hope that more of the world will, in the oft-repeated words of John Paul II, "open the door to Christ." At the same time, in our so-called developed societies, a widespread secularization increasingly descends into moral, intellectual, and spiritual nihilism that denies not only the One who is the Truth but the very idea of truth itself.

9. We enter the twenty-first century without illusions. With Paul and the Christians of the first century, we know that "we are not contending against flesh and blood,

but against the principalities, against the powers, against the world rulers of this present darkness, against the spiritual hosts of wickedness in the heavenly places." (Ephesians 6) As Evangelicals and Catholics, we dare not by needless and loveless conflict between ourselves give aid and comfort to the enemies of the cause of Christ.

10. The love of Christ compels us and we are therefore resolved to avoid such conflict between our communities and, where such conflict exists, to do what we can to reduce and eliminate it. Beyond that, we are called and we are therefore resolved to explore patterns of working and witnessing together in order to advance the one mission of Christ. Our common resolve is not based merely on a desire for harmony. We reject any appearance of harmony that is purchased at the price of truth. Our common resolve is made imperative by obedience to the truth of God revealed in the Word of God, the Holy Scriptures, and by the trust in the promise of the Holy Spirit's guidance until Our Lord returns in glory to judge the living and the dead.

    The mission that we embrace together is the necessary consequence of the faith that we affirm together.

We Affirm Together

11. Jesus Christ is Lord. That is the first and final affirmation that Christians make about all of reality. He is the One sent by God to be Lord and Savior of all: "And there is salvation in no one else, for there is no other name under heaven given among men by which we must be saved." (Acts 4) Christians are people ahead of time, those who proclaim now what will one day be acknowledged by all, that Jesus Christ is Lord. (Philippians 2)

12. We affirm together that we are justified by grace through faith because of Christ. Living faith is active in love that is nothing less than the love of Christ, for we together say with Paul: "I have been crucified with Christ; it is no longer I who live, but Christ who lives in me; and the life I now live in the flesh I live by faith in the Son of God, who loved me and gave himself for me." (Galatians 2)

13. All who accept Christ as Lord and Savior are brothers and sisters in Christ. Evangelicals and Catholics are brothers and sisters in Christ. We have not chosen one another, just as we have not chosen Christ. He has chosen us, and he has chosen us to be his together. (John 15) However imperfect our communion with one another, however deep our disagreements with one another, we recognize that there is but one church of Christ. There is one church because there is one Christ and the church is his body. However difficult the way, we recognize that we are called by God to a fuller realization of our unity in the body of Christ. The only unity to which we would give expression is unity in the truth, and the truth is this: "There is one body and one Spirit, just as you were called to the one hope that belongs to your call, one Lord, one faith, one baptism, one God and Father of us all, who is above all and through all and in all." (Ephesians 4)

14. We affirm together that Christians are to teach and live in obedience to the divinely inspired Scriptures, which are the infallible Word of God. We further affirm together that Christ has promised to his church the gift of the Holy Spirit who will lead us into all truth in discerning and declaring the teaching of Scripture. (John 16) We recognize together that the Holy Spirit has so guided his church in the past. In, for instance, the formation of the canon of the Scriptures, and in the orthodox response to the great Christological and Trinitarian controversies of the early centuries, we confidently

acknowledge the guidance of the Holy Spirit. In faithful response to the Spirit's leading, the church formulated the Apostles' Creed, which we can and hereby do affirm together as an accurate statement of scriptural truth:

I believe in God, the Father almighty, creator of heaven and earth.

I believe in Jesus Christ, his only Son, our Lord. He was conceived by the power of the Holy Spirit and born of the virgin Mary. He suffered under Pontius Pilate, was crucified, died and was buried. He descended into hell. On the third day he rose again. He ascended into heaven, and is seated at the right hand of the Father. He will come again to judge the living and the dead.

I believe in the Holy Spirit, the holy catholic Church, the communion of saints, the forgiveness of sins, the resurrection of the body, and the life everlasting. Amen.

We Hope Together

15. We hope together that all people will come to faith in Jesus Christ as Lord and Savior. This hope makes necessary the church's missionary zeal. "But how are they to call upon him in whom they have not believed? And how are they to believe in him of whom they have never heard? And how are they to hear without a preacher? And how can men preach unless they are sent?" (Romans 10) The church is by nature, in all places and at all times, in mission. Our missionary hope is inspired by the revealed desire of God that "all should be saved and come to a knowledge of the truth." (1 Timothy 2)

16. The church lives by and for the Great Commission: "Go therefore and make disciples of all nations, baptizing them in the name of the Father and of the Son and of the Holy Spirit, teaching them to observe all that I have commanded you; and lo, I am with you always, to the close of the age." (Matthew 28)

17. Unity and love among Christians is an integral part of our missionary witness to the Lord whom we serve. "A new commandment I give to you, that you love one another; even as I have loved you, that you also love one another. By this all men will know that you are my disciples, if you have love for one another." (John 13) If we do not love one another, we disobey this command and contradict the Gospel we declare.

18. As Evangelicals and Catholics, we pray that our unity in the love of Christ will become ever more evident as a sign to the world of God's reconciling power. Our communal and ecclesial separations are deep and long standing. We acknowledge that we do not know the schedule nor do we know the way to the greater visible unity for which we hope. We do know that existing patterns of distrustful polemic and conflict are not the way. We do know that God who has brought us into communion with himself through Christ intends that we also be in communion with one another. We do know that Christ is the way, the truth, and the life (John 14) and as we are drawn closer to him—walking in that way, obeying that truth, living that life—we are drawn closer to one another.

19. Whatever may be the future form of the relationship between our communities, we can, we must, and we will begin now the work required to remedy what we know to be wrong in that relationship. Such work requires trust and understanding, and trust and understanding require an assiduous attention to truth. We do not deny but clearly assert that there are disagreements between us. Misunderstandings, misrepresentations, and caricatures of one another, however, are not disagreements. These

distortions must be cleared away if we are to search through our honest differences in a manner consistent with what we affirm and hope together on the basis of God's Word.

We Search Together
20. Together we search for a fuller and clearer understanding of God's revelation of Christ and his will for his disciples. Because of the limitations of human reason and language, which limitations are compounded by sin, we cannot understand completely the transcendent reality of God and his ways. Only in the End Time will we see face to face and know as we are known. (1 Corinthians 13) We now search together in confident reliance upon God's self-revelation in Jesus Christ, the sure testimony of Holy Scripture, and the promise of the Spirit to his church. In this search to understand the truth more fully and clearly, we need one another. We are both informed and limited by the histories of our communities and by our own experiences. Across the divides of communities and experiences, we need to challenge one another, always speaking the truth in love, building up the Body. (Ephesians 4)

21. We do not presume to suggest that we can resolve the deep and long-standing differences between Evangelicals and Catholics. Indeed these differences may never be resolved short of the Kingdom Come. Nonetheless, we are not permitted simply to resign ourselves to differences that divide us from one another. Not all differences are authentic disagreements, nor need all disagreements divide. Differences and disagreements must be tested in disciplined and sustained conversation. In this connection we warmly commend and encourage the formal theological dialogues of recent years between Roman Catholics and Evangelicals.

22. We note some of the differences and disagreements that must be addressed more fully and candidly in order to strengthen between us a relationship of trust in obedience to truth. Among points of difference in doctrine, worship, practice, and piety that are frequently thought to divide us are these:

   ◆ The church as an integral part of the Gospel or the church as communal consequence of the Gospel.
   ◆ The church as visible communion or invisible fellowship of true believers.
   ◆ The sole authority of Scripture (*sola scriptura*) or Scripture as authoritatively interpreted in the church.
   ◆ The "soul freedom" of the individual Christian or the Magisterium (teaching authority) of the community.
   ◆ The church as local congregation or universal communion.
   ◆ Ministry ordered in apostolic succession or the priesthood of all believers.
   ◆ Sacraments and ordinances as symbols of grace or means of grace.
   ◆ The Lord's Supper as eucharistic sacrifice or memorial meal.
   ◆ Remembrance of Mary and the saints or devotion to Mary and the saints.
   ◆ Baptism as sacrament of regeneration or testimony to regeneration.

23. This account of differences is by no means complete. Nor is the disparity between positions always so sharp as to warrant the "or" in the above formulations. Moreover, among those recognized as Evangelical Protestants there are significant differences between, for example, Baptists, Pentecostals, and Calvinists on these questions. But the differences mentioned above reflect disputes that are deep and long standing. In at least some instances, they reflect authentic disagreements that have been in the past and are at present barriers to full communion between Christians.

24. On these questions, and other questions implied by them, Evangelicals hold that the Catholic Church has gone beyond Scripture, adding teachings and practices that detract from or compromise the Gospel of God's saving grace in Christ. Catholics, in turn, hold that such teaching and practices are grounded in Scripture and belong to the fullness of God's revelation. Their rejection, Catholics say, results in a truncated and reduced understanding of the Christian reality.

25. Again, we cannot resolve these disputes here. We can and do affirm together that the entirety of Christian faith, life, and mission finds its source, center, and end in the crucified and risen Lord. We can and do pledge that we will continue to search together—through study, discussion, and prayer—for a better understanding of one another's convictions and a more adequate comprehension of the truth of God in Christ. We can testify now that in our searching together we have discovered what we can affirm together and what we can hope together and, therefore, how we can contend together.

We Contend Together

26. As we are bound together by Christ and his cause, so we are bound together in contending against all that opposes Christ and his cause. We are emboldened not by illusions of easy triumph but by faith in his certain triumph. Our Lord wept over Jerusalem, and he now weeps over a world that does not know the time of its visitation. The raging of the principalities and powers may increase as the End Time nears, but the outcome of the contest is assured.

27. The cause of Christ is the cause and mission of the church, which is, first of all, to proclaim the Good News that "God was in Christ reconciling the world to himself, not counting their trespasses against them, and entrusting to us the message of reconciliation." (2 Corinthians 5) To proclaim this Gospel and to sustain the community of faith, worship, and discipleship that is gathered by this Gospel is the first and chief responsibility of the church. All other tasks and responsibilities of the church are derived from and directed toward the mission of the Gospel.

28. Christians individually and the church corporately also have a responsibility for the right ordering of civil society. We embrace this task soberly; knowing the consequences of human sinfulness, we resist the utopian conceit that it is within our powers to build the Kingdom of God on earth. We embrace this task hopefully; knowing that God has called us to love our neighbor, we seek to secure for all a greater measure of civil righteousness and justice, confident that he will crown our efforts when he rightly orders all things in the coming of his Kingdom.

29. In the exercise of these public responsibilities there has been in recent years a growing convergence and cooperation between Evangelicals and Catholics. We thank God for the discovery of one another in contending for a common cause. Much more important, we thank God for the discovery of one another as brothers and sisters in Christ. Our cooperation as citizens is animated by our convergence as Christians. We promise one another that we will work to deepen, build upon, and expand this pattern of convergence and cooperation.

30. Together we contend for the truth that politics, law, and culture must be secured by moral truth. With the Founders of the American experiment, we declare, "We hold these truths." With them, we hold that this constitutional order is composed not just of rules and procedures but is most essentially a moral experiment. With them, we

hold that only a virtuous people can be free and just, and that virtue is secured by religion. To propose that securing civil virtue is the purpose of religion is blasphemous. To deny that securing civil virtue is a benefit of religion is blindness.

31. Americans are drifting away from, are often explicitly defying, the constituting truths of this experiment in ordered liberty. Influential sectors of the culture are laid waste by relativism, anti-intellectualism, and nihilism that deny the very idea of truth. Against such influences in both the elite and popular culture, we appeal to reason and religion in contending for the foundational truths of our constitutional order.

32. More specifically, we contend together for religious freedom. We do so for the sake of religion, but also because religious freedom is the first freedom, the source and shield of all human freedoms. In their relationship to God, persons have a dignity and responsibility that transcends, and thereby limits, the authority of the state and of every other merely human institution.

33. Religious freedom is itself grounded in and is a product of religious faith, as is evident in the history of Baptists and others in this country. Today we rejoice together that the Roman Catholic Church—as affirmed by the Second Vatican Council and boldly exemplified in the ministry of John Paul II—is strongly committed to religious freedom and, consequently, to the defense of all human rights. Where Evangelicals and Catholics are in severe and sometimes violent conflict, such as parts of Latin America, we urge Christians to embrace and act upon the imperative of religious freedom. Religious freedom will not be respected by the state if it is not respected by Christians or, even worse, if Christians attempt to recruit the state in repressing religious freedom.

34. In this country, too, freedom of religion cannot be taken for granted but requires constant attention. We strongly affirm the separation of church and state, and just as strongly protest the distortion of that principle to mean the separation of religion from public life. We are deeply concerned by the court's narrowing of the protections provided by the "free exercise" provision of the First Amendment and by an obsession with "no establishment" that stifles the necessary role of religion in American life. As a consequence of such distortions, it is increasingly the case that wherever government goes religion must retreat, and government increasingly goes almost everywhere. Religion, which was privileged and foundational in our legal order, has in recent years been penalized and made marginal. We contend together for a renewal of the constituting vision of the place of religion in the American experiment.

35. Religion and religiously grounded moral conviction is not an alien or threatening force in our public life. For the great majority of Americans, morality is derived, however variously and confusedly, from religion. The argument, increasingly voiced in sectors of our political culture, that religion should be excluded from the public square must be recognized as an assault upon the most elementary principles of democratic governance. That argument needs to be exposed and countered by leaders, religious and other, who care about the integrity of our constitutional order.

36. The pattern of convergence and cooperation between Evangelicals and Catholics is, in large part, a result of common effort to protect human life, especially the lives of the most vulnerable among us. With the Founders, we hold that all human beings are endowed by their Creator with the right to life, liberty, and the pursuit of happiness. The statement that the unborn child is a human life that—barring natural

misfortune or lethal intervention—will become what everyone recognizes as a human baby is not a religious assertion. It is a statement of simple biological fact. That the unborn child has a right to protection, including the protection of law, is a moral statement supported by moral reason and biblical truth.

37. We, therefore, will persist in contending—we will not be discouraged but will multiply every effort—in order to secure the legal protection of the unborn. Our goals are: to secure due process of law for the unborn, to enact the most protective laws and public policies that are politically possible, and to reduce dramatically the incidence of abortion. We warmly commend those who have established thousands of crisis pregnancy and postnatal care centers across the country, and urge that such efforts be multiplied. As the unborn must be protected, so also must women be protected from their current rampant exploitation by the abortion industry and by fathers who refuse to accept responsibility for mothers and children. Abortion on demand, which is the current rule in America, must be recognized as a massive attack on the dignity, rights, and needs of women.

38. Abortion is the leading edge of an encroaching culture of death. The helpless old, the radically handicapped, and others who cannot effectively assert their rights are increasingly treated as though they have no rights. These are the powerless who are exposed to the will and whim of those who have power over them. We will do all in our power to resist proposals for euthanasia, eugenics, and population control that exploit the vulnerable, corrupt the integrity of medicine, deprave our culture, and betray the moral truths of our constitutional order.

39. In public education, we contend together for schools that transmit to coming generations our cultural heritage, which is inseparable from the formative influence of religion, especially Judaism and Christianity. Education for responsible citizenship and social behavior is inescapably moral education. Every effort must be made to cultivate the morality of honesty, law observance, work, caring, chastity, mutual respect between the sexes, and readiness for marriage, parenthood, and family. We reject the claim that, in any or all of these areas, "tolerance" requires the promotion of moral equivalence between the normative and the deviant. In a democratic society that recognizes that parents have the primary responsibility for the formation of their children, schools are to assist and support, not oppose and undermine, parents in the exercise of their responsibility.

40. We contend together for a comprehensive policy of parental choice in education. This is a moral question of simple justice. Parents are the primary educators of their children; the state and other institutions should be supportive of their exercise of the responsibility. We affirm policies that enable parents to effectively exercise their right and responsibility to choose the schooling that they consider best for their children.

41. We contend together against the widespread pornography in our society, along with the celebration of violence, sexual depravity, and antireligious bigotry in the entertainment media. In resisting such cultural and moral debasement, we recognize the legitimacy of boycotts and other consumer actions, and urge the enforcement of existing laws against obscenity. We reject the self-serving claim of the peddlers of depravity that this constitutes illegitimate censorship. We reject the assertion of the unimaginative that artistic creativity is to be measured by the capacity to shock or outrage. A people incapable of defending decency invites the rule of viciousness, both public and personal.

42. We contend for a renewed spirit of acceptance, understanding, and cooperation across lines of religion, race, ethnicity, sex, and class. We are all created in the image of God and are accountable to him. That truth is the basis of individual responsibility and equality before the law. The abandonment of that truth has resulted in a society at war with itself, pitting citizens against one another in bitter conflicts of group grievances and claims to entitlement. Justice and social amity require a redirection of public attitudes and policies so that rights are joined to duties and people are rewarded according to their character and competence.

43. We contend for a free society, including a vibrant market economy. A free society requires a careful balancing between economics, politics, and culture. Christianity is not an ideology and therefore does not prescribe precisely how that balance is to be achieved in every circumstance. We affirm the importance of a free economy not only because it is more efficient but because it accords with a Christian understanding of human freedom. Economic freedom, while subject to grave abuse, makes possible the patterns of creativity, cooperation, and accountability that contribute to the common good.

44. We contend together for a renewed appreciation of Western culture. In its history and missionary reach, Christianity engages all cultures while being captive to none. We are keenly aware of, and grateful for, the role of Christianity in shaping and sustaining the Western culture of which we are part. As with all of history, that culture is marred by human sinfulness. Alone among world cultures, however, the West has cultivated an attitude of self-criticism and of eagerness to learn from other cultures. What is called multiculturalism can mean respectful attention to human differences. More commonly today, however, multiculturalism means affirming all cultures but our own. Welcoming the contributions of other cultures and being ever alert to the limitations of our own, we receive Western culture as our legacy and embrace it as our task in order to transmit it as a gift to future generations.

45. We contend for public policies that demonstrate renewed respect for the irreplaceable role of mediating structures in society—notably the family, churches, and myriad voluntary associations. The state is not the society, and many of the most important functions of society are best addressed in independence from the state. The role of churches in responding to a wide variety of human needs, especially among the poor and marginal, needs to be protected and strengthened. Moreover, society is not the aggregate of isolated individuals bearing rights but is composed of communities that inculcate responsibility, sustain shared memory, provide mutual aid, and nurture the habits that contribute to both personal well-being and the common good. Most basic among such communities is the community of the family. Laws and social policies should be designed with particular care for the stability and flourishing of families. While the crisis of the family in America is by no means limited to the poor or to the underclass, heightened attention must be paid those who have become, as a result of well-intended but misguided statist policies, virtual wards of the government.

46. Finally, we contend for a realistic and responsible understanding of America's part in world affairs. Realism and responsibility require that we avoid both the illusions of unlimited power and righteousness, on the one hand, and the timidity and selfishness of isolationism, on the other. U.S. foreign policy should reflect a concern for the defense of democracy and, wherever prudent and possible, the protection and advancement of human rights, including religious freedom.

47. The above is a partial list of public responsibilities on which we believe there is a pattern of convergence and cooperation between Evangelicals and Catholics. We reject the notion that this constitutes a partisan "religious agenda" in American politics. Rather, this is a set of directions oriented to the common good and discussable on the basis of public reason. While our sense of civic responsibility is informed and motivated by Christian faith, our intention is to elevate the level of political and moral discourse in a manner that excludes no one and invites the participation of all people of good will. To that end, Evangelicals and Catholics have made an inestimable contribution in the past and, it is our hope, will contribute even more effectively in the future.

48. We are profoundly aware that the American experiment has been, all in all, a blessing to the world and a blessing to us as Evangelical and Catholic Christians. We are determined to assume our full share of responsibility for this "one nation under God," believing it to be a nation under the judgment, mercy, and providential care of the Lord of the nations to whom alone we render unqualified allegiance.

We Witness Together

49. The question of Christian witness unavoidably returns us to points of serious tension between Evangelicals and Catholics. Bearing witness to the saving power of Jesus Christ and his will for our lives is an integral part of Christian discipleship. The achievement of good will and cooperation between Evangelicals and Catholics must not be at the price of the urgency and clarity of Christian witness to the Gospel. At the same time, and as noted earlier, Our Lord has made clear that the evidence of love among his disciples is an integral part of that Christian witness.

50. Today, in this country and elsewhere, Evangelicals and Catholics attempt to win "converts" from one another's folds. In some ways, this is perfectly understandable and perhaps inevitable. In many instances, however, such efforts at recruitment undermine the Christian mission by which we are bound by God's Word and to which we have recommitted ourselves in this statement. It should be clearly understood between Catholics and Evangelicals that Christian witness is of necessity aimed at conversion. Authentic conversion is—in its beginning, in its end, and all along the way—conversion to God in Christ by the power of the Spirit. In this connection, we embrace as our own the explanation of the Baptist-Roman Catholic International Conversation (1988):

> Conversion is turning away from all that is opposed to God, contrary to Christ's teaching, and turning to God, to Christ, the Son, through the work of the Holy Spirit. It entails a turning from the self-centeredness of sin to faith in Christ as Lord and Savior. Conversion is a passing from one way of life to another new one, marked with the newness of Christ. It is a continuing process so that the whole life of a Christian should be a passage from death to life, from error to truth, from sin to grace. Our life in Christ demands continual growth in God's grace. Conversion is personal but not private. Individuals respond in faith to God's call but faith comes from hearing the proclamation of the word of God and is to be expressed in the life together in Christ that is the Church.

51. By preaching, teaching, and life example, Christians witness to Christians and non-Christians alike. We seek and pray for the conversion of others, even as we recognize our own continuing need to be fully converted. As we strive to make Christian faith and life—our own and that of others—ever more intentional rather than

nominal, ever more committed rather than apathetic, we also recognize the different forms that authentic discipleship can take. As is evident in the two thousand year history of the church, and in our contemporary experience, there are different ways of being Christian, and some of these ways are distinctively marked by communal patterns of worship, piety, and catechesis. That we are all to be one does not mean that we are all to be identical in our way of following the one Christ. Such distinctive patterns of discipleship, it should be noted, are amply evident within the communion of the Catholic Church as well as within the many worlds of Evangelical Protestantism.

52. It is understandable that Christians who bear witness to the Gospel try to persuade others that their communities and traditions are more fully in accord with the Gospel. There is a necessary distinction between evangelizing and what is today commonly called proselytizing or "sheep stealing." We condemn the practice of recruiting people from another community for purposes of denominational or institutional aggrandizement. At the same time, our commitment to full religious freedom compels us to defend the legal freedom to proselytize even as we call upon Christians to refrain from such activity.

53. Three observations are in order in connection with proselytizing. First, as much as we might believe one community is more fully in accord with the Gospel than another, we as Evangelicals and Catholics affirm that opportunity and means for growth in Christian discipleship are available in our several communities. Second, the decision of the committed Christian with respect to his communal allegiance and participation must be assiduously respected. Third, in view of the large number of non-Christians in the world and the enormous challenge of our common evangelistic task, it is neither theologically legitimate nor a prudent use of resources for one Christian community to proselytize among active adherents of another Christian community.

54. Christian witness must always be made in a spirit of love and humility. It must not deny but must readily accord to everyone the full freedom to discern and decide what is God's will for his life. Witness that is in service to the truth is in service to such freedom. Any form of coercion—physical, psychological, legal, economic—corrupts Christian witness and is to be unqualifiedly rejected. Similarly, bearing false witness against other persons and communities, or casting unjust and uncharitable suspicions upon them, is incompatible with the Gospel. Also to be rejected is the practice of comparing the strengths and ideals of one community with the weaknesses and failures of another. In describing the teaching and practices of other Christians, we must strive to do so in a way that they would recognize as fair and accurate.

55. In considering the many corruptions of Christian witness, we, Evangelicals and Catholics, confess that we have sinned against one another and against God. We most earnestly ask the forgiveness of God and one another, and pray for the grace to amend our own lives and that of our communities.

56. Repentance and amendment of life do not dissolve remaining differences between us. In the context of evangelization and "reevangelization," we encounter a major difference in our understanding of the relationship between baptism and the new birth in Christ. For Catholics, all who are validly baptized are born again and are truly, however imperfectly, in communion with Christ. That baptismal grace is to be continually reawakened and revivified through conversion. For most Evangelicals, but not all, the experience of conversion is to be followed by baptism as a sign of the

new birth. For Catholics, all the baptized are already members of the church, however dormant their faith and life; for many Evangelicals, the new birth requires baptismal initiation into the community of the born again. These differing beliefs about the relationship between baptism, new birth, and membership in the church should be honestly presented to the Christian who has undergone conversion. But again, his decision regarding communal allegiance and participation must be assiduously respected.

57. There are, then, differences between us that cannot be resolved here. But on this we are resolved: All authentic witness must be aimed at conversion to God in Christ by the power of the Holy Spirit. Those converted—whether understood as having received the new birth for the first time or as having experienced the reawakening of the new birth originally bestowed in the sacrament of baptism—must be given full freedom and respect as they discern and decide the community in which they will live their new life in Christ. In such discernment and decision, they are ultimately responsible to God and we dare not interfere with the exercise of that responsibility. Also in our differences and disagreements, we Evangelicals and Catholics commend one another to God "who by the power at work within us is able to do far more abundantly than all that we ask or think." (Ephesians 3)

58. In this discussion of witnessing together we have touched on difficult and long standing problems. The difficulties must not be permitted to overshadow the truths on which we are, by the grace of God, in firm agreement. As we grow in mutual understanding and trust, it is our hope that our efforts to evangelize will not jeopardize but will reinforce our devotion to the common tasks to which we have pledged ourselves in this statement.

Conclusion

59. Nearly two thousand years after it began, and nearly five hundred years after the divisions of the Reformation era, the Christian mission to the world is vibrantly alive and assertive. We do not know, we cannot know, what the Lord of history has in store for the Third Millennium. It may be the springtime of world missions and great Christian expansion. It may be the way of the cross marked by persecution and apparent marginalization. In different places and times, it will likely be both. Or it may be that Our Lord will return tomorrow.

60. We do know that his promise is sure, that we are enlisted for the duration, and that we are in this together. We do know that we must affirm and hope and search and contend and witness together, for we belong not to ourselves but to him who has purchased us by the blood of the cross. We do know that this is a time of opportunity—and, if of opportunity, then of responsibility—for Evangelicals and Catholics to be Christians together in a way that helps prepare the world for the coming of him to whom belongs the kingdom, the power, and the glory forever. Amen.

Participants: Mr. Charles Colson (Prison Fellowship); Fr. Juan Diaz-Vilar, S.J. (Catholic Hispanic Ministries); Fr. Avery Dulles, S.J. (Fordham University); Bishop Francis George, OMI (Diocese of Yakima, Washington); Dr. Kent Hill (Eastern Nazarene College); Dr. Richard Land (Christian Life Commission of the Southern Baptist Convention); Dr. Larry Lewis (Home Mission Board of the Southern Baptist Convention); Dr. Jesse Miranda (Assemblies of God); Msgr. William Murphy (Chancellor of the Archdiocese of Boston); Fr. Richard John Neuhaus (Institute on Religion and Public Life); Mr. Brian O'Connell (World Evangelical Fellowship); Mr. Herbert Schlossberg (Fieldstead

Foundation); Archbishop Francis Stafford (Archdiocese of Denver); Mr. George Weigel (Ethics and Public Policy Center); Dr. John White (Geneva College and the National Association of Evangelicals).

Endorsed by: Dr. William Abraham (Perkins School of Theology); Dr. Elizabeth Achtemeier (Union Theological Seminary, Virginia); Mr. William Bentley Ball (Harrisburg, Pennsylvania); Dr. Bill Bright (Campus Crusade for Christ); Professor Robert Destro (Catholic University of America); Fr. Augustine DiNoia, O.P. (Dominican House of Studies); Fr. Joseph P. Fitzpatrick, S.J. (Fordham University); Mr. Keith Fournier (American Center for Law and Justice); Bishop William Frey (Trinity Episcopal School for Ministry); Professor Mary Ann Glendon (Harvard Law School); Dr. Os Guinness (Trinity Forum); Dr. Nathan Hatch (University of Notre Dame); Dr. James Hitchcock (St. Louis University); Professor Peter Kreeft (Boston College); Fr. Matthew Lamb (Boston College); Mr. Ralph Martin (Renewal Ministries); Dr. Richard Mouw (Fuller Theological Seminary); Dr. Mark Noll (Wheaton College); Mr. Michael Novak (American Enterprise Institute); John Cardinal O'Connor (Archdiocese of New York); Dr. Thomas Oden (Drew University); Dr. James I. Packer (Regent College, British Columbia); The Rev. Pat Robertson (Regent University); Dr. John Rodgers (Trinity Episcopal School for Ministry); Bishop Carlos A. Sevilla, S.J. (Archdiocese of San Francisco).

NOTES

Introduction: When Trouble Knocks
1. Christopher Dawson, *The Judgment of Nations*, as quoted in *Catholic World Report*, June 1994, page 34.

Chapter One: A House Divided
1. Davis Duggins, "Evangelicals and Catholics: Across the Divide," *Moody*, November 1993, page 15.
2. Duggins, pages 12, 14.
3. Duggins, pages 14-15.
4. Duggins, page 17.
5. Rob Wilkins, "Finding the Way," *Moody*, November 1993, pages 21-22.
6. Among Peter Kreeft's many books, see his *Fundamentals of the Faith: Essays in Christian Apologetics* (San Francisco: Ignatius Press, 1988); *Between Heaven and Hell* (Downers Grove, IL: InterVarsity, 1982); *Making Sense out of Suffering* (Ann Arbor, MI: Servant, 1986).

   Three very influential books by Richard John Neuhaus are *The Naked Public Square: Religion and Democracy in America* (Grand Rapids, MI: Eerdmans, 1984), which was written while he was still a Lutheran; *America Against Itself: Moral Vision and the Public Order* (Notre Dame, IN: University of Notre Dame Press, 1992); *Doing Well and Doing Good: The Challenge to the Christian Capitalist* (New York: Doubleday, 1992).

   Thomas Howard's many books include *Evangelical Is Not Enough* (Nashville, TN: Nelson, 1984), which recounts why he was led to embrace the Roman Catholic faith; *Chance or the Dance? A Critique of Modern Secularism* (San Francisco: Ignatius Press, 1969); *Hallowed Be This House* (San Francisco: Ignatius Press, 1979).
7. John 17:11,20-23, NIV.
8. Ephesians 4:11-13, NIV.
9. John 3:16-17, NIV.

10. Galatians 3:26-28, NKJV.
11. Luke 18:9-14.
12. Matthew 19:16-26. See also John Paul II's commentary on this passage in his encyclical letter *The Splendor of Truth (Veritatis Splendor)* (Boston: St. Paul Books & Media, 1994), chapter 1.
13. Romans 10:9-10.
14. Ignatius of Antioch, "Letter to the Smymeane," in *Early Christian Fathers*, ed. Cyril Richardson (Philadelphia: Westminster, 1953), volume 8, page 12.
15. Alan Schreck, *Catholic and Christian* (Ann Arbor, MI: Servant, 1984), page 59.
16. John 13:34-35; 15:12-17; 17:11,20-26.
17. "Decree on Ecumenism," in *Vatican Council II: The Conciliar and Post Conciliar Documents*, rev. ed., ed. Austin Flannery, O.P. (New York: Costello, 1992), page 455, paragraph 3.
18. "Dogmatic Constitution on the Church," in *Vatican Council II: The Conciliar and Post Conciliar Documents*, rev. ed., ed. by Austin Flannery, O.P. (New York: Costello, 1992), pages 350-413.
19. Schreck, page 50.
20. Matthew 26:26-29, Luke 22:19-20.
21. "Dogmatic Constitution on the Church," page 350, paragraph 1.
22. Augustine of Hippo, *City of God*, 19:14-17. See also Schreck, pages 29-39.
23. "Dogmatic Constitution on the Church," page 366, paragraph 14.
24. Matthew 16:18.
25. William Barclay, *New Testament Words* (London: SCM, 1964), pages 62-64.
26. Gerhard Kittel, ed., *Theological Dictionary of the New Testament* (Grand Rapids, MI: Eerdmans, 1973), volume 2, page 770.
27. "Letters to the Editor," *Christianity Today*, 25 April 1994, page 7.
28. "Letters to the Editor," page 7.
29. "Letters to the Editor," page 7.

Chapter Two: Over the Rainbow

1. Vatican II did not alter Catholic teaching but it did lay the groundwork for changes in some practices. For instance, the liturgy would no longer be required to be prayed in Latin but in the native vernacular of the faith community. Also, the priest presiding at the liturgy would now face the worshipers rather than have his back to them while leading the service. The council also called for a renewed spirit of Scripture study and theological inquiry. Changes such as these led some Catholics to worry that the Church was either abandoning or growing soft on the faith. In reality, however, the Church was doing what she has for centuries—exercising her pastoral wisdom and adapting her practices in light of theological reflection and missionary goals.
2. Accurately, "because the one who is in you is greater than the one who is in the world" (1 John 4:4, NIV).
3. In fact, Stuart is the only traveling companion I had who has not found faith in Jesus Christ. At the time of the writing of this book, he was living in the Pacific Northeast after having returned from Japan with a wonderful wife and two children. Stuart and I have rekindled our friendship, while his spiritual hunger continues. My prayer is that his sincere desire for truth leads him finally to the One who is the way, the truth, and the life.

Chapter Three: There's No Place Like Home

1. John 6:35, NIV. See the fuller context of Jesus' comments (John 6:30-66).
2. John 2:1-10.

3. Isaiah 6:8, NIV.
4. Carl F. H. Henry, "The Christian Scholar's Task," lecture given at Oxford '88, C. S. Lewis Summer Institute, Oxford University, England, 1988.

Chapter Four: Classical Revival at a Catholic College
1. Michael Scanlan, "Making and Keeping Catholic Colleges Catholic," adapted from a presentation given at Oxford '88, C. S. Lewis Summer Institute, Oxford University, England, 1988.
2. 1 Peter 2:4-5, NIV.
3. In my book *Wounds That Heal* (Ann Arbor, MI: Servant, 1992), I spend the first chapter detailing some of the many ways Father Philip Bebie impacted my life and my family's to the glory of God. Even in his final days battling cancer, he faithfully ministered to others as he looked forward to spending eternity with the greatest Love of his life.
4. James 5:16, NIV.
5. Galatians 5:22-23.
6. *Catechism of the Catholic Church* (New Hope, KY: St. Martin de Porres, 1994), pages 224-225, paragraph 848.

Chapter Five: Fighting for Law and Justice
1. Jeremiah 20:7, NIV.
2. Many of my colleagues argue that the decision was the beginning of a downturn in judicial reasoning because it utilized the courts for social change and relied on sociological statistics over constitutional principles. That it, in effect, inserted "sociological jurisprudence" into legal analysis and injured the separation-of-power principles upon which this country was founded. In that they are probably correct. But the result, the end of legally sanctioned segregation and racism, was also correct.
3. "Chicken Little," in William J. Bennett, ed., *The Book of Virtues* (New York: Simon & Schuster, 1993), pages 443-444.
4. G. Frederick Owen, *Abraham Lincoln: The Man and His Faith* (Wheaton, IL: Tyndale, 1976), page 180.
5. *ISKCON v. Lee* (1990).
6. For example, see the fairly recent article by Amy Cunningham, "Who Are the Women Who Are Pro-Life?" in *Glamour*, February 1994, pages 154-157, 208-210. This article reports on three thousand women who responded to *Glamour* magazine's request to hear from readers who were pro-life.

   See also the fine article by Frederica Mathewes-Green entitled "Why I'm Feminist and Pro-Life," *Christianity Today*, 25 October 1993, page 13. Ms. Mathewes-Green is the vice president for communications of Feminists for Life in America. Their quarterly publication, *Sisterlife*, consistently defends pro-life causes and aggressively condemns abortion, infanticide, euthanasia, and other manifestations of a culture romancing death rather than life.

   These are just a few of the many instances that could be cited of women promoting and protecting the rights of women through the pro-life movement. Pro-life is not antiwoman; pro-abortion is.
7. Habakkuk 2:3, KJV.

Chapter Six: Restoring Liberty, Life, and Family
1. Nehemiah 4:13, NIV.
2. Nehemiah 4:16-20, NIV.
3. Nehemiah 4:14, NIV.

4. Regarding the many influences at work in the establishing of American government and culture, see John Courtney Murray, *We Hold These Truths: Catholic Reflections on the American Proposition* (New York: Sheed and Ward, 1960); Donald J. D'Elia and Stephen M. Krason, eds., *We Hold These Truths and More: Further Catholic Reflections on the American Proposition* (Steubenville, OH: Franciscan University Press, 1993); Mark A. Noll, *A History of Christianity in the United States and Canada* (Grand Rapids, MI: Eerdmans, 1992); Herbert M. Morais, *Deism in Eighteenth Century America* (New York: Russell and Russell, 1960).

5. 1 Peter 2:4, NIV.

6. 2 Corinthians 10:5, NIV.

7. Acts 22:1; 25:16; 1 Corinthians 9:3; 2 Corinthians 7:11; Philippians 1:7,16; 2 Timothy 4:16; 1 Peter 3:15.

8. Jude 3, NIV.

9. *Liturgy of the Hours* (New York: Catholic Book, 1976), volume 3, page 1447.

10. Justin Martyr, *First Apology* 2.4, as quoted by Edwin M. Yamauchi, "Justin Martyr: Defender of the Faith," in *Great Leaders of the Christian Church*, ed. John D. Woodbridge (Chicago: Moody, 1988), page 42.

11. James V. Schall, "On a New Kind of Courage," *Crisis*, May 1994, page 62.

12. Cardinal James Hickey, "Population Stabilization: Cardinals' Letter Blasts Clinton," *The American Political Network, Abortion Report*, 1 June 1994.

13. *Catechism of the Catholic Church* (New Hope, KY: St. Martin de Porres, 1994), page 241, paragraph 912.

14. Revelation 20–22.

15. Hebrews 13:12-14, NIV.

16. Appendix, "Evangelicals and Catholics Together: The Christian Mission in the Third Millennium," paragraph 30.

17. Nathan Hatch and Michael Hamilton, "Can Evangelicalism Survive Its Success?" *Christianity Today*, 5 October 1992, page 30.

18. Romans 12:1-2, NASB.

19. Matthew 11:19, NIV.

20. Saint Bonaventure, *Major and Minor Life of St. Francis*, in *St. Francis of Assisi, Writings and Early Biographies*, Marion A. Habig, ed. (Quincy, IL: Franciscan Press, 1991), 737.

21. R. Judson Carlberg, "Culture of Disrespect," *Christianity Today*, 20 June 1994, page 18.

Chapter Seven: Barbarians at the Door

1. Isaiah 5:20-21, NIV.

2. William J. Bennett, *The Index of Leading Cultural Indicators* (New York: Simon & Schuster, 1994).

3. William J. Bennett, "Getting Used to Decadence: The Spirit of Democracy in Modern America," a lecture delivered on December 7, 1993, at a special meeting of the Heritage Foundation's President's Club, the Heritage Lectures series, number 477, page 3.

4. Thomas A. Glessner, *Achieving an Abortion-Free America by 2001* (Portland, OR: Multnomah, 1990), page 23.

5. B. D. Cohen, as quoted by Nat Hentoff in the *Village Voice*, 19 December 1983.

6. Derek Humphrey and Ann Wickett, *The Right to Die* (Eugene, OR: Hemlock Society, 1990), page xi.

7. "Hospice Offers 'Dignified Death,'" *The Paper*, April 1993, page 5.

8. George M. Burnell, *Final Choices: To Live or to Die in an Age of Medical*

Technology (New York: Plenum Press, 1993), page 33.

9. Bennett, "Getting Used to Decadence," page 2.
10. Bennett, "Getting Used to Decadence," page 6.
11. Dorothy Sayers, *The Whimsical Christian* (New York: Macmillan, 1978), pages 175-176.
12. Neil Postman, *Amusing Ourselves to Death: Public Discourse in the Age of Show Business* (New York: Viking Penguin, 1985), page 4.
13. Postman, pages vii-viii.
14. James 1:27, 3:5-6, NIV.
15. C. S. Lewis, *Studies in Words*, 2nd ed. (Cambridge, England: Cambridge University Press, 1967), page 7.
16. William Dannemeyer, *Shadow in the Land: Homosexuality in America* (San Francisco: Ignatius Press, 1989), pages 10-11.
17. Dannemeyer, page 134.
18. Lewis, page 7.
19. "News Notes," *Wanderer*, 10 March 1994, page 6.
20. John 8:7, NIV.
21. Bryce J. Christensen, *Utopia Against the Family: The Problems and Politics of the American Family* (San Francisco: Ignatius Press, 1990), page 12.
22. Christensen, page 22.
23. See my article, "The ACLU's Greatest Antagonist," *Law & Justice*, October 1993, page 1.
24. John 18:36-37.
25. John 18:38, NKJV
26. John 14:6, NRSV.
27. John Paul II, *The Splendor of Truth (Veritatis Splendor)* (Boston: St. Paul Books & Media, 1994), page 9.

Chapter Eight: Sharing Foxholes—Again
1. Robert Leckie, *Delivered from Evil* (New York: HarperCollins, 1987), page 51.
2. Leckie, page 30.
3. Leckie, page 62.
4. Ephesians 2:19-22, Philippians 3:20, 1 Peter 2:9-10. See also Acts 4:13-31.
5. 1 Corinthians 12, Ephesians 4:11-16.
6. Colossians 2:8, NKJV.
7. Appendix, "Evangelicals and Catholics Together," paragraphs 52-54.
8. Hebrews 12:1, NKJV.
9. Hebrews 11:6, NKJV.
10. I relate my experience with toxic religion in my book *Wounds That Heal* (Ann Arbor, MI: Servant, 1992). Two other fine resources on this issue are Stephen Arterburn and Jack Felton, *Toxic Faith: Understanding and Overcoming Religious Addiction* (Nashville, TN: Nelson, 1991), and Ronald M. Enroth, *Churches That Abuse* (Grand Rapids, MI: Zondervan, 1992).
11. An interesting appraisal of the events and errors that led to World War II is provided in John Snell, ed., *The Outbreak of the Second World War: Design or Blunder?* (Boston: D. C. Heath and Co., 1962).
12. Luke 16:8, NIV.
13. Leckie, page 13.
14. Leckie, page 13.
15. See my book *In Defense of Life*. Another very helpful resource is Andrew Kimbrell's *The Human Body Shop: The Engineering and Marketing of Life* (New York: HarperCollins, 1993).

16. See my booklet *Religious Cleansing in the American Republic* (Washington, DC: Liberty, Life and Family, 1993).
17. Stephen L. Carter, *The Culture of Disbelief: How American Law and Politics Trivialize Religious Devotion* (New York: HarperCollins, 1993), pages 21-22.

Chapter Nine: When Unity Thrived
1. Matthew 26–28, Luke 22–24, John 18–21.
2. Acts 1:14, NKJV, italics added.
3. Acts 1:15-26.
4. Acts 1:8, NKJV.
5. Acts 2:1-4, NKJV, italics added.
6. Acts 2:42,44-47, NKJV, italics added.
7. Elvin Hatch, "Culture," in *The Social Science Encyclopedia*, rev. ed., ed. Adam Kuper and Jessica Kuper (New York: Routledge, 1989), page 178.
8. 1 Peter 2:9-10, NAB.
9. D. Edmond Hiebert, *1 Peter* (Chicago: Moody, 1992), page 142.
10. Galatians 3:28, NRSV.
11. Ephesians 4:4-6, NKJV.
12. 1 Peter 2:4-7. See also Matthew 21:42.
13. Acts 1:21-22.
14. Luke 9:1-2, NAB.
15. Matthew 28:18-20, Mark 16:15-18, Luke 24:44-49, John 20:21-23, Acts 1:8.
16. Acts 2:42, NAB. See also 4:33, 5:12-13.
17. Acts 2:42-47, 4:32-37, 5:12-16.
18. Acts 5:1-11, 15:1-35; 1 Corinthians 5:1-13; 2 Corinthians 2:3-11; Galatians 1:6-9; Colossians 2:16-23; 1 Peter 1:13–2:3, 3:13-17; Jude.
19. Alan Schreck, *Catholic and Christian* (Ann Arbor, MI: Servant, 1984), page 75.
20. Acts 11:29-30; 14:23; 20:17,27-28,35; Ephesians 4:1-16; Philippians 1:1; 1 Thessalonians 5:12-14; 1 Timothy 3:1-7; 5:17; Titus 1:5–2:1; Hebrews 13:7,17; James 5:14-15; 1 Peter 5:1-5. See also John 21:15-17, 1 Peter 2:25.
21. Acts 6:1-7, Philippians 1:1, 1 Timothy 3:8-13.
22. Schreck, *Catholic and Christian*, pages 75, 76.
23. 1 Corinthians 11:23, 15:3, NAB.
24. Gary R. Habermas, *The Verdict of History: Conclusive Evidence for the Life of Jesus* (Nashville, TN: Nelson, 1988), pages 127-128. For more information on these early creeds, see Habermas and J. P. Moreland, *Immortality: The Other Side of Death* (Nashville, TN: Nelson, 1992), chapter 4. In this latter book, Habermas notes that "critical research has shown that some of the early passages in Acts (and Peter's speeches, in particular) reflect early tradition from the Jerusalem community. The death and resurrection of Jesus are frequently recorded in these early teachings (Acts 2:22-23, 31; 3:15, 4:10, 5:30, 10:39, 13:28-29)" (page 244, note 56).
25. 1 Corinthians 3:15, NAB.
26. 1 Corinthians 1:10, NAB.
27. 1 Corinthians 13:4-8, NAB.
28. See 2 Corinthians 7. Aside from 1 and 2 Corinthians, Paul may have written as many as two other letters to the Corinthian assembly in an attempt to address their problems. One of these letters may be alluded to in 2 Corinthians 7:4 and 8, and the other in 1 Corinthians 5:9-10. For more on this matter, see Donald Guthrie, *New Testament Introduction*, rev. ed. (Downers Grove, IL: InterVarsity, 1970), pages 424-439.
29. Acts 21:20, NKJV.

30. Acts 15:9, NAB.
31. Acts 15:10-11, NAB.
32. Acts 15:12, NAB.
33. Acts 15:29, NAB.
34. Paul L. Maier, *In the Fullness of Time: A Historian Looks at Christmas, Easter, and the Early Church* (San Francisco: Harper, 1991), page 269.
35. John 16:13, Ephesians 4:11-16.
36. 1 Corinthians 11:2; 14:37-38; Colossians 4:16; 1 Thessalonians 5:27; 2 Thessalonians 2:15; 3:14; 2 Peter 3:15-16; Revelation 1:3; 2:1,8,12,18; 3:1,7,14; 22:16.
37. Clement of Rome, 1 Clement 46:1, as quoted by David Ewert, *From Ancient Tablets to Modern Translations: A General Introduction to the Bible* (Grand Rapids, MI: Zondervan, 1983), page 119.
38. Ralph P. Martin, *Worship in the Early Church* (Grand Rapids, MI: Eerdmans, 1974), page 72.
39. See Martin, chapter 6; Ewert, chapter 9; Oscar Cullman, *Early Christian Worship* (Philadelphia: Westminster, 1953), pages 20-25.
40. 2 Timothy 3:16-17, NRSV.
41. Martin, page 70.
42. Pliny, *Epistles* 10.96, as quoted by F. F. Bruce, *Jesus and Christian Origins Outside the New Testament* (Grand Rapids, MI: Eerdmans, 1974), page 26.
43. See Henry Chadwick, *The Early Church*, vol. 1 of *The Pelican History of the Church*, gen. ed. Owen Chadwick (New York: Penguin Books, 1967); Derek Tidball, *The Social Context of the New Testament: A Sociological Analysis* (Grand Rapids, MI: Zondervan, 1984); Allen Verhey, *The Great Reversal: Ethics and the New Testament* (Grand Rapids, MI: Eerdmans, 1984); George Wolfgang Forell, *History of Christian Ethics: From the New Testament to Augustine*, vol. 1 (Minneapolis, MN: Augsburg, 1979); Richard N. Longenecker, *New Testament Social Ethics for Today* (Grand Rapids, MI: Eerdmans, 1984); Hugo Rahner, *Church and State in Early Christianity* (San Francisco: Ignatius Press, 1992); John Paul II, "The Christian Family in the Modern World," in *(Familiaris Consortio), Vatican Council II: More Post Conciliar Documents*, ed. Austin Flannery, O.P. (Northport, NY: Costello, 1982), pages 815-898.
44. Ruth A. Tucker, *From Jerusalem to Irian Jaya* (Grand Rapids, MI: Zondervan, 1983), page 27.
45. Chadwick, page 56.
46. Matthew 28:18-20, NAB.
47. Acts 1:8, NAB. For more on the church's pursuit to carry out the Great Commission, see William Steuart McBirnie, *The Search for the Twelve Apostles* (Wheaton, IL: Tyndale, 1973); E. M. Blaiklock, *The Archaeology of the New Testament*, rev. ed. (Nashville, TN: Nelson, 1984), chapters 8-14; Tucker, *From Jerusalem to Irian Jaya*; Alison Jones, *Saints* (New York: W & R Chambers, 1992); John D. Woodbridge, ed., *Great Leaders of the Christian Church* (Chicago: Moody, 1988).
48. Matthew 5:13-14, NKJV.
49. Matthew 5:16, NKJV.
50. Genesis 1:26-28, 4:1, 5:3, 9:6; Psalm 8:4-8; Matthew 7:7-12; Acts 17:28; 1 Corinthians 11:7; James 3:9. For a very helpful discussion on human beings imaging God and what that means, see Henri Blocher, *In the Beginning: The Opening Chapters of Genesis* (Downers Grove, IL: InterVarsity, 1984), chapter 4; and Brian J. Walsh and J. Richard Middleton, *The Transforming Vision: Shaping a Christian World View* (Downers Grove, IL: InterVarsity, 1984), chapters 3–5.

51. Ephesians 6:12, NKJV.
52. Ephesians 6:18-20; see also Luke 18:1-8; John 11:38-44, 14:12-14; Acts 9:40-42, 12:1-18; Romans 12:12; 1 Peter 4:7; Revelation 8:3-5.
53. Luke 23:34.
54. Acts 7:60.
55. Romans 8:18.
56. Revelation 20:12-15, 21:6-8.
57. Matthew 5:44-46, NKJV.

Chapter Ten: Unity in the Face of Persecution

1. Matthew 28:11-15; Acts 2:43, 3:1-10.
2. John 11:50 in Eugene H. Peterson, *The Message: The New Testament in Contemporary English* (Colorado Springs, CO: NavPress, 1993), pages 213-214.
3. Matthew 21:12-13, Mark 11:15-18.
4. Maier, page 120.
5. Matthew 23:14-17,24,27,33-35, NKJV.
6. See John 6:14-15, Matthew 21:9, Luke 19:38-40. For a helpful overview of the many perceptions of the Messiah prevalent in ancient Israel, see F. F. Bruce's *New Testament History* (Garden City, NY: Anchor Books, 1972), chapter 10.
7. Deuteronomy 21:23, NAB.
8. See Acts 3:1–4:31, 7:1-56, 8:26-38.
9. Acts 5:41, NKJV.
10. F. F. Bruce, *The New Testament Documents: Are They Reliable?* rev. ed. (Grand Rapids, MI: Eerdmans, 1960), page 118.
11. Martin Hengel, *Crucifixion in the Ancient World and the Folly of the Cross* (Philadelphia: Fortress, 1977), page 68.
12. Michael P. Green, "The Meaning of Cross-Bearing," *Bibliotheca Sacra*, April-May 1983, page 127.
13. John 18:33-38, 19:9-22; Acts 17:6-7; 1 Corinthians 15:22-28; Revelation 19:16.
14. Luke 23:1-38, John 18:29–19:22.
15. Luke 24, Acts 1:1-11, 1 Corinthians 15:3-8.
16. Of course, not all ancient Greeks or Romans believed in an afterlife, and among those who did, some conceived of it in very vague, unattractive terms. As Ramsay MacMullen points out, "There are also explicit denials of any afterlife in various authors, as well as indications, overwhelmingly dominant in grave inscriptions and grave practices, that life was either thought to end in death or to linger only as a miserable little spark or spirit in the tomb" (Ramsey MacMullen, *Christianizing the Roman Empire [AD 100–400]* [New Haven, CT: Yale University Press, 1984], page 11). And yet, with all their differences toward life after death, the Greeks and Romans unanimously held to one belief: the human body did not rise from the dead. The Greek poet Aeschylus (525–456 BC) immortalized this understanding in the mouth of the god Apollo: "When the dust has soaked up a man's blood, once he is dead, there is no resurrection" (*Eumenides* 647-648).
17. Acts 17:16-32, NKJV.
18. Chadwick, page 25.
19. See Acts 16:16-24, 19:23-41.
20. Robert L. Wilken, *The Christians as the Romans Saw Them* (New Haven, CT: Yale University Press, 1984), page 59.
21. *Tacitus* 15.44, as quoted by Habermas, *The Verdict of History*, pages 87-88.
22. Howard F. Vos, *An Introduction to Church History*, rev. ed. (Chicago: Moody, 1984), page 29.

23. Hebrews 11.
24. Bruce, *New Testament History*, pages 423-424.
25. Bruce, *New Testament History*, page 424.
26. Luke 23:47, NKJV.
27. Justin Martyr, *2 Apology* 12, as quoted by Edwin M. Yamauchi, "Justin Martyr: Defender of the Faith," in *Great Leaders of the Christian Church*, ed. John D. Woodbridge (Chicago: Moody, 1988), page 40.
28. Leslie D. Weatherhead, *It Happened in Palestine* (London: Hodder and Stoughton, 1936), pages 267-269.
29. Stephen Neill, *A History of Christian Missions* (New York: Penguin, 1964), page 43.
30. Alan Schreck, *The Compact History of the Catholic Church* (Ann Arbor, MI: Servant, 1987), page 17.
31. Luke 1:67-79; 2:10-14,29-32; 18:31-33; 23:4,14,20,22-25; 24:7,25-27,44-48.
32. F. F. Bruce, *The Defense of the Gospel in the New Testament*, rev. ed. (Grand Rapids, MI: Eerdmans, 1977), page 57. See also Acts 13:7,12; 16:37-40; 18:12-17; 19:31,35-41; 24:1–26:32.
33. Acts 28:16,30-31.
34. Bruce, *Defense of the Gospel*, page 59.
35. Acts 9:1-22.
36. Acts 13; 17:1-4,10-12,16-34; 24:10-21.
37. Acts 21:15-26.
38. Acts 28:31, NKJV.
39. Justin Martyr, "The First Apology of Justin," in *Classical Readings in Christian Apologetics, AD 100–1800*, ed. L. Russ Bush (Grand Rapids, MI: Zondervan, 1983), page 7.
40. Justin Martyr, pages 8-9.
41. Tertullian, *Apology* 39, as quoted by Wilken, page 46.
42. Athenagoras, "A Plea for the Christians," in Bush, page 44.
43. Will Durant, *Caesar and Christ: A History of Roman Civilization and of Christianity from Their Beginnings to AD 325* (New York: Simon and Schuster, 1944), page 652.
44. Saint Augustine, *The City of God*, trans. Marcus Dods (New York: Random House, 1950), book 1, section 3.
45. Augustine, book 1, section 2.
46. Augustine, book 1, section 8.
47. Augustine, book 1, section 1.

Chapter Eleven: The Breakdown of the Family

1. Exodus 20:5, 34:7.
2. Matthew 7:9-11.
3. Alan Schreck, *The Compact History of the Catholic Church* (Ann Arbor, MI: Servant, 1987), page 43.
4. Schreck, page 43.
5. See Frank S. Mead, *Handbook of Denominations in the United States*, 9th ed., rev. Samuel S. Hill (Nashville, TN: Abingdon, 1990). At the writing of this chapter, *Christianity Today* published a report on yet another relatively new Protestant denomination called the Charismatic Episcopal Church, which since its inception two years ago has grown to more than one hundred churches. (Stephen M. Miller, "100 Churches Have Joined New Denomination," *Christianity Today*, 16 May 1994, page 51.)
6. Timothy George, "Catholics and Evangelicals in the Trenches," *Christianity*

Today, 16 May 1994, page 16.
7. Paul Weyrich, *Weyrich Insider*, 6 December 1989.
8. Romans 12:15, NIV.
9. John 17:20-23, NIV.
10. Luke 11:17, NIV.
11. Appendix, "Evangelicals and Catholics Together," paragraph 3.
12. Ephesians 4:4-6, NIV.
13. Malachi 2:10-16; 1 Corinthians 1:10-15, 3:5-23.
14. Luke 9:50, NIV.

Chapter Twelve: Sticks and Stones
1. Proverbs 27:6,17,5, NKJV.
2. "Rome," Associated Press, 13 June 1994.
3. Genesis 3.
4. Romans 5:12, NIV. Consider the entire context of Paul's comments in Romans 5 and 6, which makes it clear that Paul has separation from God in mind when he speaks of death, not just physical death. Of course, in Scripture even physical death is marked by separation, namely the separation of the soul from the body. Some other texts that speak of death as separation are Matthew 27:50, John 5:24-25, 2 Corinthians 2:15-16, Revelation 20:12-15.
5. Luke 1:42, NIV.
6. See *Catechism of the Catholic Church* (New Hope, KY: St. Martin de Porres, 1994), pages 123-124, paragraphs 490-493. For fuller treatments, see Alan Schreck's *Basics of the Faith: A Catholic Catechism* (Ann Arbor, MI: Servant, 1987), chapter 10; and his *Catholic and Christian* (Ann Arbor, MI: Servant, 1984), chapter 9.
7. Norman Geisler, *The Roots of Evil* (Grand Rapids, MI: Zondervan, 1978), pages 46-47.
8. Matthew 7:9-11, NIV.
9. Ephesians 2:8-9, NAB.
10. *Catechism*, page 482, paragraph 1989.
11. *Catechism*, page 482, paragraph 1991.
12. *Catechism*, page 484, paragraph 2001.
13. In *The Bondage of the Will*, Luther strenuously argues that "the safest and most Christian thing to do" would be to drop the term *free will* altogether in relationship to man. And though Luther appears to make allowances for man to have some independent volitional capacities in regard to matters of daily living such as sleeping, drinking, eating, and sinning, he stresses throughout his work "that the whole of Scripture fights against it [i.e., human free will]." He vigorously argues that "all we do, however it may appear to us to be done mutably and contingently [in other words, freely], is in reality done necessarily and immutably in respect of God's will." "It is a settled truth," writes Luther, "that we do everything of necessity, and nothing by 'free-will'; for the power of 'free-will' is nil, and it does no good, nor can do, without grace." Man's "will cannot change itself, nor give itself another bent. . . . Man's will is like a beast standing between two riders. If God rides, it wills and goes where God wills. . . . If Satan rides, it wills and goes where Satan wills. Nor may it choose to which rider it will run, or which it will seek; but the riders themselves fight to decide who shall have and hold it." Martin Luther, *The Bondage of the Will*, trans. J. I. Packer and O. R. Johnston (Westwood, NJ: Revell, 1957), pages 107, 169, 80-81, 105, 103-104. See also Linwood Urban, "Was Luther a Thoroughgoing Determinist?" *Journal of Theological Studies* 22 (April 1971), pages 113-139. For a different interpretation of Luther, see Robert

D. Shofner, "Luther on 'The Bondage of the Will': An Analytical-Critical Essay," *Scottish Journal of Theology* 26:1, February 1973, pages 24-39.

14. Matthew 23:37; John 1:4-12, 3:16-21; Romans 5:8-10.
15. *Catechism*, page 485, paragraph 2002.
16. *Catechism*, page 484, paragraph 1999.
17. 2 Corinthians 5:17, NAB.
18. "The practice of infant Baptism is an immemorial tradition of the Church. There is explicit testimony to this practice from the second century on, and it is quite possible that, from the beginning of the apostolic preaching, when whole 'households' received baptism, infants may also have been baptized" (*Catechism*, page 319, paragraph 1252).
19. Mark 10:14, NAB.
20. Luke 5:17-20, NAB.
21. 1 Corinthians 13:13, NIV.
22. 1 John 4:16.
23. "Dogmatic Constitution on the Church," *Vatican II: The Conciliar and Post Conciliar Documents*, rev. ed., ed. by Austin Flannery, O.P. (Northport, NY: Costello, 1992), page 400, paragraph 42.
24. 1 John 2:9-10, NIV.
25. James 2:18, NAB.
26. Galatians 5:6, NKJV.
27. Acts 17:24-28, Colossians 1:12-20.
28. John 15:5, NKJV.
29. *Catechism*, page 486, paragraph 2007.
30. James 1:16-18.
31. *Catechism*, pages 486-487, paragraphs 2008, 2010, 2011.
32. Romans 8:18-21, Revelation 20–22.
33. Philippians 2:12, NAB, NIV.
34. Hebrews 6:6, NAB.
35. C. S. Lewis, *The Great Divorce* (New York: Macmillan, 1946), page 72.
36. 2 Timothy 2:11-12, NKJV.
37. Schreck, *Catholic and Christian*, page 39.
38. 1 Corinthians 9:24-27, NAB.
39. Dave Hunt, *Global Peace and the Rise of Antichrist* (Eugene, OR: Harvest House, 1990), page 141.
40. Hunt, page 137.
41. Hunt, page 136.
42. Hunt, page 129.
43. Hunt, page 111.
44. Hunt, page 108.
45. "Anti," in Walter Bauer, *A Greek-English Lexicon of the New Testament and Other Early Christian Literature*, 2d ed., ed. William F. Arndt and F. Wilbur Gingrich (Chicago: University of Chicago Press, 1979), pages 73-74.
46. "Antichristos," Bauer, page 76. See also "Antichrist" in Colin Brown, ed., *The New International Dictionary of New Testament Theology*, 3 vols. (Grand Rapids, MI: Zondervan, 1975), volume 1, pages 124-126.
47. Ephesians 5:31.
48. An excellent analysis of the faulty methods critics such as Dave Hunt use in their attacks on fellow Christians is provided by Bob and Gretchen Passantino in their book *Witch Hunt* (Nashville, TN: Nelson, 1990).
49. Norman L. Geisler, "A New Look at the Relevance of Thomism for Evangelical Apologetics," *Christian Scholar's Review* 4:3 (1975), pages 192-193, 200. See

also his book *Thomas Aquinas: An Evangelical Appraisal* (Grand Rapids, MI: Baker, 1991).

50. John Franklin Johnson, "Thomistic Hermeneutics: An Evangelical Appraisal and Appreciation," *Bulletin of the Evangelical Philosophical Society* 3 (1980), page 20.
51. R. C. Sproul, "Thomas Aquinas," in *Chosen Vessels: Portraits of Ten Outstanding Christian Men* (Ann Arbor, MI: Servant, 1985), pages 82, 88.
52. James 3:9-10, NIV.
53. 1 John 2:9-11, NIV.

Chapter Thirteen: Humpty Dumpty Solutions

1. 1 Corinthians 13:7-8, NKJV.
2. 1 John 4:8, NKJV.
3. Romans 5:8, NKJV.
4. John 15:13, NKJV.
5. Ephesians 6:12,18.
6. Matthew 12:27-32.
7. 1 Corinthians 12:25, NKJV. Read all of 1 Corinthians 12 and compare it with 1:10-16.
8. Mark 9:39-40, NKJV.
9. Dottie Chase, "United Methodist Women Get Taste of Sophia Worship," *Good News*, January/February 1994, page 36.
10. Susan Cyre, "Mainline Denial: How Our Churches Are Responding to 'Re-Imagining,'" *Good News*, March/April 1994, page 12.
11. Faye Short, "Shocking Conference Challenges Orthodoxy," *Good News*, January/February 1994, page 35.
12. Chase, page 36.
13. Chase, page 37.
14. Cyre, pages 12-13.
15. Cyre, page 13.
16. Chase, page 37.
17. Cyre, page 14.
18. Chase, page 38.
19. Faye Short and James V. Heidinger II, "The Good News Response," *Good News*, March/April 1994, pages 24, 25.
20. Cyre, page 12.
21. William R. Cannon, "The Cult of Sophia," *Good News*, March/April 1994, pages 16-17.
22. Charles Colson, "Don't Wait for the Next Reagan Era," *Christianity Today*, 8 February 1993, page 112.
23. Colson, page 112.
24. Exodus 5–14.

Chapter Fourteen: Our Family Heritage

1. 1 Corinthians 13:9,12, NKJV.
2. Appendix, "Evangelicals and Catholics Together," paragraph 20.
3. Romans 15:12, Revelation 22:16.
4. Jude 3, NIV.
5. Hebrews 13:8, NIV.
6. 1 Corinthians 1:13, NIV.
7. Ephesians 2:14-18, NIV.
8. David F. Wright, "John Chrysostom: Master Preacher," in *Great Leaders of the Christian Church*, ed. John D. Woodbridge (Chicago: Moody, 1988), page 84.

9. A. Skevington Wood, "John and Charles Wesley and Methodism," in *Great Leaders of the Christian Church*, page 288.
10. Jay P. Dolan, *Catholic Revivalism: The American Experience; 1830–1900* (Notre Dame, IN: University of Notre Dame Press, 1978), pages 69-70.
11. Ellen H. Walworth, *Life Sketches of Father Walworth*, 2nd ed. (Albany, NY: J. B. Lyon Co., 1907), page 129.
12. Matthew 25:34-36, NIV.
13. Luke 10:30-37, NIV.

Chapter Fifteen: A Common Agenda
1. Attributed to Alexis de Tocqueville by Dwight D. Eisenhower in his Boston, Mass., campaign address of 3 November 1952. Sourced in Sherwood Eddy, *The Kingdom of God and the American Dream* (New York: Harper Brothers, 1941), page 6.
2. Eddy, page 6.
3. Richard John Neuhaus, "A Continuing Survey of Religion and Public Life," *First Things*, June-July 1994, page 70.
4. Rabbi Daniel Lapin, "Judaism Today: Men, Marriage and the Military," *Crisis*, June 1994, pages 13, 14.
5. Eusebius of Caesarea, *Preparation of the Gospel, in the Faith of the Early Fathers*, trans. W. A. Jurgens (Collegeville, MN: Liturgical Press, 1970), volume 1, page 296.
6. Appendix, "Evangelicals and Catholics Together," paragraph 27.
7. Appendix, paragraph 29.
8. Appendix, paragraph 28.
9. Appendix, paragraph 26.
10. Appendix, paragraphs 30-31.
11. Appendix, paragraphs 32-33.
12. See my booklet *Religious Cleansing in the American Republic* (Washington, DC: Liberty, Life and Family, 1993).
13. Appendix, paragraphs 34-35.
14. George Washington, from his proclamation establishing a national day of thanksgiving, given on 3 October 1789, as cited in James D. Richardson, *A Compilation of the Messages and Papers of the Presidents, 1789–1897* (published by authority of Congress, 1899), 1:64.
15. Tocqueville, as cited in Eddy, page 6.
16. Richard John Neuhaus, "The Coming Age of Religion," *First Things*, June/July 1994, page 70.
17. Appendix, paragraphs 36-38.
18. "Federal Judge Strikes Suicide Ban," *St. Petersburg Times*, 5 May 1994, section A, page 9.
19. Andrew Kimbrell, in his book *The Human Body Shop: The Engineering and Marketing of Life* (New York: HarperCollins, 1993), amply illustrates this frightening development of the culture of death.
20. Exodus 20:13, NIV.
21. Benjamin Rush, "Of the Mode of Education Proper in a Republic," in *Essays, Literary, Moral and Philosophical* (Philadelphia: n.p., 1798), as reprinted in *The Annals of America* (Chicago: Encyclopedia Britannica, n.d.), volume 4, page 29.
22. *Annals of America*, page 28.
23. Appendix, paragraphs 39-40.
24. William J. Bennett, *The De-Valuing of America: The Fight for Our Culture and Our Children* (New York: Simon and Schuster, 1992), page 51.

25. Sam Keen, *Faces of the Enemy: Reflections of the Hostile Imagination* (San Francisco: Harper & Row, 1986), page 61.
26. Appendix, paragraph 41.
27. Richard John Neuhaus, *America Against Itself: Moral Vision and the Public Order* (Notre Dame, IN: University of Notre Dame Press, 1992), page xi.
28. Steve Allen, back cover endorsement for Michael Medved, *Hollywood vs. America* (New York: HarperCollins, 1992).
29. Appendix, paragraph 42.
30. Donald J. D'Elia, "We Hold These Truths and More: Further Catholic Reflections on the American Proposition," in *We Hold These Truths and More: Further Catholic Reflections on the American Proposition*, ed. Donald J. D'Elia and Stephen M. Krason (Steubenville, OH: Franciscan University Press, 1993), page 65.
31. Appendix, paragraphs 43-44.
32. Bennett, page 172.
33. Bennett, page 211.
34. *Catechism of the Catholic Church* (New Hope, KY: St. Martin de Porres, 1994), pages 582-589, paragraphs 2422-2449.
35. Appendix, paragraphs 45-46.

Chapter Sixteen: Alliance Building: The Road Home
1. "Southern Baptists," Associated Press, 16 June 1994.
2. "Southern Baptists."
3. "Southern Baptists."
4. Edmund Burke, *Edmund Burke: Selected Writings and Speeches*, ed. Peter J. Stanlis (Garden City, NY: Doubleday, 1963), page 270.
5. Richard John Neuhaus, from a talk he gave at Franciscan University of Steubenville in the spring of 1989. Adapted from his book *The Catholic Moment* (San Francisco: Harper & Row, 1987).
6. "Neuhaus Leaves Lutheran Church for Catholicism," *Christianity Today*, 6 October 1990, page 60.
7. 1 Corinthians 9:22, NIV.
8. *Catechism of the Catholic Church* (New Hope, KY: St. Martin de Porres, 1994), page 217, paragraph 820.
9. *Catechism*, page 217, paragraph 820.
10. Philippians 2:5-8, NIV.
11. Psalm 128:6, NIV.
12. "Roman Catholics No Longer Outlaws," *Christianity Today*, 5 February 1990, page 34.
13. "Decree on Ecumenism," in *Vatican Council II: The Conciliar and Post Conciliar Documents*, rev. ed., ed. by Austin Flannery, O.P. (Northport, NY: Costello, 1992), page 459, paragraph 5.
14. 1 Corinthians 9:19-23, Acts 15.
15. Ephesians 4.
16. "Decree on Ecumenism," pages 457-458, paragraph 4.
17. T. S. Eliot, *Christianity and Culture* (New York: Harcourt Brace, 1949), page 18.
18. Charles Colson, *Against the Night* (Ann Arbor, MI: Servant, 1989), pages 104-105.
19. 1 Corinthians 6:9-10, NIV.
20. Revelation 3:15-16, NAB.
21. Philippians 4:13.
22. Hans Urs Von Balthazaar, *Convergences: To the Source of Christian Mystery* (San

Francisco: Ignatius Press, 1983), pages 14-15.
23. Matthew 1–2.
24. Isaiah 2:4, NKJV.
25. Luke 10:2, NKJV.

Chapter Seventeen: Family Alliances at Work
1. Gerry Hughes, *Leader's School: Statements from Various Cursillo Sources* (Dallas, TX: National Ultreya, n.d.).
2. Hughes.
3. Dave Hunt, "The Gospel Betrayed," *Berean Call*, May 1994, page 2.
4. Michael Scanlan, *Portion of My Spirit* (St. Paul, MN: Carillon Books, 1979), page 1.
5. Ephesians 5:22-23.
6. *Our Family Research Council* (Washington, DC: The Family Research Council, 1993).
7. *Our Family Research Council.*
8. From the underground newsletter, *The Babylonian Groundhog* (Spring 1991), by Bryan J. Brown, a leader with Northeast Indiana Rescue.
9. "The Pulpit and the Power," *Washington Post*, 18 October 1985, D-1.
10. John Stott, "The Lausanne Covenant: An Exposition and Commentary," *Lausanne Occasional Paper*, no. 3, The Lausanne Committee for World Commission (Minneapolis, MN: World Wide Publications, 1975).
11. Stott.
12. Vinson Synan and Ralph Rath, *Launching the Decade of Evangelization* (South Bend, IN: North American Renewal Service Committee, 1990), pages 105-144.

Chapter Eighteen: Restoration Begins at Home
1. Dave Hunt, "The Gospel Betrayed," *Berean Call*, May 1994, pages 1, 2.
2. Appendix, "Evangelicals and Catholics Together," paragraphs 18-19.
3. John Wesley, *Works*, vol. 10, pages 80-86, as cited in Peter Toon, *Protestants and Catholics* (Ann Arbor, MI: Servant, 1984), appendix 4, italics added.
4. Sandra Maler, "Anglican Leaders Endorse Major Anglican-Catholic Agreement," Reuter News Service, 2 August 1988, pages 7-8.
5. Augsburg Publishing House (Minneapolis, MN) has published a fascinating and informative series of books on the fruit of the Catholic-Lutheran interchange entitled *Lutherans and Catholics in Dialogue.* Another helpful resource from Augsburg is *Promoting Unity: Themes in Lutheran-Catholic Dialogue*, ed. H. George Anderson and James R. Crumley, Jr. (1989).
6. "Vatican: Pope and Lutherans Hold Historic Prayer Service at Vatican," Reuter News Service, 5 October 1991, page 2.
7. Revelation 22:21, NIV.

Appendix: "Evangelicals and Catholics Together: The Christian Mission in the Third Millennium"
1. Except for the paragraph numbering and some slight style alterations, this reprint of the accord is as it's cited in *First Things*, May 1994, pages 15-22.

AUTHORS

KEITH A. FOURNIER serves as the president of Liberty, Life and Family, and as the executive director of the American Center for Law and Justice. Keith has degrees in philosophy, theology, and law. He is a practicing attorney involved in defending pro-liberty, pro-life, and pro-family causes. He has hosted and cohosted several national radio and television programs, and he speaks throughout the country on a wide range of topics, including alliance building between Christians. An accomplished author, with special concentration in the areas of cultural commentary and apologetics, he has numerous law-review articles, editorials, booklets, and books to his credit. His books include *Evangelical Catholics, Bringing Christ's Presence into Your Home, Wounds That Heal,* and *In Defense of Life.* Among his many booklets are *Religious Cleansing in the American Republic, In Defense of Liberty,* and *Fighting for Law and Justice.* He makes his home with his wife Laurine and five children in Virginia.

WILLIAM D. WATKINS is the director of publications of Liberty, Life and Family, as well as the American Center for Law and Justice. He is also the president of William Pens, a full-service literary company. Bill has degrees in philosophy and systematic theology, with special attention paid to philosophical and cultural apologetics. He has been involved in the publishing industry for fifteen years as an author and writer, and he has served in a variety of editorial roles. Bill has had a number of books, booklets, and scholarly and popular articles published. His books include *In Defense of Life,* which he wrote with Keith A. Fournier, and *Worlds Apart,* which he coauthored with Norman L. Geisler. Bill has also worked on projects with such respected authors as Charles Swindoll, Jack Hayford, Charles Ryrie, Dallas Willard, J. P. Moreland, Jerry Jenkins, and Peter Kreeft. A member of the Evangelical Theological Society and the Evangelical Philosophical Society, Bill is also a frequent teacher and speaker nationwide. With his wife Pamela and five children, Bill lives in Tennessee.

LIBERTY, LIFE AND FAMILY

❖

Liberty, Life and Family (LLF) is a nonprofit educational and public policy organization. It is both a cultural institute and an alliance of apologists, philosophers, ethicists, lawyers, theologians, and other thinkers and activists who desire to address cultural issues from the foundation of classical Judeo-Christian thought. This alliance—which crosses confessional, racial, socioeconomic, political, and gender lines—bears witness to the universality of the Judeo-Christian worldview and is dedicated to contending for the great ideas that undergird and shape any viable, just society. Focusing in particular on liberty, life, and family, LLF seeks to speak with a contemporary voice to the issues, movements, policies, and ideologies that threaten to undermine civilization, especially in the West. LLF's goal is to help bring about the intellectual, emotional, spiritual, social, and cultural transformation of an increasingly secularized Western civilization.

To learn more about LLF, get on LLF's mailing list, or receive information about publications offered by LLF, write: Liberty, Life and Family, P.O. Box 65248, Virginia Beach, VA 23467-5248.